Images of English

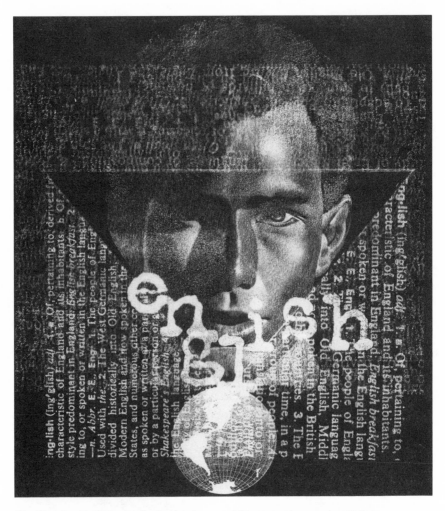

The idea that English was destined to be a world language began when Britain attempted to become a global power in the early nineteenth century. This image is still persuasive for many anglophones. Drawn by Richard Krepel to illustrate "English Out to Conquer the World" (Sanoff and Solorzano 1985). Reprinted by permission of the artist. Copyright © 1985 Richard Krepel.

Images of English

A Cultural History of the Language

Richard W. Bailey

Ann Arbor

THE UNIVERSITY OF MICHIGAN PRESS

Library of Congress Cataloging-in-Publication Data

Bailey, Richard W.
   Images of English : a cultural history of the language / Richard
  W. Bailey.
      p.   cm.
   Includes bibliographical references and index.
   ISBN 0-472-10283-4 (alk. paper)   ISBN 0-472-08242-6 (pbk: alk. paper)
   1. English language—History. 2. Language and culture.
  I. Title.
  PE1072.B33 1991
  420'.9—dc20   91-28043
                                               CIP

For Elisabeth Phelps Weld Bailey

Preface

The English-speaking peoples, riding what they believe to be the rising crest of their influence on world affairs, regularly praise the unparalleled excellence of their language, often tracing to it their economic, political, and military power. International organizations, they note, employ English more and more, and transnational discussions of science and technology are increasingly conducted in it. A Pakistani observer, somewhat hyperbolically, has suggested: "Teaching English has become a multimillion-dollar business the world over, a lucrative business next only to drug trafficking" (Larik 1981–82, 77). Yet even the most ardent English speaker, gazing with satisfaction at the huge display of dictionaries and grammars at the Singapore Book Fair in 1986, might well have wondered if truth had been epitomized in the banner displayed by a London publisher: "Sex Education & Language Skills Ensure a Better Life." Is language quite so important? Is English really deserving of such celebration?

When I was beginning this book, I asked friends in several English-speaking countries to estimate the proportion of the world's population making regular use of English. Nearly all of them offered estimates that were absurdly high; the most common answers ranged from 40 to 60 percent, and some thought that the total might be even higher. On discovering that the actual proportion is closer to 15 percent, *and declining*, many asked what competing language could possibly challenge English. Their arguments drew upon geopolitical mythology, seeking parallels between international economic competition and the linguistic scene. Surely, these friends said, French, German, and Russian are not serious competitors to English. And of course they are not. Birth rates in the countries that employ those languages do not much surpass replacement levels. But in the Third World, population increases are dramatically high, though only a few of the languages of these nations have global influence. (Arabic and Spanish are two exceptions.) Yet anglophones pay little attention to languages experiencing explosive growth—Bengali, kiSwahili, and Bahasa Indonesia, for instance. How long can our indifference to them remain in its present complacent state? As long as we believe that English is at the pinnacle of linguistic evolution.

The conviction of English superiority extends to varieties within the language. Sensitivity to prestige forms and etymological nuance are thought to be sure indicators of aptitude and are thus employed in tests that determine career choice. Some dialects of English are believed to be especially suited to intellectual or technical pursuits, and those who speak them are given opportunities denied to others. Those who accept such social practices are confronted with the same demographic facts that make the multilingual globe so rich a linguistic environment. Within the community of English speakers, diversity is continually increasing, and English itself is splitting into separate communities where some varieties are often far from intelligible across international frontiers or even beyond some neighborhoods in the largest cities of the world.

Skeptical of English triumphalism, I came to explore other beliefs about the language—ideas I had long accepted as unquestioned fact, even though they had nothing more than tradition to commend them. I soon discovered that most of our ideas about English have a long history. The journalist who fills columns on a slow news day with fulminations against linguistic deterioration embellishes centuries of complaint. The English teacher recommending the vigor of "Anglo-Saxon" words sustains an idea that began nearly four hundred years ago in ideas about racial purity. While English speakers have resisted the fiats of a language academy, public-spirited citizens continue to imagine that a few like-minded people, employing the resources of schools and the electronic and print media, can shape the language to some good purpose. Greater precision in language, they have argued, can sharpen the edge of speculation; eradication of vulgarity in language can enhance civility and moral virtue. These ideas, too, have long animated hope without obvious consequential effect. While scientific theories may be made irrelevant through intellectual progress, more broadly cultural ideas like these have greater endurance. Few of the claims about English described in this volume have been so thoroughly discredited that they no longer find adherents.

Most linguists have held that notions of laypeople are worthless when it comes to language, and few of the ideas discussed in this book have been subject to rigorous analysis. Ideas about language—and the images used to express them—are usually held to have only the most distant connection to linguistic performance or to the directions of language change. Consequently, there is little reason to study them, and it is not hard for linguists to show that what speakers claim about their own language does not match the "facts." Virtually any older list of barbaric usages or unwanted new words contains examples that successor generations find normal and distinctly useful. Language communities thought to use debased varieties of English—for instance, the United States in the early nineteenth century—have later emerged as centers of vitality and elegance. No wonder linguists have dismissed most speculations that "evaluate" English.

Another perspective invites closer attention to these comments. In *Translations*, a play by Brian Friel, a principal character suggests "that it is not the literal past, the 'facts' of history, that shape us, but images of the past embodied in language" (1981, 66). Even if these images have only the most indirect connection to language behavior and language change, they are deeply revealing nonetheless. Parents and teachers pass along notions about good and bad language to children. Adults find supposed faults in language a convenient theme to cap an argument. Direct, mother-tongue instruction now occupies a major share of the time spent in school and reflects an economic decision about the importance of English. Hence images used to discuss English are worthy of careful scrutiny. But two additional reasons have led to my investigation of this branch of the history of ideas. One is that we cannot be certain that folk wisdom about language is irrelevant until we understand it in context. The other is that these comments on language reveal patterns of cultural and political bias that may unconsciously shape belief. By a healthy skepticism toward these ideas about English, we may be less prone to confuse linguistic preferences with other kinds of judgments—ones concerning intellectual potential, ethical probity, or cultural vitality.

If images of English count little for the language, they count a very great deal to individuals, and it is from the individual viewpoint that we should begin to assess the damage caused by the most pernicious images of the language—the ones that impugn self-worth. Two nearly identical anecdotes capture this damage; both concern women.

The first is from Britain and appears in Richard Hoggart's autobiography; in it he explains how he recorded a classroom discussion in Yorkshire in the 1950s. Hearing the tape played back was extraordinarily painful to the wives of two local teachers, women who believed that their speech was close to the *standard*.

> They were Yorkshire women and to an outsider their voices would have
> sounded predominantly Yorkshire. But as wives of grammar school masters
> they belonged to the professional middle class, if to the less well-paid end of it.
> So their voices had acquired a slight gloss of educated gentility. Within their
> own heads this was what they heard; their minds filtered away the main York-
> shire strain and left them hearing the genteel elements; and those distinguished
> them importantly, crucially, from the body of the people around them in Goole.
> They believed that and so, I imagine, did the other residents of Goole with
> whom they came into contact; they were a bit different, posher. But the re-
> corder, even when one had allowed for its rudimentary falsifications, told them
> what their voices really sounded like. Overwhelmingly, and in spite of the
> genteel overlay, they sounded broad Yorkshire, more like Yorkshire comics,
> Yorkshire pantomime dames, than grammar school wives as they had imagined
> they should sound, as they wished to and had assumed they did speak; and that
> was unbearable. (Hoggart 1990, 129)

The second anecdote comes from America in William Labov's 1966 study of
the speech of New York City. Here, two women (mother and daughter) were
able to identify the sociolinguistic variables that Labov was investigating.

> The case of Debbie S. and Mrs. S. ends on an unhappy note. In the discus-
> sion of (r), both mother and daughter insisted that they always pronounced all
> of their *r*'s as (r-1). They had ridiculed Speaker LMC [Lower Middle Class]
> for dropping a single (r-1), and they could not believe that they would make
> such a mistake themselves. Unwisely, I played back the section of the tape in
> which Mollie S. recited, "Strawberry short cake, cream on top, tell me the
> name of my sweetheart." She could hear the consistent (r-0) pronunciation in
> her speech, but after a moment's thought she explained the situation as a
> psychological transference—she had imagined herself in her childhood setting,
> and had used a childish speech form. I then played a section of careful speech,
> the discussion of *common sense*, and also Debbie's reading of the standard text.
> When Mrs. S. and her daughter at last accepted the fact that they regularly used
> (r-0) in their own speech, they were disheartened in a way that was painful to
> see. An interview which would otherwise have been an exhilarating experience
> for this lady and her daughter was thus terminated in a bitter disappointment for
> them both: and once the damage had been done, there was no way to restore
> their pride in their own speech. (Labov 1966, 471)

For all four women, images of English were very important indeed, and their
pain at hearing their own careful speech should invite both compassion and
inquiry. What are the images of English that have caused such misery? This
book begins to answer that question.

The scholarly method in this book owes much to a nineteenth-century paradigm for research—the one that gave rise to the "dictionary on historical principles" of which the *Oxford English Dictionary* is the great English exemplar. Minute analysis based on actual evidence gives substance to lexicography, and I have relied on copious quotation to support my interpretations and conclusions. In historical dictionary-making, each word is allowed to tell its own "story," and I invite you to read the expressions of those who have characterized English and its varieties at length.

This material could not have been assembled in earlier times without great difficulty, and my task has been made immeasurably easier thanks to data bases (particularly the Research Libraries Information Network) and a powerful computing service (the Michigan Terminal System). I have also benefited from splendid research libraries. In particular I thank the following for access to their collections: the British Library, the Folger Shakespeare Library, the Library of Congress, the National Library of Scotland, the New York Public Library, King's College Library (Aberdeen), the Regional Language Centre (Singapore), and the School of Oriental and African Studies (London). The Harlan Hatcher Graduate Library at the University of Michigan has been an unfailing source of material and of assistance; particular thanks go to Judith C. Avery (and her staff) at Reference Services there. Various colleagues and friends have also provided help and encouragement: A. J. Aitken, John Algeo, Jacqueline Anderson, Julia Huttar Bailey, Dennis Baron, Matthew C. Benjamin, Robert W. Burchfield, R. J. C. Davies, Hilaire Davies, Marsha L. Dutton, Suzette Haden Elgin, Manfred Görlach, Norman Macleod, Michael J. McCarthy, Randolph Quirk, Allen Walker Read, Jane Powel Thomas, and Bernard van't Hul. To my son, C. A. S. Bailey, I give special thanks for assistance too richly varied to itemize.

Contents

Introduction: Standard English

Language is the thing about ourselves and our communities we know best. It is our distinctly human characteristic, and in the anglophone speech fellowship we acquire a body of lore, closely connected with other social values, about language in general and our own in particular. Children just at the threshold of speaking learn adult strategies of communication before they refine the techniques of form and content through which communication is accomplished. Differences in usage accompany various occasions, and every individual commands many possibilities that can be deployed to suit those occasions and the participants involved in them. We feel comfortable about allocating rewards and imposing punishments based on judgments about the linguistic performance of our fellow citizens (literary prizes and fines for slander are only two examples). Language is the means by which we display our origins and express our aspirations. It is, we assume, the foundation of our social selves, and since it is so closely tied to our sense of self, we are not eager to have our received wisdom about it placed in jeopardy.

As will be shown in detail in the following chapters, notions about language arise from the most diverse prejudices and incompatible presuppositions. English is in a state of perpetual decay; the history of English shows continual "progress." Linguistic saboteurs undermine the canons of good taste and logical thinking; change from "below" is the source of much that is vital in upper-class English. Usage is the only source of correctness; authorities (though fallible) dictate the standards codified in grammars and dictionaries. Great authors have profoundly influenced modern English (see, for instance, Cable 1984); anonymous bureaucrats are the principal sources of modern English (see, for instance, Burnley 1989). Linguistic "purity" is an ideal to which all should aspire; a diversity of borrowed vocabulary is a signal mark of a cosmopolitan language. Present-day English bids fair to become a universal world language; present-day English is a minority language shrinking proportionately with explosive population growth in nonanglophone countries and a stable or declining birthrate in traditionally English-speaking nations. English is as culture-free as calculus; for better and worse, English embodies the habits of thinking of its speakers. Each view, often bolstered by the citation of earlier thinkers, is briskly argued.

Nearly all who are professionally concerned with English have a fund of anecdotes describing uncomfortable encounters with self-anointed linguistic experts. The following account of "secondary responses" (utterances about language) is trenchant and rings true.

> The speaker who discourses about language sometimes adds that he himself has not a perfect command of his native language—the reasons differ with biographic details—but is aware of his weakness and tries to overcome it; he alludes patronizingly to other speakers who do not know enough to make a similar effort. In fact, it soon appears that the speaker possesses a fairly extensive stock of authoritative knowledge which enables him to condemn many forms that are used by other speakers.
>
> Several peculiarities of these secondary responses deserve further study. The speaker, when making the secondary response, shows alertness. His eyes are bright, and he seems to be enjoying himself. No matter how closely his statement adheres to tradition, he proffers it as something new, often his own observation or as that of some acquaintance, and he is likely to describe it as interesting. If he knows that he is talking to a professional student of language, he first alleges ignorance and alludes modestly to the status of his own speech, but then advances the traditional lore in a fully authoritative tone. The whole process is, as we say, pleasurable. (Bloomfield 1944, 48)

The continual reinvention of "traditional lore" by these experts is abundantly demonstrated in the pages that follow. A conservation of energy seems to apply to the many ideas expressed about English and its distinctive genius; nothing, it seems, is ever lost. English is asserted to mirror whatever the speaker or writer believes to be most distinctive of anglophone culture—whether the best or the worst. English at once liberates and enslaves, enlightens and thwarts, affirms and denies those who use it.

The emergence of the image of *standard* English—even though its metaphorical force has dissipated—is particularly consequential in establishing the terms of present-day debate about English and its varieties. This usage was succinctly identified and analyzed in Raymond Williams's *Keywords*:

In the mC19 [mid-nineteenth century] there was the curious case of **Standard English**: a selected (class-based) use taken as an authoritative example of correctness, which, widely backed by educational institutions, attempted to convict a majority of native speakers of English of speaking their own language "incorrectly." (Williams 1983, 296–97; also see Williams 1961)

Far from a nineteenth-century image, *standard* was applied to prestige varieties of a language as early as 1711, and then the term merely codified a notion already old. Before that, by the end of the sixteenth century, the phrase *King's English* had come into use to label normative forms if not actual royal usage.

(Kings and Queens have rarely been honored as exemplars of English in Britain. In one typical exchange, John Kemble, the actor, advised King George IV when he was Prince of Wales: "It would become your royal mouth much better to pronounce the word *oblīge*, and not *oblēēge*" [Lounsbury 1904,119]; Kemble in turn was roasted by a critic for pronouncing *beard* as *burd* and *Rome* as *Room* [Savage 1833, ix]. More recently, an acute observer of minute social distinctions in Britain has noted:

> the sovereign, the Queen Mother, and the heir to the throne all speak a variant of RP which is not the most widely admired or imitated accent—indeed in the mouths of other speakers it is actually ridiculed—nor is it anywhere taught. (Honey 1989, 66)

Newspapers continue to gibe at the English of the Royal family, even ones that otherwise devote many columns to fawning celebrations of their doings: "The Duchess of York takes 'miwlk' rather than milk in her tea, while the Princess of Wales believes she was married in a place called 'St. Paw's' Cathedral" (Harris 1987, 14). Similar criticism of the English of U.S. presidents has been a theme of political journalism from the beginnings of the Republic. Neither set of national leaders, in short, has been taken to articulate the *standard*.)

The early uses of *King's English* and *standard* were harbingers of doctrines that came into flower early in the nineteenth century. In 1816, an American living in London, John Pickering, published a list of departures from British usage criticized by reviewers of American publications; "how much it is to be regretted," he wrote, "that the reviewers have not pointed out *all* the instances, which have come under their notice, of our deviations from the *English* standard" (Mathews 1931, 73–74). Evidence from the *OED* suggests that the phrase *standard English* appeared in print first in 1836 in a review by an anonymous writer who, reflecting on the history of the language, alleged that "southern or standard English . . . in the fourteenth century was perhaps best spoken in Kent and Surrey," a state of affairs not supported by modern scholarship nor one those medieval English speakers would have recognized themselves. Having placed the past *standard* firmly in place, however, the reviewer continued with a description of the contemporary state of English.

> Within the English pale the matter is sufficiently clear; all agree in calling our standard form of speech the English language, and all provincial deviations from it—at least all that assume a distinct specific character—dialects. ("English Dialects" 1836, 355)

This characterization encapsulated what was to become modern wisdom in defining three varieties of English: *dialects* with "a distinct specific character"; other forms of speech unnamed which lack such "character" and are not standard; and *our* "standard form of speech" that alone merits the name of "the English language."

The presumption that every community requires a single source of authority in language is by no means self-evident, but the parallel between the royal *standard* raised over a battlefield and the quasi-regal authority of a *standard* language found ready acceptance in the English-language community. The sense of *standard* as an idealized norm to which actual instances might be compared has also been persuasive, and those who find it useful to denote one variety of English as the standard see ready parallels in other standards, for instance those of measure and volume.

One of the most careful and influential modern linguists, Leonard Bloomfield, perceived that "the most striking line of cleavage in our [American] speech is one of social class." His subsequent definition of standard, however, demonstrates a detached innocence about the consequences.

> Children who are born into homes of privilege, in the way of wealth, tradition, or education, become native speakers of what is popularly known as "good" English; the linguist prefers to give it the non-committal name of *standard* English. Less fortunate children become native speakers of "bad" or "vulgar" or, as the linguist prefers to call it, *non-standard* English. (Bloomfield 1933, 48)

Bloomfield's allegation that the terms *standard* and *nonstandard* are purely scientific and "non-committal" is not borne out by any careful investigation of the way in which they have been used.

Of course the idea of language norms is not chimerical, but the more circumspect definition by Bloomfield's contemporary, Edward Sapir, avoids the presumptions and connotations of *standard*: "there is something like an ideal linguistic entity dominating the speech habits of the members of each group, [and] the sense of almost unlimited freedom which each individual feels in the use of his language is held in leash by a tacitly directing norm" (Sapir [1921] 1949, 148). "Tacitly directing norm" does not carry the image inherent in *standard* but there is an implicit agent metaphor in *dominating* and *directing*—"Who acts to *direct* and *dominate* speech habits?" Even Sapir, more sensitive than Bloomfield to nuance in the speech community, obliges readers to consider the "unlimited freedom" of linguistic creativity "held in leash" as an animal is constrained by a leash in the hands of a superior being. The presumption of linguistic regulation is thus implied, though not explained.

In Britain, the idea of standard English emerged to shape modern debate about language in the writings to two prominent linguists of the early twentieth century, Daniel Jones (1880–1967) and H. C. Wyld (1870–1945). Jones, a specialist in phonetics at the University of London, produced a series of influential pronunciation guides and dictionaries first aimed at foreign learners but subsequently urged upon schools for use by children who were native speakers of English. In his first effort to compile a definitive account of the prestige dialect in 1907, Jones drew upon his own pronunciation (with "a few modifications" aimed at consistency or correcting instances "where my pronunciation seems to be not in accord with the pronunciation of the majority of educated Southern English speakers"). By 1908, he had enlarged upon that small social circle to encompass, with exactly the same pronunciations, the English "usually adopted by educated people in London and the neighbourhood," and, by 1912, his claim enlarged further to the "pronunciation used by the educated classes in the South of England" (quoted by Crowley 1989, 168–69).

In successive editions of his works, Jones continued to be troubled by the definition of just whose speech was being symbolized. In 1917, he hit upon the following, which continued to appear in the many subsequent editions of his *English Pronouncing Dictionary*.

The pronunciation represented in this book is that which I believe to be most usually heard in everyday speech in the families of Southern English people who have been educated at the public schools. This pronunciation is also used (sometimes with modifications) by those who do not come from the South of England, but who have been educated at these schools. The pronunciation may also be heard, to an extent which is considerable though difficult to specify, from natives of the South of England who have not been educated at these schools. It is probably accurate to say that a majority of Londoners who have had a university education, use either this pronunciation or a pronunciation not differing greatly from it. (Jones 1946, ix)

By the seventh edition in 1946, however, Jones's personal preferences had been relegated to a footnote.

The pronunciation is in the main that which I use myself. I have, however, put my pronunciation in a secondary place in all cases where another form appears to me to be the more frequent use. (ix)

In the preface of 1917, Jones described his catalog of speech habits as *PSE* 'Public School English,' and, though this definition did not come into widespread use, it occasionally turned up in later British discussions of language variety (e.g., Jagger 1940, 16). Another abbreviation for the same variety did gain general currency: *RP* 'received pronunciation' which Jones further glossed as 'widely understood pronunciation' (1946, x). *Received* in this sense is defined in the *Oxford English Dictionary* as 'generally adopted, accepted, approved as true or good' and *Received Standard* as 'the spoken language of a linguistic area (usu. Britain) in its traditionally most correct and acceptable form.' In neither case are the agents of *adopted*, *accepted*, or *approved* expressed.

Unlike later observers, Jones understood the bias introduced by the use of a standard to describe a single variety of English. This concern is amplified in the preface to his *Dictionary*.

My aim is to observe and record accurately, and I do not believe in the feasibility of imposing one particular form of pronunciation on the English-speaking world. I take the view that people should be allowed to speak as they like. And if the public wants a standardized pronunciation, I have no doubt that some appropriate standard will evolve itself. If there are any who think otherwise, it must be left to them to undertake the invidious task of deciding what is to be approved and what is to be condemned. This book will provide them with some of the materials they will require as a basis to work upon. (Jones 1946, x)

Whatever "materials" prescriptive teachers might have wanted were readily available in Jones's *Dictionary* and in other pedagogical materials derived from it. Though Jones was doubtful that *PSE* or *RP* would "meet with success" in U.S. schools, U.S. editions of his works soon appeared and were enthusiastically endorsed (though they did not widely influence U.S. speech habits). In the Empire and Commonwealth, however, Jones and H. W. Fowler (author of *Modern English Usage*) were received enthusiastically as unequivocal authorities legislating the best British usage. The range of his influence was not lost on Jones, and he was soon drawn into the "invidious task" of approval and condemnation. Eventually he became so persuaded of the connection between standards of speech and standards of conduct that, in 1937, he declared: "you cannot produce a uniform high standard of social life in a community without producing a uniform high standard of speech" (quoted by Leitner 1982, 94). By that time, his earlier "view that people should be allowed to speak as they like" had been sacrificed to the idea that linguistic uniformity is a prerequisite to "a uniform high standard of social life."

Jones's influential contemporary H. C. Wyld was an important historian of English, a lexicographer, and the author of school books concerned with grammar and pronunciation. Like Jones, Wyld claimed scientific dispassion in his description of diversity in English. Though admiring of regional dialects (at least those with a "distinct specific character"), Wyld was a proponent of a single, received variety.

> By the side of these [regional dialects], there are numerous other types of English which are not characteristic of any special geographical area, but rather of social divisions or sections of the population. Of these the chief is the type which most well-bred people think of when they speak of "English." At the risk of offending certain susceptibilities this type of English must be further described and particularized. As regards its name, it may be called Good English, Well-bred English, Upper-class English, and it is sometimes, too vaguely, referred to as Standard English. For reasons which will soon appear, it is proposed here to call it **Received Standard English**. (Wyld 1936, 2)

Wyld equated Received Standard with the English of the upper class, a class refreshed and influenced, in his view, by the "new men" who came to prominence after the Commonwealth of the seventeenth century and by the social emergence of the newly rich in the nineteenth-century industrial revolution (1914, 287). The descendents of these people were upheld as models of conduct by Wyld and by many of his contemporaries. Unlike Jones, Wyld did not require education for admission to the company of standard speakers, only wealth and social position.

> It is characteristic of R[eceived] S[tandard] that it is easy, unstudied, and natural. The "best" speakers do not need to take thought for their utterance; they have no theories as to how their native tongue should be pronounced, nor do they reflect upon the sounds they utter. They have perfect confidence in themselves, in their speech, as in their manners. For both bearing and utterance spring from a firm and gracious tradition. "Their fathers have told them"—that suffices. Nowhere does the best that is in English culture find a fairer expression than in R. S. speech. And under this should be included not merely pronunciation, but also the inflexions and modulations of the voice. If I were asked among what class the "best" English is most consistently heard at its best, I think, on the whole, I should say among Officers of the British Regular Army. The utterance of these men is at once clear-cut and precise, yet free from affectation; at once downright and manly, yet in the highest degree refined and urbane. (Wyld 1934, 614; for further discussion, see Crowley 1989, 194–204)

For Wyld, standard English need not be uniform or even elegant (though he claims that its vowels are superior in "beauty and clarity" [606]). It is fundamentally hereditary.

Wyld's view became orthodoxy in the interwar years. R. W. Chapman, secretary to the Delegates of the Clarendon Press, provided the following account for a trans-Atlantic audience.

> But standard English is now the language of a class far more than it is the language of a region. Phonetically, England is not a democracy, and the speech of London has far less uniformity than has the speech of those, who, whatever their local origin, have had in common a certain kind of education and environment. The typical custodians of this standard are not the universities, but the schools which we call public, that is the boarding schools recruited, for the most part, from our least indigent classes. In these schools, and in similar environments, the plastic youth of Britain insensibly acquires a speech which, though by no means of a drab uniformity, is sufficiently uniform, and sufficiently distinctive, to be at once recognized by those who are familiar with it. We do not expect to hear it, as a matter of course, in any given place where men congregate; when we do hear it, we know it for what it is. (Chapman 1931, 842)

Chapman saw only one standard, that derived from "the least indigent classes." If "the plastic youth of Britain" could acquire the standard only in the environment of boarding schools, what hope could there be for the majority? For their speech, Wyld conceived the term *Modified Standard*.

> It is indeed "standard" gone wrong, and "modified" either by a provincial or, as I prefer to call it, a *Regional dialect*, or by an inferior *Class dialect*. Hence the name *Modified Standard*. (1934, 605)

Thus there could be no hope that any large numbers of speakers might gain mastery of the standard.

> In so far as a speaker retains traces of a London, a Scotch, a North Country, a Liverpool, a Birmingham accent, however admirable each of these may be in its own way, and in its own district, we must say that he speaks, not Received, but Modified Standard. (1934, 616)

These varieties "gone wrong" had an equal claim to antiquity and "character" with the preferences of the rich, yet Wyld confidently designated them as deviant and hence found them distasteful. These preferences also shaped his work as a teacher, and, sixty years after his departure from his university post at Liverpool for the Merton chair at Oxford, Wyld was remembered for having reduced "women students to tears by his fierce comments on their northern pronunciation" (Kelly 1981, 222).

The heyday of the Jones-Wyld standard did not pass without dissent. In 1924, F. E. Palmer regretted that "the chimerical idea of a standard dialect still persists" and attributed the notion to only the "uninformed" (1969b, xvii–xviii). In 1925, Otto Jespersen reviewed the entire matter from the point of view of an outsider and criticized "upper-class disdain" for lower-class speech. Still, he was compelled to concede the importance of social class in British definitions of standard (1964b, 74–109).

Unlike Wyld, some British educators of the interwar years sustained a faith in the power of self-improvement while at the same time acknowledging the great gulf separating upper-class men educated at boarding schools from every other Briton. If it were impossible for those lacking a public school education to acquire a command of standard English, *standard* needed to be relaxed to make it possible for the upwardly mobile to achieve acceptable speech. A good example of the required compromise can be found in *Standard English Pronunciation with some Notes on Accidence and Syntax*, published in 1925. Though the author, Thomas Nicklin, is little known as a linguistic authority, his book was issued by the Clarenden Press, a division of Oxford University Press, as part of a series called "The World's Manuals" under the direction of a distinguished editorial board including C. T. Onions, then active as one of the principal editors of the *Oxford English Dictionary*. According to the statement printed in the endpapers, these volumes were intended for students and, most especially, "for the great body of general readers who are sufficiently alive to the value of reading to welcome authoritative and scholarly work if it is presented to them in terms of its human interest and in a simple style and moderate compass."

Nicklin took a more liberal view than Jones, Wyld, and Chapman of the accessibility of standard English. More expansively than his mentors, he viewed "all of these local dialects [—Canadian, Australian, American—as] equally entitled to be regarded as English" (1925, 9). But he saw departures from a single standard as unfortunate deviations to be remedied through the assiduous efforts of those not privileged to have acquired that standard through birth and nurture.

> There has been a disposition in some quarters to regard the use of the Standard English dialect as the prerogative of a class. It has even been said that if a representative of a trade union were regularly to adopt Standard English as the dialect he used, he would no longer be trusted by those who elected him to office, and whose spokesman he ought to be. But I will venture to contend that it is the right of everyone born in these islands, whatever the profession and whatever the property of his parents, to be taught to speak that English dialect which marks an educated man. Nothing can be more disastrous than that the accidents of history, which have led to this dialect of the educated appearing to be a special prerogative of the well-to-do, should be regarded as irretrievable. The democratic spirit must demand for every child, however humble his parents' occupation, that he shall be taught that one common dialect which can be understood everywhere, and which is the modern representative of all that has been greatest in English learning, statesmanship, oratory, poetry, and politeness. All other dialects are local. To unite all who work, whether with body or with mind, in one fellowship, a common speech must be one necessary instrument, and there is no other dialect which is spoken and is understood so widely as the Standard English dialect. (1925, 10–11)

By the time Nicklin wrote, the concept of standard English as a class-based dialect of southern British English had entrenched itself so thoroughly that these observations must have seemed commonplace. What he offered was a condescending definition, defying the "democratic spirit," by implying that standard is the only possible vehicle for "educated" expression. He alleged that this variety is "widely" spoken, though it was and is the speech of a tiny minority, perhaps fewer than 3 percent of the population of Britain (see Hughes and Trudgill 1979, 3). Yet Nicklin arrogated to this narrowly defined standard English the whole body of "English learning, statesmanship, oratory, poetry, and politeness" and recruited such disparate but revered literary figures as Chaucer, Shakespeare, and Milton to the ranks of standard English even though they differed greatly among themselves and have little in common with twentieth-century English speakers.

Like other authors of self-help manuals, Nicklin recommended assiduous yet easy practice. Hard work would allow the reader "to assimilate one's own dialect to that musical and beautiful speech which we may hear at times from the best speakers of Standard English" (1925, 11). He even associated himself with the great mass who were themselves uncertain about usages that properly belong to the standard.

Having had his "attention called" to his pronunciation of *advertise* (which "from childhood with inattention" he had pronounced with stress on the final syllable), Nicklin discovered by consulting the *OED* that his usage was typical of "good speakers" at the end of the nineteenth century, but, by 1925, old-fashioned or perhaps even verging on the nonstandard. "Nothing could better illustrate not only the law of continual change to which all language is subject, but also the necessity of alertness if any one desires to keep pace with such change" (70). Allegiance to the old thus exists in uneasy company with innovation. "Alertness" to change is recommended, but fidelity to earlier usage is also a virtue to be cultivated. In a parable of this dilemma, Nicklin memorialized someone who continued to pronounce *bicycle* and *tricycle* with "two distinct centres of stress" against the innovation of first-syllable stress. This "survivor," he remarked, "continued this pronunciation till his death ten years ago" (76). Like traditionalists yearning for the old standard measures, the linguistically hidebound denounce any supposed innovation that departs from their own notion of standard English. Far from being an easy skill to attain, Nicklin's standard English requires remarkable agility in knowing when to retain the old—and thus to qualify as a "survivor" though not an anachronism—and when to embrace the new.

Though Nicklin could argue, perhaps not very successfully, against the idea that standard English is solely "the prerogative of a class," the use of the word *standard* established the terms of the debate, one which continued long after Nicklin's work was forgotten. Although class consciousness diminished in Britain after the second World War, there was little immediate effect on thinking about standard English. Thus, A. J. Aitken has recently recalled that:

> This model and the implications of its terminology were universally accepted in most departments of English philology, so that in Edinburgh, for instance, the model of English pronunciation used for teaching English phonetics in the English language department down to the 1970s was RP. I doubt if we are wholly rid of this yet. (Aitken 1988, personal communication)

These prejudices certainly survive in Britain but even more do they influence many Commonwealth nations. A principal activity of the Department of English at the National University of Singapore, for instance, consists of instruction in RP, and active measures have been undertaken to suppress the local prestige variety of English. New Zealand is only now considering the possibility that broadcasting an indigenous standard might be preferable to the Jones-Wyld Received Standard (see Bell 1977).

Within Britain at the end of the twentieth century, a new perspective has begun to emerge, expressed in a recent work on educational practices.

> Indeed, it is one of the illusions of the epoch that the educational system can bring into harmony, singlehanded, the antagonistic social forces of capitalist society—an illusion that socialist teachers, whether as socialists or as teachers, can ill afford to share. And it is the contradictions that need, at this stage, to be stressed. "Systematic training in the use of standard English" has proved one of the most effective ways in which the exploited classes, child and adult, have been induced to consent to the conditions of their own cultural subordination. . . . Standard English appears not as a particular historical practice of language with its own appropriate occasions and limits of usefulness, but as *the* language itself, the neutral and unchanging norm (for what else does "standard" mean?) by which all other practices are judged, as quaint or deplorable, as idiom or jargon, as dialect or abuse. (Batsleer et al. 1985, 36–37, 38)

Even here, in an argument intended to repudiate the Jones-Wyld model, standard English shapes the terms of the discussion.

At the turn of the twentieth century, contemporaries of Jones and Wyld in the United States were not infected with the same degree of class consciousness and were willing to open democratic vistas in speech. "Phonetically" the United States was no democracy, but opinion makers thought it might become one if speakers were given the respect their conduct merited.

Thus, Fred Newton Scott (1860–1931) was a strong influence on U.S. educators and used his position as president of the National Council of Teachers of English to promote tolerance for speech variety. In an address to that body in 1916, he gave a moral lecture around the standard of speech.

> Whatever impression these remarks may have created, I trust I have made one point clear, and that is that when we deal with American speech we shall do well to cultivate the virtue of tolerance. It is clearly not our business to force upon the younger generation the speech of any particular section of the country, or to do them to death for want of well pronouncing shibboleth. The speech of one's own community, the speech which one hears day by day at home and on the street, is the speech which, in modified form, one will probably use all one's life long. If, as a child, I say "glăss" and "păst," I shall in all likelihood continue to do so in old age. And why not? The vowel sound in "glăss" is just as good as that in "glahss," or as the intermediate sound which, in my boyhood, teachers vainly attempted to acquire and to impose on their pupils. (Scott 1926, 14)

Such acceptance of linguistic variety became an article of faith among U.S. university teachers of the English language. In the 1920s and under Scott's influence, this small group declared itself to be the sole proprietors of the "scientific study of language" (see Fries 1927). In so doing, they separated themselves from "popular" opinions about usage that they held to be founded on ignorance and superstition rather than on what they alleged to be the only true sources of authority, language history and dialectology.

The campaign for tolerance continued with frequent and virtuous public statements. One typical expression was published in 1935 by Albert H. Marckwardt (1903–75); it carried forward the principles first articulated by Scott.

> For a period of several years, the National Council of Teachers of English, both in its meetings and through its publications, has labored in the interest of linguistic liberalism. The energies of many of the foremost language scholars of the country have been directed against the useless and out-moded freight with which a majority of our common-school textbooks are encumbered. There is no time better than the present to ask ourselves how far we have proceeded toward our goal. To what extent have we affected the attitude of English teachers toward the problems of present-day English? More important still, what changes have been wrought in actual classroom practice? (Marckwardt 1935, 283)

Improving one's English to gain social advancement became a commonplace of twentieth-century anglophone culture as the image of a *standard* English took hold. This advertisement invited the ambitious to subscribe to a series compiled by Sherwin Cody (1868–1959). Among other benefits, Cody offered unequivocally correct pronunciations for such words as *genuine*, *lamentable*, and *often*. These in turn appeared on his "National Business Ability Tests (standardized psychological tests for office employees)" to determine the suitability of applicants. Illustration from *Collier's* 55 (May 1, 1915): 37.

To his regret, Marckwardt was not able to give a strongly affirmative answer to either of his questions. Aside from compelling textbook makers to discard "the more obvious idiocies," nothing much had happened to affect "actual classroom practice." What was needed, he thought, was more study of language: "a fearless, open-minded, and accurate analysis of that level of American English which may be considered a scientifically justifiable schoolroom *standard*" (286; italics added). Yet thirty-five years later, despite the accumulation of a library of fearless, accurate analyses, Marckwardt was obliged to report "much disheartening evidence to show that the impact has been slight at best" (1971, 15). Americans, he thought, were still afflicted with "a somewhat unwholesome state of mind linguistically speaking" (1971, 28).

Undaunted, the Council continued its position of "linguistic liberalism," and university teachers attempted to indoctrinate successive generations of school teachers in the tolerance that Scott had urged. In 1974, one branch of the organization passed the following resolution, later known by its title as "Students' Right to Their Own Language."

> We affirm the students' right to their own patterns and varieties of language—the dialects of their nurture or whatever dialects in which they find their own identity and style. Language scholars long ago denied that the myth of a standard American dialect has any validity. The claim that any one dialect is unacceptable amounts to an attempt of one social group to exert its dominance over another. Such a claim leads to false advice for speakers and writers, and immoral advice for humans. A nation proud of its diverse heritage and its cultural and racial variety will preserve its heritage of dialects. We affirm strongly that teachers must have the experiences and training that will enable them to respect diversity and uphold the right of students to their own language. (Allen 1985, 144)

Like many earlier efforts, this statement attracted a firestorm of criticism from the press and from writers opposed to the "liberal" tradition. To what extent it altered "actual classroom practice" is difficult to estimate. The most likely guess is that it did no more than prior statements to wean Americans from a longing for a standard. It did, however, continue to affirm the need for "experience and training"—training that would be provided mainly by the "scientific" linguists who had formulated the statement.

In few of these disputes did the image implied by the use of standard come in for serious question. That a standard grade is not necessarily the best, at least in commerce, was fleetingly considered (Malone 1942, 237). Denials that there is any such thing as standard English did not have much impact on popular ways of thinking about the language. Judicious or skeptical statements about standard English such as those promulgated by the National Council of Teachers of English have done little to thwart the yearning for unequivocal authority in the U.S. speech community.

In both the United States and Britain, it is still true that "many citizens believe in S[tandard] E[nglish] as a semipatriotic goal that [has] contributed to national strength and unity" (Heath 1980, 31). In fact, the phrase *standard English* has, if anything, accompanied increased linguistic intolerance during the last century. As the next chapter shows, this image of the language was not discernible at the beginning.

Chapter 1

English Discerned

Diversity breeds opinion, but it would be wrong to suppose that the images modern speakers use to describe English were equally powerful in the distant past. Most scholars believe that no evaluative distinction among dialects was important before the Norman Conquest, since there was nothing resembling a norm against which variation might be measured. Whatever the attitudes toward spoken English, however, writing practices must have been influenced by normative forms associated with the courts and powerful religious houses. Even though the rich collections of manuscripts from the early Anglo-Saxon period were mostly destroyed in the devastating Norse invasions of the tenth century, the few surviving examples of written English—only four extended texts and thirty-five official documents earlier than A.D. 850 (Toon 1983, xiii)—suggest that writers acknowledged the example of Mercia in the midlands of England in providing exemplars of how English should be written. The extent to which English scribes modified their spoken language cannot easily be known, but the slight evidence of spelling has allowed scholars to conclude that a prestige variety, arising between A.D. 700 and 850, influenced the English of serious, formal *written* documents (Toon 1983, 197).

The best reason for supposing that variation in Old English led to opinions about its diversity arises from the nature of feudal social structure. Only those of high social standing were free to travel great distances or to shift their residence from the place of their birth. Others, the great majority, were tied to the land, thus establishing the conditions for social and regional dialect differences that could (and did) persist over time. Both literature and law reveal a preoccupation with mutual obligations of lords and retainers, and communication up and down the social hierarchy required a range of stylistic conventions expressed through language. Deference, respect, and fealty were articulated through language.

17

Levels of prestige expressed through spoken English are clearly evident in a story from Bede's eighth-century *Ecclesiastical History of the English People*. Bede describes Imma, a well-brought-up youth who lived in the seventh century. A follower of the King of Northumbria, Imma was captured by the Mercians and attempted to pass himself off as a peasant on the battlefield (he had been bringing supplies to the soldiers). But the Mercians were not long duped by his ruse: "Having continued with the man some time, those who attentively observed him, by his countenance, mien, and discourse ["ex vultu et habitu et sermonibus ejus" (Moberly 1881, 260)], took notice, that he was not of the meaner sort, as he had said, but of some quality" (Bede 1958, 200). This account makes plain that there were forms of discourse associated with high-ranking persons, and Imma's conversations with his captors must have been expressed in English that was not typical of local people. Though a follower of the northern king, Imma had also spent time in the south (where he had been a servant to the King's mother), and subsequently he went there to obtain the ransom that would free him from the Mercians. It would be strange indeed if his high social standing and cultivated upbringing were not somehow reflected in his speech.

Linguistic diversity increased as a consequence of the Viking invasions, not at first, when these incursions were brief, bloody raids, but after A.D. 850, when larger forces and more extended conquest led to permanent settlements in the north and east of England. Following the establishment of the Danelaw (the region under Viking jurisdiction), a long linguistic frontier was established with Norse as the predominant language on one side and English the predominant language on the other. Many English speakers remained in the area of the Danelaw, particularly in rural areas, while the Danes clustered their communities in towns. Eventually the two closely related languages influenced each other, and the result was to affect the shape of English. In present-day English, cognate pairs with similar meanings derive from Norse and Old English: *no* (English) and *nay* (Norse), *whole* and *hale*, *rear* and *raise*, *hide* and *skin*, *shirt* and *skirt*. (Recent scholarship has refuted earlier claims that Scandinavian influence on English grammar was significant; see Kirch 1959.) The choice among two possibilities, one Scandinavian and the other English, must have had a social meaning inside the Danelaw, where Norse-influenced English set off those who used it (whether English or Dane) when they traveled far from home. Unfortunately, no contemporary comment on this social meaning survives, although the mingling of the two languages, reinforced on the Norse side by continued migration from Scandinavia, went on until the end of the eleventh century. That there likely were social differences between the two varieties of English can be surmised from the description offered in 1193 by the Welsh writer Gerald:

> . . . in the southern parts of England, and especially in Devon, the speech is nowadays purer than elsewhere. It may well be that it retains more features of the original language and the old ways of speaking English, whereas the northern regions have been greatly corrupted by the Danish and Norwegian invasions. (Gerald of Wales 1984, 231)

Gerald's idea that "original languages" had been corrupted by foreign borrowings was derived from notions of what had happened to Latin after the collapse of the empire; it was an image to which subsequent writers would frequently return. And this testimony is especially important as the first expression of the image that varieties of English were differentiated on a scale of purity.

At the end of the ninth century, when Alfred the Great, King of Wessex, fostered his great enterprise of translating Latin works into English, the translators employed the variety of English most comfortable to them—the kind of English they themselves spoke. Alfred used his native West Saxon for his translation of Orosius's *History of the World*, while Bishop Werferth chose his own Mercian dialect for Englishing Gregory's *Dialogues*. Because of these differences, modern scholars deny that Alfred was "the founder or the harbinger of standard Old English" (Gneuss 1972, 68). Such judgments presume that a standard language is uniform and generally accepted as the norm. These translations represent a plurality of written Englishes that were set apart from the even greater diversity of spoken varieties.

At first glance, it seems surprising that there is no tenth-century commentary about English, since the written language was coming to be an important complement to Latin. But the surviving documents devote little attention to everyday life; most of them concern theological and liturgical issues (see Cameron 1985). Even in the absence of direct testimony, however, it is possible to make reasoned inferences about what the life of the language was like. The flourishing intellectual and creative centers of the north of England—Lindisfarne, Wearmouth, Jarrow, and York—provided an environment for the development of a prestige dialect of English that must have influenced those who were drawn to them, even though the subsequent destruction of nearly all the contents of the ecclesiastical libraries denies scholars the evidence to draw more precise conclusions. Similarly, the great religious houses of the south—Canterbury, Winchester, and Glastonbury—must have given added prestige to the kinds of English spoken in those regions. English was not discussed, perhaps, because English was not important as a vehicle for the literate imagination; Latin occupied the center of attention for those drawn to intellectual and creative endeavors. But English was the language of daily affairs for the educated as well as for those engaged in less exalted pursuits.

One consequence of the Norman invasion was to make England trilingual, with Latin retaining its position as the language of religious ceremony and intellectual work, Norman French displacing Old English as the language of the courts and of government, and English occupying a distant third in prestige but still the language of daily life for the great majority of the population. At the fringes of Norman influence, Britain was an even more diverse multilingual community. Substantial numbers of people spoke Welsh, Gaelic, Manx, Norn, and Cornish. Along the borders of English power, many people were bilingual or at least influenced by the language of their neighbors, and both Welsh and Irish show evidences of Old English and Anglo-Norman (Thomson 1984, 256). Since the degree of bilingualism is uncertain, it is difficult to discern the relative status of the languages involved before 1350, but it is clear that many people in Britain routinely spoke or heard several languages in daily life.

There is almost no documentary evidence revealing the attitudes of the English and Anglo-Normans toward this multilingualism. Other European countries varied widely in insularity, and at least a few royal courts regarded multilingualism as an "ornament." Thus, Stephen of Hungary (who ruled from 1001 to 1038) advised his successor:

> The utility of foreigners and guests is so great that they can be given a place of sixth importance among the royal ornaments. The Roman Empire, too, became powerful and its rulers glorious and august by the fact that from everywhere the wise and noble men were flocking into that country. For, as the guests come from various regions and provinces, they bring with them various languages and customs, various knowledges and arms. All these adorn the royal court, heighten its splendor, and terrify the haughtiness of foreign powers. For a country unified in language and customs is fragile and weak. Therefore I order thee, my son, to receive them with good will and to nourish them honestly in order that they abide with thee more joyfully than elsewhere. (Quoted by Jászi 1929, 39)

Whether Stephen's celebration of "various languages" expressed a sentiment also felt in Britain is not known, but literacy was highly valued there, and books in Latin and the English vernacular were treasured throughout Anglo-Saxon and Norman times.

The century and a half following the Norman Conquest was a period of crucial transformation for English. Surviving records and testimony present an obscure and conflicting image of the roles of language during that time, and modern scholarship has produced a variety of theories to explain the competing roles of English, Norman French, and Latin. As far as it is possible to tell, the Normans did little to promote their own language in the countryside, but the king's court, the major religious communities, and the great estates centered on the fortified manors were all sources of French influence. Religious life, in particular, was dominated by French speakers, though the normal written language and the spoken language of liturgy was Latin. All the kings and their feudal lords were French. Many of them spent time on their continental lands and married other French speakers. After 1080, legal documents were no longer prepared in English, and soon thereafter other records—most particularly the chronicles of events—came to be kept in Latin rather than English. The choice of language, however, was closely linked to the domain of language use and to social class. Speakers of Norman French probably numbered between 10,000 and 20,000 in a population of 1.5 million, but they occupied the positions of power at the court, in the church, and in the urban centers (Berndt 1965, 147). Anglo-French literature flourished for the entertainment and edification of courtiers, but some of this literature shows the influence of native English literary forms and thus suggests some bilingualism among the elite.

The great mass of the population in central and northern England, however, remained unilingual, and the ordinary affairs of trade and agriculture continued to be transacted in English. Lacking speakers in positions of influence, English must have been regarded as the least of the languages of England.

By the middle of the twelfth century, a balance among the three languages of England seems to have been struck. Latin was used for record keeping, for learned works in history and theology, and for liturgy in the church. French grew less usual in routine transactions except among the retinue of the king and among the most powerful of the aristocracy; it was, however, the language of the legal system, itself largely occupied with disputes among the king and his courtiers. English was still the most common mother tongue but was not much used as a written language except to record homilies and sermons directed to the laity.

A decisive event upset the balance among these languages and drew English back from the road to extinction: the conquest of Normandy by Philip II of France in 1204. That victory isolated the Norman French rulers of England from their continental lands and thus led to increased use of English among the aristocracy. Philip's victory is rightly regarded as decisive for the reemergence of English (in a form much influenced by French) as the language of the powerful in England, though it seems likely that the political separation of England from France merely hastened a process already well begun. A temporary setback to the elevation of English occurred when Henry III of England (1216–72) brought yet more French speakers from his domains in the south of France and appointed them to important positions. But the barons of England resisted and compelled Henry to accept the Provisions of Oxford (1258) by which he was obliged to renounce claims to his French territory and to expel the supporters he had imported from France. These Provisions were disseminated in English, the first act of government promulgated through English for more than a century and a half.

Political separation from France, however, did not end the use of spoken and written French in England. More and more, French came to be regarded as the proper language of government records, and, by 1300, it had virtually replaced Latin in most official documents—writs, charters, and petitions to Parliament. Not for another century did English gradually come to be accepted for such purposes, and such was the weight of tradition that law French did not entirely disappear until finally Parliament acted to eliminate it in 1733 (6 George II 6).

Another extraordinarily important influence on the development of English began in 1348 when the series of plagues known as the Black Death spread through England, eventually claiming as much as half the population. Modern estimates suggest that the population of England was between 4.5 and 6 million in 1348; a century later, following the plagues, it may have stood at only 2 to 2.5 million; by 1525 it had increased only to 2.75 million (Hatcher 1977, 68– 69; see Wrigley and Schofield 1981, 528). As population fell, per capita wealth increased; the wool trade and tin mines, both principal sources of export wealth, flourished. Consumption of goods and lavish expenditures likewise increased; people anticipating imminent death, after all, are unlikely to hoard and save. Prices of farm products were high; towns and cities grew rapidly by drawing population from the rural areas. The resulting social instability had consequences for the status of English. People of high social standing were more likely to survive than the poor, who lived in overcrowded and squalid housing—rats and the fleas that carried the plague were not quite so common in palaces of stone or in places where sanitation was at a relatively high standard. But the rich shared in the general catastrophe. Thus positions in the church and in government were made vacant for the survivors, and these opportunities were seized by English speakers. The plagues helped to accelerate the decline of French by speeding the demise of the minority ruling class who used it and thus hastened the rise of English both as a spoken and as a written language. The balance among French, Latin, and English is revealed by an act adopted in 1362, during the reign of Edward III (1327–77), requiring that:

> all pleas which shall be pleaded in any courts whatsoever, before any of his justices whatsoever, or in his other places, or before any of his other ministers whatsoever, or in the courts and places of any other lords whatsoever within the realm, shall be pleaded, shewed, defended, answered, debated, and judged in the *English* tongue, and that they be entered and inrolled in *Latin*. (36 Edward III 15)

It did not seem odd to those in authority that English should be mandated for the oral language of court proceedings and Latin for the written record of decisions while the law setting forth these requirements was enacted in French. But French and Latin now served merely archival purposes; English was the vital language of the adversarial process. At the lowest end of the justice system, official multilingualism presented considerable difficulties. One Robert Goodgroome, in 1440, concluded a long and highly self-incriminating deposition with the plea that the Court transcribe his declaration "in my moder tonge, f[or] I understond noyþer latyne nor frensshe" (Aston 1963, 90), a request that on that occasion, at least, was honored.

The preamble to Edward's law of 1362 provides useful insight into the rationale behind the change it mandated. "Great mischiefs," it asserted, arose from general ignorance of the laws, statutes, and customs that were compiled in French since, by the mid-fourteenth century, French was "much unknown in the said realm." Other countries were seen as better governed because their laws were "learned and used in the tongue of the country." Requiring the courts to use English in conducting the business of justice would keep citizens from "offending the law" and help them to "better keep, save, and defend [their] heritage and possessions."

Some hint of the views of linguistic variety emerges in the deliberations of Parliament. Protesting in 1347 against the appointment of foreigners to church posts in England, English speakers pointed to the fact that "aliens" were unable to carry out priestly duties because of their inability to communicate: they "do not know or understand either the patois or the language of England, and the ordinary people do not understand their language either" (*Rolls of Parliament* [Edward III] 2:173a [1347]). Whether this problem was genuine or the debate merely a piece of special pleading on behalf of native candidates is not easy to determine. It would be tempting (though wrong) to give much weight to the apparent distinction between a local "patois" and a national "language" since the modern French distinction between *patois* and *langue* had not yet arisen (see Dobson [1955]1969, 435). Even so, explicit commentary about language—even oblique commentary as in this example—was the mark of growing self-consciousness about the conflict between a language for local purposes and a national means of expression.

The first extended discussion of the linguistic diversity in Britain is found in the *Polychronicon*, a Latin history of the world, written by Ranulf Higden, a Benedictine monk of St. Werburg's, Chester. Higden, who died in 1364, speculated about the origins of the various languages spoken in the land, and his views were much elaborated by John Trevisa (1326–1412), who translated and expanded the *Polychronicon* in 1387. Higden found it remarkable that English was so various while French, he believed, was uniform. Trevisa dissented and alleged that French was diverse as well. For Trevisa, this variety in English had social meaning, and in a well-known passage he wrote that "Al þe longage of þe Norþhumbres, and specialliche at ʒork, is so scharp, slitting, and frotynge and vnschape, þat we souþerne men may þat longage vnneþe vnderstonde" (1869, 2:163). Just how unintelligible northern English was to southerners like Trevisa is a matter of dispute, although complaints about the speech of Yorkshire had been a commonplace since they had first been articulated by William of Malmsbury about 1125. Higden called it *stridet*, by which he meant that it had a whistling, hissing sound that he found distasteful. Trevisa's amplification of *stridet* into "scharp, slitting, and frotynge and vnschape" extends the description and intensifies the distaste; *slitten* is not elsewhere used for the sounds of language in Middle English, but it does occur for the sound of ripping cloth. *Frotynge* only survives in this passage and is glossed by the *Middle English Dictionary* as "strident or harsh (speech)." Southern contempt for northern English was probably long established when Higden wrote. This contempt persisted, and in 1560 a later proponent of southern English, Thomas Wilson, heaped scorn on a speaker who "barkes out his English Northren-like" (Wilson [1560]1909, 219).

Northern English struck southerners as an outlandish, frontier variety. Higden and Trevisa attribute its distinctiveness to three causes: the influence of nearby foreigners, the fact that the English kings seldom went north (and when they did, they took their southern retainers with them), and the prosperity of the south ("better corne londe, more peple, more noble citees, and more profitable hauenes"). All three are good reasons for supposing northern English to be different, but the best reason is the one that Higden and Trevisa ignore: the influence of the Scots on their southern neighbors. Because of their proximity to the Danelaw, the Scots acquired Norse loanwords early and used them in place of the cognates usual in Old English: *kirk* and *church*, *breeks* and *beeches*, *skirl* and *shrill*. Gaelic, formerly the language of both highlands and lowlands, also provided distinctive vocabulary: *loch, glen,* and *bog.* When Flemish weavers were brought to Scotland to encourage the manufacture of finished cloth, Scots borrowed such Dutch words as *golf, pinkie*, and *scone* (Murison 1979). Independent changes in the evolution of the language added to the distinctiveness of Scots and northern varieties of English, though Scots were ambivalent about whether to call their language "Inglis" or "Scottis" (McClure 1981).

Unfortunately, there is no comparable commentary from a northern Higden or Trevisa evaluating the language of the south. Yet the author of the *Cursor Mundi*, writing about 1300 in Northumbria, felt the need to translate a southern text for a northern audience: "In sotherin englis was it draun, /And turnd it haue i till our aun / Langage o northrin lede / Þat can nan oiþer englis rede" (Morris 1875, 1148). Such differences gave the northerners a distinctive linguistic independence.

A recently rediscovered record of a bigamy trial held at York in 1364 helps makes clear that linguistic variety within English had definite social meaning by that time. Having heard a deposition in the case, the judge discounted the testimony because the witness "often" shifted among three kinds of English: Scots (*Scoticum per modum Scotorum sonando ydioma Anglcanum*), southern English, and "pure" northern English (*Borialem mere*). Such "deliberate" shiftiness, as the judge saw it, was sufficient to discount the honesty of the witness, though both his childhood in Peebles (in the Scottish borders) and his long residence in England might also have explained his dialect (Clark 1981, 505). A similar view of southern English from a northern perspective appears in *The Second Shepherds's Play* (1385) in which a Yorkshire writer presents his principal character as a trickster able to disguise himself as an important southern official by speaking in "southern tooth" to the discomfiture of his friends. Comic as this piece of stage business is, it embodies the idea that an important personage would speak in a southern variety of English. By the end of the fourteenth century, northerners had apparently accepted the notion that "good English," the sort associated with important public business, was southern. Northerners were likely to be poorer, as Higden noted, and to resist the expansion of southern power; they also came to share the southerner's estimate of their English. For southerners, then and later, this difference in language came to be seen as a problem in need of solution. Writing about 1450, another southern author declared "that the commen maner of spekyng in Englysshe of some contre can skante be vnderstonded in some other contre of the same londe" (Blunt 1873, 8). National unity required that the language be made uniform, conforming to that of the south.

Varieties of English at the frontiers of English authority were considered, in Trevisa's word, *uplandish*—glossed by the *Oxford English Dictionary* as "rustic, rude, uncultivated, boorish." Beyond those frontiers lay the homelands of other languages spoken by militant peoples whose languages yielded loanwords: *clan* (< Scots Gaelic *clann* 'tribe'), *gael* (< Scots Gaelic *gaidheal* 'a Gaelic person'), *kern* (< Irish *ceithern* 'a band of foot-soldiers'), and *truant* (< French *truant* < Celtic *trudanach* 'vagabond'). Few named by these words rushed willingly to embrace the English, and their modern descendants retain, if not their languages, their separate identities: Scots, Cornish, Welsh, and Irish.

In Cornwall in the far southwest, the Cornish language sustained a vital oral tradition with occasional, minor uses of it in written form. Cornwall's political independence was effectively extinguished by the beginning of the tenth century. English rule separated it from its cognate languages—Breton on the continent, Welsh to the north—thus isolating the Cornish-speaking community except for those involved in fishing and other seafaring activities. Through ocean fishing and trade, Cornish survived and eventually contributed to the Atlantic lingua franca that began with the Newfoundland fishery in the sixteenth century. Along its landward boundaries, however, Cornish culture was almost defenseless and thus, following a military engagement concluded in 836, powerless to resist the encroachment of the Saxons and, after the Conquest, of their Norman-French successors.

As speakers of Cornish were few and powerless, they were unable to support institutions that would have strengthened their language community:

formal education, legal procedures, and the record keeping that accompanies routine occasions of civic life. Only as Cornish speakers verged on political power did the question of their language for such official purposes arise. When Henry Tudor returned from exile in Brittany to defeat Richard III and to assume the throne of England in 1485, he was assisted by a large rebel army from Cornwall and Wales. Some of his supporters from these two regions were awarded positions of authority, but "they adopted the English language, manners, and clothes and many of the Welsh who returned to Wales were nicknamed *Sais* (Englishman)" (Ellis 1974, 53). Certainly this label did not reflect enthusiasm for those who yielded to anglophone power and abandoned the resistance so long a distinctive trait of Cornish (and especially Welsh) politics. Nonetheless, it shows the attraction of English for those who wished to participate in the wider arena for power and wealth afforded by the English court.

Stern measures were at first employed in forcing English on the Welsh. A much more populous region than Cornwall, Wales had not been much influenced by English before the sixteenth century. With the Acts of Union of 1536 and 1542, however, Welsh speakers could only gain access to law courts if they were willing to seek justice in English. Even more persuasive for language choice was the provision in the 1536 act that

> henceforth no person or persons that use the Welsh speech or language shall have or enjoy any manner office or fees within this realm of *England, Wales*, or other the King's dominion, upon pain of forfeiting the same offices or fees, unless he or they use and exercise the *English* speech or language. (27 Henry VIII 20)

The only persons likely to be awarded "offices or fees" in the first place were anglicized Welsh people or English appointees, and thus the statute had little immediate effect in disseminating the use of English among the majority. But for the ambitious, the choice of English was made even more powerfully attractive. Parliament had flatly denied Cornish prayer books in 1549, but, in 1563, the government passed an Act for the Translation of the Bible and the Divine Service into the Welsh Tongue. Church politics thus transcended language policy, and the regular use of Welsh in Protestant religious observance helped to maintain the language among the mass of people unlikely to be granted offices or fees by the London government.

(The subsequent fate of Welsh is of interest since it has been the language community most resistant to English in Britain. After the beginning of the seventeenth century, Welsh bishops of the Anglican church sometimes provided clergy able to conduct services in Welsh, but the normal practice was to assign the "livings" to absentee English speakers while services were conducted in Welsh by resident curates. So pervasive was Welsh that, in the mid-nineteenth century, Parliament was obliged to provide for English speakers by authorizing churches for any ten petitioners who could provide a building and a stipend for an English-speaking minister. In the courts, Welsh speakers were again allowed to use their language in 1942, but only if they could prove that the use of English would put them at a disadvantage. Following passage of the Welsh Language Act of 1967, anyone could demand legal proceedings in Welsh without claiming such disadvantage.)

In medieval England, the severity of official action against other languages of the British Isles seems to have increased with the distance from London, and particularly strenuous efforts were made to maintain English at the expense of Irish. Speakers of English had first settled in Ireland early in the twelfth century as retainers of the Normans who imposed the feudal system on the Irish peasantry. Since English was not supported by those of the highest social rank—the Normans used French in the castles and towns—these English settlers were rapidly assimilated to the Irish language and customs. In 1366, at the same time that Edward III was making English the language of judicial proceedings in England, a parliament at Kilkenny issued an edict to regulate the behavior of those English who had forsaken "the English language, fashion, mode of riding, laws, and usages" thought fit for English people. These so-called statutes attempted to suppress intermarriage (as well as "fostering of children, concubinage, or amour") and stated that all English people—those descended from English immigrants—would henceforward use the English language and abandon the Irish language and the Irish surnames that many of them had adopted. The penalties imposed for disobedience were severe: loss of land and property, or, if those refusing to comply with the statutes owned no land, imprisonment (Curtis and McDowell 1943, 52– 59).

These laws had little effect on the use of English in Ireland, however. When most of their provisions were reaffirmed under Henry VII in 1485, those concerning the use of English were scrapped since the language was so little used in Ireland by that time that enforcement would have been impossible. English survived only in enclaves in the extreme south of the country and among a few of the educated who lived in towns and cities. After Henry VIII seized control of the church, the Irish language became strongly identified with Catholicism, even though its use was only occasionally and inconsistently supported by the bishops. Henry's Parliament required Protestant clergy in Ireland to preach in English and to provide schools for the instruction of the young in that language (28 Henry VIII 15), but these measures seem to have had almost no success in promoting English in family, commercial, and civic life. Late in the sixteenth century, English travelers found that Irish people able to speak English refused to do so, since the language implied allegiance to a foreign power and Protestantism (Bliss 1977, 7–8). The use of English diminished even within the pale of English power. Richard Stanihurst's *Description of Ireland* (1577) provides a glimpse of the social and linguistic scene:

> Of all other places, Weisforde with the territorye bayed, and perclosed within the riuer called the Pill, was so quite estranged from Irishry, as if a trauailer of the Irish (which was rare in those dayes) had picht his foote within the pile [= pale] and spoken Irishe, the Weisefordians would commaunde hym forthwith to turne the other ende of his tongue, and speake Englishe, or else bring his trouchman [= translator] with him. But in our dayes they haue so aquainted themselues with the Irishe, as they haue made a mingle mangle, or galla-maulfrey of both the languages, and haue in such medley or checkerwyse so crabbedly iumbled them both togyther, as commonly the inhabitants of the meaner sort speake neyther good English nor good Irishe. (quoted by Bliss 1979, 20–21)

The nature of this "medley" of English and Irish is difficult to reconstruct in the absence of contemporary representations, and we know virtually nothing of the *truchmen* and *truchwomen* who served to bridge the linguistic divide. The use of English, however, continued to diminish. Only with the settlements fostered in the north of Ireland by James I early in the seventeenth century, subsequently strengthened by aggressive colonization, did English become firmly and finally established in Ireland. Irish-influenced English appeared in London before 1530 and was especially associated with hawkers who sold fruits and vegetables in the streets of the city. Later in the same century, the Irish in London were commonly employed as house servants, and their variety of English was sufficiently known to become a staple of comedy in plays and other forms of popular entertainment. With civil strife in Ireland came the first of a series of migrations to England; since those who arrived were poor and uneducated, their English (like that of the Scots and Welsh before them) was regarded as a debased variety. By the late seventeenth century, this English had come to be known as "a brogue on the tongue" (? < Irish *bróg* 'shoe').

After nearly a thousand years, the English and Irish peoples continue a bitter warfare. From 1567–78, Henry Sidney represented England as Lord Deputy of Ireland; he was constantly engaged in combat with Irish forces led by The O'Neill, chief of Tyrone. This illustration appeared in John Derricke's *The Image of Irelande* (1581) and shows O'Neill's troops engaged with Sidney's forces. Despite penalties contrived in England to punish the use of Irish customs and language among English settlers, Ireland continued to assimilate migrants until well into the seventeenth century. Illustration courtesy of the University of Michigan Library.

What happened to accented English on the frontiers of English power also happened to the dialects nearer the center. Though diversity in the speech of the highest social class had been tolerated in earlier times, the emergence of modern Britain called forth forces of prescription. Education in the sixteenth century was perceived as a vehicle for linguistic change, even though only a handful of people had the opportunity to attend school. Many authors reflected on the right preparation for the governing classes, and, though the classical languages remained the focus of instruction, new roles were carved out for English. Writing in 1540, John Palsgrave argued (in a dedicatory preface to Henry VIII) that reading and writing in English could have valuable benefits. Such instruction would be especially important for those destined for the priesthood; many of them enrolled at the universities lacking "sufficient perfection in our owne tongue."

... yet for all this partely bycause of the rude language vsed in their natyue countreyes, where they were borne and firste lerned (as it happened) their grammer rules, & partely bycause that commyng streyght from thense, vnto some of your graces vniuersities, they haue not had occasions to be conuersaunte in such places of your realme, as the pureste englysshe is spoken, they be not able to expresse theyr conceyte in theyr vulgar tonge, ne be not suffycyente, perfectly to open the diuersities of phrases betwene our tonge and the latyn (which in my poore iudgemente is the veray chiefe thynge that the schole mayster shulde trauayle in). In so moche that for want to this sufficient perfection in our owne tongue, I haue knowen dyuerse of theym, which haue styl continued theyr study in some of your graces vniuersities, that after a substanciall encrease of good lernynge, by theyr great and industrious study obteyned, yet whan they haue ben called to do any seruice in your graces commen welthe, eyther to preach in open audience, or to haue other administration requiringe theyr assiduous conuersantynge with your subiectes, they haue then ben forced to rede ouer our englyshe auctours, by that means to prouyde a remedy vnto their euident imperfection in that behalfe. And when it hath fortuned any suche for theyr good name and estimation to be called from your vniuersities, to instructe any of your graces noble mennes chyldren, then euidently hath appered their imperfection in that case to be notable, and that to no smal detriment and hinderaunce of suche as they haue taken charge to enstruct and brynge forwarde. (Palsgrave 1540, A-iii[v]–A-iv[r])

Palsgrave's description of the setting for linguistic variety has a modern ring. In this statement he reflects the conventional wisdom of the time, but he also makes a new claim by suggesting the possibility of his book's contributing to making English "uniforme throughe out all your graces domynions." In his observation that English had, by 1540, reached "the hygheste perfection that euer hytherto it was" (B-i[v]), he expressed an idea that was not typical of his day, when the inadequacies of English in comparison to other languages were frequently anatomized. But Palsgrave's view would eventually prevail (see Jones 1953).

The problem that Palsgrave found so vexing lay in the diversity of English throughout the kingdom, and, in 1551, John Hart similarly characterized the varieties of the language.

We see that few of ani nation, doo come to the perfait speche of their mother toung in all their life. . . . So that yf they heare their neyghbour borne of their next Citie, or duelling not past one or two dais Iouney from theim, speaking some other word then is (in that place) emongest theim used, yt so litell contenteth their eare, that (more than folishli) they seem the stranger were therfore worthie to be derided, and skorned. (Danielsson 1955,115)

Both Palsgrave and Hart saw linguistic differences as a source of social discord and thought it necessary to select a perfected English that would fix the language for eternity. Once that decision had been made, all that remained was to determine the mechanism for keeping it stable. That need was addressed by William Bullokar a generation later.

> ... whereas men be of opinion, that our language is at this present time in perfect and sensible vse: my opinion is, that it is the great goodnes of God, if the same be now staied in that perfectnes, which may continue as long as letters shal endure: whereas before time (through the vnperfect writing and printing thereof) the same is changed (more or lesse) in euerie two or three ages, as may appeere by the antiquities. (Bullokar [1580a]1966,16–17)

For Bullokar it was not the English language in general that had achieved perfection but one particular variety of it which he designated on his title page "right speech."

The locus of this "right speech" had, by Bullokar's time, been settled: it was the English of the educated (though not of those at the universities or of preachers or schoolmasters), of those at the center of political power (though not secretaries, merchants, or others influenced by foreign languages through contacts abroad), and of the people living close to London (though not those engaged in productive labor nor the gentry who *condescend* to identify with *common people* through language). All the varieties of English from which an idealized norm might be selected presented distinct difficulties, and it is apparent that some degree of social condemnation attached to each variety. Elizabethans saw the divisiveness of varying kinds of English as a problem to be solved. Their consensus is best described by George Puttenham in a much-quoted passage from *The Arte of English Poesie*, published in 1589 but composed somewhat earlier.

> Then when I say language, I meane the speach wherein the Poet or maker writeth be it Greek or Latine, or as our case is the vulgar English, & when it is peculiar vnto a countrey it is called the mother speach of that people: the Greekes terme it *Idioma*: so is ours at this day the Norman English. Before the Conquest of the Normans it was the Anglesaxon, and before that the British, which as some will, is at this day, the Walsh, or as others affirme the Cornish: I for my part thinke neither of both, as they be now spoken and pronounced. This part in our maker or Poet must be heedyly looked vnto, that it be naturall, pure, and the most vsuall of all his countrey: and for the same purpose rather

than which is spoken in the kings Court, or in the good townes and Cities within the land, then in the marches and frontiers, or in port townes, where straungers haunt for traffike sake, or yet in Vniuersities where Schollers vse much peeuish affectation of words out of the primatiue languages, or finally, in any vplandish village or corner of a Realme, where is no resort but of poore rusticall or vnciuill people: neither shall he follow the speach of craftes man or carter, or other of the inferiour sort, though he be inhabitant or bred in the best towne and Citie in this Realme, for such persons doe abuse good speaches by strange accents or ill shapen soundes, and false ortographie. But he shall follow generally the better brought vp sort, such as the Greekes call [*charientes*] men ciuill and graciously behauoured and bred. Our maker therfore at these dayes shall not follow *Piers plowman* nor *Gower* nor *Lydgate* nor yet *Chaucer*, for their language is now out of vse with vs: neither shall he take the termes of Northernmen, such as they vse in dayly talke, whether they be noble men or gentlemen, or of their best clarkes all is a matter: nor in effect any speach vsed beyond the riuer of Trent, though no man can deny but that theirs is the purer English Saxon at this day, yet it is not so Courtly nor so currant as our Southerne English is, no more is the far Westerne mans speach: ye shall therfore take the vsual speach of the Court, and that of London and the shires lying about London within lx. myles, and not much aboue. I say not this but that in euery shyre of England there be gentlemen and others that speake but specially write as good Southerne as we of Middlesex or Surrey do, but not the common people of euery shire, to whom the gentlemen, and also their learned clarkes do for the most part condescend, but herein we are already ruled by th'English Dictionaries and other bookes written by learned men, and therefore it needeth none other direction in that behalfe. Albeit peraduenture some small admonition be not impertinent, for we finde in our English writers many wordes and speaches amendable, & ye shall see in some many inkhorne termes so ill affected brought in by men of learning as preachers and schoolemasters: and many straunge termes of other languages by Secretaries and Marchaunts and trauailours, and many darke wordes and not vsual nor well sounding, though they be dayly spoken in Court. Wherefore great heed must be taken by our maker in this point that his choise be good. And peraduenture the writer hereof be in that behalfe no less faultie than any other, vsing many straunge and vnaccustomed wordes and borrowed from other languages: and in that respect him selfe no meete Magistrate to reforme the same errours in any other person, but since he is not vnwilling to acknowledge his owne fault, and can the better tell how to amend it, he may seeme a more excusable correctour of other mens: he intendeth therefore for an indifferent way and vniuersall benefite to taxe him selfe first and before any others. (Puttenham 1936, 144–46)

This long passage is so illuminating that it merits special attention. Many of the subsequent images used in discussions of English are articulated here, not as new discoveries but as received wisdom. Positive and negative characterizations are expressed as moral opposites: gracious, natural, and pure; affected, false, ill-shaped, and strange. The "indifferent way" should be followed by the writer, a detached and impartial view of the language, one in which the judicious author rises above the vulgarity of variety to an ideal usage. Following much classical precedent, Puttenham acknowledges the Celtic, Old English, and Anglo-Norman examples that ought to decide questions of propriety and decorum, just as Cicero had been regularly invoked to settle norms for postclassical Latin usage. Though they should be "heedyly looked vnto," however, these exemplars have little contemporary relevance since "at these dayes . . . their language is now out of vse." Likewise the northern varieties, though they have a greater claim to the "purity" inherent in the "Saxon" ideal, must be examined and then dismissed because they are not "so Courtly nor so currant" as southern English. For Puttenham, the contradiction between classical ideal and current fashion is to be settled in favor of "the usual speach of the Court." Even though innovation is not to be desired, it must be accepted, since currency is a higher virtue than antiquity. People who are "vnciuill" or "of the inferior sort" have, in his view, no claim to influence this ideal; in uncivil, he draws upon the Latin etymon and asserts that those remote from the center of power, whether geographically or socially, cannot claim the traits associated with full citizenship— urbanity, grace, courtesy, and judgment. Good writers provide the best guide for linguistic choice, yet they too are given to "errours" which must be judicially rejected.

Even though no monolingual English dictionary had yet been published, Puttenham, Bullokar, and others foresaw how reference works could be employed to guide the formation of norms. Thus all the lines of modern thinking about the English language were laid out: the example of the past, the consent of the present, the behavior of those who wield power, the usage of the best writers, the authority of the "ruled" English of dictionaries. But Puttenham provided no principle for adjudicating controversies when these norms can be applied to support competing choices among usages. In the end the choice of a variety depends upon a compact between author and audience, speaker and listener. For a usage to be deemed worthy, there must be a willingness to regard it as acceptable. "The pureste englysshe" of which Palsgrave had spoken is not located in a vocation, region, or social class; it is an ideal arising from the persuasion of power.

What is especially consequential at the end of the sixteenth century is the creation of books to promote such ideas about English and to disseminate particular practices in its use. While the printing press had served as a source of uniformity in the written language for more than a century, monolingual grammars and dictionaries of English emerged to make the ideal of a "pure," national language attainable. Early in the sixteenth century, Thomas Elyot had laid out the principles for the education of young men "that hereafter may be demed worthy to be gouernours of the publike weale" (Elyot [1531] 1970, A2v), and he was particularly eager that such youth hear only Latin spoken around them:

> if it be possible / to do the same: or at the leste way / that they speke none englisshe but that / whiche is cleane /polite / perfectly / and articulately pronounced / omittinge no lettre or sillable as folisshe women often times do of a wantonness / wherby diuerse noble men / and gentilmennes chyldren (as I do at this daye knowe) haue attained corrupte and foule pronuntiation. (L3v)

By the end of the century, the solution to the problem of "corrupt and foul pronunciation" was to spread the knowledge of the norms deemed fitting not only for "governors" but for the "comminalitie."

Two instances will suffice to illustrate the nature of the apparatus that was designed to enforce consensus. The first is from Edmund Coote's *English Schoole-Maister* of 1596. In it, Coote laid out his plan of education for teachers who kept primary schools. These teachers and pupils were not merely from the gentry:

> The learneder sort are able to vnderstand my purpose, and to teach this treatise without further direction, I am now therefore to direct my speech vnto the vnskilfull, which desire to make vse of it for their owne priuate benefit: And vnto such men and women of trades (as Taylors, Weauers, Shop-keepers, Seamsters, and such other) as haue vndertaken the charge of teaching others. Giue me leaue therefore (I beseech thee) to speake plainly and familiarly vnto thee . . . thou maiest sit on thy shop-bord, at thy loomes, or at thy needle, and neuer hinder thy worke, to heare thy scholers, after thou hast once made this little booke familiar vnto thee. (Coote [1596] 1968, A3r)

In lessons teaching spelling, Coote made clear that there was a normative pronunciation and a normative spelling undergirded by an array of rules and exceptions. The assumptions of his school book are familiar to modern readers, since it was Coote who provided the foundation for subsequent teaching;

The English Schoole-Maister was published in fifty-four editions until it went out of print, at last, in 1737.

Even more propitious for modern English was the first monolingual English dictionary for a popular audience, Robert Cawdrey's *Table Alphabeticall* of 1604. Cawdrey restricted himself to "hard vsuall English wordes" (rather than attempting to define the common words of the language or the "outlandish English" and "strange ynckhorne termes" of the traveled and the learned). His title page declared his purpose: to provide

> the interpretation therof by *plaine English words, gathered for the benefit & helpe of Ladies, Gentlewomen, or any other Vnskilfull persons.* Whereby they may the more easilie and better vnderstand many hard English words, vvhich they shall heare or read in Scriptures, Sermons, or elswhere, and also be made able to vse the same aptly themselues.

Like Coote's schoolbook, Cawdrey's dictionary was aimed at a wide audience of the "unskillful" (those who did not know Latin); it was designed and served to spread a particular kind of knowledge for the use of the language. Scattered prejudice had begun to coalesce into a national image of the purest English.

Chapter 2

Emergent English

By 1600, English writers had begun the conversation that continues to this day concerning the virtues and faults that enhance or sully English. With the emergence of a consensus about the respectability of the language, there ensued disputes about just what the best English was and which expressions properly belonged to it. The literate and the learned recognized that the ideals of good English were being diffused through the social structure. Consequently, they created an ideology that persuaded some people to aspire to improve their usage, others to determine which aspirants could join the linguistic gentry, and still others to assume authority over the shape and development of the language. The recognition of English as a language worthy of serious use had an immediate consequence in differentiating its varieties.

Writing in 1592, Thomas Nashe credited "the Poets of our time" as the sources of that authority and influence.

> First and formost, they haue cleansed our language from barbarisme and made the vulgar sort here in *London* (which is the fountaine whose riuers flowe round about *England*) to aspire to a richer puritie of speach, than is communicated with the Comminaltie of any Nation vnder heauen. (Nashe 1966, 1:193)

The notion that the shapers of the norm had an opportunity—and subsequently an obligation—to "communicate with the Comminalitie" is, ostensibly at least, a democratic ideal. Anyone making the effort should be able to join the speech companionship of good English and, as a consequence, make use of that English to participate in the pleasures and profits that ought to flow from membership. What was accomplished by the diffusion of this belief, however, was not democratic at all; language became an additional means

of social discrimination, and those who were not full participants were readily identifiable by their speech. (Richard Carew wrote that a foreigner could
not master the intricacies of English; through a foreign accent such a person
"carrieth evermore a watch-word upon his tong to descrie him by" [Camden
1984, 40]; 350 years later, George Orwell wrote with more optimism than
hope for his English contemporaries: "No one should be 'branded on the
tongue'" [Orwell and Angus 1970, 3:51].) By the beginning of the seventeenth century, the inchoate linguistic biases described in the previous chapter had begun to be anatomized and codified.

In Elizabethan England, scholars and wealthy collectors fostered copious speculation about English and its origins. Many were antiquaries who
examined everything—documents, coins, ruins, place and family names,
heraldry, and, most especially, languages—to support their imaginings about
the history of Britain. From a modern point of view, these inquirers seem to
be merely eccentric dilettantes, but they were among the first to give respectability to English. An impecunious member of this company was Richard
Verstegan (ca.1550–1620). Of humble background, he enrolled at Oxford
as "Richard Rowlands" and deeply immersed himself in the history of England and its language. As a result of his enthusiasm for the Germanic
background of English, he assumed his grandfather's Dutch surname on
leaving the University. A zealous Catholic, he went abroad in 1587 and never
returned to England, although he retained his fervid patriotism and scholarly
interests in antiquarian subjects bearing on the national character.

In 1605, Verstegan published *A Restitution of Decayed Intelligence*,
which began with the Biblical account of the flood and the tower of Babel.
After the collapse of that structure, he wrote, the source of the "English-
Saxon language" appeared at an instant: "This language vndoubtedly is that
which at the confusion of *Babel*, the Teutonic people (those I mean that were
conducted by *Tuisco*) did speak. And as the people took their name after their
conductor, so the language consequently took the name of the people"
([1605] 1976, 188). In this speculation, Verstegan considered but did not
endorse the more radical view of Joannes Goropius Becanus (John Van Gorp)
who held that the "Teutonic" language was not among the residue of Babel
but, in fact, was "the moste ancient language of the world; yea the same that
Adam spake in *Paradise*" (Verstegan [1605] 1976, 190). Though he reluctantly dismissed this opinion—one that achieved considerable popularity in
Becanus's day (see Jones 1953, 215–19)—Verstegan nonetheless concluded
that "yf the Teutonic bee not taken for the first language of the world, it
cannot bee denied to bee one of the moste ancientest of the world" ([1605]

1976, 192). In finding special virtue in its "Saxon" and monosyllabic component, he provided an extended argument, one still commonly articulated,
that the Latin-Romance elements of the English wordstock are a linguistic
blemish on an otherwise excellent tongue.

Verstegan's conjecture was that, on naming-day in Eden (Gen. 2:19),
Adam created words for "every living creature" and that these words were
monosyllables: "This our ancient language consisted moste at the first of
woords of monosillable, each hauing his own proper signification, as by
instinct of God and nature they first were receaued and vnderstood" (189).
Subsequently, human beings contrived to combine these monosyllabic words
and increase the range of meaning they could express. Nonetheless, Verstegan thought, the "Teutonic" monosyllables were close to the primitive,
prelapsarian lexicon ordained by divine providence, and these words were
thus a testimony to the antiquity and excellence of English. In this view, he
echoed conventional regrets that polysyllables had crept in to defile the language. This "corruption," Puttenham wrote,

> hath bene occasioned chiefly by the peeuish affectation not of the Normans them
> selues, but of clerks and scholers or secretaries long since, who not content
> with the vsual Normane or Saxon word, would conuert the very Latine and
> Greeke word into vulgar French, as to say innumerable for innomerable,
> reuocable, irreuocable, irradiation, depopulation & such like, which are not
> naturall Normans nor yet French, but altered Latines, and without any imitation
> at all: which therefore were long time despised for inkehorne terms, and now
> be reputed the best & most delicat of any other. (1936, 117)

Yet as regrettable as the importation of polysyllables was, Verstegan felt
borrowings did not drastically alter the Teutonic nature of English. In an
ingenuous extension of Puttenham's argument, Verstegan declared that "the
old and true French, was in effect all one with our ancient English" ([1605]
1976, 201), and it too suffered from the importation of Latin words, though
he thought he could discern the ancient Germanic substratum "mingled" with
the Latin. Though the true "Saxon" English had been corrupted by French
borrowings, its claim to excellence was not thereby much diminished since
French was, at its base, a Teutonic language as well.

For Verstegan, the special virtues of English were to be found in the
Saxon monosyllables whose preservation reflected the steadfast and conservative character of the people who spoke the language. The French, less
staunchly loyal to their ancient language, were thus to be pitied, and their

In 1631, Cambridge University undergraduates published a comedy satirizing Garbriel Harvey (1545?–1630). The frontispiece of this work, *Pedantius*, shows a foppishly dressed teacher with two admiring pupils; behind them is a library of the Latin authors from whom Renaissance English scholars drew to enrich their vocabulary. Ridiculed by Thomas Nashe for his "fine leg and a daintie foot . . . in pumps and pantoffles," Harvey appears in the *Oxford English Dictionary* for such usages as *perfidy* 'betrayal,' *recumbentibus* 'a knock-down blow,' and *vagation* 'wandering.'

infidelity was further confirmed by their abandoning French in England after the Conquest and acquiring English "howbeit . . . they much mingled and tempred it with their French" (203). As a consequence of these arguments, Verstegan allied himself with those who were alarmed by the contemporary impulse to add to the primitive Saxon wordstock even more borrowed words.

> For myne own parte I hold them deceaued that think our speech bettered by the aboundance of our dayly borrowed woords, for they beeing of an other nature and not originally belonging to our language, do not neither can they in our toung, beare their natural and true deryuations: and therefore as wel may we fetch woords from the Ethiopians, or East or West Indians, and thrust them into our language and baptise all by the name of English, as those which wee dayly take from the Latin, or languages thereon depending: and heer-hence it cometh (as by often experience is found) that some Englishmen discoursing together, others beeing present and of our own nation, and that naturally speak the English toung, are not able to vnderstand what the others say, notwithstanding they call it English that they speak. (204–05)

By such sentiments, Verstegan articulated, for the seventeenth century, the purist and nativist views of English that would shape later thinking about the language. He admitted that English people "delight in strange language-borrowing" (206) but warned that such innovations diminish the true and ancient character of the language, create needless problems of communication among English speakers, and invite the scorn of foreigners, who regard borrowing as evidence of insufficiency in the language.

To this discussion, Verstegan appended an alphabetical list of obsolete words of Germanic origin in the hope that poets would assist him in reviving them for current use: *bead* to replace *prayer*, *fuglas* for *fowls*, *gyfta* for *marriage*, *rood* for *cross*, *scypman* for *mariner*, *wrec* for *revenge*, and many others. (This saxonizing was forgotten when he conceived *A Restitution of Decayed Intelligence* as the title of his book, since all three of its principal words are of Latin-Romance origin.) As with successors bent on improving the language, he noted that English omits needful distinctions, in particular failing to differentiate male from female friends; to this end, he proposed *freundine* or *freundina* for *shee-freind*. Still more Germanic words were to be found, he thought, "among the countrey people that neuer borrow any woords out of the Latin or French" (195). Yet as the reliance of his list on literary sources shows, he was chary of seeking the true foundation of the language among such folk since some of them were influenced by the "il pronountiation of their yong children." Even so, these rustics were the repository of the best that is in English; like Puttenham, Verstegan saw the innovators and borrowers as the source of what made English so unfortunately various—clerkes, scholars, secretaries, and those who find borrowings "very sportefull in [their] own ears" (206).

Almost as soon as it was published, Verstegan's *Restitution of Decayed Intelligence* evoked a reply, *The Excellencie of the English Tongue* by Richard Carew (1555–1620). Carew was Verstegan's near contemporary; both matriculated at Christ Church, Oxford, in 1565. Verstegan was a Catholic, the son of a cooper; he did not complete his degree at Oxford (because he declined to declare allegiance to the established church) and subsequently made his living abroad as a printer and engraver. Carew, on the other hand, was a Protestant, the child of a landed family in Cornwall, a lawyer educated in the Middle Temple, a member of Parliament and lord-lieutenant for Cornwall, and an accomplished poet. Carew's essay was a patriotically English reply to his classmate's arguments (see Wood 1977).

A member of the Society of Antiquaries since 1589, Carew had been favorably impressed by the publication of William Camden's *Remains Concerning Britain* in 1605, and he wrote admiringly about the book, in April of that year, to his friend Robert Cotton. In a chapter devoted to the languages of Britain, Camden had celebrated the Germanic origins of English with the same pride Verstegan had expressed in his book of the same year: "This English tongue is extracted, as the nation, from the Germans the most glourious of all now extant in Europe for their morall, and martiall vertues, and preserving the libertie entire, as also for propagating their language by happy victories . . ." (Camden 1984, 23). Though apparently aware of Becanus and his theories, Camden did not venture an opinion on "the antiquity of our language," but he regarded English monosyllables as "most fit for expressing briefly the first conceipts of the minde, or *Intentionalia* as they call them in schooles" (30), even though (as Puttenham and others had remarked) they made it difficult for English poets to imitate classical verse meters. Camden's observations were full of linguistic patriotism: "pardon me and thinke me not overballanced with affection, if I thinke that our English tongue is (I will not say as sacred as the Hebrew, or as learned as the Greeke,) but as fluent as the Latine, as courteous as the Spanish, as courtlike as the French, and as amorous as the Italian, as some Italianated amorous have confessed" (30).

Carew apparently found these sentiments congenial and probably immediately wrote down his own extension of Camden's observations while replying to Verstegan's opinions. *The Excellencie* was published as a separate chapter of the 1614 edition of Camden's *Remains,* and the continuing popularity of that work kept his views alive. In 1644, a pamphlet published without attribution at Oxford, *Vindex Anglicus, or the Perfections of the English Language Defended and Asserted,* borrowed copiously from Carew's essay; eighteenth- to twentieth-century editions of Carew's prose masterpiece *The Survey of Cornwall* included the essay entire. In 1688, the grammarian Guy Miège paraphrased with enthusiasm and approval the ideas he found in *Vindex Anglicus* (A6r), and in this way Carew's ideas continued to be influential long after Verstegan had been forgotten. A genteel and accomplished member of the establishment, Carew reflected more certainly than Verstegan the views that were coming into fashion at the beginning of the seventeenth century.

Like Camden, Carew set out to prove that the English language was "matchable, if not preferrable before any other in use at this day" (Camden 1984, 37). English, he thought, is superior because it has more letters in its alphabet than Greek, Latin, French, or Italian (thanks to the use of *w*); its interjections are more naturally connected with the emotions they express (to support this claim he instanced *alacke, phy, haa, whowpe,* and *wahahowe*). Compound words are graceful, brief, and "significant" (which he illustrated by pointing to the metaphoric meaning contained in the constituents of such words as *moldwarp* 'mole' [composed of *earth* + *thrower*], *upright,* and *wisdome*). Carew declared that foreigners never gain a full mastery of English, but English people quickly command other languages so that they "nothing differ from the patterne of that native language" (40). English authors are a match for classical ones:

> . . . will you have *Platoes* veine? reade Sir *Thomas Smith,* the *Ionicke?* Sir *Thomas Moore, Ciceroes? Ascham, Varro? Chaucer, Demosthenes?* Sir *John Cheeke* who (in his treatise to the Rebels) hath comprised all the figures of Rhetorick. Will you reade *Virgill?* take the Earle of Surrey, *Catullus? Shakespeare* and *Marlowes* fragment, *Ovid? Daniell, Lucan? Spencer, Martial?* Sir *John Davies* and others: will you have all in all for Prose and verse? take the miracle of our age Sir *Philip Sidney.* (Camden 1984, 42–43)

The celebration of English writers, many of them Carew's contemporaries, was remarkably prescient (or at least in accord with the preferences of his successors) and certainly novel in its suggestion that his contemporaries were the equal of the revered authors of antiquity.

In his most direct dissent from Verstegan's views, Carew claimed that the many borrowed words in English were a sign of its virtue and richness. Prevailing opinion, echoed by Verstegan, held that ancient languages were "pure" and their "purity" was somehow sullied by words from other languages. But Carew asserted that classical example provides ample evidence that the revered writers of ancient Greece and Rome borrowed words when "either necessitie or convenience" inclined them to do so (41). That justification is sufficient, for "in other languages there fall out defects" that their speakers have not the wit or the inclination to repair as English speakers do through borrowing. The result is that English is rich and copious.

> . . . the long words that we borrow being intermingled with the short of our owne store, make up a perfect harmonie, by culling from out which mixture (with judgement) you may frame your speech according to the matter you must worke on, majesticall, pleasant, delicate, or manly more or less, in what sort you please. (43)

Such "harmonie" makes English a copious language and thus, in Carew's view, an excellent one.

Carew found much to praise in English, and his essay is correspondingly expansive. For instance, he is the first on record to regard the diversity of English dialects as one of the ornaments of the language.

> Moreover the copiousnesse of our language appeareth in the diversitie of our Dialects, for wee have Court and we have Countrey English, wee have Northerne, and Southerne, grosse and ordinarie, which differ each from other, not onely in the terminations, but also in many words, termes, and phrases, and expresse the same things in divers sorts, yet all right [= write] English alike. . . . (42)

The idea that is strikingly modern here is that a single form of written English encompasses the diversity of spoken varieties. By Carew's time, the conventions of written English had stabilized and served equally the needs of the quite different speakers who made use of them. Carew was capacious in his admiration, treating southern and northern English on an equal footing, "court" English as parallel to "countrey" (by which he means the speech of the gentry living at a distance from the capital), and "grosse" (describing the English of the illiterate and uncultivated, *OED* sense 14.b) as akin to "ordinarie" (the language of the next highest social class, *OED* sense 5). He found in all this variety an argument for the "excellencie" of English.

Carew went far beyond Camden in the extravagance of his claims for English in comparison to other languages (which he knew well).

> The Italian is pleasant but without sinews as a still fleeting water. The French, delicate, but over nice as a woman, scarce daring to open her lippes for feare of marring her countenance. The Spanish majesticall, but fulsome, running too much on the O, and terrible like the divell in a play. The Dutch manlike but withall verie harsh, as one readie at everie word to picke a quarrell. Now we in borrowing from them, give the strength of consonants to the Italian, the full sound of wordes to the French, the varietie of terminations to the Spanish, and the mollifying of more vowels to the Dutch, and so (like Bees) gather the honey of their good properties and leave the dregges to themselves. And thus when substantialnesse combineth with delightfulnesse, fulnesse with finenesse, seeme-linesse with portlinesse, and currantnesse with stayednesse, how can the language which consisteth of all these, sound other than most full of sweetnes? (43)

Others before him had suggested that English was not worse than other vernaculars; Carew was among the first to say that it was better.

Carew's enthusiasm for English was soon imitated by those who wished to proclaim their linguistic patriotism.

> . . . what Englishman of vnderstanding is there, but may be delighted, to see the prety shifts our tongue made with her owne store, in all parts of learning, when they scorned to borrow words of another? Albeit now sithence wee haue taken that liberty which our neighbours doe; and to requite them more then for need, our language is improued aboue all others now spoken by any nation, and become the fairest, the nimblest, the fullest; most apt to vary the phrase, most ready to receiue good composition, most adorned with sweet words and sentences, with witty quips and ouer-ruling Prouerbes: yea able to expresse any hard conceit whatsoeuer with great dexterity; weighty in weighty matters, merry in merry, braue in braue. Tell me not it is a mingle-mangle; for so are all: but the punishment of confusion we marke not so much in other tongues, because wee know not them and their borrowing so well as our owne: and this also is delightfull to know. (L'Isle 1638, fol. 3)

These observations, written about 1623, echo Carew's enthusiastic celebration of variety in English vocabulary with its combination of Germanic and Romance words. They further illustrate that not all "Saxonists" were as stiff-necked as Verstegan had been. (This appreciation comes from one of the first anthologies of Old English texts, compiled by William L'Isle [1569?–1637].)

Some of the virtues that Carew listed were widely accepted as signs of the approaching (or even actual) perfection of English. Thus, many old arguments against the language lost some of their force: English was no longer regarded as "rude, rusty, cankered, and dull" (all words used by John Skelton to describe the language at the beginning of the sixteenth century [Rollins and Baker 1954, 77]); denunciations of borrowings from other languages were less firmly expressed; the influence of poets was viewed as beneficial and their writings as evidence that English was at least the equal of other languages ancient and modern; as knowledge of earlier English texts was spread, the idea that English could claim a respectable history emerged (laying the foundation for the idea that English is an "old," and consequently a good, language). The arguments fulfilled the agenda set out by Richard Mulcaster (1532?–1611) at the end of the previous century for demonstrating the "sufficiency" of English: "the antiquitie of our tung, the peples wit, their learning, and their experience" (Mulcaster [1582] 1970, 79). The emerging celebration of English was thus brought to maturity.

Nonetheless, the diversity of English dialects continued to trouble observers, and many prejudices of the past were repeated and codified. Though Carew had declared that "the copiousnesse of our language appeareth in the diversitie of our Dialects," few were inclined to share that opinion. One typical opposing view was expressed by Alexander Gill (1565–1635), the headmaster of St. Paul's School (where he was Mulcaster's immediate successor and John Milton's teacher). Like the others so far discussed, Gill was an antiquarian with an interest in the history of English, but he was also (like Carew) an enthusiastic admirer of contemporary authors (regarding Spenser's *Faerie Queene* as an epic superior to Homer's). An acute observer of the spoken English of his own day, Gill proposed spelling reforms, wished to reduce borrowing when "Saxon" equivalents could be used or fabricated by compounding, and desired a grammatical analysis for English so it could be "ruled" as the ancient languages had been and thus reduced to order. On the subject of dialects, he had firm opinions. In England, he explained, there are six dialects: common, northern, southern, eastern, western, and poetic (Gill 1621 [1903], 31). These he described and evaluated:

> among all dialects, none is so flavored with barbarism as the western; among the country folk in the rural parts of Somerset, one can readily question whether they are even speaking English or some foreign idiom. (33)

Gill's word *barbariem* in his Latin text draws upon the relatively neutral notion of the Greeks and Romans, who used this concept to name languages other than their own. But as the word was borrowed into English at the beginning of the sixteenth century, it acquired an additional connotation, one that is clearly seen in the definition for *barbarism* provided by Cawdrey in his *Table Alphabeticall*: "rudenesse, a corrupt forme of writing or speaking." To regard the dialect of Somerset (or any other region) as "barbaric" was to view it as a corrupted form of some originally "purer" language. Gill seems to approve of the fact that these country folk "still retain ancient usages," but (what to him is reprehensible) they also invent some words of their own and "corrupt legitimate words" (*legitima corrumpunt*), "sometimes by applying them in the wrong way and sometimes by mispronouncing them." Such practices, however, are only found among the folk.

> The things I have said here about dialects you will understand to pertain, for the most part, to country folk, for among those of gentle nature and cultivated upbringing [*mitioribus ingenijs & cultius enutritis*] every place is as one in language and accent and meaning. (34)

This notion, rather than Carew's, emerged as the "right" way to look at variety in English; the gentry and the genteel, though regionally dispersed, were a unified social class with a single kind of English against which others could be measured and found wanting or regarded as "barbaric."

What is most remarkable in these disputes is how linguistic arguments are adapted to suit political allegiances and antagonisms. Just as Gill found it easy to argue that the gentlefolk (whose children attended St. Paul's, the universities, and the Anglican Church) best represented the unsullied language, so the republicans and royalists, Puritans and adherents of the "high church," preferred arguments on the merits of English. Following the theme established by Nashe and Carew, the dramatist Thomas Heywood wrote (probably in 1607) *An Apology for Actors* to defend dramatic performances against ever more vigorous attacks from the Puritans, who would succeed in closing the theaters in 1642 as a step in their efforts to purify and modernize English social life. Heywood's view of the history of the language was of ever-increasing improvement.

> . . . our *English* tongue, which hath ben the most harsh, vneuen, and broken language of the world, part *Dutch*, part *Irish, Saxon, Scotch, Welsh*, and indeed a gallimaffry of many, but perfect in none, is now by this secondary means of playing, continually refined, euery writer striuing in himselfe to adde a new

flourish vnto it; so that in processe, from the most rude and vnpolisht tongue,
it is growne to a most perfect and composed language, and many excellent
workes, and elaborate Poems writ in the same, that many Nations grow
inamored of our tongue (before despised). . . . Thus you see to what excellency
our refined *English* is brought, that in these daies we are ashamed of that
Euphony & eloquence which within these 60 years, the best tongues in the land
were proud to pronounce. (Heywood [1612] 1941, fol. 3)

Heywood's views were opposed by one I. G. (initials expanded to "John
Green" by subsequent readers), who regarded plays as an institution of the
Devil (Green [1615] 1941, 58).

Green's *Refvtation of the Apology for Actors* appeared in 1615, three
years after Heywood's essay had been published. In it he responded, point
by point, to Heywood's arguments, especially emphasizing, through Biblical
and classical citation, the immorality of the stage. When he at last arrived at
the effect of acting on English, he introduced a novel theme to the dispute.

. . . [Heywood] sheweth (and to the disgrace of his mother-tongue) that our
English was the rudest language in the world, a Gallymafry of Dutch, French,
Irish, Saxon, Scotch, and Welsh, but by Play-Poets it hath been refined. But
doth he not forget, that whiles they adde Greeke, Lattine, and Italian, they
make a great mingle-mangle. Nay, before the Conquest by Bastard *William*
that the French came in, our English tongue was most perfect, able to expresse
any Hebruisme, which is the tryall of perfection in Languages, and now it will
very hardly expound a Greeke Lecture. For after that the French had once
corrupted it, it was but of late years that it would recouer a common Dialect
againe. Since which againe it hath indeed been more refined, but thereby it is
become more obscure, and vsed amongst few, for the simple vulgar people
cannot vnderstand it: And a plaine man can scarce vtter his mind, for want of
Phrases (as I may say) according to the fashion. But what refinednesse is in our
language, it's not from Poets, but from other learned mens writings, from
whom they borrow all the refined words they haue. (Green [1615] 1941, 41–42)

This diatribe was a new turn on the old theme of linguistic borrowing.
However, Green introduced a new idea in arguing that borrowing is socially
divisive. The "simple vulgar people cannot understand" the English that
reflects the classical education afforded to the few (who cannot resist importing vocabulary from Greek and Latin) or the English of those who have had
opportunities for leisurely travel abroad, a privilege limited to the offspring
of the gentry (from which the language obtains vocabulary from Italian and

French). The linguistic dispute (paralleling the political divisions that would eventually culminate in the English civil war) was ultimately class based, and Green (like other Puritans) argued on behalf of ordinary people against the "authority" of the higher social classes. His argument was not elaborated beyond the passage quoted, and the Puritan divines were themselves zealous coiners of arcane vocabulary that required special explanation to "simple vulgar people." Yet he argued along democratic lines that some were denied participation in the common discourse as a consequence of innovations from the highest social class.

The urgency of establishing a reputable image for English is revealed in the vituperative language Gill adopts in the closing sentences of his chapter on dialects.

> About that poisonous, rotten sore of our nation it is shameful to speak. The disgusting refuse of society, the wandering vagabonds, have not so much their own dialect as a cant or language which no law or punishment ever controls (until the day when Justice by public edict shall compel its authors to be crucified). But because this whole dialect, along with the murderous scum who use it, is described in its own book (and because nothing useful may be added for the benefit of outsiders), I will forego discussion of it in my work. (Gill [1621] 1903, 34)

Gill did not bother to name the particular "refuse of society" whose language caused him such anger; their identity was obvious to any contemporary reader and most particularly to someone who spent his life close to St. Paul's in London, as Gill did while headmaster of its school. He meant the thriving, linguistically creative, and highly organized society of criminals who regularly cruised the aisles of the huge church in search of victims.

There were several published collections of criminal argot by the time Gill wrote, and it is not clear just which "book" he had in mind (see Salgado 1972 and 1977). Then, as now, the criminal underworld was viewed by the respectable with a mixture of curiosity and revulsion, and, from the mid-sixteenth century forward, popular publications presented ballads, biographies, and even dictionaries describing criminal practices and language. Frequent use of specialized criminal slang in the plays of Shakespeare, Jonson, and their contemporaries shows that these varieties of English were widely known. Some vocabulary still in current use is first recorded in these sources: *cant* (1640) and *canting* (1567) 'the language of the underworld' and the use of that language; *doxy* 'prostitute' (1530); *duds* 'ragged clothing' (1508);

fence, both the receiver of stolen property and the act of receiving it (1610); *foist* (now mainly used as a verb, 'to put forth or allege fraudulently') the act of introducing a palmed die into a gambling game (1545) or, as a noun, 'a pick-pocket' (1591); *pimp* (1607); *slang* (1756) 'language of tramps and thieves' (> 'vividly informal language' [1818]); and *swigman* (1561) or, later, *swagman* 'peddlar, tramp.'

To focus only on the words that survive from this source is, however, to neglect the rich and complex sociolinguistic background that Gill's dismissive comment draws to modern attention. As is the case with later and better documented "secret languages," the primary purpose of Elizabethan cant was to assert the solidarity of those engaged in the criminal subculture. While a few of these terms might well convey information among thieves within the hearing of unwitting gulls or victims, most of it was used within the subculture itself and served to identify the participants and practices in the remarkably differentiated world of crime. In a much-quoted passage from the *Description of England*, William Harrison speculated about the origins of this language.

> It is not yet fifty years sith this trade began: but how it hath prospered sithens that time, it is easy to judge; for they are now supposed, of one sexe and another, to amount unto above ten thousand persons, as I have harde reported. Morover in counterfeiting the Egyptian roges, they have devised a language among themselves, which they name Canting, but others Pedlars French, a speache compact thirty years since of English, and a great number of odde words of their own devising, without all order or reason; and yet such it is as none but themselves are able to understand. The first deviser thereof was hanged by the neck, as a just reward, no doubt, for his desartes, and a common end to all of that profession. (quoted in Grose 1963, 8)

Pedlar's French, first attested in English in 1530, suggests the international flavor of this language (precisely parallel to the sources of borrowing for "respectable" English): *cant* itself from Latin; *kinchin cove* 'little boy' and *kinchin mort* 'little girl' from German, *bonaroba* 'wench' from Italian, *palliard* 'professional beggar' from French. An even more important source of this vocabulary is to be sought in Harrison's allusion to "Egyptian rogues," the gypsies whose language, Romani and Angloromani, contributed significantly to the technical terminology of the Elizabethan underworld (see Hancock 1984). From the words *Egyptian* and *gypsy* comes the term *gibberish* (1554), originally applied contemptuously to unintelligible speech and

A CADGER'S MAP OF A BEGGING DISTRICT.

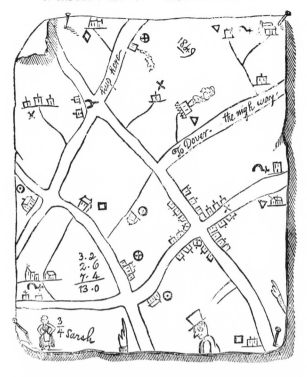

EXPLANATION OF THE HIEROGLYPHICS.

No good; too poor, and know too much.

Stop,—if you have what they want, they will buy. They are pretty "*fly*" (knowing).

Go in this direction, it is better than the other road. Nothing that way.

Bone (good). Safe for a "cold tatur," if for nothing else. "*Cheese your patter*" (don't talk much) here.

Cooper'd (spoilt) by too many tramps calling there.

Gammy (unfavourable), likely to have you taken up. Mind the dog.

Flummuxed (dangerous), sure of a month in "*quod*," prison.

Religious, but tidy on the whole.

Criminal subcultures have provided a rich source of vocabulary for English, and seventeenth-century dictionaries attempted to increase sales by listing words from them. In John Camden Hotten's *Slang Dictionary* (1864), "slang, cant, and vulgar words" were given full treatment and illustrated through quotations from such literary figures as Shakespeare, Middleton, and Thackeray. "Hieroglyphs" used by beggars to signpost the lay of the land were imagined to share with other English usage a descent from remote antiquity. "How strange it would be if some modern Belzoni, or Champollion [scholars who deciphered the Rosetta stone], discovered in these beggars' marks traces of ancient Egyptian or Hindoo sign-writing!" ([Hotten] 1874, 31—32).

expressive of the consternation and alarm felt by respectable people overhearing the "secret" language of the underworld. Borrowings from Romani are a significant part of *cant*: *cove* (1567) 'chap, fellow,' freely combined with other cant or English in, for instance, *bene cove* 'good fellow' and *gentry cove*; *filch* 'pilfer' (1561), *jarkman* 'forger' (1561); *maund* 'beg' (1567) and *maunder* 'beggar' (1609); *rum* 'good, excellent, strong' (1567), which occurs in a remarkable number of combinations (e.g., *rum mort* 'the Queen,' *rum booze* 'good liquor or wine,' and *rum cull* 'a man whose wealth is ready for the taking').

Elizabethan cant reflects other linguistic creativity in the period. While the learned were pouring "inkhorn" classical vocabulary into English, the counterculture of crime enriched its technical language through borrowing and creative use of the existing English wordstock. Various phrases for the specialized roles, practices, and settings of the underworld reveal this verbal exuberance: *bene faker of gibes* 'skilled forger of documents,' *counterfeit crank* 'pretended epileptic,' *knight of the post* 'hired character witness,' *prigger of prancers* 'horse thief,' *stalled to the rogue* 'initiated as a beggar,' *vaulting house* 'brothel.' In discussions about the dimensions of English, Carew and other commentators divided the world into court and country, northern and southern, "gross and ordinary." The criminal subculture made its division between rogues and honest folk, and language was a primary vehicle by which the separation was made. The language of the criminals and prisoners is "overlexicalized" with a broad range of near synonyms for practices, objects, and roles of considerable interest (see Halliday 1978). Just as the criminal world closely imitates the value system of respectable society (with salient differences, of course), so in its attitudes toward language the Elizabethan underworld mirrored the linguistic preferences of its time. The innovations fostered by Renaissance rhetoricians, natural scientists, and physicians were, in principle, no different from those of the "canting crew" (see McMullan 1984, esp. 95–116).

Criminal argot shows a playfulness with language as well as a desire to create a special vocabulary to describe the minute particulars of professional life. Lawyers, doctors, scholars, and theologians were all enthusiastic borrowers of new words, drawing first upon Latin (from which writers drew most extravagantly between 1520 and 1650) and then Greek (after 1800 with the explosive growth of science). The rage for new words was praised for adding copiousness to the language and condemned for tending toward obscurity. Ben Jonson's *Poetaster* (1601) satirized the practice of ornamenting the language with new words in a scene of extravagant vulgarity; Crispinus, a character based on John Marston, is given an emetic and thus forced to expel a series of "terrible, windy words": *barmy froth, chilblained, clumsy, clutched, conscious, damp, defunct, fatuate, furibund, glibbery, incubus, inflate, lubrical, magnificate, oblatrant, obstupefact, prorumpted, puffy, quaking custard, reciprocal, retrograde, snarling gusts, snotteries, spurious, strenuous, turgidous, ventositous.* Virgil, the character reflecting Jonson's view of linguistic propriety, then declares how this malady of inventiveness can be cured.

> You must not hunt for wild, outlandish terms,
> To stuff out a peculiar dialect;
> But let your matter run before your words:
> And if, at any time, you chance to meet
> Some Gallo-Belgic phrase, you shall not straight
> Rack your poor verse to give it entertainment;
> But let it pass: and do not think yourself
> Much damnified if you leave it out;
> When, nor your understanding, nor the sense
> Could well receive it.
>
> (Jonson [1640] 1981, 1:216–19)

Two things are striking about Jonson's list of "wild, outlandish terms": many of them come from medicine (which, then as now, was famed for obscure language); several have become part of the core vocabulary of English and are now regarded as indispensable and "standard" (a kind of evolution that has often been the undoing of linguistic proscription).

The argument about English thus resolved itself into two distinct and opposing views. One side sought to enhance the "purity" of English and to foster simplicity and uniformity: Verstegan, Gill, Green, and Jonson brought quite different assumptions and aspirations to bear in that quest. The other celebrated "copiousness" and "eloquence": Carew, Heywood, and many unnamed innovators and borrowers wished to increase the range of usage (even at the expense of uniformity). Yet both sides reflected an advocacy of English despite their differing ideas of what sort of English was the ideal. Palsgrave's notion that students could perfect their English through Latin translation had been reversed; English, assisted by dictionaries and grammars, could be a vehicle for the appreciation of the classical languages. To that end, English speakers needed to persuade themselves that "purity" and "copiousness" were not irreconcilable opposites. Words needed to be "authenticated" by inclusion in dictionaries; linguistic structure needed to be shown to have the same sort of grammatical regularity discerned in Greek and Latin. When Ben Jonson turned his hand to the latter task about 1623, he found just the linguistic virtues he had been seeking. By compiling a grammar of English (on the model of Latin), he insisted:

> wee free our Language from the opinion of Rudnesse, and Barbarisme, where-
> with it is mistaken to be diseas'd; We shew the Copie [= copiousness] of it,
> and Matchablenesse, with other tongues; we ripen the wits of our owne Chil-
> dren, and Youth sooner by it, and advance their knowledge. (Jonson [1640]
> 1972, 33)

These arguments were increasingly appealing to teachers when Jonson wrote. In 1624, John Hewes published a Latin grammar whose title sums up his effort to give order to English by conforming it to Latin: *A Perfect Survey of the English Tongve, Taken According to the Vse and Analogie of the Latine*. Such attempts to reduce English to rules like those found in William Lily's ubitiquous Latin grammar soon prevailed and remain part of anglophone cultural bric-a-brac to this day.

As the celebration of English emerged, English writers began to question the assumption that Latin was the only proper vehicle through which an international audience might be reached and the best means for ensuring that one's works would be read by posterity. (Both Bacon and Newton composed scientific works in Latin, and Milton considered and then rejected the idea of writing *Paradise Lost* in that language.) For early seventeenth-century intellectuals, the choice between Latin and English was a real one, but Edmund Waller's poem, written at midcentury, reflected what, by that time, had become a minority opinion.

> But who can hope his lines should long
> Last, in a daily changing tongue?
> While they are new, envy prevails;
> And as that dies, our language fails.
>
> When architects have done their part,
> The matter may betray their Art;
> Time, if we use ill-chosen stone,
> Soon brings a well-built palace down.
>
> Poets that lasting marble seek,
> Must carve in *Latin* or in *Greek*,

We write in sand, our language grows,
And like our tide, our work o'erflows.

(Waller 1904, 2:69–70)

To say that English "overflows," as Waller wrote, was to declare that it had exceeded its bounds or become excessive or inordinate (*OED* sense 5.b). "Classical" ideas of constraint and formality, in his view, were incompatible with an exuberant, ever-changing language.

Waller's contemporary, John Dryden, better expressed the view at the end of the seventeenth century. In a prefatory poem to a Latin schoolbook, Dryden declared:

Latine is now of equal use become
To Englishmen, as was the Greek to Rome:
It guides our language, nothing is exprest
Gracefull or true but by the Roman test.

(Barnard and Hammond 1984, 586)

As the Greek language (through the ancient rhetoricians and grammarians) had provided a "guide" to eloquence in Augustan Rome, so now could Latin serve the same role for English. Taking Latin as an ideal provided a model for language reformers who wished to recreate English with "musical" suffixes, to improve it with explicit grammatical gender, or even to hope for the ineffable eloquence of the Latin gerund (see below, p. 183). Though most such proposals were visionary and impracticable, the notion that Latin "guides our language" became a staple of grammatical instruction in English. Acknowledging that English lacked the formal case-marking system of Latin, textbook writers nonetheless introduced English speakers to the array of cases to which English might aspire. Thus in *Grammar of the English Language* (1795), the most influential school book in both Britain and the United States for more than a century, Lindley Murray (1745–1826) criticized other grammarians for multiplying distinctions and objected to the idea that English has "as many cases as in the Latin tongue." Nonetheless, he listed the six Latin cases in singular and plural with English equivalents: *Nominative* 'A Lord, Lords'; *Genitive* 'Lord's, of a Lord, Lords', of Lords'; *Dative* 'To Lord, To Lords'; *Accusative* 'A Lord, Lords'; *Vocative* 'O Lord, O Lords'; *Ablative* 'By a Lord, By Lords' (Murray 1816, 45). Such was the consequence of Dryden's "Roman test" applied to English.

The anxiety that language change made English an unsuitable vehicle for important writings, however, continued to arouse linguistic jeremiads for many subsequent observers, but Waller's notion that growing "copiousness" made the language "overflow" was a special preoccupation of his contemporaries. What is of special interest is that the increasingly compendious dictionaries served a double function and supported both sides of the controversy between purity and copiousness. By being incorporated in dictionaries—most especially Thomas Blount's *Glossographia* (1656) and Edward Phillips' *New World of English Words* (1658)—the vocabulary was both authenticated (by being "registered") and increased (since dictionaries became larger and larger as earlier words were joined by new inclusions). Each lexicographer thus set out to make earlier dictionaries obsolete by adding entries, and if the newly added words were not "pure English" (as conceived by Verstegan and like-minded critics), they were seen as English nonetheless. The trend toward inclusiveness reached a recognizably modern shape in Elisha Coles's *English Dictionary* of 1676 with: "a large addition of many words and phrases that belong to our English Dialects in the several Counties" ([1676] 1971, 5); "Old Words" to give readers access to *"Chaucer, Gower, Pierce Ploughman, and Julian Barnes"* (6); "difficult Terms that are used in Divinity, Husbandry, Physick, Phylosophy, Law, Navigation, Mathematicks, and other Arts and Sciences" (title page); and even "Canting Terms" (whose inclusion "may chance to save your throat from being cut, or (at least) your Pocket from being pickt" [6]).

Writing just after the restoration of the monarchy, Thomas Sprat found a typically English solution to the problem of selecting among the varieties of the language. Reflecting on the tumult of the civil war, he declared that such times were inevitably innovative both for ideas and the language used to express them.

> In the Wars themselves (which is a time, wherein all Languages use, if ever, to increase by extraordinary degrees; for in such busie and active times, there arise more new thoughts of men, which must be signifi'd, and varied by new expressions) then I say, it receiv'd many fantastical terms, which were introduc'd by our *Religious Sects*; and many outlandish phrases, which several *Writers*, and *Translators*, in that great hurry, brought in, and made free as they pleas'd, and with all it was inlarg'd by many sound, and necessary Forms, and Idioms, which it before wanted. And now, when mens minds are somewhat settled, their Passions allai'd, and the peace of our Country gives us the opportunity of such diversions: if some sober and judicious Men, should take the whole Mass of our Language into their hands, as they find it, and would set a mark on the ill Words; correct those, which are to be retain'd; admit, and establish the good; and make some emendations in the Accent, and Grammar:

I dare pronounce, that our *Speech* would quickly arrive at as much plenty, as it is capable to receive; and at the greatest smoothness, which its derivation from the rough *German* will allow it. (Sprat [1667] 1958, 42)

His proposal for an English Academy to regulate the language by "marking the ill Words" and "establishing the good" did not come to fruition in explicit public action. Yet how to sort varieties of the language into better and worse continued to occupy the thoughts of commentators. (With the exception of Sprat and a few others, the Royal Society showed little interest in English, though many of its seventeenth-century members were occupied with constructing perfected artificial languages.)

The consensus that emerged in the seventeenth century was to select a linguistic middle way between the perils of polysyllabic eloquence and the bluntness of very short words. Sprat believed that "fantastical terms" and "outlandish phrases" had led to civil unrest in the generation of his youth; "*eloquence*," he thought, "ought to be banish'd out of all *civil Societies*, as a thing fatal to Peace and good Manners" (1958, 111), and the "easie vanity of *fine speaking*" (112) corrupted and distorted intellectual inquiry. Members of the Royal Society, he believed, had hit upon the best form of the language.

They have exacted from all their members, a close, naked, natural way of speaking; positive expressions; clear senses; a native easiness: bringing all things as near the Mathematical plainness, as they can: and preferring the language of Artizans, Countrymen, and Merchants, before that, of Wits, or Scholars. (113)

The ideal English thus became centered firmly in a conceptual midpoint between the florid and the inarticulate, the aristocracy and the folk, the overly learned and the uneducated. Subsequent disputes turned to the issue of just what sort of English lay in that middle ground and just which expressions from intellectual and geographical voyagers would be admitted to it.

Chapter 3

English Abroad

As English speakers discarded feelings of linguistic inferiority, they began to declare that their language was at least as good as any other, and it was inevitable that the opinion makers should not stop with asserting its mere equality. Searching for evidences of English superiority, writers soon discovered one in its diverse vocabulary. Opposing purists (who saw in the variety of English vocabulary a defect), Richard Mulcaster declared, in 1582, that the tendency to borrow from other languages was a sign of English wit and intelligence:

> If the spreading sea, and the spacious land could vse anie speche, theie would both shew you, where, and in how manie strange places, theie haue sene our peple, and also giue you to wit, that theie deall in as much, and as great varietie of matters, as anie other peple do, whether at home or abrode. Which is the reason why our tung doth serue to so manie vses, bycause it is conuersant with so manie peple, and so well acquainted with so manie matters, in so sundrie kindes of dealing. Now all this varietie of matter, and diuersitie of trade, make both matter for our speche, & mean to enlarge it. For he that is so practised, will vtter that, which he practiseth in his naturall tung, and if the strangenesse of the matter do so require, he that is to vtter, rather then he will stik in his vtterance, will vse the foren term, by waie of premunition [= forearming], that the cuntrie peple do call it so, and by that mean to make a foren word, an English denison. (Mulcaster [1582]1970, 81–82)

Richard Carew, whose ideas were discussed in chapter 2, conceived receptiveness to borrowings in a mercantile metaphor: "we employ the borrowed ware so farre to our advantage that we raise a profit of new words from the same stocke, which yet in their owne countrey are not merchantable" (Camden 1984, 41). These ideas became, almost immediately, a commonplace in the celebrations of English that continue to excite matrilingual sentiments. Mulcaster's and Carew's successors find a ready audience by repeating this idea: "English has been growing fast for 1,000 years, promiscuously borrowing words from other lands. 'English accepts new words and is more friendly to change than other languages'" ("Why English Is So Easy to Mangle" 1985, 53).

The English were late participants in the great expansion of European power that began in the fifteenth century; the Portuguese, Spanish, and Dutch languages, in particular, reached around the world long before English was much used outside the British Isles. From 1375 to 1550, a time of great prosperity in England, there was little urgency to seek riches overseas for there was so much wealth at home. But as the English population increased, personal income and productivity fell, and Britain began to consider exporting its "excess population." Economic and demographic factors thus became a spur to the spread of English. Just as the plague had been an impetus to the consolidation of English as the language of public life in the fourteenth century, so at the end of the sixteenth, as population outstripped resources, and hunger, unemployment, and growing poverty again became stark facts of life in Britain (see Hatcher 1977, 70), the language, through emigration, went abroad.

Individual voyagers and nations brought varying assumptions and expectations to the people they met in the "remote" places they visited, and one of the striking facts about the effect of exploration and colonialism on English is how the late start is mirrored in word borrowing. Many words were first borrowed, adapted, and used in *other* European languages and from those languages came into English. That process is illustrated in the first word of North American origin to be used in English, *guaiacum* (a Caribbean tree whose resin was used as a medicine), which was borrowed by the Spanish from the Taino language of the Bahamas, given a Latin form in a medical treatise, and thence used as an English word in 1533. By a similar process, English obtained from the Americas (among many other words) *canoe*, *chocolate*, *potato*, *tobacco*, and *tomato* through Spanish and *caribou*, *bayou*, *sassafras*, *toboggan*, and *totem* through French. Such secondhand borrowings reveal how much of the contact with aboriginal peoples was mediated through other European explorers and settlers, at least some of whom were more likely to integrate themselves into the North American cultures than their English successors (see Malkiel 1976).

The situation was the same outside North America, where English came into contact with other cultures. *Tea* and *typhoon*, both ultimately of

Chinese origin, came into English first through Dutch and Portuguese, respectively. The Portuguese were world travelers, and accounts of their voyages brought vocabulary, often adapted or modified through intermediate stages, into English: *Bonze* 'priest' was the first Japanese loanword to enter English (in 1588); *assagai*, a slender spear formerly widely used as a weapon in Africa, derived from a Berber language and reached English in 1523; *betel*, the plant that yields a stimulant usually chewed with palm nuts and lime, had its origin in the Tamil language of India and Sri Lanka and entered English in 1553; *junk*, the Asian sailing vessel, first appeared in English in 1555; *mango*, the fruit, from Malay or Tamil in 1582; *proa*, another sailing ship, in 1582. All these words came to English through Portuguese. While there were certainly many direct borrowings from "remote" languages later, it was the precursors of European expansionism who provided the initial vocabulary. Their sense of racial superiority made English voyagers less receptive to borrowings that had not already been, in part, authenticated by other European travelers.

The dependence on continental European languages for words from remote places and exotic languages has usually been ignored in the ritual celebrations of the excellence of English, where secondhand words have been regarded as freshly borrowed by intrepid English travelers. *Bazaar* reached English in 1599 from its ultimate Persian source through Turkish and then Italian; *caravan* and *divan*, likewise from Persian, entered English through French. The principal agents in this borrowing process were not the seafarers or merchant explorers, but travel writers who explored new worlds in books. Typical of such writers, Richard Hakluyt explained his practice in the preface to his *Principall Navigations*.

> Whatsoever testimonie I have found in any authour of authoritie appertaining to my argument, either stranger or naturall, I have recorded the same word for word, with his particular name and page of booke where it is extant. If the same were not reduced into our common language, I have first expressed it in the same termes wherein it is originally written, whether it were a Latine, Italian, Spanish or Portingall discourse, or whatsoever els, and thereunto in the next room have annexed the signification and translation of the wordes in English. (Quoted by Finkenstaedt and Wolff 1973, 57)

Hakluyt and his like did their adventuring among volumes of European origin and, thus, were anglicizers of the innovations made elsewhere. Yet their "new" words were almost immediately declared to be signal evidence of English as "receptive" to exotic foreign borrowings.

The circumstances of English language contact do not support this romantic notion of linguistic accommodation. In North America, where the French had earlier come to foster trade with native peoples and to draw them to Christianity, the first English settlers were explicitly colonists, living in self-contained communities, depending upon Britain for supply and resupply, and indifferent, until necessity drove them to seek help, to the indigenous peoples. There was little two-way linguistic contact to influence English. When they discovered that the areas of their intrusion did not abound in precious gems and metals, most English adventurers quickly subdued or displaced the native peoples. It was a pattern repeated elsewhere. In the Caribbean, English invaders challenged and then displaced the Spanish and seized control of plantation agriculture with its slave-based work force. Along the West African coast, English adventurers began to trade early in the sixteenth century, but they followed the long-established Portuguese routes and were obliged to make use of a trade language strongly influenced by Portuguese. Cook's late eighteenth-century voyages to the northern Pacific, Australia, New Zealand, and the Oceanic civilizations of Polynesia and Melanesia opened these regions to English influence, but the Spanish had initially explored the areas in the north and east, while Abel Tasman (a Dutchman who was probably preceded by Spanish and Portuguese explorers) had discovered and partly charted Fiji, Australia, and New Zealand in the 1640s (see Sharp 1963).

English voyages to North America began with seasonal fishing trips from the Bristol and other west of England ports to the Grand Banks, New-foundland, and the islands off Cape Breton. Though Giovanni Caboto, a Venetian sailor hired by the Bristol merchants whom he obliged by adopting the name John Cabot, is credited with the "English" discovery of the continent of North America in 1497, his successors were not colonists but fisher-folk, who paid seasonal visits and saw little reason to remain in the harsh, northern regions during the winter. Only in 1583 did a Devonshire entrepreneur, Humphrey Gilbert, declare a colony at present-day St. John's, New-foundland, and claim the land on behalf of Queen Elizabeth I before an indifferent audience of Breton, Welsh, Portuguese, and English fisherfolk then engaged in using the port to dry rack upon rack of cod for the European market. (The supposed place of Gilbert's landing is today marked by a monument, and, in 1983, Newfoundlanders celebrated on that spot, memorializing the "four-hundredth anniversary" of the British Empire.) The earliest lexical borrowings arriving home from North America are, unsurprisingly, from the European languages used in the fishery rather than Amerindian words: *baccalao* 'codfish' (from Portuguese, 1555), *penguin* 'the great auk, *Alca impennis*' (from Breton, 1578), and *Canada* itself (from French, where it had been borrowed and adapted from Iroquoian by 1536 and employed in English by 1568). Even *tobacco*, one of the early loanwords from the Americas and an important product of colonial trade, reached English only in 1577, nearly fifty years after both the word and plant had been introduced to Europe by the Spanish. Before the end of the sixteenth century, there was little English used abroad and, consequently, little direct influence on English from the languages outside Europe.

Colonizing began in earnest with Walter Raleigh, Gilbert's brother-in-law. In 1584, the Queen granted him letters patent "to discover search fynde out and viewe such remote heathen and barbarous landes Contries and territories not actually possessed of any Christian Prynce and inhabited by Christian people as to him his heyres and assignes and to every or any of them shall seme good and the same to haue holde occupy and enioye to him his heyres and assignes for ever with all prerogatives comodities iurisdiccions and royalties priviledges Fraunchises and preeminences there or thereaboutes bothe by sea and lande" (Quinn 1955, 82). Raleigh's voyages to Roanoke in present-day North Carolina are consequential for the spread of English, since they mark the first extended interaction between English people and aboriginals. Yet what brought English people to North America was not, primarily, the desire for exploration or colonies but rather the search for a port from which English privateers could attack Spanish shipping and thus open a western front in the anticipated European war with Spain (6).

Given the rapid destruction of the Amerindian community by the European intruders, it is difficult to determine just how the native population regarded the newcomers beyond disputes (as the Europeans construed them) over whether the fair-skinned visitors were gods or reincarnations of ancestral heroes. The English expeditions found it easy to impute to the people they encountered the same acute sense of rank and hierarchy that was so much the distinctive trait of European society, and so they readily identified the people they encountered as of high or low "birth" without imagining that the cultures might have a different system of social organization. Among the first English visitors, there was a readiness to impute to the Amerindians the political prejudices that the English themselves held—for instance Miles Philips (who was cast away in a mutiny in 1568 and struggled until 1582 to return home from the Caribbean basin) "learned . . . the Mexican tongue very perfectly" and found that the inhabitants were "a courteous and loving kind of people, ingenious, and of great understanding, and they hate and abhor the Spaniards with all their hearts" (Hakluyt 1985, 150).

On their way to the proposed base on Roanoke Island, the English travelers were especially aware of the Spanish and other Europeans who had been to the region before them. After their first encounter with the Algonquian inhabitants, whose language they could not understand, the English determined to return better prepared to evaluate and understand the land and its peoples. Thomas Harriot (1560–1621), hired by Raleigh to tutor him in mathematics so that he could improve his navigation, is a remarkable figure in this encounter. Engaged on the 1585 voyage to Roanoke as a mapmaker, he was also expected to conduct an economic analysis of the resources the explorers encountered. Harriot was given special responsibility for two Amerindians brought back to England, and he had the double task of teaching them English and learning what he could of their language. Harriot is the first to have elicited directly from native speakers a list of Amerindian words for the English reader, and those who followed him (particularly John Smith and William Strachey) were also assiduous recorders of Native American vocabulary. But aside from personal names (like *Powhatan* and *Pocahontas*) or place names (like *Virginia*, named for the virginal Elizabeth I but influenced by the name of the chief who welcomed the English to Roanoke, *Wingina*), Harriot's transcriptions of words for the plants, animals, and social practices of North America gained little currency in English, though *manitou* and *skunk* endure from his *Briefe and True Report of the New Found Land of Virginia* (1588). Harriot's work reflects a curiosity about these newly encountered people and a willingness to learn from them. His account, coupled with the drawings by his companion, John White, shaped English understanding of native American peoples for the half century that followed.

The two Amerindians who visited England after the 1585 voyage, Manteo and Wanchese, represent (with Harriot) the intersection of cultures and languages that eventually had important consequences for the development of an interlanguage, bilingualism, and mutual influence on the languages involved. The long sea voyages typical of these journeys of exploration allowed leisure that could be used in learning languages, and in nearly every report of explorations, some (usually unnamed) member of the ship's party was available at crucial junctures to act as a translator. These interpreters seem to have been part of the polyglot crew of nearly every expedition and, in English, were called first *linguoa* (< Portuguese, 1554) and later *linguists* (1711). Such *linguists* were essential to the British everywhere they

C.Smith taketh the King of Pamavnkee prisoner 1608

When the Age of Discovery finally took hold in Britain, English gained a reputation as a language receptive to borrowings from far-away languages. Illustration from John Smith's *Generall Historie of Virginia, New England and the Summer Isles* (1624). Courtesy of the William L. Clements Library, University of Michigan.

went, whether on sea or ashore; in New England, such helpful individuals were known as *linguisters* (ca. 1649). Words borrowed from the newly encountered languages came first from them and subsequently to the narrators of the journey and to the reading public. Bookish and obsolete as many of the words surviving from these contacts often now seem, the fact of their borrowing is important for the idea of English as a receptive language for loanwords.

Brought to England with the first Roanoke expedition, Manteo and Wanchese were the objects of great curiosity. According to one contemporary account, "their usual habit was a mantel of rudely tanned skins of wild animals, no shirts, and a pelt before their privy parts. Now, however, they were clad in brown taffeta. No one was able to understand them and they made a most childish and silly figure" (quoted by Quinn 1955, 116, n. 6). Manteo, a Croatoan, was a willing traveler and quickly became highly anglicized; Wanchese, his companion and a Roanoke, possibly kidnapped, was less enamored of England and the English (Quinn 1985, 39). Apparently both quickly learned to speak English, however, and soon were supplying information about their homeland. According to a recent study of the surviving accounts:

> they are referred to specifically as a source—"as these men which we have brought with us into England have made us to understand." A two-way exchange of information was now taking place and we are strongly inclined to give Thomas Harriot credit for this. (43)

Manteo's two visits to England, the first from September, 1584, to April, 1585, and the second from July, 1586, to April, 1587, led first to his being regarded as a valuable informant and then as a client of the London government, and Raleigh declared him to be the "lord" of Roanoke and the surrounding territory under the English crown (Quinn 1955, 531). Exactly how he regarded that status, or whether his people saw him in any new light, is impossible to reconstruct. The English, however, viewed him as their special friend, and when the colonists vanished from their settlement between 1587 and 1590, it was first assumed that they had gone away under Manteo's protection. This story is the foundation of a persistent myth that underpins even present-day ideas about the expansion of English power: relatively cordial initial contacts, a helper who befriends the settlers, and subsequent hostilities between emigrants and aboriginals in which the native peoples are much blamed.

Wanchese and, particularly, Manteo are thus representative figures in the early spread of English beyond the British Isles. Though regarded as "silly and childish," they were involved in an information exchange that influenced the knowledge and languages of both cultures. Harriot prepared a dictionary, later destroyed in the Great Fire of London in 1666, of the Algonquian language of Roanoke and devised a phonetic alphabet to record its sounds. His writings on the language were used by subsequent explorers, and his work inspired others to compile word lists and seek knowledge of North American languages. While most of the words Harriot recorded for newly encountered plants did not remain in English—Harriot's *metaquesunnauk* is now known as the *prickly pear*, for instance—he and others treated the newly encountered peoples with a measure of respect that was reflected in their linguistic studies. Nothing is known of what Manteo brought back from England to his people; David Quinn is probably correct in speculating that his reports may have been influential (1985, 236). But the cultural exchanges were not immediately useful to either side. Only after long struggle did the English finally learn that tobacco would provide an export economy for continuing colonies. The native Americans acquired the use of metal tools, edged weapons, and firearms. Quinn's conclusion is a succinct summary of the longer term consequences.

> The Eastern Woodland culture, encountered by the Elizabethans and Jacobeans, had existed with some considerable degree of stability since roughly the time of the Norman conquest of England. Within fifty years after 1585 it had begun to be shattered by English intrusions, by English diseases, by English arms. The Roanoke colonies can be seen as striking the first blow at this culture in eastern North America. (423)

The enlarging of the English vocabulary was thus purchased at enormous cost to native cultures; allegedly a language "friendly to change," English has accumulated its wordstock as an incidental consequence of the extension of anglophone power.

Far from an expression of internationalism or intellectual curiosity, British expansion flowed from economic and political motives. John Smith, promoter of Roanoke's successor colony in Jamestown, articulated the rationale for England's exportation of its excess population.

> Who can desire more content that hath small meanes, or but onely his merit to advance his fortunes, then to tread and plant that ground he hath purchased by

the hazard of his life; if hee have but the taste of vertue and magnanimity, what to such a minde can bee more pleasant then planting and building a foundation for his posterity, got from the rude earth by Gods blessing and his owne industry without prejudice to any, if hee have any graine of faith or zeale in Religion, what can he doe lesse hurtful to any, or more agreeable to God, then to seeke to convert those poore Salvages to know Christ and humanity, whose labours with discretion will triple requite thy charge and paine; what so truly sutes with honour and honesty, as the discovering things unknowne, erecting Townes, peopling Countries, informing the ignorant, reforming things unjust, teaching vertue and gain to our native mother Country; a Kingdome to attend her, finde imploiment for those that are idle, because they know not what to doe: so farre from wronging any, as to cause posterity to remember thee, and remembring thee, ever honour that rembrance with praise. (Smith 1986, 2:420–21)

This view—that English people of "small means" or none and who might otherwise be idle—describes the justification for North American and subsequent imperialism. The notion that the native inhabitants be converted to Protestant Christianity was, as Smith clearly states, designed to provide a pliant work force for the kingdom overseas that would yield wealth (and leisure) for the colonists and gain to "our native mother Country." (The unwillingness of the Amerindians to become servants and agricultural workers had, as one of its consequences, the beginning of the coerced migration of Africans to North America from the Caribbean and Africa.) Smith's colonizing efforts in Virginia also gave loanwords to English: *hickory* (1618), *hominy* (1629), *moccasin* (1612), *moose* (1603), *oppossum* (1610), *pone* (1612), *raccoon* (1608), and *sagamore* (1613), but on the English side the integrative phase was short lived.

Roanoke, Jamestown, and the Massachusetts Bay settlements provide a legendary backdrop to what is now seen as the beginning of American history. The names of prominent figures from these colonies are taught to U.S. schoolchildren: Virginia Dare, the first North American–born Englishwoman, at Roanoke; John Smith and Pocahantas at Jamestown; William Brewster, Miles Standish, John Alden, and Priscilla Mullens in Massachusetts. For the purpose of understanding the linguistic setting, however, the most interesting of these well-remembered people is Tisquantum (or Squanto), the special helper who emerged from the forest to assist the Mayflower pilgrims in their struggle to survive in an environment for which they were utterly unprepared.

From the Native American point of view, Tisquantum was a traitor to his people, since he enabled distinctly unwelcome outsiders to gain a foothold on the mainland of North America. It was he, after all, who, in William Bradford's grateful recollection, directed the Pilgrims "how to set their corn, where to take fish, and to procure other commodities, and was also their pilot to bring them to unknown places for their profit, and never left them till he died" (Bradford 1952, 81). Tisquantum had been kidnapped by an English slaver in 1614, taken to Spain, and (in Bradford's words once again) eventually "was entertained by a merchant in London, and employed to Newfoundland and other parts" (81). Returning to Cape Cod in 1618, he discovered that the Patuxets, his tribal group, had been exterminated by disease, and so he attached himself to Massasoit and the Wampanoag, with whom he remained until the English colonists arrived and shortly found themselves in dire need of his technical and linguistic skill. "Squanto continued with them," Bradford wrote, "and was their interpreter and was a special instrument sent of God for their good beyond their expectation" (81).

What was especially remarkable, though little discussed in popular accounts of the colony, is that Tisquantum appeared almost immediately after the Mayflower arrived and spoke fluent English. Through his agency, the colonists avoided the difficulties their counterparts had faced at Roanoke and Jamestown, and, thanks to more abundant records from Massachusetts Bay, it is possible to discern some of the impulses that must have motivated Tisquantum to adopt the colonists and assist them. The plague that wiped out his people while he was in Europe, probably a disease of European origin, left him as an outsider of uncertain status with the Wampanoag. The English colonists commanded a technology (most particularly medicine) that the Wampanoags desired, and Tisquantum made good use of his command of languages to mediate the mutual needs of the two groups. Though some of his behavior was viewed by the Europeans as greedy and childish, he was almost certainly using the power their presence offered to further his own claims as a shaman. His motive was to advance his power among his adopted people, and thus his interests, in some respects, coincided with those of the colonists, since by helping them sustain themselves he could maintain them as a source of gifts and military force on behalf of the Wampanoag (see Shuffelton 1976). From the contacts initiated through Tisquantum emerged most of the first enduring loanwords from native American languages indigenous to New England: *papoose* (1634), *powwow* (1624), *sachem* (1622), *squash* (1634), *squaw* (1634), *wampum* (1636), and *wigwam* (1628). Like the words from Virginia, these reflect English curiosity about native life and customs and direct contact between English speakers and aboriginal peoples.

This curiosity led a few scholars to investigate Amerindian languages in detail. The first was Thomas Harriot, and though he spent little time in North America, his investigation of Amerindian languages prepared the way for intercultural communication. A second major figure in this effort was John Eliot (1604–90), who became a school teacher in England after taking a degree from Cambridge and, finding his increasingly Puritan views unsupported by the established church, migrated to Massachusetts in 1631. Like Harriot and Smith, he had a special interest in the Native American peoples, and he too had a purpose for them in mind—not to learn about their resources or to subdue them for physical labor, but to convert them to Christianity. With the help of a young Amerindian whom he took into his household, he translated the Ten Commandments and the Lord's Prayer into the Massachusetts dialect of Algonquian. By October, 1646, he was able to preach in the language; in 1653, he published a *Catechism*; and finally, in 1664, he completed and published a translation of both Old and New Testaments. Unflagging in his efforts, Eliot produced schoolbooks—*Indian Dialogues* (1671) and *Logic Primer* (1672)—to foster literacy, and by the time of his death, missionary work in Amerindian vernaculars had reached its height in New England.

In order to convert the Native Americans to the seventeenth-century idea of Christian piety, it was first necessary to undermine their existing culture. Wearing European clothes, adopting contemporary hair styles, and dividing the work of agriculture and spinning according to received ideas of the appropriate roles for men and women were prerequisites to conversion. Removed from their traditional villages and their communal life-style, the converts were herded into "praying towns" where they could have, once they had been declared "civilized," the benefit of preaching by Eliot and others drawn to the cause, the opportunity to send their children to school, and access to agriculture and trade paralleling the practices of the colonists. For the Native Americans whose culture had not been impaired through English influence, these were not popular attractions. While some efforts were made to educate the converts and to ordain them as ministers, including a short-lived Indian college at Harvard started in 1654, almost all of these programs were unsuccessful (see Salisbury 1974).

Interaction between Native Americans and English people in the mid-seventeenth century had many of the traits that lead to linguistic influence: substantial numbers of bilinguals in regular communication, literacy and written documents in both languages, and shared economic and cultural experiences. Yet on the English side, there is little surviving trace of this influence beyond place and personal names. Some words formerly in use

have become obsolete: *matchit* 'bad' (attested in 1638; "But, at last, he
entertained the distinction, that there were 'matchet' Englishmen as well as
'matchet' Indians, . . . that is to say, naughty or wicked" [1705, quoted by
Mathews 1951 and Goddard 1977, 38]); *netop* 'friend, companion' ("The
Indian . . . shooke her . . . by ye hand, and asked her where her netop was"
[1662, quoted by Mathews 1951], widely used as a term of address from
Virginia to New England [Goddard 1977, 39]); *peag* 'shells used as money'
("No peage, white or black, [shall] bee paid or receiued, but what is
strung . . . sutably, and not small and great, vncomely and disorderly mixt"
[1648, quoted by Mathews 1951]). For the most part, however, the flow of
borrowings at the outset of English migration to North America slowed to a
trickle as the Europeans consolidated power and had less need for interaction
with the long-resident peoples. The native population, on the other hand,
experienced debilitating and eventually genocidal destruction; their languages were hastened to extinction.

Another side of the attempt by the English to "civilize" Native Americans appears in the work of Eliot's near contemporary, Daniel Gookin
(1612–87). Gookin first migrated to Virginia with his father, who had been
engaged to transport colonists and their livestock from Ireland. As a noncon-
formist in religion, Gookin was expelled from Virginia and migrated to New
England in 1643–44. In 1656, he was named Superintendent of the Indians
in Massachusetts, a position he held until the end of his life. About 1674,
he wrote a petition to English philanthropists that includes a chapter "Con-
taining Proposals, as an Expedient for Civilizing the Indians, and Propagating the Gospel Among Them"; this document illuminates the cultural and
linguistic assumptions of the English colonists in North America.

> That which I shall here offer, may be comprehended under two heads. First,
> that utmost endeavours be used, with all industry and diligence, that the Indi-
> ans, especially the children and youth, may be taught to speak, read, and write,
> the English tongue.
>
> For this end I propose, first, that as many of their children as may be
> procured, with the free consent of their parents and relations, be placed in sober
> and christian families, as apprentices, until the youths are twenty one years, and
> maids eighteen years of age: the males to be instructed in the trade practised
> by their masters; and the females in good housewifery of all sorts: with this
> provision in all contracts and indentures, that they shall be taught to read and
> write the English tongue at the cost of their masters. And this may be easily
> accomplished, because servants are scarce in New England. The ordering of
> this affair must be committed to the management of prudent persons, that have

an interest in the Indians, and that may be able, by their authority and wisdom, so to argue this case with the Indians, as to convince them that this way is for their children's good; for they are generally so indulgent to their children, that they are not easily persuaded to put them forth to the English.

Secondly, another way for bringing this matter to pass, is by setting up one or two free schools, to learn them to read and write English. But because this thing hath some difficulty in it; partly because, first, a suitable pious person for a schoolmaster will not be willing to leave the English society, and to live constantly among the Indians, as such a work will require: and, secondly, how the Indian children that are sent to school, shall be provided with diet and clothing, without charge to the Indian stock,—excepting only a blue coat for each of them once a year, which will not cost much, but may greatly encourage the Indians:—and therefore it must be contrived, for effecting this thing, that those difficulties may be obviated. (Gookin 1792, 79)

There is something repellent in his judgment that the Amerindians were "so indulgent to their children" that they were unwilling to place them, as the poorest British were used to doing at home, as servants in the houses of more prosperous members of the community. The intended audience for Gookin's proposal, however, was the community in England financially supportive of efforts to persuade the native population to Christianity. This group would, of course, have seen the "putting forth" of children as servants as a normal social practice, for, at the time Gookin wrote, 14 percent of the English population was in service, and half the total population of England were, or had been, servants (Bailyn 1986a, 22). The response to his appeal was a substantial gift of funds. An index of settler enthusiasm to the idea of fostering education and English among the indigenous peoples can be guessed from the fact that no money was raised locally to support the projects that Eliot and Gookin championed (Salisbury 1974, 31).

The English intended to recreate the social structures of their homeland in the new world. Gookin, Eliot, and others well disposed to the native population were seldom able to find clergy and schoolmasters "willing to leave the English society, and to live constantly among the Indians." Philanthropists in Britain, however, persisted in urging that such missionary work continue. Cotton Mather (1663–1728), the influential Puritan divine in the generation after Eliot and Gookin, was urged by the London-based Corporation for Propagating the Gospel to prepare a new edition of Eliot's "Indian Bible." Resisting this idea, Mather wrote:

In the mean time 'tis the opinion of many, That as little Money as would be expended on a New Edition of the Bible (and not much time) would go very far towards bringing them to be a sort of *English Generation*. It is very sure, The best thing we can do for our Indians is to Anglicise them in all agreeable Instances; and in that of Language, as well as others. They can scarce retain their Language, without a Tincture of other Salvage Inclinations, which do but ill suit, either with the Honor, or with the design of Christianity. The Indians themselves are Divided in the Desires upon this matter. Though some of their aged men are tenacious enought of Indianisme (which is not at all to be wondred at) Others of them as earnestly wish that their people may be made English as fast as they can. The Reasons they assign for it are very weighty ones; and this among the rest, That their Indian Tongue is a very penurious one (though the Words are long enough!) and the great things of our Holy Religion brought unto them in it, unavoidably arrive in Terms that are scarcely more intelligible to them than if they were entirely English. But the English Tongue would presently give them a Key to all our Treasures and make them the Masters of another sort of Library than any that ever will be seen in their Barbarous Linguo. And such of them as can speak English, find themselves vastly accommodated for the entertaining and communicating of Knowledge, beyond what they were before. And it is hoped, That by good English Schools among the Indians, and some other fit methods the grand intention of Anglicising them would be soon accomplished. (Quoted in Sewall 1886, 1:401–2)

Bible translating continued, of course, and by the end of the nineteenth century at least thirty-two Amerindian languages north of Mexico had been reduced to writing and given all or parts of the Bible. As a matter of policy, however, *anglicizing*—Mather is the first writer known to have used this word—became the usual policy in British North America, and no revision of Eliot's translation was published.

The consequences of reluctance to confront the new linguistic environment are found not in the few loanwords but in the adaptation of the English wordstock to suit, however approximately, the experience of the new world. *Corn*, hitherto a general term for grains of many kinds in Britain, was employed in the combination *Indian corn* (attested in Virginia, 1617, though in New York the same plant and its products were called *Indian wheat* in 1609). It was planted in *corn hills* (attested in Massachusetts in 1622), in a *corn field* (attested in Virginia in 1608), a *corn lot* (attested in Rhode Island in 1640), or on *corn land* (attested in New England in 1654); its *ears* (another adaptation of an existing English term also attested in 1622) twisted from the *cornstalk* (attested in Connecticut in 1645), gathered in *corn baskets* (attested in Connecticut in 1648), the outer leaves *husked* (attested in Virginia in

1624), stored in a *crib* (still another long-standing English word given a new, specialized meaning, attested in New York in 1687), eaten in the form of *roasting ears* (attested in Virginia in 1650), ground into *Indian meal* (attested in New York in 1609) or *corn flour* (attested in South Carolina in 1674), cooked into *Indian cake* (attested in Virginia in 1607) or *Indian bread* (attested in New England in 1654), brewed into *corn beer* (attested in Massachusetts in 1662), or even used in the currency-poor colonies as *corn money* (attested in Massachusetts in 1691) or *corn pay* (likewise in Massachusetts in 1671). This cluster of innovations, all from the seventeenth century, shows the most frequent linguistic practice on the cultural frontier. Though *maize*, a word borrowed into English by 1555 from the Spanish who had discovered the plant and the Amerindian name for it in the Caribbean, was a term available for their use, the simpler expedient was to adapt the English word *corn*, first as *Indian corn* before being shortened, sometimes to *Indian* alone, and then to *corn* for the distinctive staple of the colonial diet.

Combining *Indian* with a familiar word was a usual process of word formation in the early period of anlophone migration to the New World, particularly for plants and animals: *Indian dog* (1672), *Indian fig* (1622), *Indian hemp* (1619), *Indian pea*, *Indian purge* (1687), and *Indian weed* (1687). Similarly, when British forces seized Jamaica in 1655, it became a common practice to describe exotica with the word *Spanish*: *Spanish arbour-vine*, *Spanish carnation*, *Spanish elder*, *Spanish elm*, *Spanish rosemary*, and *Spanish woodbind* (all first attested in a botanical catalog of island vegetation published by Hans Sloane in 1696). That linguistic approach to novelty also appeared when Canada came under British rule in 1763: *Canada goose* (1795), *Canada jay* (1772), *Canadian balsam* (1793), *Canadian breed* 'a horse' (1774), *Canadian bullock* (1764), and *Canadian horse* (1798). So, too, in the years following the arrival in Australia of the *First Fleet* in 1788: *Australian fringed violet* (1819), *Australian hedgehog* (1827), *native bear* (1827), *native box [thorn]* (1835), *native bread* 'an edible fungus' (1831), *native cat* (1804), *native dog* (1788), *native hen* (1804), *native pheasant* (1826), *native pepper* (1826), *native pine* (1838), *native plum* (1835), *native porcupine* (1834), *native potato* (1833), *native rose* (1827), *native tiger* (1832), *native tulip* (1826), *native turkey* (1822), and *native yams* (1827).

New words were also invented for new worlds, but most often they were made from the familiar English wordstock: *bullfrog* (1698), *bullhead* (1674), *catfish* (1612), *mouse squirrel* (1662), and *pignut* (1666) are typical North American examples. Features of the landscape were named with English elements but with semantic differences: *bluff* (1687) for the steep bank of a river rather than, as in England, an abrupt rise of land along the seashore; *creek* (1622) for a freshwater stream rather than an inlet of the sea, *opening* (1663) in a newly specialized sense describing a place where a swamp might be crossed safely; *slough* (1665) for a narrow backwater or inlet in addition to its British use to describe a marshy pond. Adjustment and adaptation along these lines became, in North America (as elsewhere in the spread of English), the common pattern of linguistic adaptation.

Lest it appear that the response of the English colonists to the new land and its people was the inevitable result of contact between two materially different cultures, one need only examine the conduct of other European migrants to North America. When Henry Hudson sailed along the North American coast in 1609, he found that the natives who visited his ship could speak some words of French (Feister 1973, 29). Under the leadership of Samuel de Champlain, French outposts had been established on the Atlantic coast and along the banks of the St. Lawrence. Gradual expansion of the trading network in the interior spread French to the Great Lakes and down the Mississippi and Ohio rivers to New Orleans. Since the fur trade was the principal source of wealth, the French needed a language in which to negotiate with the Native Americans who supplied them with pelts. At the same time, missionary efforts were led by priests who did not displace, but rather joined, the indigenous society. From these two sources of contact emerged a pattern of bilingualism on both sides of the cultural divide, frequent intermarriage, and a relatively settled community, disrupted only by intertribal wars, until the expulsion of the French by the English in 1763. For a century and a half, the interaction of French and native populations led to language mixture and borrowing, some of which carried over into English and influenced the lingua franca that came to be used over a wide area in communication between Native Americans (with their various languages) and Europeans (with their various languages).

Reliable reports of the lingua franca are scarce, but the situation is illuminated by a Dutch missionary, Jonas Michaelius, who, in 1628, bewailed the difficulties he found in communicating with the Native Americans in the vicinity of the colony of New Netherland:

> It is true one can easily learn as much as is sufficient for the purposes of trading, but this is done almost as much by signs with the thumb and fingers as by speaking, and this cannot be done in religious matters. It also seems to us that they rather try to conceal their language from us than to properly communicate it, except in things that have to do with everyday trade, saying that it is sufficient

for us to understand them to this extent; and then they speak only half sentences, shortened words, and frequently name a dozen things and even more, yea, all things that have only a rude resemblance to each other, they frequently call by the same name. On the whole, it is a made-up, childish language, so that even those who can best of all speak with the savages, and get along well in trade, are nevertheless altogether in the dark and as bewildered, when they hear the savages talking among themselves. (Quoted in Feister 1973, 32)

Bilingualism joining Europeans and Native Americans seems to have been rare in the areas of Dutch influence, with the most fluent speakers drawn from the offspring of intermarriage who could serve as interpreters between the two communities. A few enterprising traders may have mastered a pre-European pidgin Delaware for use in the fur trade, but this language had little influence on the language of the immigrants (Thomason 1979). When the English ousted the Dutch from their mainland North American colonies in 1664, the virtual segregation of Europeans from Native Americans persisted until the native population of the Hudson River valley was entirely displaced by the newcomers. English in North America did gain loanwords drawn from Dutch—*boss* (1649), *sleigh* (1696), *scow* (1669), and *stoop* (1679) are early examples—but none of these words has any connection with a Native American language, as is so commonly the case with American borrowings from French.

In the English settlements, as in the Dutch, there were some bilinguals among the immigrants. With the exception of Eliot, Gookin, and a few others especially appointed to interact with native peoples, most of those who could communicate effectively across cultures were marginal rather than central figures in the respective social hierarchies. On the English side, these were escaped indentured servants and a few social renegades who found life more congenial among the Indians than in the colonies. Writing to Governor John Winthrop of Massachusetts in 1637, Roger Williams reported a typical case.

Sir, I heare that there is now at Pequat with the Monahiganeucks one William (Baker I thinck his name is) who was pursued, as is said, by the English of Qunnihticut for vncleanenes with an Indian squaw, who is now with child by him. He hath there gotten another squaw & lies close, vnknown to the English. They say he came from a trading howse which Plymouth men haue at Qunnihticut, & can speak much Indian. If it be he, when I lived at Plymmouth, I heard the Plymmouth men speake much of his evill course that way with the natives. (Williams 1863, 215)

Such fugitives were unlikely to transmit much from native cultures to the English, but they certainly provided their hosts with a source of information about the immigrants, at least those who came, like Baker, to "speak much Indian." Even so, it is likely that these assimilated immigrants used pidginized forms of the Amerindian languages and were baffled when confronted with the unsimplified use of them (see Goddard 1977, 41).

The structure of the interlanguage of partial bilinguals in seventeenth-century North America follows a familiar pattern, one perhaps influenced by the long-standing maritime pidgins that were widely used in the Atlantic trade. Early attestations of it are few and of doubtful accuracy, since those who recorded it are English speakers with their own ideas about what seemed to be broken in the "broken" English they wrote down. But the pattern that emerges is one that appears again and again in later, better documented, contacts: reduction of the inventory of sounds, deletion of unstressed syllables, infinitives of verbs and singulars of nouns generalized to other functions, negation expressed by *no* or *not* in place of the broader array of negators in English, topicalization by various strategies rather than subject-first as in most English sentences. All of these appear in the few surviving specimens (see Leechman and Hall 1955).

The impact of English on Amerindian languages was profound, and it reveals the other side of the contact between the two cultures. Reliable, early evidence comes from an account of the Abenakis written by a French-speaking priest, Joseph Maurault, who worked among the small surviving community in Canada in the second quarter of the nineteenth century. In his judgment, the tribe had left their traditional homeland on the Maine coast by the end of the seventeenth century, and all their subsequent contact with Europeans was with French speakers. The English words he found thoroughly assimilated in their language must have predated that migration: *akson* 'ox,' *ases* 'horse,' *azip* 'sheep,' *bastoniak* 'Americans,' *bastonimôni* (<'Boston' + 'money') 'American currency,' *bastonki* (<'Boston') 'the United States,' *inglismôn* 'Englishman,' *kabits* 'cabbage,' *manistel* 'minister,' *melases* 'molasses,' *piks* 'pig,' *sanda* 'Sunday,' *sidel* 'cider,' *silôn* 'shilling,' *sogal* 'sugar,' *ti* 'tea,' *timli* 'chimney,' *tlaps* 'trap,' *tsannaps* 'turnip' (Maurault 1866, vii–ix). The character of these borrowings reveals the nature of the cultural contact—European goods, food, and social practices provided the Abenakis with loanwords just as English received parallel loans from Amerindian languages.

Some Native Americans vigorously resisted assimilation in culture and language and held themselves aloof from the invading English. Others found it useful, as did, for instance, the Mohicans, to form alliances with the English. According to Maurault, the Mohicans were relatively recent arrivals in Massachusetts when the English appeared; constantly engaged in warfare with the established tribes, they welcomed the seasonal fishing fleets and bartered furs for European goods. "In this trade," he writes, some of them "learned to speak English in a passable fashion," adding, parenthetically, that "all the Indians of New England showed a great aptitude for learning the English language and introduced in the course of time many English words into their languages" (39).

The social conditions of contact in North America were repeated elsewhere as English speakers encountered new cultures. The English arrived full of confidence in their accomplishments and persuaded that their own hierarchies were universal conditions of human community life (hence they projected onto those they encountered such titles as *priest, queen, prince,* and *doctor*). They persuaded themselves that their language could, by one means or another, respond to any novelty they might encounter. And everywhere they went, they were in quest of economic advantage and profit. It is no surprise that the fishing fleet turned to the fur trade even before colonists arrived in eastern North America, nor that Raleigh's voyage to Guiana was motivated by the supposition that gold fields lay up the Orinoco.

In other overseas adventures, the English typically adjusted their own usage or appropriated the vocabulary already borrowed by their European forerunners. In South Africa, English took permanent hold with the settlers who formed Cape Colony about 1820 and founded the cities of Cape Town, Port Elizabeth, and Grahamstown. Of the lexical innovations from this period, most were adapted from existing English (e.g., *Cape Smoke* [1834], a potent brandy; *Dutch medicines* [1833], household remedies; *kaffir beer* [1837], a beverage brewed from sorghum; *good-for* [1821], an I. O. U.). A few were borrowed from Afrikaans (e.g., *dopper* [1815], a member of the Gereformeerde Kerk in South Africa; *predikant* [1821], a minister in that church; *sosatie* [1833], a kabob). Only a tiny number of such borrowings entered English from the African languages of the region, often as loan translations (e.g., *eat-up* (1827), to take revenge by taking an enemy's property [< a Nguni language]) or as synonyms that coexisted with more familiar terms (e.g., *tshwala* [1826] 'Kaffir beer' [< Zulu]) (Branford 1987, 430–31). With the spread of English to present-day Malaysia and the founding of Singapore in 1819, the same linguistic pattern repeated itself. Adaptations and extensions from existing English were numerous, for example, *Malacca cane* (1856), a walking stick; *the Resident* (1814), chief colonial official in

Java. Portuguese influence through international maritime pidgin remained strong, for example, *amah* (1839), a nursemaid; *peon*, worker—with the eventually specialized sense of an office messenger, and the impact of local languages was slight, for example, *Jawi* (1808), the Malay vernacular (Platt and Weber 1980, 83–85).

Circumstances were rather different when the English approached a culture confident of its superiority and indifferent to European technology. These conditions presented themselves with the commencement of increased trade with China in the mid-eighteenth century as the English attempted to extend the influence of their long-established trading outpost at Guangzhou (then known as Canton).

In 1759, the governor-general of the Liangkwang Provinces, Li Shih-yao, speculated on the means by which foreigners gained a knowledge of Chinese.

> Foreigners who live in the distant seas do not normally understand the Chinese language. Formerly, when they came to Canton to trade, they relied upon Chinese translators to conduct their business. Lately foreign merchants like Hung Jen-hui [James Flint] have proved to be not only familiar with Cantonese as well as Mandarin but also able to read Chinese words and understand their meanings. There are several who have achieved this proficiency. How could they possibly have achieved it, had not some traitorous Chinese secretly taught them? (Li 1969, 29)

Shortly after the first official delegation arrived from Britain in 1793, the Emperor Ch'ien-lung replied to the letter the emissaries had brought from George III, King of England.

> Despite the fact that your country is located in the distant seas, you, as its ruler, have expressed your sincere desire to partake of the great civilization of China. You have sent your envoys to my court across the high seas: on your behalf they have presented a memorial, kowtowed on the occasion of my birthday, and presented to me native products as tribute. How earnest and sincere a king you must be! As I read your memorial, I am particularly impressed with the sincerity with which you express yourself, indicating the fact that you, as the king of your country, are truly respectful and obedient. How much I am really pleased! (41)

The Emperor concluded his letter by rejecting the King's offer to send a trade representative to Beijing: "We in China," he wrote, "do not attach great importance to strange or clever objects, and we have no need of your manu-factured products" (42–43). Monarchs of both countries expected respect and deference from each other, each presuming the superiority of his own civili-zation. What is consequential in this exchange is that the English traders were eager to learn new languages when they perceived it was in their interest to do so in order to pursue their economic ambitions.

Loanwords from Chinese at the end of the eighteenth and beginning of the nineteenth century show a rather different pattern from the borrowings that enter as a result of earlier adventures abroad. As already noted, much of the distinctive vocabulary of Chinese origin had entered English at second hand, through the writings of other European explorers: *Japan*, introduced to Europe by Marco Polo; *ketchup* and *mandarin* through Dutch and Portu-guese. The firsthand borrowings of direct English contact retained a distinctly "foreign" quality: *chow-chow*, the dog (1886); *cumshaw*, a present or tip (1839); *fan-tan*, the gambling game (1878); *kowtow*, an act of obsequious deference (1804); *loquat*, the tree and its fruit (1820); *oolong* (1850) and *souchong* (1760), kinds of tea; *taipan* (1834), a foreign merchant in China; *tung* oil (1881). Today such borrowings retain their denotations to things oriental and have not achieved the broader currency of *ketchup*, *mandarin*, or *tea*.

Late in the eighteenth century, voyages to the South Pacific reproduced the patterns of contact formed in the early expeditions to North America. Just as Amerindians had been brought to Britain to be inspected by the homebound, so South-Sea Islanders were collected by the later travelers and invited to admire the accomplishments of English society and to provide information for subsequent expeditions. A thoroughly documented account of one of these visitors provides confirmation that the welcome given Wan-chese and Manteo in the 1580s was repeated in the 1770s when Omai, a native of Raiatea (an island northwest of Tahiti), returned to England with the expedition to Polynesia led by James Cook and Tobias Furneaux (McCormick 1977).

During his two-year stay in England, Omai toured the country, met George III, and was the object of considerable curiosity. Shortly after his arrival, he visited Dr. Charles Burney and his family in July, 1774. Dr. Burney's son, James, had been a member of Furneaux's expedition; his daughter, Frances, later well known as a novelist, recorded her impressions of the encounter in a letter to her sister.

He was dressed according to the fashion of his Country, & is a very good looking man—my Father says he has quite an *interesting* Countenance. He appeared to have uncommon spirits, & laughed very heartily many Times. he speaks few English words—& Capt. Furneaux a few Otaheite words.—they had got Mr Banks [later Sir Joseph; he had traveled to the Pacific with James Cook's 1768–71 expedition] there on purpose to speak with him—but Mr Banks has almost forgot what he knew of that language. But you must know that we are very proud to hear that our *Jem* [James Burney] speaks more Otaheite than any of the Ship's *Crew*.—this Capt. F. told my Father, who was Introduced to this Stranger, as Jem's Father—he laughed, & shook hands very cordially, & repeated with great pleasure the name thus *Bunny*! O! *Bunny*! immediately knowing who was meant. & the Capt. Says that he is very fond of *Bunny*, who spent great part of his Time in Studying the Language with him. (Quoted in McCormick 1977, 95)

What is striking in this report is not so much James Burney's linguistic accomplishment but the apparent indifference of other members of the crew to Omai's language. In the course of his visit, Omai acquired some competence in English, learned to avoid "low" companions and to be deferential to his "superiors," and tolerated constant inspection and interrogation from those he met in society.

Neither Joshua Reynolds's full-length portrait of Omai in "oriental" costume nor the widely publicized disquisitions on him and on Polynesia resulted in any very profound understanding of Pacific culture. Returned to his homeland by Cook, Omai arrived with a European wardrobe, furniture, tools, firearms, and a collection of English livestock so the Polynesians could establish flocks and herds. Speculating from Cook's narrative of the journey, an English writer suggested that "such is the strange nature of human affairs, that it is probable we left him in a less desirable situation, than he was in before his connection with us" (quoted in McCormick 1977, 264). Though these are not Cook's words, they are consonant with his strongly held opinions about the consequences of European contact with other cultures.

> . . . what is still more to our Shame . . . we interduce among them wants and perhaps diseases which they never before knew and which serve only to disturb that happy tranquility they and their fore Fathers had injoyed. If any one denies the truth of this assertion let him tell me what the Natives of the whole extent of America have gained by the commerce they have had with Europeans. (Cook 1971, 128)

Omai survived only thirty months after Cook's departure; his goods were dispersed, the animals died, but the memory of his riches and his adventures had not been forgotten when a subsequent expedition revisited Tahiti in 1788 and sought information about him.

Returning to Tahiti in 1792, William Bligh found striking changes in the greeting he then received when compared to his first visit there in 1773.

> . . . there was very little of the ancient Custom of the Otaheitean—all that was laid aside. [I]t is rather a difficulty to get them to speak their own language without mixing a jargon of English, and they are so generally altered, that I believe no European in future will ever know what their ancient Customs of receiving Strangers were. (Bligh 1976, entry for April 16, 1792)

The invasion of a "jargon of English" may, of course, have been less devastating than Bligh's account suggests; the use of a mixed language with outsiders may not have immediately affected the language and style thought fit for monolingual conversations. Even so, the influence of English was rapid. Finding the Australian Aboriginals unwilling to work in the sugarcane fields of Queensland, entrepreneurs in the nineteenth century began the practice of *blackbirding* (attested in print in 1871) through which Polynesians and Melanesians were impressed as contract laborers and thrown together in work crews. These workers developed a pidgin language with English elements that they brought back to the islands when they returned home on the completion of their contracts. Thus the "jargon of English" Bligh observed in Tahiti became consequential for the indigenous languages of the region.

In the western Pacific, English accumulated vocabulary in much the way it had when Amerindian words returned from Roanoke and its successor settlements. Cook's voyages, like Raleigh's, were partly motivated by scientific curiosity, but Harriot's ethnography had not been nearly so influential as the reports from Joseph Banks and his companions, who visited the Antipodes in the eighteenth century, would become. Prior experience of discovery had given an English audience a sense of what to expect, and mass-market publications disseminated the results of the voyages rapidly. For instance, the first European sighting of a *kangaroo* occurred on June 23, 1770; by the end of July, Banks and Cook had learned from the Endeavour River Aboriginals to call it by that name. In June, 1773, John Hawkesworth published an *Account* of their voyages and introduced *kangaroo* to the published wordstock; in August of that same year, Samuel Johnson apparently discoursed on the animal and even mimicked its movements (Pottle and

Shown in English clothing on his return to the South Seas in 1777, Omai had
spent more than four years among the British but his people expressed little
interest in his possessions and less in his accomplishments. Within a short time
after Cook's departure, he died. Despite the benefits of English, he was unable
to transform his culture as his sponsors had hoped he would. Illustration from
James Cook, *A Voyage to the Pacific Ocean* (1784), detail of pl. 16. See
McCormick 1977.

Bennett 1936, 98, n. 6). In the year following, its habits were described in a volume of natural history. When the first flotilla of immigrants sailed into Botany Bay in 1788, the English settlers recognized *kangaroos* and called them by that name; the Aboriginals who met them were puzzled since they called the animals "pat-ag-a-ran." An account of *that* voyage published in 1793 noted dryly: "Kanguroo was a name unknown to them for any animal, until we introduced it."

While *kangaroo* achieved the peculiar status of a borrowing from one Aboriginal language subsequently introduced by Europeans to another Aboriginal language through English, the vocabulary of South Sea voyaging achieved immediate popularity in Britain and the United States. *Tattoo* and *taboo* are other words Banks and Cook brought from the Pacific to English (see Gray 1983); *boomerang* (attested c.1790), *dingo* (1789), *koala* (1798), and *wombat* (1798) are all early borrowings from the Aboriginal languages of Australia that became part of international English. Settlement of New Zealand led to loanwords from Maori—*biddy-biddy* (< Maori *piripiri*, 1866; 'plant with prickly brown burrs'), *kit* (< Maori *kete*, 1834; 'a basket plaited from flax'), *kiwi* (attested in 1835), *mako* (1848), *Maori* (1843), *moa* (1842)—but few of them have wide circulation in international English (see Burchfield 1986; Gordon and Deverson 1985, 34–38). As had been the case in North America, these borrowed words were almost always nouns for new or unfamiliar things. And, once again, colonists settling in Australia and New Zealand preferred adapting the existing wordstock to cope with new surroundings: *mob* 'group of Aboriginals,' 'herd of cattle, flock of sheep' (both attested in 1828) and *paddock* 'any field or piece of land enclosed by fencing' (1808) in Australia; *gully* 'a valley' (1840) and *shanty* 'bar, public-house' (1862) in New Zealand. The same enthusiasm for compounding seen in the North American combinations of *corn* was also a trait of the new English of Australia and New Zealand. Examples employing *bush* 'wild uncultivated district' abound: *bush carpenter* (Australia, 1848), *bushcraft* (New Zealand, 1871), *bushdray* (Australia, 1848), *bushfire* (Australia, 1832), *bush flats* (New Zealand, 1847), *bush hand* (Australia, 1850; New Zealand, 1863), *bush lawyer* (Australia, 1835), *bush hawk* (New Zealand, 1882), *bush hut* (Australia, 1830), *bush land* (Australia, 1827), *bush pig* (New Zealand, 1840), *bushranger* 'escaped convict' (Australia, 1801), *bush road* (Australia, 1827), *bush telegraph* 'means of spreading gossip and other information' (Australia, 1864), *bush track* (Australia, 1837), *bushwacker* 'a person who clears land' (both Australia and New Zealand, 1898), and *bush wren* (New Zealand, 1887). Familiar techniques of English word formation also yield *bush* (v.) 'to camp in the bush' (Australia, 1825, and New Zealand, 1827) and *bushie* 'a dweller in the bush' (Australia, 1843; see Ramson 1988).

English abroad, then, has been the weapon of English imperialism. Acquisitions from the languages encountered in the new worlds were incidental consequences of cultural invasion. As confidence grew in the mission of civilizing the world, English speakers became more and more indifferent to the societies they encountered. These themes are captured in an address given to an assemblage of Australian Aboriginals gathered to celebrate Queen Victoria's birthday in 1838.

> Black men—
> We wish to make you happy. But you cannot be happy unless you imitate good white men. Build huts, wear clothes, work and be useful.
> Above all you cannot be happy unless you love God who made heaven and earth and man and all things.
> Love white men. Love other tribes of black men. Do not quarrel together. Tell other tribes to love white men, and to build good huts and wear clothes. Learn to speak English.
> If any man injure you, tell the Protector and he will do you justice.
> (Quoted in Franklin 1976, 47)

Through such statements, the English shouldered the "white man's burden," the obligation to transplant English institutions and to protect client peoples from their own desires.

Americans, arriving last as an anglophone colonial power, had influential British models to imitate, and American English is even more aloof from direct foreign influence than its parent language. Yet the idea of a far-flung linguistic empire animated U.S. optimism. Americans "opening" Japan to diplomacy and trade sparked the belief that American English could be a model for universal democracy. On May 21, 1872, Arinori Mori, the first Japanese envoy to Washington, wrote a remarkable letter to the internationally known philologist William Dwight Whitney. In it, he declared:

> The spoken language of Japan being inadequate to the growing necessities of the people of that empire, and too poor to be made, by a phonetic alphabet, sufficiently useful as a written language, the idea prevails among many of our best educated men and most profound thinkers, that if we would keep pace with the age, we must adopt some copious, expansible, and expanding European language, print our laws and transact all public business in it as soon as possible, and have it taught in our schools as the future language of the country,

to the gradual exclusion of our present language, spoken and written. (Quoted in Kinney 1873, 189)

Coining a word that later would achieve considerable currency to describe the conversion of the Pacific to an "American pond" and Asia to an anglophone district, Coates Kinney greeted the Mikado's "rapid and radical progress in *westernization*" (190, italics added). That monarch's absolute power, he thought, could make such a transformation "an accomplished fact by 1880." The obstacle to Mori's otherwise welcome idea was his conviction that for English to be suitable for Japanese purposes, it would have to be fitted to a phonetic spelling system and reduced to consistent regularity in grammar and word formation (for instance, *seed* for 'saw' and 'seen,' *speaked* for 'spoke' and 'spoken,' and *bited* for 'bit' and 'bitten' [see Upton 1873, 327; Hall 1973, 192]).

In a characteristically xenophobic response, the *New York Times* commended "the almond-eyed islanders" on their perspicacity, but demurred from the idea of reform, preferring instead "this awkward and barbarous tongue of Shakespeare and Milton" ("A Modest Proposal," 1873, 4). Deriding the "priceless boon of being able to converse with casual Japanese with perfect ease and freedom," the paper asserted that "the labor of revising the English language is wholly unnecessary." Imperial sentiment favored the idea, however, and Kinney exclaimed: "How grand an opening for the school-teaching talent of our New England!" (195). President Ulysses S. Grant caught the idealism of a universal language, and Kinney was eloquent in describing the sweeping consequences of the spread of his language.

But the details of execution may appropriately be left to Mr. Mori and the Japanese government. If he can influence it to undertake and carry out his project, immortality is assured for him in his own country; and when the new language shall have pushed west and proselyted China, winning Ah Sin from his monosyllabic nasals and his Pigeon English; absorbed the Indies and conformed to itself the British speakers there; then, careering north and west, swept the continent clean of Turanian, and Semitic, and dead Aryan; and finally, coming into Europe by the old route of its ancestry, conquered at last its kindred continental tongues, Great Britain and America, having already Japanned their English and naturalized it in Africa and the Isles long before; then the mighty benefaction of Mori shall be fully appreciated, and gratefully celebrated in eloquence and song that shall be intelligible round the world. (195)

What a heady notion for Americans fearful that their variety of English was somehow inferior to that of Britain. Not only would American English be the model for the Pacific, it could "conform to itself" British imperialists on their colonial ground and, in a joint effort with them, sweep westward around the globe through Africa and Asia to Europe itself.

Though Mori's audacious idea quickly evaporated, Americans soon found a practical opportunity to spread their language to Asia. Victory in the Spanish-American War, a four-month campaign in 1898, gave Americans an empire consisting of Puerto Rico, Guam, and the Philippines. The opportunity to govern a huge Asian nation brought into practice the theoretical ideas about language spread formed in the previous generation, and Congress soon appointed a commission to "Americanize" the Philippine educational system. Early reports described the satisfying popularity of English as a school subject, and the commissioners reported in 1900:

> The young Filipinos display a considerable aptitude for learning new tongues and it is believed that if this policy is followed out English can within a short time be made the official language of the archipelago. . . . The introduction of English, wherever made, had been hailed with delight by the people, who could hardly believe that they were to be encouraged to learn the language of those in authority over them. (Quoted in Yule 1925, 112)

The *New York Times* welcomed the prospect of American women teachers' effecting the transformation of the Philippines to an American English–speaking nation ("Filipinos Learn Readily" 1901, 6), and, by 1903, a thousand Americans had migrated to administer and teach in Philippine schools.

Some U.S. voices resisted the idea that English should be imposed, and Bryan J. Clinch, writing in the *American Catholic Quarterly Review*, was scathing in his attack on "the cult of the English language" (1902, 388). His eloquent defense of linguistic self-determination arose, in part, from consternation that the United States, with its Protestant majority, had conquered a nation governed by a Catholic elite and was about to augment (or replace) long-established Catholic schools, where Spanish and local languages were used in instruction, with publicly supported, English-medium, secular education. Clinch argued that the proper course was to foster Philippine languages and that U.S. policy was mimicking the despotism of the Czar and Kaiser; he recalled that "the policy of Metternich, in seeking to obliterate the various national languages and institutions, brought the whole Empire to the verge of destruction in 1848" (378). Given prevailing ideas about the universal excellence of English and U.S. yearning for imperial power, however, it is not surprising that Clinch's carefully argued position did not prevail.

Examination of the emerging English of the Philippines clarifies the actual transformation that U.S. teachers facilitated. Early Philippine English was typified by Spanish loanwords (including *buenos dias* and *buenos noches* as greetings) and phonological interference among language learners who carried Spanish patterns into English (in, for instance, the use of epenthetic vowels to break up consonant clusters). What was accomplished was not the democratization of the Philippines (as the commissioners of 1900 had hoped), but a conversion of the ruling elite from Spanish to English usage. That change can be quite precisely dated to 1920 with the first speech in English made in the officially bilingual (though in practice Spanish-speaking) national Assembly. A contemporary observer who recognized the significance of this event predicted that the general election of 1928 would produce a legislative majority of English speakers (Yule 1925, 115). In short, it took only a quarter century for English to displace Spanish as the language of the governing elite of the Philippines, but while the elite switched from one European language to another, the vast majority of the population was little affected.

From the evidence of word borrowing, U.S. teachers and administrators had only the most superficial contact with monolingual Filipinos. Most loanwords involved terms of Spanish origin (e.g., *bueno attitude* 'tendency to procrastination' [1929]), and the few borrowings from Philippine languages had either entered English before the American hegemony (e.g., *ylang-ylang*, 'a shrub, its flower, and the perfume made from it' [1876]) or were restricted to local use. The only Philippine borrowing to gain widespread currency in American English was *boondocks*, 'jungle, a remote rural area' (1925 < Tagalog *bundok* 'mountain'). Another enduring innovation was *Gook* (unknown etymology), first used by English speakers as a term of opprobrium for anyone speaking Spanish in the Philippines [1935], and later extended to any Asian, particularly an enemy soldier, during the conflicts in Korea and Viet Nam. In the years the Philippines were regarded as a U.S. territory, 1898–1946, an interlanguage developed known as *Bamboo English* (1929), parallel to the *Babu English* of British colonies in Asia. Derided by resident Americans, this language showed frequent Spanish influences (e.g., *shoe-hombre* 'clerk' [1938]) and occasional borrowings from indigeneous languages (e.g., *quan* 'thing' [1929]). Since 1946, English in the Philippines has emerged as a distinctive national variety with U.S. English traits (see

Llamazon 1969), but the consequences of cultural contact for the international language were negligible (see Barry 1927; Struble 1929; Darrach 1930; Mencken 1960c, 241–43).

The Pacific War of 1941–45 gave most Americans their first taste of Japanese culture. Like borrowings from earlier territorial expansion, *banzai* (< Japanese, literally 'ten-thousand years') had entered English through a travel writer (in 1893 to signify the cry used to salute the Emperor). Early twentieth-century mariners in the Pacific brought it into English usage in the phrase *banzai party* 'spree,' but wartime reintroduced it to refer to a reckless attack by Japanese fighter pilots (*Banzai run* [1945]) or by infantry (*banzai charge* [1945]). Similarly, *kamikaze* (< Japanese, literally 'divine wind'] acquired small currency through travel writing describing Japan (1896) but achieved international prominence when applied to 'suicide aircraft' and their pilots at the end of the war; later evolution of the term retained the idea of 'suicide,' either literally (*kamikaze porpoises* [1966] or *kamikaze dolphins* [1974], animals trained to approach vessels while harnassed with explosives) or figuratively (*kamikaze* [taxi-]*cabs* [1964] or *kamikaze liberals* [1968] 'idealistic but ineffectual politicians').

At the close of hostilities, U.S. military forces took up extended residence in Japan—for which the term *Occupation*, first used in Britain to describe areas under German influence in 1940, was adopted. Peaceful contact between Americans and Japanese fostered yet another interlanguage for which the term *Bamboo English* was imported from the Philippines. Veterans of this Occupation recalled *shack-up* 'cohabit' as a distinctive term, though it had been in prewar African-American usage. A Japanese woman entering into such a relationship was called a *moose* (< Japanese *musume* 'daughter, girl' 1953), and *butterfly* was used as both noun and verb to describe those engaging in such contacts (*butterfly* 'to flirt' had been in nineteenth-century British English but the usage in Japan was likely an independent development). The term *honcho* (< Japanese *hancho* 'squad or group leader,' 1947) achieved international currency meaning, derisively, 'boss,' while *hootch* (< Japanese *uchi* 'shelter or dwelling,' 1952) was in local use for 'barracks' or an Asian dwelling. For the most part, however, English speakers merely rediscovered terms used in the language earlier: *hibachi* 'brazier' (1863), *kimchi* (< Korean) 'spicy pickled vegatables' (1898), *tatami* 'straw floor mat' (1614), *torii* 'ceremonial gateway' (1727). The honorific suffix *-san* (< Japanese *sama*) had first been noticed in English in 1878 and even appeared in James Joyce's *Ulysses* (1922), but the Occupation made it extremely productive among U.S. troops though without its "honorific" force:

mama-san 'matron, brothel keeper' (1949), *papa-san* 'elderly Japanese man, servant,' *boy-san* 'male adult menial,' and *baby-san* 'young Japanese woman.' Mimicking Japanese adaptations of English loanwords to their native syllable structure produced such English pronunciations as *biru* 'beer' and *isukrimu* 'ice cream.' Reduplications regarded as typical of 'pidgin' languages also gained increased currency: *changee-changee* 'exchange currency,' *samee-samee* 'identical,' *washee-washee* 'launder, laundry.' A few of these were actually connected to Japanese expressions (e.g., *mushee-mushee* 'a telephone greeting'). Since English-speaking forces were sent to Japan for *R and R* 'leave' (< *rest and recreation*, 1953) during the Korean conflict of 1950–53, most distinctive borrowed vocabulary of that war was of Japanese origin, though troops in Korea stationed along the *DMZ* 'truce line' (< *Demilitarized Zone* [attested in 1960, likely in earlier use]) made some use of Korean borrowings that have not achieved international currency (see Norman 1954 and 1955; Algeo 1960; Webster 1960).

Indifference to local languages characterized U.S. intervention in the Vietnamese civil war of the 1960s. Words arising in English from that conflict were almost exclusively formed from the existing American-English wordstock: *air cav* (1965 < air cavalry [1915]); *ARVN* or *arvin* 'a soldier in the Army of the Republic of Vietnam' (1965); *body bag* 'a rubberized, zippered sack for holding and transporting a corpse' (1967); *body count* 'the number of soldiers killed in a specific period or in a particular military action' (1965); *frag* and *fragging* 'to throw a fragmentation grenade at one's superior officer, esp. one who is considered overzealous in his desire for combat' (1970); *peacenik* 'a member of a pacifist movement, esp. when regarded as a "hippy"; an opponent of the military intervention of the United States in Vietnam' (1965); *strategic hamlet* 'a settlement for accommodating potential terrorists or their supporters' (1963); *Victor Charlie* 'a Viet Cong or the Viet Cong' (1965 < military communications code); *vietnik* '(a usually pejorative term applied to) an active opponent of U.S. military involvement in the war between North and South Vietnam' (1965). Direct borrowings were rare: *ao dai*, tunic worn by Vietnamese women (< Vietnamese *aó* 'jacket' + *dái* 'to be long' 1969); *Viet Cong* (< *Viêt Nam công-san* 'Vietnamese communists' 1957). Other terms associated with that conflict often were earlier coinages or borrowings: *boondocks, hooch, punji* or *punji stick* 'a sharpened (frequently poisoned) bamboo stake set in a camoflaged hole in the ground as a trap for enemy soldiers' (1872 ?< a Tibeto-Burman language); *slant* (1942) and *slope* (1948) 'an oriental, later specifically a Vietnamese.' A few U.S. soldiers, early in the war, distinguished *gook* 'Korean' from *dink* 'Vietnamese' (of unknown origin, 1969), but both terms soon came to be used by Americans for Asians of any nationality (Lifton 1974, 205; see also Clark 1990, Reinberg 1991).

Far from its conventional image as a language congenial to borrowings from remote languages, English displays a tendency to accept exotic loanwords mainly when they first have been adopted by other European languages or when presented with marginal social practices or trivial objects. Anglophones who have ventured abroad have done so confident of the superiority of their culture and persuaded of their capacity for adaptation, usually without accepting the obligations of adapting. Extensive linguistic borrowing and language mixture arise only when there is some degree of equality between or among languages (and their speakers) in a multilingual setting. For the English abroad, this sense of equality was rare. Linguistic borrowing reflects intimate contact between speakers of different languages; coping with new worlds usually has been accomplished by using existing English to fit the circumstances. Whether it is a language more "friendly to change than other languages" has hardly been questioned; those who embrace the language are convinced that English is a capacious, cosmopolitan language superior to all others.

Chapter 4

World English

Longing for a universal language has stimulated human hope since the earliest recorded times, and many cultures have regarded linguistic diversity as a curse. Since there has been no universal language in recorded history, mythologies have invented one and located it in a past, golden age. Most of the stories that explain the disappearance of this unifying human tongue invoke some catastrophe that has thrust humankind into the misfortunes of diversity. Some of them make linguistic variety a punishment for challenging the gods, and tales on this theme have been told among the peoples of India, Burma, middle America, and, of course, in all those cultures influenced by the Biblical story of the tower of Babel.

The Babel story elucidates antagonism between God and his people. Those who found themselves on the plain of Shinar after the flood were "of one language and of one speech" (Gen.11:1). They built their tower so they would not "be scattered abroad upon the face of the whole earth" (11:4). The tower, with the top reaching toward heaven, has been interpreted in terms of the builders' desire to "make us a name," but commentators seldom give due weight to the additional reason that concludes the verse: "lest we be scattered abroad upon the face of the whole earth" (11:4). In the standard view, it was for their *pride*, their desire for a *name*, that God came down to "confound the language" (11:9). But Genesis repeats as a consequence the fear that motivated them to build the tower in the first place—being scattered "upon the face of all the earth" (11:8). This terror of being "scattered" is a key to understanding this central myth of Western language culture.

Historically, the point of emphasis in the Babel story has been the inference that linguistic diversity arose from divine punishment. Other narratives that explain the multiplicity of languages follow the same pattern. For the Greeks, an age of peace and linguistic unity was ended when Hermes created separate nations and languages which in turn led to warfare and discord. Other explanations trace diversity of languages to a similar catastrophe: a famine that dispersed the people in Kenya and thus caused them to speak different languages. An ill-tempered old woman, according to aboriginal peoples of Australia, "walked about with a big stick in her hand to scatter the fires round which other people were sleeping." When she died, to the satisfaction of all the victims of her mischief, they ate a celebratory banquet (instead of mourning) and thereafter began to speak in different languages (see Gaster 1969,135–38).

Having explained the source of linguistic diversity, some traditions have also described its effects. Dante, for instance, assumed that the architects at Babel were more culpable than the laborers and concluded that architects had been punished by being given worse languages: "to the extent that their skills were more noble, to that extent their language was now more crude and barbaric." Those who dissented from the project altogether continued to speak Hebrew (Dante 1973, 9, 11). Renaissance expounders of Babel, as noted in chapter 2, were similarly inclined to presume gradients of excellence in the languages arising at Babel, typically locating their own among the most favored (see pp. 38–39). But most writers have dwelt on misfortune. Thus Noah Webster wrote in 1834: "The diversities of language among men may be considered as a curse, and certainly one of the greatest evils that commerce, religion, and the social interests of men have to encounter" (Webster 1843, 289). Or J. Hubert Jagger in 1940: "The unfortunate incident that happened in Babylon some few millenia ago is one of the predisposing conditions leading to war, and perhaps the chief of them" (1940, 119).

Unwilling to resign themselves to the loss of linguistic unity, Renaissance thinkers set themselves the task of doing something about it. Proposals were of two kinds: first, the creation of an artificial language; second, the spread of an existing natural speech. Articulating the first in 1629, Descartes proposed (though he did not design) a language that would be absolutely regular, logical, and unchanging. Artificial languages were devised to meet these standards by several seventeenth-century philosophers: Thomas Urquhart, John Wilkins, and Gottfried Leibnitz are among the best remembered, and their influence reaches as far as designs for artificial intelligence systems in our own day. The second kind of proposal began with the educational ideas of Johann Komensky ("Comenius") whose *Janua linguarum reserata* (1631) suggested two language territories: one in eastern Europe relying on Russian, the second in western Europe employing French and English. Modern derivatives of his idea have offered as candidates, at one

The Tower of Babel continues to be an influential image in speculations about
English. British illumination drawn from about 1300. Reprinted by permission
of the British Library from B. M. Egerton 1894, fol. 5v.

time or another, many of the languages of the world including some that must have seemed unlikely candidates for spread even at the time they were put forward: Danish (proposed in 1905), Dutch (1869), Italian (1922), German (1938), Hungarian (1832), and Malay (1909) (see Pei 1958, 105).

In Renaissance Britain, the idea that English might become a universal world language formed slowly, partly because Latin already occupied the position of a pan-European language for learning. Before 1600, the idea that English would have any importance in such a role was regarded as absurd, the character of the language being tarnished by so many faults that it could not be a contender, even in competition with living foreign languages. Thus in 1542, Andrew Boorde praised Britain, not as a lamp unto other nations, but merely as an attractive destination for travelers from abroad.

> Wherfore, all nacyons aspyeng thys realme to be so commodyous and pleasaunt, they haue a confluence to it more than to anye other regyon. I haue trauayled rownd about Chrystendom, and out of Christendom, and I dyd neuer se nor know .vii. Englyshe men dwellynge in any towne or cyte in anye regyon byyond the see, excepte marchauntes, students, & brokers, not theyr beyng parmanent nor abydyng, but resorting thyther for a space. In Englande how manye alyons hath and doth dwell of all maner of nacyons! (Boorde [1542]1870, 144)

If Boorde's testimony is to be trusted, there were few English speakers settled abroad. Certainly there were no colonies, nor had the British yet begun the practice of foreign travel that would eventually lead young gentlefolk on a "Grand Tour," first to the principal European cities and then to the remotest regions of the world.

Writing in 1582, Richard Mulcaster reflected Boorde's assumption that English would inevitably be confined to the British Isles (where it was by no means universal) and was virtually useless in traveling abroad. Even so, he declared in the format of a dialogue, it would still be worth perfecting even if only for domestic uses:

> But it maie be replyed again, that our English tung doth nede no such proining [= 'preening, adorning'], it is of small reatch, it stretcheth no further than this Iland of ours, naie not there ouer all. What tho? Yet it raigneth there, and it serues vs there, and it wold be clean brusht for the wearing there. Tho it go not beyond sea, it will serue on this side. And be not our English folks finish, as well as the foren I praie you? And why not our tung for speaking, & our pen for writing, as well as our bodies for apparell, or our tastes for diet? But our

state is no *Empire* to hope to enlarge it by commanding ouer cuntries. What
tho? tho it be neither large in possession, nor in present hope of great encrease,
yet where it rules, it can make good lawes, and as fit for our state, as the biggest
can for theirs, and oftimes better to, bycause of confusion in greatest gouern-
ments, as most vnwildinesse in grossest bodies. (Mulcaster [1582] 1970, 256)

Not all of Mulcaster's contemporaries were sure that the insularity of English
would remain a permanent condition. In 1599, Samuel Daniel raised the
possibility that English might reach beyond the British Isles in the often-
quoted stanza from his poem, *Musophilis*:

> And who in time knowes wither we may vent
>> The treasure of our tongue, to what strange shores
>> This gaine of our best glorie shal be sent,
>> T'inrich vnknowing Nations with our stores?
> Which worlds in th'yet vnformed Occident
> May come refin'd with th'accents that are ours.

(Daniel 1950, 96)

At the time they were composed, Daniel's speculations were pure patriotic
pipe dream. He imagined, as his predecessors had not, the possibility that
English might reach "unknowing Nations" beyond the sea and around the
world.

Writing half a century later, Richard Flecknoe, himself fluent in the
major European languages, found that for the traveler abroad, English still
had little use beyond communicating with other English people and for "stop-
ping holes."

> . . . for my part I account it altogether as necessary for those who travel to
> make provision of Languages as of money, & therefore I never travail any
> where, but first I provide me with furniture enough of Languages for so vast a
> Room as those Countries I travail through; and if you demand of me which
> Language I found the most large and spreading, and of greatest latitude and
> extension, the best way to answer you, is to give you first the plane of the
> Room, and next to let you see the several pieces of Languages to furnish it.
> First then for *French* it serves you thorough all *Flanders, Spain, Savoy* up to
> *Italy* (exclusively) as through the *Neitherland* up to *Sweadland, Denmark* and
> *Poland*, the other way, where almost all the people of quality speak *French*.
> Then for *Italian* it serves you not only through all *Italy*, but *Sicily, Malta*, and
> almost all the Isles of the *Archipelago* and *Mediterranean Sea*, up to *Con-*

stantinople[,] where your Language begins to change, and fails you in travelling further *Levant*, wherefore to return back again, It serves thorough all *Dalmatia*, and beyond the *Venetians* Territory up to *Austria*, where tis spoke commonly in the Emperours Court, as almost in all the Princes Courts of *Germany*. Now for *Spanish* it not only serves you thorough all *Spain* and *Portugal*, but along all the Coast, and the Isles of *Affrique* to the *Brasils*, and either *Indies*. For *Dutch* next, it not only serves you in *Germany, Switzerland*, the *Low Countries, Denmark, Sweadland*, but every where by Sea, which is as properly the *Hollanders* Country, as any Land they or any other Nation Inhabit and possesse; and lastly for *Latine* and *English* (to tell you true) they only served me to stop holes with; the *English* Language out of our Dominions being like our *English* money current with much adoe in neighbouring Countries who traffick with us, but farther off you must go to *Banquiers* of your own Nation, or none will take it of your hands. And for *Latin*, it being no where a Vulgar Language, but the *Sacred* and *Erudite* Tongue, take even the *Clergy* and *Schoolmen* themselves (whose proper Language it ought to be) out of the *Church* or *Schools*, and you cannot doe them a greater displeasure, than speak *Latin* to them, so as it rather serves to *interlard* other Languages, than to make an intire meal of discourse, and but upon great necessity is never to be used. (Flecknoe 1665, 103–5)

Despite the spread of English to colonies in the Caribbean and in North America in his lifetime, Flecknoe saw only two languages of any use outside Europe—Spanish for Africa, South America, and the Far East, and Dutch for seafarers generally. English was currency with no international value, and he urged his compatriots to follow his example in preparing for their travels by investing in several languages.

The notion that English speakers were particularly inept in learning foreign languages arose only when English power had reached around the world; the prevailing sentiment in the seventeenth century was that they were accomplished polyglots. As Richard Carew expressed that opinion: "turne an Englishman at any time of his age into what countrie soever allowing him due respite, and you shall see him profit so well that the imitation of his utterance, will in nothing differ from the patterne of that native language" (Camden 1984, 40).

In the eighteenth century, however, optimism about the value of English outside of Britain had begun to increase. In 1754, in the first of his two celebrated periodical essays welcoming the publication of Johnson's *Dictionary*, the Earl of Chesterfield looked with "honest English pride" on the spread of the language abroad.

I have therefore a sensible pleasure in reflecting upon the rapid progress, which our language has lately made, and still continues to make, all over Europe. It is frequently spoken, and almost universally understood, in Holland; it is kindly entertained as a relation in the most civilized parts of Germany; and it is studied as a learned language, tho' yet little spoke, by all those in France and Italy, who either have, or pretend to have, any learning. (Stanhope 1777, 2:168)

Though French had become "almost an universal" language for Europe through military conquest, English, he wrote, "has made its way singly by its own weight and merit" and the influence of English authors; hence its spread was "a nobler sort of conquest, and a far more glorious triumph, since graced by none but willing captives!"

Military success was seen by others as a legitimate means by which to extend the use of English. In 1740, a letter writer who adopted the pseudonym of "M. Briton" declared that it was a wise policy of Louis XIV to bring "*his own national language* to so great a Reputation, as to become the common Dialect of the learned and polite Part of the World." By carrying out negotiations toward the Treaty of Utrecht in French and signing the resulting document written in that language, the British envoys had missed a chance to promote their own language (and perhaps had been less successful negotiators through their imperfect knowledge of French).

The Opportunities we have lost for propagating *our Language* on the Continent, are more to be lamented, since perhaps the same, or so great, may never again be offer'd . . . how easily might we have made the *Frenchmen* eat their own Words, and obliged them to speak plain *English*. (Briton 1740, 600)

Such ardent sentiments in favor of English were part of a century of struggle between Britain and France. French was the language of international diplomacy, and English nationalists set out to challenge the influence of French and to "propagate" their own language. In 1766, another anonymous writer alluded to French as "that fashionable, that universal language" and thought that the limited circulation of English was owing to the negligence of its speakers rather than to any excellence in other languages.

The last objection that occurs to me at present, is, that our tongue wants universality, which seems to be an argument against its merit. This is owing to the affectation of Englishmen, who prefer any language to their own, and is not to be imputed to a defect in their native tongue. But this objection, if such it be, is vanishing daily; for I have been assured, by several ingenious foreigners, that in many places abroad, Italy in particular, it is become the fashion to study the English tongue. ("Some Thoughts on the English Language" 1766, 195)

Such tentative estimates came to be more and more influential as British writers became more globally minded.

Prevailing opinion can be sensed in a letter from David Hume to Edward Gibbon written in 1767. Gibbon had drafted some portions of a proposed history of the Swiss revolution and sent them to Hume for his comments. Hume counseled him to abandon his plan to write this work in French.

> Why do you compose in French, and carry faggots into the wood, as Horace says with regard to the Romans who write in Greek? I grant that you have a like motive to those Romans, and adopt a language much more generally diffused than your native tongue: but have you not remarked the fate of those two ancient languages in following ages? The Latin, though then less celebrated, and confined to more narrow limits, has in some measure outlived the Greek, and is now more generally understood by men of letters. Let the French, therefore, triumph in the present diffusion of their tongue. Our solid and increasing establishments in America, where we need less dread the inundation of Barbarians, promise a superior stability and duration to the English language. (Hume 1932, 170–71)

Hume's argument was an interesting one. He presumed that language change takes place through "inundation" by speakers of other languages (which he saw as unlikely in North America). He further assumed that a geographically dispersed language is a source of "stability" and a promise of "duration," since distance and continued communication retards the process of language change. But the point of comparison, for both Gibbon and Hume, was the spread of French in their own time.

The success of the French in establishing the dialect of Paris as the language of international diplomacy and even of domestic politics in Germany and Russia was an admired and envied example upon which anglophone observers discoursed. In the course of the eighteenth century, however, the influence of French outside Europe had begun to diminish, particularly with the military defeat by the British of French forces in India (1757) and in Canada (1759). Even so, the Royal Academy of Sciences in Berlin proposed a competition in 1783 for the best essay on the "universality of the French language." (Founded by Frederick the Great in 1700, the Academy continued to have a strongly French bias throughout the century.) The winning submission (among twenty-one entered) was by Antoine de Rivarol (1753–1801);

his essay reviewed both the political prospects of competing European languages and the internal merits of them from the point of view of euphony, adequacy, and logic. The aesthetic and conceptual blemishes of German, he declared, descended to its daughter language, English (Rivarol 1929, 85); English faults included an unstable pronunciation, obscure vocabulary, bizarre syntax, and "rules that have fewer applications than they have exceptions" (86). English is full of circumlocutions and obsequious expressions that he found astonishing in the speech of a free people; thus (in examples provided by his modern editor), it was impossible for English people to speak the words *belly, shirt, pants, Hell,* or *God* while French people uttered the corresponding words without the least embarrassment. Though English literature had some evident merits, Rivarol found it generally lacking in good taste, charm, and scope in presenting the full range of human experience. Most important, French reflected a "natural" logic superior to all other languages. Employing a celebrated aphorism, Rivarol stated: "that which is not clear is not French" (90); the following words are equally forceful: "that which is not clear is *merely* English, Italian, Greek, or Latin" (90–91; italics added). None of these opinions, he wrote, arose from "blind love of country or from national prejudice" (87); any dispassionate observer would naturally accept his views since they were based on the plain evidence of the facts.

Rivarol's assumptions about the political issues involved in the spread of languages were similarly directed toward supporting the inevitable "universality" of French. Science, philosophy, and literature were all the special province of French; the recent, marvellous balloon ascent in Paris had been, to him, an evidence of the superiority of French scientific thinking and, hence, a further testimony to the merits of the language. English, he thought, had no share in the flowering of scientific inquiry, nor did he detect any effort to spread English beyond the borders of Britain. When British people traded abroad, he alleged, they did not use English but employed the languages of their customers; hence, economic forces seemed to him unlikely to foster its spread (85). Even though he acknowledged that Britain had commercial relations with countries around the world, these enterprises merely subjected the country to hatred, fear, and envy (61). By overextending itself and becoming dependent on foreign markets, England put itself in peril. But even if England should succeed economically and militarily, France would prevail in the "realm of human opinion" (63), an empire far superior to mere temporal kingdoms.

Rivarol placed great emphasis on the role of the French in assisting the American colonists in achieving their freedom; in the ringing conclusion of his essay, he asserted: "American history will henceforth be condensed into three epochs: butchered by Spain, oppressed by England, and delivered by France" (111). The well-being of a language conforms to the well-being of its speakers (66); hence, the excellence of the French language expressed with unparalleled aptness the "nearly democratic liberty" of its people (86). People who want to liberate themselves, he believed, were especially well served by the French language. This idea was an important one in the years that followed, since France itself was a multilingual country, and "for millions of French citizens, the French revolution was conducted in a foreign language" (Lyons 1981, 264). But Rivarol was not thinking locally when he speculated on the qualities that made for a universal language.

Rivarol's argument that the political circumstances of a nation were directly connected to the excellence of its language has, of course, a distinctly circular contour: good languages make good nations and vice versa. This circularity was, however, characteristic of eighteenth-century linguistic thought, but it allowed for an escape from the viciousness of circularity through managed change. "Improvement" could be effected in two ways. By "refining and elevating" the language, national greatness might emerge; by "ameliorating" political and social conditions, an improved language would evolve. While these ideas about change were not necessarily mutually exclusive, the former line of argument was preferred by those who, like Jonathan Swift, urged a language academy to regulate the progress of the language or by those who proposed less bureaucratic means to enhance the excellence of language. The latter, especially toward the end of the century, concentrated on social conditions and their linguistic consequences: politically healthy nations will direct language toward excellence.

Not long after Rivarol's celebrated essay was published, another writer considered the claims of French to "universality," Jean Marie Roland (1734–93). Roland was an enthusiastic supporter of the Revolution whose reputation was much enhanced by the efforts of his wife, Manon Jeanne Philipon, who presided over a salon in Paris at which Robespierre and others elaborated political ideas. (Mme. Roland eventually fell under Marat's enmity and was guillotined in 1793; her husband, then in hiding, committed suicide two days later.) While still living in Lyons in 1789, Roland prepared a "communication" on the language question; like his later and more influential political writings, it may have been composed by his wife but circulated under his name. Whatever its authorship, however, the essay adopts Rivarol's idea that the claim of a language to universality "resides in the state of that language and in that of the nation which speaks it" (Baldensperger 1917,

475). Crediting his knowledge to St. Jean de Crèvecoeur's *A Farmer's Letters in Pennsylvania* (1782; translated into French in 1784), Roland declared that American English met the conditions necessary for universality. English in Britain had intrinsic merits (comparable to those of classical Greek), but shortcomings of British society, particularly in "generosity" and "tolerance," prevented the language from reaching its potential. Among the Americans of the United States, on the other hand, people were bound by a sense of equality that embraced African Americans, Native Americans, and immigrants from every European nation. Such a cosmopolitan mixture of people would, Roland claimed, inspire other nations to the example provided by the Americans, since they are related to every member of the human family. "It seems to me," he concluded, "that the language of such a nation will one day become the universal language" (1917, 476).

Roland's notion that political aspirations are related to language occurred independently to the Americans. In a letter of 1774, an anonymous author writing to the *Royal American Magazine* in Boston asserted:

> The dispensations of Providence, and the present aspect of the world, make it evident, that America will soon be the seat of science, and the grand theatre where human glory will be displayed in its brightest colours. The present age may lay a foundation for the shining improvements which shall adorn future periods, and thereby contribute to all the splendor and felicity which shall illumine this New World through the successive areas of its duration. And as Language, is the foundation of science, and medium of communication among mankind, it demands our first attention, and ought to be cultivated with the greatest assiduity in every seminary of learning. The English language has been greatly improved in Britain within a century, but its highest perfection, with every other branch of human knowledge, is perhaps reserved for this Land of light and freedom. As the people through this extensive country will speak English, their advantages for polishing their language will be great, and vastly superior to what the people in England ever enjoyed. (An American 1774, 6)

This letter, attributed to John Adams, mirrors the linguistic patriotism that formed one part of American aspirations for independence from Britain.

In later reflections on English, Adams proposed to the Congress the formation of an academy to assist citizens of the new Republic in realizing the potential for their language made possible by their political freedom.

> English is destined to be in the next and succeeding centuries more generally the language of the world than Latin was in the last or French is in the present

age. The reason of this is obvious, because the increasing population in America, and their universal connection and correspondence with all nations will, aided by the influence of England in the world, whether great or small, force their language into general use, in spite of all the obstacles that may be thrown in their way, if any such there should be. (Adams 1852, 250)

The Academy founded by Congress would set "a public standard for all persons in every part of the continent to appeal to, both for the signification and pronunciation of the language" (249–50). While no serious steps were taken to establish an "American Academy" along the lines Adams suggested, the impulse toward a national standard and the means to achieve it was widely acclaimed. Despite persistent folklore promulgated by subsequent writers, there were no serious attempts to adopt some language other than English for the new nation. (French, German, Hebrew, and ancient Greek are sometimes mentioned as having been considered as candidates [see Baron 1982b, 11–13].) There was, however, considerable attention paid to the future of English and the role of the United States in its development.

Among the most influential of those who addressed the question of the future of English in the United States was Noah Webster. In his *Dissertations on the English Language* (1789), Webster carried earlier speculations a step further and foresaw a linguistic schism between Britain and America.

. . . several circumstances render a future separation of the American tongue from the English, necessary and unavoidable. The vicinity of the European nations, with the uninterrupted communication in peace, and the changes of dominion in war, are gradually assimilating their respective languages. The English with others is suffering continual alterations. America, placed at a distance from those nations, will feel, in a much less degree, the influence of the assimilating causes; at the same time, numerous local causes, such as a new country[,] new associations of people, new combinations of ideas in arts and science, and some intercourse with tribes wholly unknown in Europe, will introduce new words into the American tongue. These causes will produce, in a course of time, a language in North America, as different from the future language of England, as the modern Dutch, Danish and Swedish are from the German, or from one another: Like remote branches of a tree springing from the same stock; or rays of light, shot from the same center, and diverging from each other, in proportion to their distance from the point of separation. (Webster [1789] 1951, 22–23)

Webster's notion of a "future separation" of the varieties of English was a novel argument, particularly so in that he welcomed that prospect (as Rivarol

FEDERAL LANGUAGE

Inventing a pedigree for the American language was part of Noah Webster's effort to make English independent of Britain. In 1788, Webster was among the founders of the Philological Society of New York, and in July of that year the members took part in a parade anticipating ratification of the U.S. Constitution. Among other patriotic paraphernalia was a "standard" displaying the arms of the society. The illustration above recreates these "arms" from Webster's description: "Argent three tongues, gules, in chief; emblematical of *language*, the improvement of which is the object of the institution. Chevron, or, indicating firmness and support; an *eye*, emblematical of *discernment* over a pyramid, or rude monument, sculptured with Gothic, Hebrew, and Greek letters. The Gothic on the *light* side, indicating the *obvious* origin of the American language from the Gothic. The Hebrew and Greek, upon the reverse or *shade* of the monument, expressing the remoteness and *obscurity* of the connection between these two languages and the modern. The *crest*, a cluster of cohering magnets, attracted by a key in the centre; emblematical of *union* among the society, in acquiring *language*, the *key* of knowledge; and clinging to their *native* tongue in preference to a *foreign* one. The *shield*, ornamented with a branch of the oak, from which is collected the *gall*, used in making ink, and a sprig of *flax*, from which paper is made, supported on the dexter side, by CADMUS, in a robe of Tyrian purple, bearing in his right hand, leaves of the rush or flag, *papyrus*, marked with Phonecian characters; representing the introduction of letters into Greece, and the origin of writing. On the sinister side, by HERMES, or Taaut, the inventor of letters, and god of eloquence, grasping his caduceus or wand. Motto—*Concedat Laurea Linguae*—expressive of the superiority of *civil* over *military* honors." By this means, Webster traced the descent of the American language without once mentioning English. See Read 1934, 133–34. Illustration copyright © 1991 David Zinn.

had done) as a natural consequence of the vitality of the New World and the separate cultural development that he anticipated in the United States.

The typical views of the nineteenth century were not those of Hume, Adams, or Webster. Instead, writers anticipated that English would spread to a worldwide speech community as a consequence of the extension of British (and later U.S.) enterprise. A representative prediction was expressed by the British philologist, Julius Charles Hare (1795–1855).

> And as of all the works of man language is the most enduring, and partakes the most of eternity, and as our own language, so far as thought can project itself into the future, seems likely to be coeval with the world, and to spread vastly beyond even its present immeasurable limits, there cannot easily be a nobler object of ambition than to purify and better it. (Hare 1832, 665)

Hare was one of the founders of the Etymological Society at Cambridge and an editor of the influential, though short-lived, *Philological Museum*. Having met Goethe and Schiller in his youth (as a result of his parents' residence in Weimar), he conceived an admiration for German scholarship that was unusual among English intellectuals of his day, and he did much to convey ideas about emerging Germanic philology from the continent to Britain. His notion that language "partakes the most of eternity" was consonant with the Biblical basis of his thinking (and anticipated his move from Trinity College, Cambridge, to a succession of increasingly influential positions in the Church of England); his claim that English "seems likely to be coeval with the world," on the other hand, mirrors the robust optimism that animated so much subsequent commentary on the future of the language.

Views like Hare's began to flourish as the imperial impulse coalesced in a linguistic ideology.

> *1801.* However, my idea is, that, if the English language be cultivated *as it ought to be*, regulating and improving its harmony, and adapting it, as far as can be with propriety, to the several European dialects, derived from Latin, it will *ultimately supersede* the *French*. It is already the most general in *America*. Its progress in the *East* is considerable; and if many schools were established in *different* parts of Asia and Africa to instruct the natives, *free of all expence*, with various *premiums of British manufacture* to the most meritorious pupils, this would be the best preparatory step that Englishmen could adopt for the *general* admission of their commerce, their opinions, their religion. This would tend to conquer the heart and its affections; which is a far more effectual conquest than that obtained by swords and cannons: and a

thousand pounds expended for tutors, books, and premiums, would do more to subdue a nation of savages than forty thousand expended for artillery-men, bullets, and gunpowder. (Russel 1801, 93–95)

1829. It is evident to all those who have devoted any portion of attention to the subject, that the English language would, if proper care were devoted to its advancement, stand an excellent chance of becoming more universally diffused, read, and spoken, than any other now is, or ever has been. In Europe, the study of it seems to be gradually spreading. In Germany, Russia, and Scandinavia it is esteemed an essential, in France a highly useful, branch of education; in Africa it is gradually superseding the Dutch, and becoming the medium of valuable information. In Australasia it is not only widely spoken, as the only European language known on that vast continent, but written and printed in an almost incredible number of newspapers, magazines, and reviews. In Asia so great is the desire manifested to learn it, that it was thought by Bishop Heber, that, if proper facilities were afforded, it would, in fifty years, supersede Hindoostanee, and become the court and camp language of India. In America, millions already speak, write, and read it, as their mother tongue; and it is rapidly obliterating the savage languages and French from Canada, and the rest of the north of the Northern Continent. Never before did a language look forward to so bright a prospect as this, and nothing could retard its swift march but our own incredible folly. By stupidly and (I may almost say) wickedly introducing French into our books, we are, as it were, compelling all those who wish to study English literature, to acquire the French language also. (A. C. C. 1829, 121–22)

1846. In this literary combat for supremacy, it is, therefore, England against the world—the English language contending for dominion in the primeval habitation of every other dialect spoken among men. Homogeneous and consolidated in its own birth-place, it has no distractions with the Celtic fragments of Ireland, Wales, or Scotland. The Cornish or Pictish, the Saxon or Norman vestiges which remain, only serve to enrich the other classic and vernacular treasures of the imperial tongue. In British colonies and the United States, the population which increases is the Anglo-Saxon race speaking English. In South Africa, in Australia, New Zealand, and in the West Indies, this is the language which prevails, and which natives acquire as the means of wealth, improvement, and power. (Eclectikwn 1846, 7)

1847. This brief survey of the extensive use of our language must be gratifying to every person who possesses it; but more especially to those to whom it belongs as their birthright. It also clearly shows the God of providence has a hand in doing it,—that he is pushing it onwards to accomplish some great purpose arising from his good-will to all men. We, as a nation, ought to be very thankful to him for exalting us to such a conspicuous situation, and for causing our language to be employed so extensively; for while every nation will be profited by the great event of its becoming universally used for international purposes, ours will reap the greatest advantage. The prevalence of it must, of course, carry with it British influence; and if we continue to manifest the same mild and benevolent spirit which has, of late, characterized our movements, and sweetened our influence in the world, the respect we have already attained will continue to increase in proportion as the nations become familiarized with us. We shall be a kind of moral sun, diffusing the light of knowledge; and by our genial influence promoting the spread and growth of every beneficial institution. (Bradshaw 1847, 30–31)

1848. In its easiness of grammatical construction, in its paucity of inflection, in its almost total disregard of the distinctions of gender excepting those of nature, in the simplicity and precision of its terminations and auxiliary verbs, not less than in the majesty, vigour and copiousness of its expression, our mother-tongue seems well adapted by *organization* to become the language of the world. To boast of its wealth is needless, with such a literature as exists to prove it. It is now spoken by sixty millions of people—and before the termination of the present century will in all human probability be spoken by two hundred millions: in the British Islands, in the United States, in Canada, in Central America, in Guiana, in the West Indian group of islands, on the seaboard of Africa, in Hindustan, in the Asiatic archipelagoes, and in Australia and the vast islands of the surrounding seas—a population nearly equal to that of the whole of Europe! To what extent the revolutions of science, the progress of free institutions, and the developements of civilization generally may contribute to spread the English language on the neighbouring continent it is not so easy to determine: but it need scarcely be supposed that a language which has already belted the world and established itself permanently in every latitude will prove unable in the future, with new advantages in its favour, to fix itself firmly in the countries of Europe. (Review of Bradshaw's *Scheme* (q.v.), 1848, 82)

1850. At present the prospects of the English language are the most splendid that the world has ever seen. It is spreading in each of the quarters of the globe by fashion, by emigration, and by conquest. The increase of population alone in the two great states of Europe and America in which it is spoken, adds to the number of its speakers in every year that passes, a greater amount than the whole number of those who speak some of the literary languages of Europe, either Swedish, or Danish, or Dutch. It is calculated that before the lapse of the present century, a time that so many now alive will live to witness, it will be the native and vernacular language of about one hundred and fifty millions of human beings. (Watts 1850, 212)

1855. And this, in our tongue, is a very hopeful feature not observable in any other language that has fallen within our observation. Wherever it may go, the force of our institutions, our character, our literature, and policy accompany it; the vigor of the race that uses it, almost as surely triumphs over all opposing obstacles as do their arms over all opposing nations. It seems to be a providential decree; and, no doubt, a wise and beneficient object underlying it.

The language of the seas is already our own. Nine tenths of the commerce of the ocean is transacted through the copious and flexile medium of our tongue, and claims the protection of the Anglo-American fraternity.

The barbarism of Australia, the heathen institutions and worn-out languages of India, the superannuated hieroglyphs of China, and the rude utterances of important parts of Africa and of numberless islands in the Eastern seas, are fast giving way to the institutions and the languages of our race.

But the great field for its most splendid and extensive development, we believe, must be looked for in our own youthful and magnificent republic [i.e., the United States], and the supremacy she is yet destined to exercise over the whole of this Western world. ["Our Language Destined to be Universal" 1855, 311)

Such ideas would have been almost unthinkable in the eighteenth century; two centuries earlier, they could hardly have been imagined. For writers of the last century and a quarter, they are taken to be commonplaces of received wisdom.

Perhaps the most influential prediction about the future of English came not from Britain or the United States but from the preeminent linguistic scholar of the time, Jakob Grimm (1785–1863). Speaking to the Royal Academy of Berlin in January, 1851, Grimm discussed the origin of language and trends apparent in modern languages. Published in 1852, his views quickly reached the English-reading audience.

Of all modern languages, not one has acquired such great strength and vigour as the English. It has accomplished this by simply freeing itself from the ancient phonetic laws, and casting off almost all inflections; whilst, from its abundance of intermediate sounds, tones not even to be taught, but only to be learned, it has derived a characteristic power of expression such as perhaps was never yet the property of any other human tongue. Its highly spiritual genius, and wonderfully happy development, have proceeded from a surprisingly intimate alliance of the two oldest languages of modern Europe—the Germanic and Romanesque. It is well known in what relation these stand to one another in the English language. The former supplies the material groundwork, the latter the higher mental conceptions. Indeed, the English language, which has not in vain produced and supported the greatest, the most prominent of all modern poets (I allude, of course, to Shakespeare), in contradistinction to the ancient classical poetry, may be called justly a LANGUAGE OF THE WORLD: and seems, like the English nation, to be destined to reign in future with still more extensive sway over all parts of the globe. For none of all the living languages can be compared with it as to richness, rationality, and close construction, not even the German—which has many discrepancies like our nation, and from which it would be first obliged to free itself, before it could boldly enter the lists with the English. (S. H. 1853; see Grimm [1851] 1965)

Citation of Grimm's opinions became a regular feature of subsequent speculation. Some indication of the willing reception of his optimism appears as early as 1856, when Walt Whitman declared that "the English language is by far the noblest now spoken—probably ever spoken—upon this earth" and cited Grimm to confirm his view (Whitman 1856,185).

When F. A. March published his oration to graduates of Amherst College, he included mention of Grimm's opinion (March 1861, 19). Like other observers in Britain and North America, he was confident of the destiny of English and eager to see its benefits spread around the globe.

It is the glory of the English speech that its idioms speak for truth and freedom, and law and religion. It grew up in the midst of struggles for religion,—in the midst of the contests of freemen,—in the midst of a people fond of nature and home. Its idioms have been dyed in the blood of matryrs, or taken their festive colors in the heart of patriots or poets; they are tinted less in the colors of fancy than in the veritable hues of sky and cloud, wood and field, and ocean, wrought into unity of meaning under the solemn and earnest gaze of imagination. (15)

Florid rhetoric and extravagant comparisons of this sort became commonplace. English, though beset with an orthography that Grimm and others decried, was the "natural" language of the highest human ideals, and the zeal that propelled economic and cultural imperialism was coupled with the use of English. The intrinsic qualities of the language were believed to be so superior for all manner of intellectual activity that it was easy to confuse altruism with self-interest and generosity with exploitation.

Within the community of English speakers, self-congratulation continued to flow as writers contemplated their own language. But it was foreign observers like Grimm who certified the correctness of these views. In the 1840s, writers began to speculate about the number of people who would speak English by the beginning of the twentieth century—150 and 200 million were both approximations concocted for domestic consumption. Such numbers were based on the assumption that English would replace the other languages spoken in the British Empire at an increasingly rapid pace and that the North American communities where English was not spoken (for instance, the French in Canada or Germans in the United States) would soon succumb to English influence. A more conservative guess in the 1860s put the current number of anglophones at 61 million (Brackebusch 1868, 22). Instead of comparing the spread of English to the diffusion of Latin in the Roman Empire as had by then become customary, this writer (who was awarded a German Ph.D. for his predictive speculations) called to mind other conquerers—Carthaginians, Vikings, and the Dutch—whose languages did not permanently alter the balance of linguistic power (48). Such comparisons, needless to say, were not popular in a time when the Empire of Rome, not that of Carthage, was the model for British political conduct.

The most extravagant projections were the most satisfying to the anglophone community and, therefore, the most popular. The Swiss botanist Alphonse de Candolle (1806–93) turned his attention to the question in the early 1870s. Drawing on census returns, he calculated the following "at the present time":

> English-speaking peoples in England, 31,000,000; in the United States, 40,000,000; in Canada, &c., 4,000,000; in Australia and New Zealand, 2,000,000; total, 77,000,000. (Candolle 1875, 241)

From that beginning, he projected a wildly optimistic set of numbers for English speakers a century thereafter.

> Now, judging by the increase that has taken place in the present century, we may estimate the probable growth of population as follows:
> In England it doubles in fifty years; therefore, in a century (in 1970) it will be 124,000,000. In the United States, in Canada, in Australia, it doubles in twenty-five; therefore it will be 736,000,000. Probable total of the English-speaking race in 1970, 860,000,000. (241–42)

Candolle's astonishing number does not include any estimates for English speakers in Africa, the Caribbean, India, or the Far East. Others were quick to supply that deficiency.

Writing in 1883, Foster Barham Zincke computed estimates for the same regions that Candolle had considered and conjectured that there would be 998,050,000 mother-tongue speakers of English by 1980. What would occur, he believed, was that the superior wealth (the "dollar") and abundant energy (the "plough") of anglophones would overwhelm the "worn-out" world.

> In half a century the Englishry of the United States having overflowed into Canada, and bought up Mexico in detail, will number 200,000,000, and will then be increasing at the rate of 8,000,000 annually. This will oblige them to spread over Guatemala, Columbia, Bolivia, and Peru in the fashion in which they will have already occupied Mexico. All these vast tracts are now only waiting for their advent. They, too, will be acquired by the dollar and the plough. The impetus to increase, and multiply, and advance will as yet have received no check. In the following half century, it will carry the flood of American cultivators down the valley of the Amazon, and along the whole range of the Andes, and wherever in South America men of European descent can live by their own labour. Before, however, this will have been effected, they will have spread as settlers over the islands of the Pacific, and will have joined hands with their kindred in New Zealand and Australia. (Zincke 1883,13–14)

Eccentric as this vision now seems, it reflected the prevailing opinion and unbounded optimism of the imperialists who looked with pride on their own culture and its influence.

In 1884, W. E. Gladstone wrote to a correspondent of the *New York Tribune* in answer to a request for his views of two subjects that had been raised in conversation at "a country house in Scotland": George Washington (whom Gladstone regarded as "the purest figure in history") and the spread of English.

> The other subject is one on which I hardly like to touch in a few lines; for the prospect it opens to me is as vast as it is diversified, and it is so interesting as to be almost overwhelming.
>
> Mr. Barham Zincke, no incompetent calculator, reckons that the English-speaking peoples of the world 100 years hence will probably count a thousand millions. Some French author, whose name I unfortunately forget, in a recent estimate places them somewhat lower; at what precise figure I do not recollect, but it is like 600 or 800 millions. A century back I suppose they were not much, if at all, beyond 15 millions; I also suppose we may now take them at 100.
>
> These calculations are not so visionary as they may seem to some; they rest upon a rather wide induction, while the best thing they can pretend to is rough approximation . . . . What a prospect is that of very many hundreds of millions of people, certainly among the most manful and energetic in the world, occupying one great Continent, I may also say two, and other islands and territories

not easy to be counted, *with these islands at their head*, the most historic in the world. In contact, by a vast commerce, with all mankind, and perhaps still united in kindly political association with some more hundreds of millions fitted for no mean destiny, united, almost absolutely, in blood and language, and very largely in religion, laws, and institutions. (Gladstone 1885, 7, col. 4; italics added)

As "scientific" estimates like those provided by Candolle and Zincke entered the realm of established truth, visions emerged of little England made globally large.

It is, then, not only within the limits of possibility, but, unless something quite unforseen should arise to hinder the action of the causes now at work, it is as likely as anything prospective can be in human affairs, that the Englishry of 1980 will amount to about 1,000,000,000 souls. . . . [A]ll these people will speak the same language, read the same books, and be influenced by the same leading ideas. (Axon 1888, 204)

Subsequent estimates for the year 2000 suggested that English speakers might number 850,000,000 (Matthews 1898–99, 103) or even 1,100,000,000 (Babbitt 1907–8, 9905). All of these predictions drew, naturally enough, on the uniformitarian principle—the expectation that past trends would continue into the future. Such speculations presumed that "the causes now at work" would mean yet further extension of commerce, colonization, migration, and language. What makes them especially anachronistic in light of the actual history of the past century is that they do not presume multilingualism as an important fact of social demographics in the future.

There were some observers who took a rather longer view, one influenced by ideas about the Roman Empire, which, thanks to their education and predisposition, continued to influence speculative thinkers. Latin, they well understood, was a dead language, though they quickly observed that it survived in the modern Romance languages. Would the same evolutionary trend toward linguistic dissolution influence English?

The past of Rome seemed a powerful predictor of the future of English, and the notion Webster had expressed earlier—that English would eventually evolve into several separate languages—was considered by some at midcentury to be a likelihood. Thus in 1860, an anonymous American reviewer declared:

It has for some time been the fashion, among a certain class of semi-political critics, to favor the impression that the language of the two great branches of the Anglo-Saxon family is gradually diverging into two appreciably distinct dialects. (Review of George P. Marsh's *Lectures on the English Language,* 1860, 507)

Though dismissed by most, the prospect of trans-Atlantic division in English was seriously mooted by a few eminent writers. One of the most prominent was the philologist Henry Sweet (1845–1912). Predicting a century into the future, he wrote: "It must also be remembered that by that time England, America, and Australia will be speaking mutually unintelligible languages, owing to their independent changes of pronunuciation" (Sweet 1877,196). (As Randolph Quirk has explained, this guess has "proved dramatically wrong" [1985, 3].)

Reflecting on the future of the language at the jubilee of Victoria's reign in 1897, another philologist, Richard J. Lloyd, enlarged on Sweet's prediction.

. . . the Latin language, carried by the legions out of Italy over Gaul and Spain, soon fell into a dozen mutually uncomprehended types, of which the victorious Tuscan and Castilian and Norman-French are merely the literary examples. No doubt it will be said that there is no such danger for English, because at the present time all Anglian (i.e., English-speaking) men readily understand each other. This proposition cannot be denied in the main. Still, there are degrees of comprehensibility. I, an Englishman of Liverpool, am conscious of no effort in talking to an educated Northern Englishman, or Virginian, or Upper Canadian; but in talking to a born Londoner or Bostonian I have to use some attention in rightly catching occasional sounds which are not quite familiar to me; and in talking to a London cockney, or Glasgow Scotchman, or nasal Northerner, the effort of attention, though always successful, is wearisome and at last painful. This shows that our mutual comprehensibility is very far from absolute; it shows that we have advanced many steps towards mutual incomprehensibility. For never since Babel, have two dialects become mutually incomprehensible at one stroke; the change creeps upon them unawares; and once attained, it is irrevocable. There is thenceforeward no longer one language but two, distinct and irreconcilable. (Lloyd 1897, 287)

Lloyd was among the first to articulate for modern readers a theme that became a dominant one for subsequent observers, the erosion of "standard" English because of rapid change in urban models: in London, "the corruption of language seems to proceed chiefly from below" (291), but not only because of the unbridled tendencies of the lower orders. Those of higher social standing also participate in the emerging "slovenliness of utterance." A "fine scholar and great London preacher, known in both hemispheres," and "the average well-dressed person . . . [in] a good London restaurant" (291) were singled out as harbingers of linguistic discord. For instance, the "disappearance" of preconsonantal and final *r*, was denounced by Lloyd as a London innovation, "slipshod and emasculate" (1895, 53); for Charles Remy, an American, it seemed "grossly incorrect" (1900, 419). Such novelties, they thought, were all too typical of the rifts separating British and American English.

Lloyd's speculations alarmed W. H. Stead, editor of the *Review of Reviews*. Though less inclined than Lloyd to forsee the imminent dissolution of English, he agreed that if "change" was creeping upon the community "unawares," something should be done to prevent it.

> Hence the suggestion that I venture to make is that this, the year of the great Jubilee, should be utilised in some way or other to begin a systematic attempt, on however humble a scale, to fix the character of the language, to prevent its degradation or disintegration into a congeries of mutually unintelligible dialects, and, in short, to perpetuate for the benefit of future generations one tongue, one language, that will be mutually understood by all the children of men. (Stead 1897, 338)

Having quoted Grimm's opinion that English deserved worldwide use on its intrinsic merits, Stead proposed an academy to ascertain the standard and promote its use. Philologists, "leading men of letters," and the editors of magazines in New York and London (including himself) could make up the membership: "Such an Association, however humble and insignificant it might be at the beginning, would contain within itself the germ of an Academy of the English-speaking world" (339). His proposal did not meet with much sympathetic response. The *Spectator* declared that "all this talk about unintelligibility is a delusion" ("Shall English Become a Dead Language?" 1897, 621), poked fun at the pretense that editors make good academicians, and opined: "We would rather see the English language grow so disunited that it would cease to be a single language than see it perish by being confined in an academic strait-waistcoat" (620).

These skirmishes about correctness were a digression from the mainstream of thought about English and global politics. At the end of the nineteenth century, the British Empire was at its height and the United States had just extended its influence with military campaigns that brought the Caribbean and the Philippines into its sphere. Most observers believed that English would follow the two flags and spread beyond the political outposts to all nations of the world. (Dissent from the imperial theme is rare even today.) Without the least uncertainty, most observers have declared that culture, religion, literature, technology, and wealth are all tied to the use of English.

> *1846*. Let the speech of Britain obtain access to the markets and the schools of those regions as the medium of mercantile correspondence and religious intercourse;—let it become the ambition of the young and the reward of the studious; let it be the ladder of power and the door to office and emolument; let the treasures of English literature be diffused amidst the people from Cape Comorin [at the southern tip of India] to the Himalayas, from the Indus to the Burrampooter, and British dominion will be consolidated, equal British rule will be cherished, British commerce will be paramount, and the Christian religion and literature will diffuse their influences in the plain and among the mountains. (Eclectikwn 1846, 12)
>
> *1849*. Ours is the language of the arts and sciences, of trade and commerce, of civilization and religious liberty. It is the language of Protestantism—I had almost said, of piety. It is a store-house of the varied knowledge which brings a nation within the pale of civilization and Christianity. As a vehicle of our institutions and principles of civil and religious liberty, it is "belting the earth," pushing east and west, and extending over the five great geographical divisions of the world, giving no doubtful presage that, with its extraordinary resources for ameliorating the condition of man, it will soon become universal. Already it is the language of the Bible. More copies of the sacred Scriptures have been published in the English language, than in all other tongues combined. And the annual issues in this language, at the present time, beyond all doubt, far surpass those of all the world besides. So prevalent is this language already become, as to betoken that it may soon become the language of international communication for the world. This fact, connected with the next, that *the two nations speaking this language have, within a few years past, gained the most extraordinary ascendancy*, holding in their hands nearly all the maritime commerce and naval power of the world, giving tone to national opinion and feeling, and sitting as arbiters among the nations, dictating terms of peace and war, and extending their empire over the nations of the East, holds out a glorious presage of the part *America* is destined to act in the subjugation of the world to Christ. (Read 1849, 48)
>
> *1873*. Fashion has been the forerunner in this extraordinary and significant movement. It is sufficient to give us pause, when we reflect that the tailor has done more toward the unification of mankind than Alexander, and that

the hatter has woven a bond of union among them which is of adamant in comparison to that which the Caesars forged. The pantaloons and dress-coat may be seen as frequently in Constantinople now, as in Paris or London. Even the *fez* is slowly receding before the inevitable stove-pipe hat. . . . Commerce, geographical situation, and probably increase in numbers [of English speakers], are the governing and absolute factors in the problem. (Upton 1873, 326–27)

1889. The English language as spoken by the American people is subject to great and rapid changes. Among a people so little conservative every one seems to feel at liberty to coin words and take liberties with his mother tongue. The varied foreign elements pouring into our country from every nation under the sun, the extent and variety of our territory, the vast sectional industries carried on, the cosmopolitan and migratory character of our people, their omnivorous habit of taking intellectual pabulum from all nations and languages and tongues—all these are constantly transforming our language. While these things may prevent a tendency to distinct dialects and serve in a measure to knead our language into a compact whole, yet they keep pouring into the mass an endless variety of new elements, and thus it is at the mercy of an infinite number of fluctuating forces. (Campbell 1889, 127)

1890. Surely, a language which combines such extreme simplicity with all the qualities demanded of a language expressing the thought of the most advanced civilization ought to have the first claim to becoming the language of the world, or, at least, the basis upon which the universal language of the future is to develop. And this, indeed, seems to be the destiny of the English language. All English-speaking people are agreed on this point, while the other nations do not seem inclined to contest it; there is, at least, no one nation which puts forth a claim for its own speech as superior to that of English. (Knoflech 1890,17)

1894. It has been suggested by some that several centuries hence these four branches [of English (the European, the American, the South African, and the Australasian)] will have developed into as many different languages. The difference, however, cannot, we think, ever be of great extent, as the universality of printing, of electric communication, of steam-ships, and other facilities for travel, should have a tendency to check anything like organic disruption of the language, always excepting of course the changes which must accrue from the addition of local phrases to the general vocabulary. ("The Future of the English Language" 1894, 296)

1908. The spread of a language and its general acceptance depend very little upon its own qualities, and very largely upon the qualities of the race that has it for a mother-tongue, and upon the commanding position this race holds in the struggle for economic mastery. (Matthews 1908, 431)

1908. The conclusion is this: the only way to advance the interests of a community is to advance the tongue of that community, and conversely the only way to harm the interests of a country is to diminish its language. The only way to advance the interests of England is to advance the English tongue, and the only way English interests can be damaged is by damaging the English language. The sole way of advancing English interests is to *increase the English-speaking* population. To increase the *not-English-speaking* population is of no use to England; on the contrary, it is enormously harmful to her . . . . (Alderson 1908, 69)

1909. The English tongue has become a rank polyglot, and is spreading over the earth like some hardy plant whose seed is sown by the wind. It has crossed seas to continents remote—it has taken root in foreign soil—it has become cosmopolitan—it has grown forgetful of early forms—it has mixed with noisome weeds—it has blown new blossoms—it is putting forth strange buds, and will continue to grow, to change, to expand, to decay, to take fresh root again throughout the ages to come; but it will never dissociate itself from the island which gave it birth. The English language and the Union-Jack seem almost to stand for the same thing: the glory of England. (Bell 1909, 3–4)

1920. If discovery and conquest have coloured the language-map over vast but thinly-peopled regions of the earth it is the more permeative influence of the personal contact of the trader, and of the missionary of religion, philosophy, science or education—served in these later days by almost miraculous and constantly advancing means of transport, transit and communication—that has broken down, and is daily breaking down, with cumulative energy, the barriers of racial, national and linguistic isolation, alike in the old world and the new.

And if the Briton has, in the past, played a master-part in these processes, it is due to those national characteristics of which Emerson wrote with such luminous sympathy in Victorian days—to that happy combination of physical vigour and mental complexity which have made him so pregnant a paradox in the history of the race. (Hayes 1920, 199)

1924. Many must be taught to see and hear the beauty that is around them; others have seen and heard it from childhood on, and have known early in life that to be born a heritor of the history and beauty of the English language was a veritable gift of the gods—a gift that should be cherished equally by all whose mother tongue has practically become the world-language—English, the Lingua Franca of to-day. (De Witt [1924], 9)

1927. English is the most modern of the great languages, the most widely spoken, and the most international; for it contains more foreign words than any other. Yet, because of its frequent lack of agreement between spelling and pronunciation, its great variety of vowel sounds, the idiomatic character it shares with all natural tongues, and, above all, its lack of political neutrality, English would not be acceptable to all nations. (Pankhurst 1927, 44)

1929. To-day, however, steam navigation, printing, railroads, postal and telegraphic service are enough to accentuate or maintain uniformity of language within each nation and within its colonies or within the colonies which it once held. This process by which many local dialects fuse into a single language which for one reason or another reaches a position of preëminence and becomes the national language will tend to repeat itself in the broader field of world languages. For the means of communication mentioned above are now augmented by aviation, motion pictures, and the wireless telephone, and not only do rivers and valleys offer no obstacles to communication, but even the highest mountain ranges and the broadest oceans have been overcome. (Domínguez 1929, 110)

1935. Three-quarters of a century ago, that shrewd judge of current topics, Walter Bagehot, put the matter clearly, if somewhat unkindly, into the nutshell phrase, "French is the patois of Europe, while English is the language of the World." No ambition on our part, no organised efforts to seize such a sovranty has brought about this long-forseen result, but simply the course of events and the spread of the English-speaking peoples and their dominant place in the world. (Haines 1935, 55)

1943. Germany *sees with crystal clearness the need for a common speech in Europe if unity is to be attained. Das Reich*, the Berlin newspaper, wrote, "There is only one language that will be spoken by Europe in the future, and that language is German, which will be the international *lingua franca* between the nations of the New Order." Are the Allies blind to the stark logic of the idea? . . .

Here then is a clear-cut policy that the Allies can adopt in their peace terms. Mix the Europeans—a process largely achieved by the Germans. Give them English as a common speech. The neutral countries, Sweden, Spain, and Turkey, could be left out, since they would not constitute a threat to an English-speaking Europe. Germany must be occupied by this mixed European race, the Germans themselves being dispersed. Russia, having contributed the lion's share to the defeat of Nazism, could be given authority over the part-Slav races in Finland, Estonia, Poland, and Bulgaria. Being unaggressive by nature, added to the fact that she is socialist, she would not disturb the peace. Doubtless her communism, the result of an extreme swing to the left from Tsarism, will become modified. (Harrison 1943, 55, 58)

1945. The roots of English spread into the continent, and the influence of English spreads throughout the world. There is no language anywhere in any continent of the world, which has the importance of English. In poetry, in literature, in philosophy, in technical subjects—I was going to say in mathematics, but I am not sure of that—our language has spread much more than any other, and on the top of others. (Follick 1946, 12)

1955. Therefore the change to English [beyond the anglophone world] would have to be forced on the leaders and politicians and also on the population because the latter, owing to sameness of language, are entirely in the hands of their leaders, who would tell them it was some deep-laid scheme of the Americans to enslave them or some equally idiotic drivelling humbug, which they would implicitly believe. There is no limit to the utter rubbish the populace, and sometimes even the educated classes, who ought to know better, of any country will swallow.

The point to be decided, then, is whether it would pay the United States and Great Britain to compel the change by force. The answer is that it would be one of the most profitable undertakings, in every respect, that those countries had ever been engaged in. Financially it would pay profits hitherto unheard of, because once the cost of the change had been met, there would be no further expense whatever, nothing but profit. It costs North America nothing to keep up the English language in Great Britain, and England pays nothing to maintain the English tongue in North America. Likewise, once the change was made, China herself would willingly keep up the English tongue because it would be her tongue as well, the only one she knew.

We need not repeat the political and strategic benefits of the change not only for China, North America and England, but for the whole world. The interests of the three Powers would be identical and no combination of other Powers would dare to attack them: China would not be the weak, distraught country she is to-day but a second United States. Needless to say we are not suggesting any connection, political, governmental or other between the three countries, they would all be free as air, sovereign and independent. (Alderson 1955, 234)

1974. English is winning (to borrow a French expression) by a *tour de force.* It is by far the most useful from the standpoint of business, science, and literature generally. More is written in English in every field. More television programs use it. There are English-language newspapers in most important non-English-speaking cities. If one language is to win, it's almost certain to be English. (McGhee 1974, 6)

1984. . . . the centripetal forces making English the world language are stronger: the media of mass communication that spread the word instantaneously around the global village; pop songs; mass tourism, in which the package holiday to foreign parts is a fundamental annual right; above all the printing press, which still flies the standard even if it is no longer at the top of the pyramid. (Howard 1985, 6)

1985. English has also become a lingua franca to the point that any literate, educated person on the face of the globe is in a very real sense deprived if he does not know English. Poverty, famine, and disease are instantly recognized as the cruellest and least excusable forms of deprivation. Linguistic deprivation is a less easily noticed condition, but one nevertheless of great significance. (Burchfield 1985, 160–61)

1986. The worldwide spread of English is remarkable. There has been nothing like it in history. Spanish and French, Arabic and Turkish, Latin and Greek have served their turn as international languages, in the wake of the mission station, the trading post or the garrison. But none has come near to rivalling English. ("The New English Empire" 1986,127)

1990. Fundamentally, the invention of the communications satellite as the prime mechanism for international communications has allowed penetration of vast new areas of the world. This is particularly true of opportunities to transmit television over long distances and to receptors deep inside of nations not reachable by normal ground transmissions. Not only has the space program brought about the means to disseminiate great volumes of English information, but the U. S. leadership in space technology meant that the *lingua franca* of the space business also became English. This caused another mighty penetration of the world's advanced technology. (Freitag 1990, 7)

In the twentieth century, some of the themes expressed in this anthology of extracts have diminished (for instance, the expression, if not the conviction, of anglophone racial superiority) while others have been amplified (for example, the supposed power of popular culture in spreading English through the media). For the most part, however, the linguistic ideas that evolved at the acme of empires led by Britain and the United States have not changed as economic colonialism has replaced the direct, political management of third world nations. English is still believed to be the inevitable world language; the reasons for the prominent place of English in global affairs are the same ones that were first elaborated in the nineteenth century. The metaphors used to describe its spread are drawn consistently from the language of economic, political, and military competition: "*ladder* of power," "*bond* of union," "breaking down *barriers*," market "*penetration*," "*sovereignty*," "*winning*," and "*rivalling*." The old metaphors have held good in an era that is quite different from that in which they were coined and far from that even more distant time when English began to spread.

Chapter 5

English Transplanted

With the dispersal of English, its speakers established permanent communities in remote areas, and, as innovations emerged at home and abroad, English in the new regions began to diverge from the London fashion. As the images used to describe these new kinds of English coalesced into practice, the reputation of the colonists was a crucial factor in the way their language was evaluated. When the speakers of transplanted English were esteemed, their language was likewise highly valued (often for having an ancient "purity," since lost at home). When the speakers were scorned, their English was regarded as debased, vulgar, and unpolished. Many reports of these new kinds of English survive in the writings of cultivated travelers and expatriates, most of whom disparage the quality of English on foreign shores. For instance, the usual meaning of *bluff* 'steep rise of land' as seen from the sea was shifted, in South Carolina and Georgia before 1666, to 'steep river bank.' The first English visitor to record this innovation, Francis Moore in 1735, categorically declared that usage to be "barbarous English" even though the meaning shift seems a natural one and the normative sense against which he measured the change belonged to the technical vocabulary of mariners rather than to that of the literati (Moore [1744]1840, 94). (Moore's comment is the first recorded British objection to an American usage [see Read 1979].) As exploration pressed westward, *bluff* was transferred from riverbank to lakeshore, then (from the fact that such declivities were often wooded) to a grove of trees rising like an island from the western prairies. As the historical record shows, this sense shift took about a century to complete (see Avis 1967, s. v. *bluff*), and the result, barbarous or not, was a distinctive use of English on the North American continent. Naturally enough, those who used *bluff* in its "new" sense were hardly aware of the change; only foreign visitors, especially those from Britain, regarded it as evidence of a colonial blot on the excellence of English.

123

At first, those who speak the transplanted varieties are likely to accept the valuation that outsiders provide, and linguistic self-doubts, once introduced, are surprisingly enduring. Even when the variety is fully established (as in the case of modern American, Canadian, New Zealand, and Australian Englishes), there remains a persistent belief that the prestige norms of southeastern England still provide a model for the "best" English, at least for some purposes. In the performance of Shakespeare's plays, for example, pronunciation according to present-day British ideas of "proper" English is widely accepted wherever the plays are performed, even though that style is remote from Shakespeare's own, and dozens of jokes and puns are thereby lost in the process, many of which would be obvious if local pronunciations were employed. The prevailing view was articulated by Ngaio Marsh, who drew on "30 years or so of directing student actors in the plays of Shakespeare."

> Over those years I never encountered a student who, after being invited to think about it, did not agree that the New Zealand dialect was an unsatisfactory vehicle for the magnificent words he was called upon to use, nor a student who was not ready and able to abandon it. Pinched "O's," tinny "A's," long drawn-out "E's" and neglected consonants all righted themselves and nobody a penny the worse. (Marsh 1978, 23)

Not content with praising stage English, Marsh expressed regret that few of her students adopted this "Shakespearean" English in their offstage conversations. (This "colonial cringe" about New Zealand English continues to animate discussion there [see Bell 1977; Bell and Holmes 1990; Horrocks 1985].) Like many others, Marsh asserted the general excellence of contemporary British norms at the expense of all others.

Colonial English begins, as far as the historical record extends at least, with the variety of Old English spoken by the English followers of the Normans who settled in Ireland shortly after the Conquest. As already described, English gradually disappeared as the migrants were assimilated into the Irish-speaking population. In a few small enclaves, however, English survived, and, in 1577, the English traveler, Richard Stanihurst, observed that in two districts of county Wexford "the dregs of the old auncient Chaucer English" still remain (quoted in Bliss 1979, 21). A century later, another English visitor made the same comparison.

> Itt's notorious that itt's the very language brought over by Fitzstephen [= Robert Fitz Stephen, leader of the Welsh and Anglo-Norman forces in the

capture of Wexford in 1169], and retained by them to this day. Whoever hath read old Chaucer, and is at all acquainted therewith, will better understand the barony of Forth dialect than either an English or Irishman, that never read him, though otherwise a good linguist. (Solomon Richards, writing in 1682, quoted in Bliss 1979, 22)

While the connotation of the word *dregs* is hardly a positive one, the implication of antiquity through the invocation of Chaucer invites the idea that this transplanted English has a quaintness that distinguishes it from dialects spoken closer to home that have only innovation to commend them. Even today, when the dynamics of language change are better understood, some isolated communities (for instance, in the east-central United States) are "explained," and thereby approved, as retaining qualities of "Elizabethan English." Hence, the allegation of antiquity counts as a commendation, though one granted only to speakers who appear to be simultaneously "authentic" and powerless.

A second transplantation occurred at about the same time the language spread to Ireland, the penetration of English northward to Scotland. Immediately after the Normans gained military supremacy in southern England, the survivors of the Old English–speaking royal family fled to Edinburgh, accompanied by retainers of various ranks. Unlike the situation in Ireland, however, there was already some use of English in Celtic Scotland through missionary efforts from the English church. Adventurous Scots had, before the Conquest, been attracted to the southern religious houses and royal courts. Fleeing Macbeth, Malcolm Canmore spent fourteen years at the English court of Edward the Confessor; returned to Scotland, where he reigned as Malcolm III from 1058 to 1093; and in 1068 married Margaret (the sister of Edgar Aetheling, who had been dispossesed by the Normans). Margaret is credited with bringing Celtic Christianity into conformity with English practices, but her role as a harbinger of the English language and of English mores at the highest levels of society is more consequential for the extension of English, even though the anglicization of the Scottish court was not completed in her lifetime. The displacement of Gaelic by English was complicated by the subsequent immigration of French-speaking Normans (and yet more English retainers), but support for English remained in high social circles in church and state, and the development of the royal burghs provided a nascent urban environment where, as so often later, multilingualism provided a linguistic mixture that eventually led to the predominance of English. By the fourteenth century, English based on northern models was the first language of Scots of all ranks except in the remote regions of the north and southwest (Aitken 1985, ix). Unfortunately, no comments on this early development of a distinctive Scottish English survive, but in Scotland the transplantation of English quickly took root (as it did not in Ireland) and eventually flourished (see Murison 1979).

As English travelers later visited even more remote regions, the language acquired loanwords. These were often welcomed as signs of the vitality of the language, as yet more treasures (by metaphoric extension) brought home by foreign adventurers. But welcoming new vocabulary from abroad was not the same as acknowledging an independent English with features differing from those in the mother country. From the English perspective, the English of Ireland and Scotland long remained merely "outlandish."

Of the overseas types, maritime English was first to be seen as distinct. Because it was thought to be flawed, maritime English was shunned in the search for an ideal; in Puttenham's view, coastal towns (including London) could not provide models for cultivated English at the end of the sixteenth century, since there "straungers haunt for traffike sake" (quoted above, p. 33) and seafarers introduce unwanted innovations. Even so, the dictionaries of the seventeenth century contain increasing numbers of "nautical words," often grudgingly included but nonetheless significant additions to the vocabulary from the sea (see Osselton 1958, 170–72). Maritime English, moreover, was a harbinger and vehicle for transplanted English, and, as in Moore's complaint about the American use of *bluff*, one of the influences of this variety was the transfer of terms from naval to terrestrial life. This tendency is apparent in a report by a visitor to the Caribbean at the end of the eighteenth century.

> There are some peculiarities in the habits of life of the White Inhabitants, which cannot fail to catch the eye of an European newly arrived. . . . Another peculiarity in the manners of the English in the West Indies (in Jamaica especially) is the number of nautical expressions in their conversation. Thus they say, *hand such a thing*, instead of bring or give it. A plantation well stocked with Negroes, is said to be *well handed*; an office or employment is called *a birth*; the kitchen is denominated the *cook-room*; a warehouse is called a *store*, or *store-room*; a sopha is called *a cot*; a waistcoat is termed *a jacket*; and in speaking of the East and West, they say to *windward* and *leeward*. This language has probably prevailed since the days of the bucaniers. (Edwards 1819, 2:9–10)

Such shifts in the existing English wordstock were one effect of maritime usage on transplanted English.

Borrowings from other languages used on the seas, a second feature of maritime English, continued a tradition begun when Old Norse seafarers provided vocabulary that was adopted by English speakers in the fourteenth century (for example, *keel* and *stern*). Sea terms derived from the languages of Europe were already commonplace and widely known as the period of colonization began: *smack* (first attested in 1611), *sloop* (1629), *yacht* (1557), and *yawl* (1670) from Dutch; *brigantine* (1525), *caravel* (1527), and *corvette* (1636) from French; *galleon* (1529) from Spanish; *junk* (1555) from Portuguese (with its ultimate source in the Far East). But more profound changes were at work in the development of pidgin varieties.

Shipboard multilingualism led to innovations in spoken English, even though most of the borrowings from non-European languages are only attested from bookish sources. The difficulty in identifying the influence of maritime English lies in the fact that the sharp social stratification of life ashore was recreated in the crowded conditions of life at sea. Passengers were not much affected by the language of sailors, but the crew were almost as likely as paying passengers to be migrants, and the social and linguistic distance that kept them apart on board was not necessarily maintained once the ship had reached its destination. Illiterate sailors did not leave testaments describing their own usage, but *berth* 'office, employment' and *cot* 'sofa' in Jamaican usage show their influence.

The lingua franca of the Mediterranean in medieval times persisted into the age of exploration in the larger seas, eventually enhanced by contributions from the diverse groups that were recruited or impressed into service on board British ships (see Yule and Burnell [1903]1968, xviii–xix). It is likely that maritime English provided much more than vocabulary to transplanted English, and pidgins ashore in ports and their hinterlands have much in common with the language of the sea. Recognition of the contribution of maritime English to the various transplanted varieties is only now becoming apparent (thanks, especially, to the work of J. L. Dillard). The following are a few examples of the words that even the most conservative etymologists trace to maritime English: *buckra* 'a white person' (attested in English, 1744), *fetish* 'icon' (1613), *mosquito* (1539), *nigger* 'a black person' (1574), *palaver* 'talk, parley, conference, discussion' (1735), *pickaninny* (1653) 'a child, usually black' (in widespread and early use in North America, the Caribbean, and Australia), *savey, savvy* 'understand' (v.), 'know-how' (n.) (1785), *yam* and *nyam* (v.) 'to eat heartily' (1725; associated with *yam* 'potatolike tuber' [1588]).

During the early seventeenth century, small groups began to establish

Maritime English introduced travelers to the new speechways developing
abroad. Nineteenth-century emigrants to Australia were depicted during their
first days at sea in the *Illustrated London News* 90 (February 12, 1887): 192–93.

themselves permanently abroad in circumstances that fostered the development of new varieties of English. Some of these colonies were short lived
(for example, Providence Island in the Caribbean [1630–41]); others attracted emigrants and endured as English-speaking communities. In either
case, commentators were silent in describing language differences even
though there were early and detailed observations about other facets of colonial life.

Before the Revolution, American visitors to Britain were rare, yet not
so uncommon that any great linguistic difference in their English would be
overlooked. Samuel Johnson, a severe critic of American disloyalty to the
Crown and a careful observer of English, seems to have said nothing about
the language of, for instance, Benjamin Franklin, Arthur Lee, Benjamin
West, and other Americans of his acquaintance in London. But if the facts
of linguistic difference were little noticed, the *idea* of difference and the

supposed "corruption and barbarity" of transplanted English had certainly become an accepted idea about English by the end of the eighteenth century.

The situation is usefully described in Benjamin Silliman's account of his visit to England in 1805 and 1806. Silliman (1779–1864) had been appointed professor of chemistry at Yale at age 23. To find how this new subject was taught abroad, Silliman investigated chemical study in England and Scotland. In his journal, he recorded a conversation at dinner in Cambridge where the company consisted "principally of masters or presidents, professors and fellows."

> Our sitting lasted four hours; my seat was next to Mr. C———, and, in the course of a very free conversation, he took occasion to observe, that it was impossible that any man born and educated 3000 miles from England, should speak the language so perfectly, that even an Englishman could not distinguish the difference between a stranger's speech and his own. This, he was pleased to say, was just the case between us; and he then, with much good nature and urbanity, insisted that I had been all the while amusing him with the story that I was an American, when it was so evident that I must be an Englishman, or must, at least, have been educated in England. I succeeded however, at length, in removing this gentleman's incredulity, although not his surprise. Probably every American traveller in England can relate similar occurrences with which he has been personally acquainted. We must not infer from them that the English do not know that their own language is spoken in the United States. Although we may pardon a Russian, or an unlettered Englishman for such a mistake, we must look for more correct information in a peer of the realm and a learned fellow of one of the universities. They, and all well-informed people in England, unquestionably know that the Anglo-Americans speak the English language; but they imagine that it is a colonial dialect, with a corrupt and barbarous pronunciation, and a vocabulary, interspersed with strange and unknown terms of transatlantic manufacture. That this is the result of prejudice or ignorance, is proved by the fact that a well-educated American may travel from London to John a Groat's house, and thence to the Land's-end, and every where pass for a Londoner; this is the universal presumption concerning him, as will appear from the incidental remarks of the people of the country and their questions concerning the news of the day. (Silliman 1812, 2:227–28)

Just a few days after this dinner, Silliman continued his tour by coach. Among his companions was a young boy, "the son of an Englishman," on his way to an English school from his native Tobago. Though the purpose of Silliman's mentioning him is to describe the youth's wonder at seeing frost for the first time, he characterized the boy's colonial dialect as "broken English" (237). If some native speakers of English from abroad could pass for Londoners, others were quickly recognized and stigmatized though their language.

English transplanted, then and now, is not monolithic, but Britons often lack a discriminating array of stereotypes and evaluations for the diversity of English abroad. (*Abroad* as an English noun often has negative connotations in domestic use: "'abroad,' that large home of ruined reputations" [George Eliot, 1866]; "beastly abroad" [Kenneth Grahame, 1895]; "'Abroad' was a slightly terrifying word of adventure [H. G. Wells, 1934]; "abroad is unutterably bloody and foreigners are fiends" [Nancy Mitford, 1945].) Domestic comment on transplanted English begins with the Caribbean, and, as a reflex of British racism, those varieties influenced by Africans, as Silliman's journal shows, were the first to be scorned. For mainland American English, domestic opinion took somewhat longer to form. For British intellectuals, the idea of American English did not emerge until the 1840s, two hundred years after the two varieties began to drift apart (see Read 1947). Once it was acknowledged as distinct, however, American English was usually despised, and that fate provides a model for other transplanted kinds of English to be evaluated.

Early comments on transplanted English form a cluster of images that derive from differing assumptions about the language. The following extracts illustrate some of the typical reports.

> *Jamaica* (1740). To talk of a *Homer*, or a *Virgil*, of a *Tully*, or a *Demosthenes*, is quite unpolite; and it cannot be otherwise; for a Boy, till the Age of Seven or Eight, diverts himself with the Negroes, acquires their broken way of talking, their Manner of Behavior, and all the Vices which these unthinking Creatures can teach; then perhaps he goes to School; but young Master must not be corrected; if he learns 'tis well; if not, it can't be helped. After a little Knowledge of reading, he goes to the Dancing-school, and commences Beau, learns the common Topicks of Discourse, and visits and rakes with his Equals. (Leslie 1740, 36–37)
>
> *United States* (1781). The vulgar in America speak much better than the vulgar in Great-Britain, for a very obvious reason, viz. that being much more unsettled, and moving frequently from place to place, they are not so liable to local peculiarities either in accent or phraseology. There is a greater difference in dialect between one county and another in Britain, than there is between one state and another in America. I shall also admit, though with some hesitation, that gentlemen and scholars in Great-Britain speak as much with the vulgar,

in common chit-chat, as persons of the same class do in America: But there is a remarkable difference in their public and solemn discourses. I have heard in this country, in the senate, at the bar, and from the pulpit, and see daily in dissertations from the press, errors in grammar, improprieties and vulgarisms, which hardly any person of the same class in point of rank and literature would have fallen into in Great Britain. (John Witherspoon [1781], quoted in Mathews 1931,16)

Newfoundland (1794). As this Island has been inhabited for such a number of years and was peopled by British and Irish, you frequently meet with Familys whose Grandfathers were born in Newfoundland. These are what I call the Natives. They speak English but they have a manner peculiar to themselves—the common people Lisp. When I came among them I thought some of the old Dimerips of Fashion from the perilus of Rathbone Place and Portman Square had been transported as Convicts here, for every Out-harbour I viseted on coversing with the people, they would on answering my enquirys say—"Yes, *dat* is the way" or "O No, we *tant* do it so; but *den* we do it the other way, *tafter* we bring it home because it is *taffer*."

I believe that about ten years ago, amongst the Bon Ton, it was a fashionable qualification to Lisp. I have heard some Women of Rank say—"O T*hear*, p*ay* do not *thrubble yourthelf*" for "O Dear, pray do not trouble yourself." But how the common people of Newfoundland got this *accomplish'd* malady I have not yet been able to learn. (Thomas 1968, 137)

United States (1797). The future history of the other three quarters of the world will, probably, be much affected by America's speaking the language of England. Its natives write the language particularly well; considering they have no dictionary yet, and how insufficient Johnson's is. Washington's speeches seldom exhibited more than a word or two, liable to the least objection; and, from the style of his publications, as much, or more accuracy, may be expected from his successor Adams. (Croft [1797] 1968, 2n)

Jamaica (1802). The Creole language is not confined to the negroes. Many of the ladies, who have not been educated in England, speak a sort of broken English, with an indolent drawling out of their words, that is very tiresome if not disgusting. I stood next to a lady one night, near a window, and, by way of saying something, remarked that the air was much cooler than usual; to which she answered, "Yes, ma-am, *him rail-ly too fra-ish*." (Nugent 1907, 132)

United States (1806). They [a Scottish couple formerly resident "several years" in the United States] observed that the Americans possessed the power of expressing their thoughts with a degree of facility which, when they first heard it, astonished them. It made little difference whether the speaker understood his subject or not, whether he were a man of sense or a fool; in either case there was a copiousness and elegance of expression which seemed to pervade all ranks.

They had listened with surprise, to hear young ladies, in particular, convey their ideas with such beauty and fluency of diction, as was rarely found in the old world; and they did not confine this observation to high life; for, in North Carolina, they had heard a poor woman, who, with a husband and five children, inhabited a miserable hut, with only one room, deplore her sufferings in such language as a lady of the Court of St. James would have been proud to equal. (Silliman 1812, 2:341–42)

Australia (1820). The children born in those colonies, and now grown up, speak a better language, purer, more harmonious, than is generally the case in most parts of England. The amalgamation of such various dialects assembled together, seems to improve the mode of articulating the words. (Dixon 1984, 46)

Australia (1827). A number of the slang phrases current in St. Giles's *Greek* ['criminal argot'] bid fair to become legitimized in the dictionary of this colony: *plant, swag, pulling up*, and other epithets of the Tom and Jerry school [i.e., the boisterous urban world described in Pierce Egan's *Life in London* (1821)], are established—the dross passing here as genuine, even among all ranks, while the native word *jirrand* (afraid) has become in some measure an adopted child, and may probably puzzle our future Johnsons with its *unde derivatur* [<Dharuk *jiran* 'afraid']. In our police-offices, the slang words are taken regularly down in examinations, and I once saw a little urchin not exceeding ten years *patter* it in evidence to the bench with the most perfect fluency. Among the lower classes, these terms form a part of every common conversation; and the children consequently catch them. (Cunningham 1827, 2:59)

South Africa (1829). The tutor, who teaches the ingenuous youth of Southern Africa, is generally a discharged English soldier, and leads a kind of middle life, a connecting link between the family and the slaves: his salary is very small; but then he is fed, and found in brandy, and for this, instructs the younger branches in polite literature and performs various trifling acts of servitude for the elders. . . . He brought forward several of the boys to exhibit their proficiency in the English language: the sounds that came from the unwilling urchins might be any thing; but they drew forth a compliment on the skill and industry that had been so successful. (Rose 1829, 254–55)

Canada (1832). It is really melancholy to traverse the Province [viz., Ontario], and go into many of the common schools; you find a herd of children, instructed by some anti-British adventurer, instilling into the young and tender minds sentiments hostile to the parent state . . . and American spelling-books, dictionaries, and Grammar, teaching them an anti-British dialect, and idiom; although living in a Province, and being subjects, of the British Crown. (Rolph 1836, 262)

Britain (1833). We seldom meet with a Scot, an Irishman, or an English rustic, that does not boast of the superior orthoepy and dialect of his native soil; yet Boswell apologised for being a Scotchman and years after boasted of his improved pronunciation. Irishmen are almost impertinent in their appeal to you upon the subject, and there exists a joke that Curran once seeing a man with his mouth wide open, said he was catching the English accent. Entitled to the same privilege we claim regal dominion for the parlance of the metropolis, and totally denegate the capability of any man to decide upon the enunciation of the English language; unless he not only have been bred in London, but circulated also in good society. (Savage 1833, xxv)

New Zealand (1887). I think it may be admitted that the pronunciation of the colonies as a whole, is purer than can be found in any given district at Home. . . . For months after I had commenced my investigation on this subject, the unfailing answer to my enquiries in the different Australian colonies was, "We can hear no distinction between ourselves and visitors." It was only since coming to New Zealand that I have been able to definitely say "There is another type here." Even this is difficult to define, and, as young people grow up, may alter and perhaps assimilate to that prevailing in Australia, as I found it doing in Wellington more than any other place. (Samuel McBurney, Christchurch *Press*, October 5, [1887], quoted in Gordon and Deverson 1985,15; see also Gordon 1983; McGeorge 1984)

Australia (1911). But it is not so much the vagaries of pronunciation that hurt the ear of the visitor. It is the extraordinary intonation that the Australian imparts to his phrases. There is no such thing as cultured, reposeful conversation in this land; everybody sings his remarks as if he were reciting blank verse after the manner of an imperfect elocutionist. It would be quite possible to take an ordinary Australian conversation and immortalise its cadences and diapasons by means of musical notation. Herein the Australian differs from the American. The accent of the American, educated and uneducated alike, is abhorrent to the cultured Englishman or Englishwoman, but it is, at any rate, harmonious. That of the Australian is full of discords and surprises. His voice rises and falls with unexpected syncopations, and, even among the few cultured persons this country possesses, seems to bear in every syllable the sign of the parvenu. (Valerie Desmond, *The Awful Australian* [1911], quoted in Hornadge 1980, 20)

As these examples show, attitudes toward transplanted varieties of English have taken many forms, from categorical denunciation of an entire national variety to niggling criticism of minute details of local usage. Identification of a poor woman in North Carolina with an English socialite or of the speech of the Newfoundland outports with the fashionable slang of London society characterizes one side of the matter; denunciation of the "brokenness," discordance, and vulgarity of the transplanted variety presents the other, and more commonly expressed, idea.

Though widely diverse, these opinions reveal a social and political ideology that is as enduring and repetitious as the ideas described in the earlier chapters. Linguistic stereotypes eventually emerge with opprobrious social evaluations attached to them; once a given feature is associated with that stereotype, it joins the value system already established for it. Received wisdom declares that transplanted English must be somehow different, and probably worse; the image, in short, anticipates the evidence.

The transplanted English thus far discussed concerns English-speaking emigrants and their offspring. Though one justification for the monolingual grammars and dictionaries of the seventeenth century was to make it possible for foreigners to learn English, there was little organized attempt to proselytize on behalf of the language until the notion of empire emerged as a driving force for governmental policy, and English people discerned that they had a political as well as a cultural interest in fostering the use of their language. Efforts to induce others to learn English by fiat had not been notably successful in Wales and Ireland, but these failures did not strike anyone as germane to the situation at the beginning of the nineteenth century (since more subtle cultural influences were accomplishing the anglicization of those regions [see Agnew 1981]). Instead, the question turned on the issue of who should be obliged to learn an additional language, colonial administrators or subject peoples. The central arena for this struggle was India.

In the East India Act of 1813, the British government responded to those who valued Asian learning and provided that

> a sum of not less than one lac [= *lakh* '100,000'] of rupees in each year shall be set apart and applied to the revival and improvement of literature and the encouragement of the learned natives of India and for the introduction and promotion of a knowledge of the sciences among the inhabitants of the British territories in India. (Bhatt and Aggarwal 1977,1)

In the years that immediately followed its adoption, this policy led to the support of higher education. But the curriculum was the traditional one, and students were trained in the traditional texts written in Sanskrit and Arabic. The rationale for that instruction derived from the idea that the people of India should be governed under a legal system derived from their own ancient codes. At the end of the eighteenth century, European orientalists had made the literature of Persia and India well known in the West, and Sir William

Jones (1746–94), the principal English translator of these works and subsequently a judge of the Supreme Court in Calcutta, provided the foundation of a policy that fostered the use of the languages of India in the affairs of the East India Company. Other British officials (notably Henry Thoby Prinsep [1793–1878]) who followed Jones were also accomplished linguists and supported the policy that literature and learning should be "revived" on the subcontinent rather than imported from abroad. This policy was consonant with other practices of the East India Company, whose British "servants," military officers and civilian officials, were ostensibly only advisors to the Indian rulers of the districts under British control. But these limits had not restrained the extension of European wars to India or inhibited the British in expanding their sphere of influence against native opposition.

As British and U.S. missionaries began to arrive, sympathy and respect for the classical languages of India and for its vernaculars began to be challenged as the newcomers encountered obstacles to their purpose of eradicating the ancient religious and social practices of the subcontinent. When the agents of the London Missionary Society proposed to erect a college in Bangalore in 1826, they circulated a proposal stating their intention to offer instruction in English. Having dismissed Sanskrit literature as worthless, they stated their conclusion with a prefatory disclaimer.

> Without the charge of predilection for our own country, we think we are justified in asserting that Britain stands unrivalled by any ancient or modern nation in the study of universal knowledge, and that through the English language India will receive from her conquerors and legislators an intellectual treasure far more valuable than all she has in her power to give in exchange. (Quoted in Massie 1840, 2:422)

Making translations from English scientific works into Indian languages was inconvenient. But if practical difficulties did not seem persuasive, there were moral obstacles to consider. In an extreme of racist argument, these missionaries even suggested that Indian languages would poison the European mind.

> A knowledge of the English tongue and its authors, therefore, appears to hold a place of the first importance in a plan for the intellectual and moral elevation of the Hindoos. The English language will not only prove a more correct medium of giving public instruction to the students, but it will facilitate their progress in useful knowledge. All the Indian languages have been for so many ages the vehicle of every thing in their superstition which is morally debasing or corrupting to the mind, and so much is the grossly impure structure of

heathenism wrought into the native languages, that the bare study of them often proves injurious to the mind of a European. (425)

Should any rationale be required to avoid the "bare study" of Indian languages, this argument provided the ethical foundation for doing so.

In these arguments, the missionaries were abetted by an influential Bengali, Ram Mohan Roy (1774–1833), who had embraced European learning and argued that English provided Indians with "the key to all knowledge—all the really useful knowledge which the world contains." Roy urged that English be used as the language of education "until the spoken, living dialects of India become ripened by the copious infusion of expressive terms for the formation of a new and improved national literature" (quoted in Massie 1840, 2:439). In 1830, the Emperor at Delhi sent Roy on a diplomatic mission to England, where he presented evidence to the House of Commons, met British intellectual and political leaders, and, as he contemplated travel to the United States, succumbed to "brain fever." Regarded as an "enlightened" Indian, on the grounds of his support for British values, Roy's advocacy of English influenced public opinion against the orientalists who wished to continue the practice of education in the languages of the subcontinent.

Even though Roy and the missionaries were persuasive advocates, the evolution of English-medium education was stoutly resisted by some transplanted English people. Acting in what they believed was the Indian's best interests, they argued that English-medium schools would thwart, or at least divert, the continued development of indigenous literature. Most important, they asserted, was the argument that education in English would be inevitably elitist and probably not very successful. In a series of letters published in the *India Gazette* in 1833, an anonymous English writer articulated this view in opposition to that of the missionaries.

The case stands thus:—We come out to this country after enjoying the advantages of a liberal education; most of us have spent five or six years in studying the abstruse languages of antiquity, and very few are altogether unacquainted with those of the foreign nations of Europe; our minds must, therefore, be well imbued with the general principles of grammar; we find here a variety of books intended to facilitate the acquisition of one or two languages in addition to those we have already attained; we are surrounded by teachers ready enough to lend their assistance, and above all, we possess the incalculable advantage of being in the country where the languages are vernacular, and where consequently we learn a good deal insensibly. With all this we are perpetually complaining of the difficulty of mastering the native languages, and yet expect that the Natives without any of those means, with little or no knowledge of grammar, destitute of adequate books, and with few and limited opportunities of conversation shall very perfectly master ours, which is allowed to be one of the most difficult and idiomatic of the European tongues. (*The Letters of T on the Employment of the English Language as a Medium for Native Education* 1834, 6)

Whatever the cultural claims for English might be, this writer declared the proposed changes in education as unsound for the most practical of reasons—they would not create the effect their proposers desired.

The reforming Parliaments of the 1830s recognized a need for change in the relations among the government in London, the company, and the people of India. No individual was more influential in the evolution of British policy than historian and essayist Thomas Babington Macaulay (1800–59). Macaulay applied his famous eloquence to the debate on the government of India bill in 1833 and provided the broad historical context that justified the imposition of more direct control on the country.

But what constitution can we give to our Indian Empire which shall not be strange, which shall not be anomalous? That Empire is itself the strangest of all political anomalies. That a handful of adventurers from an island in the Atlantic should have subjugated a vast country divided from the place of their birth by half the globe; a country which at no very distant period was merely the subject of fable to the nations of Europe; a country never before violated by the most renowned of Western Conquerors; a country which Trajan never entered; a country lying beyond the point where the phalanx of Alexander refused to proceed; that we should govern a territory ten thousand miles from us, a territory larger and more populous than France, Spain, Italy, and Germany put together, a territory, the present clear revenue of which exceeds the present clear revenue of any state in the world, France excepted; a territory, inhabited by men differing from us in race, colour, language, manners, morals, religion; these are prodigies to which the world has seen nothing similar. Reason is confounded. We interrogate the past in vain. General rules are useless where the whole is one vast exception. The Company is an anomaly, but it is part of a system where everything is anomaly. It is the strangest of all governments; but it is designed for the strangest of all Empires. (Macaulay 1952, 699–700)

The notion of a heroic "handful of adventurers" pressing eastward beyond the farthest advance of the empires of Greece and Rome was a heady vision, and the government rewarded Macaulay's eloquence more than his expertise by naming him to a seat on the newly established Supreme Council of India. In February 1834, he set out for Calcutta to assume the duties of that office.

On his arrival, Macaulay was given added responsibilities as president of the Committee of Public Instruction, which he found evenly divided between supporters of the existing policy of devoting the lakh of rupees to oriental higher education and those who wished to introduce English-medium colleges in India. After listening to the arguments of the two sides of the controversy, Macaulay prepared a minute for the governor general, Lord William Bentinck (who had apparently decided to support education in English even before Macaulay appeared on the scene). Macaulay began by heaping scorn on the idea that the act of 1813 could possibly have been intended to support Arabic and Sanskrit learning, which he regarded with contempt. He then asserted that

> the dialects commonly spoken among the natives of this part of India, contain neither literary nor scientific information, and are, moreover, so poor and rude that, until they are enriched from some other quarter, it will not be easy to translate any valuable work into them. (Macaulay 1952, 721)

He further stated that he had never found an English orientalist "who could deny that a single shelf of a good European library was worth the whole native literature of India and Arabia" (722). Moreover, he alleged that the Indians educated at the Sanskrit and Arabic colleges did not find employment on completing their studies, that the books published in those languages with government subsidies were unread and were "of less value than the paper on which they are printed was while it was blank" (730), and that Indian students would pay for instruction in English, though they learned Sanskrit and Arabic only when offered government stipends to do so.

Macaulay concluded with a vision of the future for India that has often been quoted in subsequent discussions of his impact on the spread of English in India (e.g., Kachru 1986, 5).

> In one point I fully agree with the gentlemen to whose general views I am opposed. I feel with them, that it is impossible for us, with our limited means, to attempt to educate the body of the people. We must at present do our best to form a class who may be interpreters between us and the millions whom we govern; a class of persons, Indian in blood and colour, but English in taste, in opinions, in morals, and in intellect. To that class we may leave it to refine the vernacular dialects of the country, to enrich those dialects with terms of science borrowed from the Western nomenclature, and to render them by degrees fit vehicles for conveying knowledge to the great mass of the population. (Macaulay 1952, 729)

Residence in India afforded middle-class colonists a way of life attainable only by the upper classes at home. In the illustration above a *punkah* is shown overhead; framed of wood with a cloth suspended beneath it, the punkah was drawn back and forth by a cord connected to an adjoining room where it was operated by a *punkah-wallah*, a servant employed in this effort to provide a cooling breeze. Colonial officials appointed before 1856 disparaged their successors selected for service by an examination system as *competition wallahs*. Modern Indian English makes extensive use of *-wallah* in compounds: *box wallah* 'traveling salesman,' *police wallah* 'police officer,' and even *OUP wallah* 'employee of Oxford University Press branches in Bombay, Calcutta, New Delhi, and Madras' (Nihalani, Tongue, and Hosali 1979). Illustration from Atkinson 1860, pl. 35.

The conflict, as Macaulay presented it, was between funding for instruction in contemporary English and support for the ancient classical languages of India; beyond the disparaging characterization of the Indian vernaculars as "poor and rude . . . dialects," he had nothing to say about the languages in current use. In opposition to Macaulay, Brian Houghton Hodgson declared that English education would only produce a "host of grandiloquent grumblers." Pointing to the 100,000 village schools in Bengal, he challenged Macaulay's plan: "You have an indigenous system of vernacular education which has grown naturally out of the wants of the people. Build upon it" (quoted in Marriott 1932, 201). But Macaulay's views prevailed. The following year, Lord Bentinck gave his "entire concurrence to the sentiments expressed in this minute" and declared that the funds administered by the Committee on Public Instruction should be "henceforth employed in imparting to the native population a knowledge of English literature and science through the medium of the English language" (Bhatt and Aggarwal 1977, 4–5).

While Macaulay was a thoroughgoing imperialist, he was committed to freedom of the press and to equality of Europeans and Indians in the administration of justice. Before returning to England in 1838, he drafted a penal code embodying these principles and thereby earned the enmity of expatriate Britons who were not enamored of due process when summary justice had worked so much to their advantage. His views on the question of English were not merely those of a European who held Eastern cultures in contempt (as he certainly did), but those of an imperialist who anticipated the eventual "refinement" and "enrichment" of the languages of India through English influence, so that they might become the vehicles for "European" scientific, historical, and literary expression. Having persuaded himself of the intrinsic merits of English, he favored imparting those merits to other languages. Just as Roy had done before him, Macaulay articulated an ameliorist idea of the influence of English, one that still prevails in many places and fosters the importation of vocabulary that allegedly "enriches" the receptor languages.

What Macaulay did not notice was the flow of influence that led from the languages of India into English, "enriching" the jargon of colonial administration. As British authority expanded from its original, small centers of trade after Clive's conquests in the mid-eighteenth century, the administrative language used within the East India Company was crammed with loanwords for the various economic practices that were involved in the extraction of riches from the subcontinent. Without the aid of a glossary, the letters sent from one English officer to another from the beginning of the Raj until its end are now virtually unintelligible. Such official correspondence shows how rapidly loanwords from Asian languages became part of local administrative English (see, for instance, Islam 1978). Throughout the period of the Raj, loanwords became a constant and distinctive feature of Indian English as used by English bureaucrats, military personnel, and civilians. Others are now part of the international vocabulary of the language (e.g., *cheroot* [attested in 1669], *chit* [1785], *cowrie* [1662], *curry* [1598], *dinghy* [1794], *khaki* [1837], *loot* [1788], *nabob* [1612], *pajamas* [1800], *polo* [1842], *seersucker* [1722], *thug* [1810], *toddy* [1609], and *veranda* [1711]). Many others had a more restricted distribution but nonetheless widespread currency among English people both in India and when they returned home (in the specialized sense that became current in many colonies, where *home* meant 'England' even for people who had never been there; see Nihalani, Tongue, and Hosal 1979; Yule and Burnell [1903] 1968).

Though Macaulay's aim was to educate "a class who may be interpreters between us and the millions whom we govern," the consequence of his educational reform was not quite as he had anticipated. In 1854, in a dispassionate and insightful review of "The State and Prospects of the English Language in India," David O. Allen (1799–1863) resisted the then flourishing notion that English was destined to be the "future universal language." (As a U.S. missionary in Bombay from 1827 to 1853, Allen had overseen the completion of the translation of the Bible into Marathi, a language in which he had become fluent.) He regarded the literature of southern Asia with respect, but, more importantly, he recognized that the people's opinion of their own language was consequential for their interest in English.

> They have some science, and the Sanskrit and Tamil people especially have much literature, ancient and modern, sacred and profane, which they hold in great veneration, and to which they are strongly attached. (Allen 1853–54, 266)

English speakers, he thought, were unlikely to form self-perpetuating, permanent communities; Eurasians (though regarded as "English") would not form a large group; colonial officers were required to acquire proficiency in Indian languages before being appointed and, hence, did not often use spoken English in their duties; and English was not much spoken (nor did he expect it to be) outside the port cities. In these circumstances, Allen could not believe that English would become a language of a large community in southern Asia.

Macaulay had seen Indians as different from Europeans; Allen saw them as very much the same in their attitudes toward their languages.

> To the educated natives of India the idea or plan of making any one language supersede those now in use, and so become the common language of the whole country, would appear as unreasonable, as it would appear to the educated people of Europe, were it proposed to select some language, as the English, or the French, or the German, and endeavor to make it supersede all the others, and so become the general and common language of all the people of Europe. (Allen 1853–54, 270)

As English sovereignty spread across the region, more and more places became available for Indians to act as interpreters and subordinates to British administrators. Yet Allen recognized that these opportunities were not limitless, and he discerned that "all the more honorable and highly remunerating places have been filled by Europeans, and only those of the second or third rate are given to the natives" (272). By the 1850s, those who learned English were in no better position than the earlier generation educated in Arabic and Sanskrit.

> This desire to learn English has been increasing for some years past, and probably the number now engaged in acquiring it, is three times as large as it was fifteen or twenty years ago. But, even at the present time, many who become thus educated, find it very difficult, and some find it impossible, to obtain such employment as they expected. The supply of such educated talent is increasing faster than the demand, and it will not be many years before the principal motives in which this strong desire for English education had its origin, will cease, or at least will exert less influence than they have had for some years past. (274)

Allen was certainly wrong in expecting the "strong desire for English education" to "cease," but he was right in foreseeing that colonial administrators would not offer positions beyond "the second or third rate" to Indians who had taken the trouble to learn English.

English in India has always been restrained in comparison to American English. In the United States, there has been no numerous cadre of teachers and officials from Britain to censure the natives for departures from the latest in London linguistic taste and fashion. In India, of course, exactly those conditions prevailed. Alleged "imperfections" in Indian English were held up to scorn, a tendency perhaps nowhere better illustrated than in the book by Arnold Wright, *Baboo English as 'tis Writ, Being Curiosities of Indian Journalism* (1891). Though commending the Anglo-Indian newspapers "printed in the most irreproachable English" (8), Wright examined the English papers written and published by Indians. These he regarded as "badly printed, badly written," and full of "ridiculous blunders" (17) typical of the *babus*, a scornful term defined (s. v. *"baboo"*) in Yule and Burnell's Anglo-Indian glossary.

> In Bengal and elsewhere, among Anglo-Indians, [baboo] is often used with a slight savour of disparagement, as characterizing a superficially cultivated, but too often effeminate, Bengali. And from the extensive employment of the class to which the term was applied as a title, in the capacity of clerks in English offices, the word has come often to signify 'a native clerk who writes English.'

What Wright found offensive in the *baboo* press was not only linguistic innovation or infelicity but also a tendency toward grandiloquence. Indian delight in the learned and arcane portion of the English vocabulary had become a stock source of humor among those who ridiculed Indians attempting to become "English in taste, in opinions, in morals, and in intellect" (see Aberigh-Mackay 1881, 40–55; Parry 1946). Though some of the newspapers Wright described were "capable of taking quite an Imperial view of public questions" (1891, 21), many joined the vernacular press in espousing the cause of Indian independence. It was the use of English in opposition to the economic and political influence of Britain that provoked his criticisms of Indian English.

Like other translators on the margin of two cultures, Babus were scorned by both sides; their reputation suggests the difficulties of remaining Indian in national feeling while English in taste. When Arnold Wright criticized Bengali anglophones from the imperial perspective, Bankin Chandra Chatterjee in 1874 had already written of the Babu from the Indian viewpoint. His scathing portrait was styled after one of the epics of the subcontinent.

> *Vaisampayana* said, O best of men, I will speak of those Babus variously-talented, skilled in eating and sleeping, attend and listen. I extol the character of the Babu, spectacle-adorned, belly-minded, many-tongued and news-loving, attend and listen. O king, those who have patterned clothes, cane in hand, dyed hair and large boots, they are Babus. Those who are invincible in speech, adept in a foreign language and hostile to their mother-tongue, they are Babus. Great

King! in this way many Babus, endowed with great intellect, will be born who will be incompetent at conversing in their own language. Those whose ten sense-organs are in a natural state, and hence impure, whose sense of taste alone is purified by the spittle of foreigners, they are Babus. . . . He whose deity is the Englishman, preceptor the Brāhmo Samājist *Vedas* the Bengali newspapers and place of pilgrimage the National Theatre, he is a Babu. He who is a Christian with the missionaries, a Brahmo with Keshabchandra [= Kesava Chandra Sen (1838–91)], a Hindu with his father and an atheist with begging priests, he is a Babu. He who takes water in his own house, wine in his friend's house, insults at the prostitute's house and beatings at his English master's house, he is a Babu. He who despises oil when bathing, his own fingers when eating and his mother-tongue when conversing, he is a Babu. He whose only enthusiasm is for clothes, whose only zeal is for soliciting a job, whose only devotion is for his wife or mistress, and whose only contempt is for good books, undoubtedly he is a Babu. (1986, 27–29)

Chatterjee's diatribe was, naturally enough, written in Bengali. It reflected the view, found in many cultures invaded by foreign rulers, that those who mimic foreign ways are marginal people, unworthy of regard. In it he expressed an image of English that is by no means unknown today.

The national language for multilingual India was (and is) complex, and the role of English under the Raj and afterward has been a subject of constant debate. In 1908, Mohandas K. Gandhi (1869–1948) stated a view that he frequently rearticulated for the rest of his long and influential life.

To give millions a knowledge of English is to enslave them. The foundation that Macaulay laid of education has enslaved us. I do not suggest that he had any such intention, but that has been the result. . . . Is it not a painful thing that, if I want to go to a court of justice, I must employ the English language as a medium; that, when I became a Barrister, I may not speak my mother-tongue, and that someone else should have to translate to me from my own language? Is not this absolutely absurd? Is it not a sign of slavery? Am I to blame the English for it or myself? It is we, the English-knowing men, that have enslaved India. The curse of the nation will rest not upon the nation but upon us. (Gandhi 1958, 5)

Gandhi's objections were founded on his vision of an embracing unity for all of India's diversity. English, he believed, "has caused a deep chasm between the educated and politically-minded classes and the masses" (41); the use of English is responsible for the "impoverishment" of the vernaculars in the development of science (41); the English language in India is a "cultural usurper" (43). Though he foresaw its use in international diplomacy, Gandhi declared that "English cannot become the national language of India" (38).

Gandhi's allegation that English-knowing Indians were responsible for the political oppression of the country was not a new idea when he wrote, nor is it now obsolete in arguments about language policy in India. Two viceroys had expressed opposition to the educational system based on English that was Macaulay's legacy; their arguments anticipated Gandhi's.

> *Richard Southwell Bourke, Sixth Earl of Mayo, viceroy from 1869 to 1872.* I dislike this filtration theory. In Bengal we are educating in English a few hundred Babus at great expense to the State. Many of them are well able to pay for themselves, and have no other object in learning than to qualify for Government employ. In the meanwhile we have done nothing towards extending knowledge to the million. The Babus will never do it. The more education you give them, the more they will keep to themselves, and make their increased knowledge a means of tyranny. If you wait till the bad English, which the 400 Babus learn in Calcutta, filters down into the 40,000,000 of Bengal, you will be ultimately a Silurian rock instead of a retired judge. Let the Babus learn English by all means. But let us also try to do something towards teaching the three R's to "Rural Bengal." (Quoted from a letter to a friend in Marriott 1932, 203)
>
> *George Curzon, Lord Curzon, viceroy from 1899 to 1905.* The vernaculars are the living languages of this great continent. English is the vehicle of learning and advancement to the small minority; *but* for the vast bulk it is a foreign tongue which they do not speak and rarely hear. If the vernaculars contained no literary models, no classics, I might not be so willing to recommend them. But we all know that in them are enshrined famous treasures of literature and art; while even the secrets of modern knowledge are capable of being communicated thereby in an idiom and in phrases which will be understood by millions of people to whom our English terms and ideas will never be anything but an unintelligible jargon. (Quoted in Marriott 1932, 207–8)

The issues at dispute in this argument remain unresolved.

Meanwhile, Indian English has emerged as a self-perpetuating national variety, though one used mainly by Indians whose native language is not English. A minority tongue and yet the language of national affairs, its status as a transplanted English continues to be called into question, not only by foreign visitors who bring outside ideas of proper English to bear in criticizing it, but also by Indians who remain ambivalent about its distinctive features and uncertain about its future.

Postindependence views of Indian English properly belong to the next

The question whether English has been (or ought to be) "nativized" remains a matter of dispute. International intelligibility competes as a measure of excellence with national or local values expressed through the language. Illustration from the *Illustrated Weekly of India* 101 (November 9, 1980): 63. Reprinted by permission.

chapter, but this brief history of a transplanted English can best be concluded by illustrating recent opinions of Indian poets writing in English. Those associated with the Writers Workshop in Calcutta were asked by the organizer of that institution, P. Lal, to respond to a series of questions for an anthology of *Modern Indian Poetry in English* (1969); among them was "Why write in English?" These are some of their answers.

> *M. P. Bhaskaran.* Obviously, people [who do not write in it] are afraid of English. Or they are jealous. Perhaps both. The Hindi imperialists fear that English, unless it is rooted out, may not allow Hindi to dominate India. They are jealous of the world-wide audience that those who write in English have, actually or potentially. They are scared of the poverty of Hindi in contrast with the richness of English, and the inadequacy of Hindi to deal with the world of today and tomorrow in contrast with the ability of English. (Lal 1969, 45)

Deb Kumar Das. The England which gave the world the language which is at issue has lost its claim to imperial status; "English" is now a world language, its spread across other countries and cultures is now a historical event. (86)

R. de L. Furtado. The English language has been with us for a good number of years; it has cemented the bonds of thought between the north and south of the country; it has kept going a continuous dialogue between India and the rest of the world. (185–86)

Paul Jacob. . . . anglo*phobia* is a lower-class attitude. (Attitude is the key-word). In Kerala, where I come from, there is still much misdirected ill-feeling about speaking in English. Indeed, a euphemism for that particular activity there, is "shitting in English." (216)

Adil Jussawalla. No. English is not an Indian language and never will be. Unlike West Indian English, ours is not used at all levels of society, nor are the idiosyncracies consistent enough to amount to a language. (230)

Meera Pillai. The only reason I write in English in preference to any other language is that it is the tongue I am best acquainted with. I was born and brought up in the north and have only a superficial speaking knowledge of my mother-tongue Malayalam. I had my entire school and college education in English-medium institutions run by nuns. (402)

Rakshat Puri. . . . I believe English is now an Indian language—in the way that English is an American language in the USA, an Australian language in Australia, West Indian in the West Indies, Ghanaian in Ghana . . . and will become more Indian as time passes. (411)

C. Raju. English is certainly not one of the Indian languages unless we try to give a special designation to "Babu English." (437)

Such opinions are a sign of the health of English in India, but these creative writers have very different views of its status and role. These many reasons for using it provide a continuing justification, and as one argument loses force, another grows in importance to take its place.

Yet one more of these transplanted varieties deserves mention here, though it no longer survives: the Pidgin English associated with China and the maritime trade of the western Pacific. Like other makeshift derivatives of English, Chinese Pidgin English drew the scorn of mother-tongue observers. In the mid-nineteenth century, this variety seemed to some to be evolving from a limited contact language to a full-scale derivative of English.

It is not very satisfactory to look forward even to the bare possibility of such a caricature of our tongue becoming an established language. Should this ever be the result, translations into it of our classic authors will become a necessity. Shakespeare and Milton turned into Pigeon English are fearful even to think of. . . . The Missionary "pigeon" will also in due time demand a translation of the Bible into this very vulgar tongue. Death has many consolations, and to the number may be added this new one, that before the consummation foretold above can be realized, we will have passed away, and our ears will be deaf to the hideous result. (Simpson 1873, 47)

A similar, though less censorious, view was expressed by the adventurous nineteenth-century English explorer, Richard Burton.

If English, as appears likely, is to become the cosmopolitan language of commerce, it will have to borrow from Chinese as much monosyllable and as little inflection as possible. The Japanese have already commenced this systematic process of "pidgeoning," which for centuries has been used on the West African Coast, in Jamaica, and, in fact, throughout tropical England, Hindostan alone excepted. (Burton 1875, 1:159, n. 2)

By the end of the century, another observer who examined Pidgin in detail saw that its use "has spread to . . . an incredible extent, thereby leading the way towards making English the language of the Pacific" (Leland 1892, 2). But it was rare indeed for English speakers to regard Pidgin as a "valuable medium of communication" (Mahaffy 1893, 789).

Pidgin English did not develop along the lines of the other varieties of transplanted English and evolve into a distinctive and institutionalized language in the nations in which it had been used. (The exception to this generalization is present-day Papua New Guinea, where Tok Pisin, a collateral descendant of Chinese Pidgin English, has a tenuous hold as the national language of that recently independent nation [see Mühlhäusler 1982; Wurm 1984].) The reasons for this outcome are clear: this variety never became the language of preference of an economically and politically influential people; it existed in a culture where most speakers were fluent in other languages that they regarded as "proper" and nearly all who used it acknowledged that Pidgin was "flawed" (e.g., "piebald English," "horrid trash," "gibberish" ["Canton-English" 1857, 451–52]; "a grotesque or absurd jargon" [March 1888, 449]; "a sort of jabbering" [Follick 1934, 89]). Spoken in widely separated places, it never had a cultural center and such trappings of modernity as a stable spelling, an educational system in which it was used, and publications that would make literacy in it worthwhile. In short, there was nothing in the emerging variety of English that empowered its speakers and enabled them to fulfill their aspirations.

Transplanted English of the kinds so far discussed became, for the most part, institutionalized abroad as the language of national affairs with a full range of styles, including modes of literary expression. Nearly all of these varieties have been scorned in Britain: "boisterous" and "vivid" American English corrupting the homeland of the language; "ten-thousand horse-power English words and phrases" from Indians and Africans taught from the Bible and from the classical literature of England challenging the "simple" elegance of mother-tongue nations (Aberigh-Mackay 1881, 53); "a peculiar dialect of English, corrupted with African words" from the Caribbean and from West Africa threatening to displace the "decent" English of Europeans and their descendants (Dallas 1968, 1:92). By the end of the twentieth century, most of them have achieved linguistic independence, though not necessarily freedom from censure. Even today, many of these kinds of English are still so attuned to the *idea* of a foreign standard of propriety (if not the actual linguistic norms proclaimed from abroad) that their independence remains partial. This vulnerable condition is well described by one observer of the situation in Ghana: "The surest way to kill Ghanaian English, if it really exists, is to discover it and make it known" (Sey 1973, 10).

Chapter 6

Postcolonial English

As the American colonies were the first to wrest political freedom from Britain, so the United States was the first to declare linguistic independence. John Adams and Noah Webster hoped that new conditions of social life in the United States would change English for the better, but their idea did not win approval from all Americans, especially those who treasured a cultural attachment to Britain or feared a linguistic schism across the Atlantic. It alarmed such critics when Webster's used *American* in *An American Dictionary of the English Language* (1828) and exemplified usage in American writings—for instance, those of Franklin, Washington, Adams, Jay, Marshall, and Irving. Such a step, they thought, might even presage the evolution of separate languages (see Read 1935).

An anonymous writer in the *Southern Literary Messenger*, then edited by Edgar Allan Poe, presented a view typical of the early years of U.S. independence.

> The preservation of a pure English diction is not sufficiently aimed at in America. Some are so entirely Britannic, as to receive every thing for legal tender in letters, which comes across the water. This is thenceforward duly '*marqué au coin.*' Others are so patriotically republican, as to set about the task of nursing the countless brood of cis-Atlantic words, into literary respectability. Both are in error. It is not enough to avoid Americanisms; nor is it expedient to manufacture a pye-bald dialect, of vulgarisms and provincialisms, for the mere satisfaction of calling it our own. In England, no less than here, the language is growing to an unhealthy exuberance, and many of the words which are fathered on the poor Americans, are distempered excrescences of the over-grown British trunk. Nothing but the appeal to a standard of former golden days of literature and classic taste, can save the noble tongue of freemen from becoming an unwieldy, cacophonious, inconsistent mass of crudities. How

> much more is there danger, lest the other party, by encouraging unauthorized and American inventions in language, lay the foundation for provincial dialects, which shall hopelessly diverge from one another, until the Mississippian and the Virginian shall be as diverse as were the Athenian and the Macedonian. ("Borealis" 1836,110–11)

This writer draws upon the metaphors by then conventional for discussing English—lamented "former golden days of literature and classic taste"; a contrast between "pure English diction" and crudity, cacophony, and vulgarity. What was distinctly American at that time, however, was the hope that "the noble tongue of freemen" might develop in the United States. Even though the writer claimed that "it is an *English*, not an *American* language which we are called upon to nurture and perfect" (111), he asserted that even Americans have a role to play in the development of the language.

As Americans began to articulate their own ideas about their language in the nineteenth century, they were inclined to self-congratulation on the grounds that American English had no regional dialects. In this respect they were affirmed by the many censorious English travelers who otherwise abused their institutions and their English. Thus, Frederick Marryat, typical of many visiting Britons, wrote in 1839:

> The Americans boldly assert that they speak better English than we do. . . . What I believe the Americans would imply by the above assertion is, that you may travel through all the United States and find less difficulty in understanding, or in being understood, than in some of the counties of England, such as Cornwall, Devonshire, Lancashire, and Suffolk. So far they are correct; but it is remarkable how very debased the language has become in a short period in America. (Quoted in Mathews 1931, 131)

Marryat believed that English in the new nation was uniform but poor. James Fenimore Cooper expressed the same opinion in 1838.

> While it is true that the great body of the American people use their language more correctly than the mass of any other considerable nation, it is equally true that a smaller proportion than common attain to elegance in this accomplishment, especially in speech. Contrary to the general law in such matters, the women of the country have a less agreeable utterance than the men, a defect that great care should be taken to remedy, as the nursery is the birth-place of so many of our habits. (Quoted in Mathews 1931, 123)

So frequent were the observations that the United States had no regional dialects that historians have wondered how British regionalisms could have survived without being noticed.

Statistics of emigration from Britain at the end of the eighteenth century help to clarify the linguistic situation that emerged in the newly independent United States. The great majority of migrants from the urban centers of southern England were young men who had completed an apprenticeship and who indentured themselves for a term of years in order to pay the passage across the Atlantic. Few women and children joined these young men; most of them traveled alone and were settled in the established towns and villages offering the highest prices for their work contracts. Migrants from northern England and Scotland, on the other hand, were likely to travel in large family groups. Women and small children were well represented, and the basic economic unit was usually a family prepared for immediate independence through agriculture on the fringes of settled areas (Bailyn 1986b, 202–3).

On arrival, the two groups selected different places to settle. The migrants from the south of England began their New World lives in Pennsylvania, Maryland, and Virginia; the northerners overwhelmingly chose New York and North Carolina (Bailyn 1986b, 205). The consequences of these demographic differences for language are obvious. Once freed from indentured servitude, single men could settle anywhere in the country, but most remained in the communities that first offered them work. They were also obliged to seek wives from the resident population and from immigrant groups with no connection to their places of origin in England. Whatever linguistic idiosyncrasies they brought with them were not likely to be perpetuated, and from initial diversity emerged eventual uniformity. For the northerners, although the New World offered immediate opportunities for settlement, the seaboard was already occupied. Hence, these families settled the interior regions, particularly in New York, western Pennsylvania, and North Carolina. Finding themselves near others from home, they created communities that preserved linguistic and other cultural distinctiveness. (The present-day boundaries between American varieties that delete *r* after vowels and those that retain it show one vestige of this pattern; various lexical survivals from Scots and northern English still identify areas of eighteenth-century settlement [see Carver 1987].) While these interior communities were forming, cities on the Atlantic were most likely to be visited by foreign travelers, and it is from their observations that the idea arises in the early nineteenth century that there were no regional differences. Of course, localized speech patterns akin to those of tiny England did not emerge in the

United States, but new regionalisms created boundaries on a larger scale. The idea of a uniform language, however, appealed to Americans (and visitors) looking for uniformity and a national "character" in a culturally diverse nation.

Having struggled to persuade themselves that American English was equal to that of southern England, U.S. writers in the early nineteenth century began to test the argument that it was better. This trend produced extravagant claims, and the most extreme views reveal enthusiasm for the separation of the two traditions. One U.S. observer, writing in 1860, found a useful comparison in the physical basis of speech.

> As regards articulation, the Americans, we think, have a natural advantage over the English in a superior delicacy of structure of the vocal organs. Very many Englishmen apparently have to contend with a thick and unmanageable conformation of the organs of speech, which occasions the spluttering and mouthing so common in their public speaking. That the Americans have great natural facility for clear and fine articulation, is shown by the readiness with which they acquire the pronunciation of foreign tongues, and by the fact that, with proper early training and care, they do attain to remarkable grace of utterance. ("The English Language in America" 1860, 525)

Such a claim was far removed from the defensive and self-critical views expressed by Cooper and others a generation earlier.

Another attempt to vindicate American English appeared in a story that began with the visit of an "American scholar" to Britain in 1880. It was his aim to puncture English smugness about the perfection of their language, and his effort was a success. This episode must be seen at twice remove: first, in a report of the "scholar's" audacity in a U.S. newspaper; second, in the expression of wounded pride by a British journalist who knew the "scholar" only from the U.S. paper.

> Printed as an "editorial" in a New Orleans newspaper, I have lately seen the following, which may even now be going "rounds of the press":
> "The other day an American scholar stood before an English audience in Bedford, England, and declared that he was astonished to find the American language so well understood in that country. His announcement was received with roars of laughter; but he contended that he spoke the tongue of Chaucer and of Shakespeare, and that the innovations and the greater part of everything which tended to corrupt 'the well of English undefiled' originated on that side of the Atlantic. He defended his position by instancing no less a body than the

House of Lords, and he went so far as to say that their excellencies, eminences, serenities, or whatever they may be pleased to be called, even misplace their '*h*'s.' It was impossible, he said, sometimes to determine whether they said ''igh' or 'high.' People of the greatest pretensions to literary culture said '*ivery*' or '*hivery*' for '*every*,' although some of them had diplomas from Oxford or Cambridge. All that was very unaccountable to him; but he had been converted to the theory of a high patriotic tariff in the interests of the purity of American speech, and in order to prevent the introduction of certain crudities and absurdities in English idioms—such, for instance, as 'very pleased.'"

. . . Our American cousin prides himself upon his contempt of forms, his fertility of invention, and claims entire freedom from "old world" ways, customs, and methods of thought. If he discover anything new, from a fixed star to an egg-whip, he is delighted, and takes care that all the world shall know it. (Fonblanque 1881, 330–31)

The "scholar's" satire in his address at Bedford was compounded by the editorial writer for the New Orleans newspaper (who tweaked British sensibility by deliberately obfuscating the etiquette of titles in the House of Lords). The English essayist who brought this editorial to the British public responded just as Americans had when charged that their language was defective. The examples alleged were, he wrote, not accurately characterized, or, where they were indeed cisatlantic errors, they were equaled by transatlantic mistakes. Defensiveness about difference and anguish over linguistic details, hitherto typical of American victims of British scorn, thus came home to England.

The "scholar" whose views the editorial reported was very likely Franc B. Wilkie (1832–92), a journalist who left home at age twelve to become a boatman on the Erie Canal and, after two years of college and a stint as proprietor of a newspaper on the western frontier, the chief war correspondent for the *New York Times*, covering "every important battle of the West and Southwest." From 1863 until his retirement in 1890, he was an editorial writer for the *Chicago Times*; in 1877–78 and 1880–81, he served as European correspondent for that paper. According to the *Dictionary of American Biography*, "he had a fertile imagination and a fund of sarcasm, which he employed effectively in his editorials." These habits were fully at play in his discourse on English, first published in the *Chicago Times* in 1877 and reprinted in his book *Sketches beyond the Sea*.

Declaring himself an impartial observer, Wilkie regretted that "the English are losing the English language, and substituting a jargon that is totally unlike that speech bequeathed to us by our Saxon and Norman ancestors" (1880, 140). He exemplified this claim with an extensive list of innovations and linguistic differences that have their origin in the idea that "the original and pure English of America" (142) is the fixed reference point from which to judge the vagaries and innovations of "English English." His comparison stretched beyond the usual view that American English was essentially an archaic dialect sprung wholly from British stock, and he argued that things unknown to the Saxons and Normans were named in the United States in ways these "founders" would have recognized. On those grounds, the U.S. *freight-car* was superior to the British *goods-van* and the U.S. *street-sprinkler* better than the British *hydrostatic van*. Wilkie simply turned the usual British argument on its head; British, not American English, was the source of unwanted innovation and debasement of the common language. If, as he predicted, the two nations would become linguistically separate "in a century," that outcome would be the fault of British "philological eccentricities" (136).

This lively address attracted public attention on both sides of the Atlantic. The conclusion of one commentator must have pleased the satirical Wilkie: "Now, all this, unless it is intended for an elaborate (and exceedingly feeble) joke, is absurd on the face of it" (Proctor 1881, 170). Like all good satirists, Wilkie was unwilling to explain himself further; if his readers took him at his word, they were obliged to accept the consequences. The wounded pride of the British writers who thought Wilkie's claims worthy of rebuttal is evidence of a more important development—the grudging recognition of American English as an independent, postcolonial variety.

By the end of the century, Americans had become sufficiently confident of their linguistic autonomy that they could look to themselves for the future lines of development of the language. Writing for an English audience in 1900, Brander Matthews of Columbia University described the drift of "the literary centre of the English language" and speculated that, by the middle of the twentieth century, "the largest portion of the brain, as well as the largest body of the English-speaking race, will have its residence on the western shore of the Western Ocean" (Matthews 1900, 239).

> What then will happen to the English language in England when England awakens to the fact that the centre of the English-speaking race is no longer within the borders of that little island? Will the speech of the British sink into dialectic corruption, or will the British resolutely stamp out their undue local divergences from the normal English of the main body of the users of the language in the United States? Even now, at the end of the nineteenth century,

more than half of those who have English as their mother-tongue are Americans; and at the end of the twentieth century the numerical superiority of the Americans will be as overwhelming as was the numerical superiority of the British at the beginning of the nineteenth. Will the British frankly accept the inevitable? Will they face the facts as they are? Will they follow the lead of the Americans when we shall have the leadership of the language, as the Americans followed their lead when they had it? Or will they insist on an arbitrary independence, which can have only one result—the splitting off of the British branch of our speech from the main stem of the language? (Matthews 1900, 239–40)

Matthews's answers to these many questions rested on some assumptions that the twentieth century has proved distinctly wrong—for instance, his estimate that "all signs" indicate "not only to a continuance of the British Empire, but also to its steady expansion" (240). Nonetheless, he articulated a view that would have seemed irresponsibly speculative a century earlier but in this century has become a commonplace: American English has become independent of its British parent.

Confirmation that even British linguistic xenophobes were obliged to recognize the shift of the linguistic "centre" of the language to North America appeared early in the twentieth century when British scoffing at American English was replaced by anxiety. Writing in the *New Statesman* for June 25, 1927, an anonymous author declared:

The English language proper belongs to the people who dwell south of Hadrian's Wall, east of the Welsh hills and north of the English Channel. . . . We obviously cannot admit that the English language contains "Anglicisms"—because that admission would imply that our language belongs to everybody who uses it—including negroes and Middle-Westerners and Americanised Poles and Italians. That is the fundamental point. "Anglicisms" are English *tout court*. And on the question of what words and idioms are to be used or to be forbidden we cannot afford any kind of compromise or even discussion with the semi-demi-English-speaking-populations of overseas. Their choice is to accept our authority or else make their own language. (Quoted in Malone 1928, 271–72)

By the end of the Second World War, such linguistic jingoism had become a minority view. Nevertheless, anti-American sentiment expressed in judgments about language is by no means extinct in Britain. Thus, in 1979 an English peer declared in the House of Lords: "if there is a more hideous language on the face of the earth than the American form of English, I should like to know what it is!" (Hansard 1979, 164)

Despite attacks on their language, Americans in the generation after independence began to take pride in the authenticity of their English. For other countries less removed from British political influence, progress toward that state of mind was considerably slower. Indifference to swings of linguistic fashion in the south of England was more difficult to achieve in places where colonial officials and expatriate teachers continally imposed British norms.

Early in the nineteenth century, political independence movements often took language as an arena for rebellion against imperial domination. To achieve freedom was to choose an alternative to the administrative language of the Empire. This development took place throughout Europe, among Greeks and Palestinian Jews restive under Turkish rule, Norwegians attempting to put themselves at a distance from Danes and Swedes, Czechs wishing independence within the Austrian empire. In all of these cases, the languages of the subject peoples became a focus for larger nationalistic aspirations. Some colonies in the British Empire showed signs of following the same path. For instance, the Boers in South Africa rejected English as part of their attempt to displace the British both before and after the Anglo-Boer War (1899–1902). The most accessible case to represent linguistic nationalism in areas under British control, however, is provided by Ireland; its accessibility arises from the fact that the debate over Irish and English was conducted almost wholly in English.

The number of monolingual speakers of the Irish language had begun to decline at the beginning of the seventeenth century. Though the geographical territory dominated by Irish speakers did not much change from 1700 to 1800, their social-class distribution did. English became associated with the cities and the professions that were open to Catholics (particularly the law and commercial enterprises). Irish was the language of rural and peasant life; in the cities, Irish speakers were the uneducated poor. Although Daniel O'Connell (1755–1847), Ireland's great advocate, led the movement to provide Irish Catholics with civil rights, he did not view the Irish language as a significant symbol in the struggle for home rule. Instead, he viewed it as an obstacle to a unified Ireland powerful enough to free itself from British political domination.

The great famine of 1846–48 reduced the population of Ireland by 20 percent; a million people starved and another million emigrated. The effects of this catastrophe fell with disproportionate harshness on speakers of Irish, and the survivors saw a knowledge of English as an essential skill if they wished to flee the countryside for the cities or to emigrate to North America or Australia. By midcentury, the linguistic situation had shifted entirely in favor of English.

> Contrary to popular persuasion, the schools did not kill the Irish language. Even before the famine the country was predominantly English-speaking. O'Connell spoke in English because most of his east-of-Ireland audiences understood it better than Irish. By 1851 less than ten per cent of the population were unable to speak English, while only thirty per cent were able to speak Irish. The language committed suicide before 1845, aided and abetted less by the national schools than by the hedge schools cherished in nationalist mythology. (Lee 1973, 28)

The abruptness of the language shift occurred as part of a people's desperate struggle to escape from the intolerable reality of oppression and famine. While the national schools offered instruction only in English, the attitudes that led to the suppression of Irish were more important than the official policy.

> The whole paraphernalia of tally sticks, wooden gags, humiliation and mockery—often enforced by encouraging children to spy on their brothers and sisters, or on the children of neighbouring townlands—were not the product of any law or official regulation, but of a social self-generated movement of collective behaviour among the people themselves. Most of the reasons adduced for the suppression of the Irish language are not so much reasons as consequences of the decision to give up the language. (Fréine 1977, 84)

The result of this turmoil was the drastic reduction in the use of Irish throughout the country.

Just as this linguistic revolution was taking place, Irish found a hero in Thomas Davis (1814–45), who argued in favor of a "traditional" Ireland. In 1843, he published "Our National Language," an essay that asserted the link between linguistic community and nationhood.

> The language, which grows up with a people, is conformed to their organs, descriptive of their climate, constitution, and manners, mingled inseparably with their history and their soil, fitted beyond any other language to express their prevalent thoughts in the most natural and efficient way.
> To impose another language on such a people is to send their history adrift among the accidents of translation—'tis to tear their identity from all places— 'tis to substitute arbitrary signs for picturesque and suggestive names—'tis to

cut off the entail of feeling, and separate the people from their forefathers by a deep gulf—'tis to corrupt their very organs, and abridge their power of expression. . . .

A people without a language of its own is only half a nation. A nation should guard its language more than its territories—'tis a surer barrier, and more important frontier, than fortress or river. (Davis [1914]1982, 172–73)

Davis's equation of an "authentic" language with political liberation became, later in the century, a source of the agenda for Irish nationalism. His words had an almost proverbial ring: "To lose your native tongue, and learn that of an alien, is the worst badge of conquest—it is the chain on the soul" (174). The loss of Irish names for persons and places, the disappearance of songs and poetry, the lack of a scientific vocabulary because Irish had been neglected—all of these were subjects for regret and humiliation (see Friel 1981). Davis's metaphors suggest the maiming of the body politic by means of "cutting off" Ireland's heritage and "corrupting the very organs" of its people. For these misfortunes, Ireland had the English to blame; to put things to right, the Irish people needed to revive their language and to cast off "the speech of the alien, the invader, the Sassenagh tyrant" (175). Yet Davis, son of an English military surgeon and a Protestant, was later celebrated for his own English poetry and for contributing to the development of Irish literature in English. And Davis probably had only a rudimentary knowledge of the Irish he so fervently celebrated.

Davis's argument well represents the views articulated by later linguistic patriots who have discerned creative salvation in casting off the "chain on the soul" represented by English. Douglas Hyde (1860–1949) echoed Davis's sentiments but from the firmer foundation of a deep knowledge of Irish. (A founder of the Gaelic League, Hyde translated Irish literature into English and consequently influenced such authors as Yeats, Synge, and Gregory.) In 1892, he reiterated Davis's arguments.

The losing of [our once great national tongue] is our greatest blow, and the sorest stroke that the rapid Anglicisation of Ireland has inflicted upon us. In order to de-Anglicise ourselves, we must at once arrest the decay of the language. We must bring pressure upon our politicians not to snuff it out by their tacit discouragement merely because they do not happen themselves to understand it. We must arouse some spark of patriotic inspiration among the peasantry who still use the language, and put an end to the shameful state of feeling—a thousand-tongued reproach to our leaders and statesmen—which makes young men and women blush and hang their heads when overheard speaking their own language. (Hyde 1973, 236–37)

When Hyde became president of Ireland in 1938 under the newly adopted constitution of the Republic, he had the pleasure of being welcomed to office in a congratulatory address spoken first in Irish and then in English (Moynihan 1980, 354). That constitution declared Irish as the "first official language," but English remained the first language of the Irish people. The notion that Irish is the "real" language of Ireland persists. Conor Cruise O'Brien bluntly characterized the present-day situation.

> The official national aims, I need hardly remind you, are the restoration of the Irish language and the reunification of the national territory. Most people in the Republic don't give a tinker's curse about either of these aims: if anything they are opposed to both of them. But they do like to elect people who proclaim their dedication to these aims. (O'Brien 1982, 429)

Other nations considering alternatives to English can anticipate a rather different outcome, since multilingual societies can designate a living language for national use. For Ireland, the choice dwells in theoretical and nostalgic speculation about reviving a moribund language (see Ó Murchù 1985).

Even though the circumstances of British control were quite different, colonial Americans and Irish nationalists had in common a quest for liberation from British power through a linguistic alternative to the language of England. In the United States, escape from English was accomplished through the assertion of linguistic independence. America's own xenophobes and linguistic conservatives found their "authentic" identity by asserting a special link with Chaucer, Shakespeare, or other tributaries of the ancient and undefiled "wellsprings" of English; America's patriots and progressives were inclined to accept the anti-American evaluation that their language was undisciplined, exuberant, vulgar, democratic, or, in short, "free" of restraint, but they regarded these qualities as meritorious. In Ireland, the mythology of the Irish language as the liberating alternative settled into uncomfortable alliance with two distinguishable streams of literature in English, one more "English"—that of Spenser, Steele, Goldsmith, Burke, Wilde, and Shaw; the other more "Irish"—that of Edgeworth, Moore, Yeats, Synge, O'Casey, Joyce, O'Brien, and Behan. Both traditions have been called into question. Writing soon after the Republic was established, an Irish Jesuit declared: "Even 'Irish-hearted' literature in English is a source of danger in Irish education" (Corcoran 1923, 269). Even now, official endorsement of the Irish language among the "national aims" gives these two traditions of writing in English a somewhat uncertain status.

The search for an "alternative language" is itself part of an English tradition, one expressed by Dryden in his effort to modernize the English of earlier poets and by Coleridge and Wordsworth in seeking to return literary language to the domain of the "real" language of ordinary people. Wresting control of (and changing) the means of expression, in short, is a perennial theme of English and English-influenced language cultures. In Ireland and North America, however, the choice of language dwelt mainly in the details of English; in other nations, the array of choice is much wider.

Multilingual nations provide real alternatives, and the choice of English or another language continues to animate lively debates. Some of the principal themes of these debates are displayed in African comments on the choice of a privileged language.

> *Nigeria* (1842). One thing I want for beg your Queen, I have too much man now, I can't sell slaves, and don't know what for do for them. But if I can get some cotton and coffee to grow, and man for teach me, and make sugar cane for we country come up proper, and sell for trade side I very glad. Mr. Blyth tell me England glad for send man to teach book and make we understand God all same white man do. If Queen do so I glad too much, and we must try do good for England always. (King Eyo, quoted in Waddell 1970, 664)
>
> *Liberia* (1862). The spirit of the English language is the spirit of Independence, both personal and national; the spirit of free speech and a free press, and personal liberty; the spirit of reform and development; the spirit of enterprise; the spirit of law, of moral character, and spiritual beneficence. (Crummell 1862, 51)
>
> *Sierra Leone* (1876). It is unfortunate for the English and other European languages that, in this part of Africa, they have come to the greater portion of the natives associated with profligacy, plunder, and cruelty, and devoid of any connection with spiritual things; while the Arabic is regarded by them as the language of prayer and devotion, of religion and piety, of all that is unworldly and spiritual. (Blyden 1967, 68)
>
> *Commonwealth Africa* (1965). English has always lain beyond the reproach of tribalism, and is widely accepted as a politically and culturally neutral language, now largely disassociated from former political dependence on Britain. Even more than in Asia, English provides a window on the world and a widespread common language which can aid African unity and development. But in this context English must be seen as an African language—albeit an acquired one—and must be ready to serve as the vehicle for distinctively African cultural values. (Perren and Holloway 1965, 20)
>
> *Uganda* (1967). The English language as a partial embodiment of Anglo-Saxon

SHOOTING IN WEST AFRICA—THROUGH A MANGROVE SWAMP

English became nativized in Asia and Africa mainly through the efforts of missionaries, traders, and the military. While the Empire spread through a mixture of commerce and idealism—especially in campaigns to eradicate slavery—there was in Britain an undercurrent of anti-imperial feeling expressed in satirical treatments of exploration and exploitation. Illustration from the *Graphic* 42 (December 6, 1890): 656.

habits of thought must therefore carry with it seeds of intellectual accultura-
tion for the Africans who learn it. That is why learning English was, to a
non-Westerner, a process of Westernization. And to the extent that an English-speaking African was thus partly "Westernized" he was indeed partly
detribalized. (Mazrui 1973, 66)

South Africa (1975). But why do Africans want to learn English? So that they
may absorb the British tradition and study its great books? I doubt it. I doubt
it very much. They want English primarily because they need a lingua franca
which is also a world language. They want English because, thanks mainly
to the missionaries (whom it is now popular to sneer at), it is the traditional
language of education. They want English because it is not the language of
the political party that imposes apartheid. They will learn the language to
serve their own ends; and those ends may well change the language itself.
(Butler 1975, 3)

South Africa (1976). For myself, English has offered, above all, the challenge
of a new medium: a challenge to myself, to try and convey to a public remote
from Africa something of my African experience; but also a test of and a
challenge to the language. (Brink 1983, 113)

Nigeria (1982). The adoption of Nigerian Pidgin for national literature will
arrest our writers's flight to English, a difficult foreign language which even
a writer of [John] Munonye's standing "doesn't know enough," let alone his
much less privileged countrymen. Not only is Pidgin a much simpler language, syntactically, but it is also a practical, viable, flexible language dis-
tilled in the alembic of our native sensibility and human experience. This
lusty language, which transcends our geographical and political boundaries,
grows daily before our very eyes. It is our natural, unifying weapon against
the divisive forces of English. In West Africa, English splits; Pidgin unites.
(Okeke-Ezigbo 1982, 34)

South Africa (1983). But learning and using English will not only give us the
much-needed unifying chord but will also land us into the exciting world of
ideas; it will enable us to keep company with kings in the world of ideas and
also make it possible for us to share the experiences of our own brothers in
the world: men such as black Americans W. E. Burghardt DuBois, Ralph
Ellison, James Baldwin, Richard Wright, Langston Hughes; Chinua Achebe
of Nigeria, Ghana's Ayi Kwei Armah, Sembene Ousmane from Senegal,
South Africa's Es'kia Mphahlele, Peter Abrahams and a host of other men
of letters. (Mashabela 1983, 17)

Kenya (1986). We African writers are bound by our calling to do for our
languages what Spenser, Milton and Shakespeare did for English; what
Pushkin and Tolstoy did for Russian; indeed what all writers in world history
have done for their languages by meeting the challenge of creating a literature
in them, which process later opens the languages for philosophy, science,

technology and all the other areas of human creative endeavours. (Ngũgĩ 1986, 29)

South Africa (1986). . . . there are many reasons why [English] cannot be considered an innocent language. The problems of society will also be the problems of the predominant language of that society. It is the carrier of its perceptions, its attitudes, and its goals, for through it, the speakers absorb entrenched attitudes. The guilt of English then must be recognized and appreciated before its continued use can be advocated. (Ndebele 1986, 14)

As these extracts show, English involves both positive and negative cultural values: economic development and yet exploitation; political and cultural ideas and institutions (some welcome, some offensive to revered traditions); enrichment of English but deprivation of one's own language; opportunities to communicate with readers around the world yet at the expense of one's local audience.

Alternatives to English have been intensely discussed in postcolonial, sub-Saharan Africa. Various nations there have favored different language policies and achieved correspondingly different results (see Spencer 1971; Whiteley 1971). The older motives for using English still draw people to learn the language, but there is also an undercurrent of resistance now being articulated as part of the quest for appropriately "African," postcolonial ideologies. Four possibilities have been given serious consideration: the designation of a pan-African language; the use of vernaculars; adherence to "international" English norms; and the creation of a distinctly "African" variety of English. All four are accompanied by arguments that derive from the same set of issues that earlier emerged in other postcolonial settings; they revolve around the themes of personal and national identity.

The earliest attempt to impose a pan-African language accompanied the spread of Islam with its emphasis on classical Arabic as the language of devotion and of the Holy Koran. Though never the language of a large, politically defined territory in sub-Saharan Africa, Arabic penetrated southward to various regions, especially those influenced by Zanzibar. European languages that arrived with the colonizers were also widespread: Portuguese in Guinea-Bissau, Angola, and Mozambique, for instance; Dutch and its successor language Afrikaans in South Africa; French in West and Central Africa; German, for a brief but crucial period, in present-day Tanzania; and English in West Africa and in the states that ran from Cape Town to Cairo. Most of these European languages were not perceived by anyone to be "African" but rather extensions of the metropolitan influence of Lisbon,

Berlin, Paris, Brussels, or London, and, though promulgated mainly by Christian missionaries, they were most forcefully presented as the sole appropriate vehicles for economic life and high culture.

The postcolonial search for an African language that could unite the peoples of the continent derives from faith in a common African culture. The following observation, published in 1949, sums up that faith.

> . . . notwithstanding all the factors and handicaps arrayed against them[,] it is still the simple truth about our African languages *that they are ours*—the only vehicles of our thoughts, the facile messengers upon whose wings our ideas take flight. The majority of Africans can never employ the English language as the majority of Englishmen and Americans employ it; they can or should never build a national literature upon it, because the original language of a people carries with it that people's peculiar genius. And the African genius dwells as much in African languages as the Anglo-Saxon and Hindu spirits dwell in English and Hindustani. (Jones-Quartey 1949, 24)

This sense that only an African language can be a fit vehicle for "the African genius" was the impulse that led to the adoption of a resolution to affirm a single, pan-African language (from a list of six candidate languages) at the Congress of Negro Writers and Artists held in Rome in 1959 ("Résolution de linguistique" 1959). Later, at the All-African Union of Teachers meeting held in Algiers in 1975, a more practical step was offered in a proposal that the single language for schooling be selected from Hausa, Arabic, and kiSwahili. Brought up again and again, this idea continues to gain popularity (if not practicality), even among writers of African English who have achieved an international readership.

By 1971, Wole Soyinka (the Nobel Laureate for Literature for 1986) had begun to urge the selection "from the existing languages of Black Africa" a single "official language for the black continent including the black peoples of America" (1971, 6). Subsequently, he identified kiSwahili as the most appropriate candidate for that purpose, and, though he does not expect to learn it himself, Soyinka has offered to assist in translating his English works so they can inspire a successor generation to devote creative energies to that language (see Jeyifo 1984; Soyinka 1979). He has been joined in the effort to make kiSwahili the pan-African language by another internationally known writer in English, Ayi Kwei Armah.

> Once adopted, that African language will be taught as a compulsory language in all African schools, alongside the current official languages it will eventually

THE SLEEPING SICKNESS.
CUTTING A CONTINENT OUT FROM UNDER HIM.

The division of Africa into spheres of influence centered in the northern hemisphere has shaped modern nation states on that continent. English in east, west, and southern Africa has emerged in distinct varieties, each with a full range of literary expression. See Bailey and Görlach 1982. Illustration from *Puck* 70 (October 25, 1911): 6–7.

replace. No African will be denied access to foreign languages, but all educated Africans will be competent in that one African language, so that by the time the continent is wholly literate, Africans conversing with one another will no longer need interpreters. (Armah 1985, 832)

The intellectual appeal of such a linguistic future needs no explanation; Soyinka, Armah, and others assert the fellowship of a larger community (either one defined by the continent of Africa or, in Soyinka's case, one defined by race, since he wishes to induce Black people from the African diaspora to acquire kiSwahili in order to come into communion with those who have remained at home). But there is a more profound result to be achieved, escape from the "chain on the soul" implicit in European languages.

Arguments in favor of the "enrichment" of individual African languages derive from the same sources as the grander scheme of pan-African linguistic unity: self-sufficiency, community, and adequacy (actual or potential) of one's own language for every important purpose in life. It is a measure of the image of English that so many of the proponents of the vernaculars feel obliged to argue against the backdrop of the alleged benefits of English, making English a norm (if not an ideal) against which to measure the alternatives.

The arguments for the vernaculars vary depending upon the nation and region. In Tanzania, for instance, kiSwahili has the strongest support and widest use in national affairs, partly because it was encouraged during German colonial rule (1885–1920), which had an influence on the policies of subsequent British occupation (1920–1961). In Cameroon, on the other hand, the remarkable number of vernaculars presented a problem that was "solved" by the use of English and French for education in the regions controlled by the two colonial powers, and in the postcolonial era this heritage has led to continued reliance on these languages, though not without controversy (see Fonlon 1969).

What is important for understanding the image of English among Africans is that the European languages are sustained in Africa not only by colonial legacies and postcolonial elites but by popular sentiment as well. A report from Zambia explains the dilemma.

[The Zambian vernacular writer] is not slow to notice that the favourable emphasis which society has placed on English has had the inevitable consequence of cultivating in the educated Zambian generations a corresponding attachment to English, but a profound disdain for the local languages. And the Zambian vernacular writer (who in any case must depend for his livelihood on the proceeds from his writings), quite understandably, becomes less inclined to write in the mother tongue. Nor does he regret taking this step. After all, even an illiterate old woman in the remotest of Zambia's villages is today demanding to be taught the basic skills of reading and writing in English, arguing that literacy in the vernacular does not pay. English, I am afraid, has come to signify for many in this country—including the prospective Zambian vernacular writer—both the key to a lucrative occupation and the passport to considerable social prestige. (Kashoki 1970, 32)

As long as these economic and ideological conditions prevail, writers (and "development specialists" of all kinds) will find it difficult to claim the sufficiency of the vernaculars, however strong their emotional attachments to them.

The use of "international" English for African expression was implicit in colonial times. More localized, English-based alternatives were viewed as "broken," evidence of imperfect education rather than of creative adaptation to African conditions (see Bobbins [ca.1951] n.d.). Writers who shared the assumptions of the metropolitan critics were likely to look to the use of English (and French) as part of a movement toward what former President Léopold Sédar Senghor (himself a member of the French Academy) called "Euroafrica, a decisive stage towards the *Universal Civilization*" (1975, 98). Senghor's celebration of the African subdomain of European culture reveals an attempt to embrace English as an African language without altering its basic foundations.

One last remark on the English language: it has, since the eighteenth century, been one of the favourite instruments of the New Negro, who has used it to express his identity, his *Négritude*, his consciousness of the African heritage. An instrument which, with its plasticity, its rhythm and its melody, corresponds to the profound, volcanic affectivity of the Black peoples. And indeed, the Nigerians, and the Ghaneans and the black Africans have produced masterpieces in prose; though they are less convincing in poetry, no doubt because poetry demands a more complete mastery of the language, as indicated by the flowering of Negro-American poetry since the abolition of slavery; and today by the prodigious vitality of the young generation of Negro-American poets, such as Don Lee, Leroy Jones. And the young Niki [sic] Giovanni whose works, if translated—I myself am incapable of translating them, not being familiar with slang—would infuse new life into poetry. All over the world. (Senghor 1975, 85)

In his famous dismissal of Senghor's assertion of *négritude*, Wole Soyinka declared: "A tiger does not proclaim his tigritude: you know it when he pounces. The duiker does not proclaim his duikeritude: you see it in his elegant leap" (1979, 23). Yet Soyinka's rejection of English is partial. While he scorned too much self-congratulation, he did not question the use of "international" English to reach a global audience. Enthusiasm for explaining and justifying the African experience (and the use of "good" English to express it) was an inevitable consequence of colonial condescension and scorn. In an effort entirely consonant with Senghor's desire to authenticate the Black experience, an anthologist in 1973 even felt obliged to compile selections "to prove one point: that African authors have produced good and interesting English prose" (Bown 1973, xii).

Ambivalence as expressed by nineteenth-century Americans anxious about "Americanisms" was repeated in Africa. Only as political independence appeared a likely possibility did African writers begin to see themselves as afforded the same independence in the use of the language. Chinua Achebe expressed this idea in 1964.

> The price a world language must be prepared to pay is submission to many different kinds of use. The African writer should aim to use English in a way that brings out his message best without altering the language to the extent that its value as a medium of international exchange will be lost. He should aim at fashioning out an English which is at once universal and able to carry his peculiar experience. . . . I feel that the English language will be able to carry the weight of my African experience. But it will have to be a new English, still in full communion with its ancestral home but altered to suit its new African surroundings. (1975, 62)

In the early postcolonial era, Achebe was similarly doubtful about possibility of writing in an African language.

> Where am I to find the time to learn the half-a-dozen or so Nigerian languages each of which can sustain a literature? I am afraid it cannot be done. These languages will just have to develop as tributaries to feed the one central language enjoying nation-wide currency. Today, for good or ill, that language is English. Tomorrow it may be something else, although I very much doubt it. (58)

Between 1964 (when these words were written) and 1974 (when Achebe compiled a book of his essays), his opinion had changed.

. . . the fatalistic logic of the unassailable position of English in our literature leaves me more cold now than it did when I first spoke about it in the auditorium of the University of Ghana with that formidable Irishman, Conor Cruise O'Brien, in the chair and the great African revolutionary, Kwame Nkrumah, in Flagstaff House. (xiv)

The warmth of support for English as a literary medium for African expression has continued to cool, not only for Achebe but also for other African writers.

Just how English should be "altered" to bring out the "message" of "African experience" had been illustrated in Achebe's internationally acclaimed novels (with an "African" colloquial style to convey the dialogue of his characters). Even more dramatic and controversial was the use of a drastically altered English in the novels and stories of Amos Tutuola, beginning with his novel *The Palm-Wine Drinkard* (1952), which was celebrated in Britain and the United States but more circumspectly viewed by many African writers who alleged that Tutuola was only a "natural" whose English was imperfectly learned rather than artistically contrived. Nonetheless, Tutuola, Achebe, Gabriel Okara (and many others) continued to explore the means and consequences of making English a distinctly African language without, as Achebe put it, losing its "value as a medium of international exchange." In so doing, they experienced a spectrum of responses ranging from high praise to rancorous abuse (see Achebe 1975). The following is representative of one theme of the argument.

We have examined the hegemonic intentions of eurocentric criticism of African literature and how it has led African poetry astray, how it has attempted to scotch African nationalist consciousness in African literature and attempted to replace it with a pro-European pseudo-universalist, individualist consciousness and values. This foreign domination of African culture is long overdue for overthrow. (Chinweizu *et al.* 1980, 301)

Arguments along these lines have been directed primarily against non-African critics and their supposed affrontery in considering African literature as a branch of European tradition. (The volume from which this extract is taken was dedicated to more than thirty "giant voices of the Black World calling us to liberation." Achebe and Senghor were included among the "giants," but Tutuola was not.) What is being rejected is not writing in English but "eurocentrism" in taste and culture.

Tutuola's experiments were anticipated in nineteenth-century North America by a rich popular literature in which an "Americanized" dialect was extensively used. Today mostly excluded from the pantheon of canonical authors, its writers presented an image of the country through language. Much of this writing was satirical, mixing humor with a serious social purpose. Its authors often employed comic pseudonyms—Sam Slick, Sut Lovingood, Widow Bedott, Petroleum Vesuvius Nasby, and Josh Billings are examples—and they created or refined stereotypes of hayseed philosophers, stubborn farmers, roistering ripsnorters, and a host of one-dimensional North American types to serve as the backdrop for literary adventures and moral reflection (see Blair and McDavid 1983). Present-day readers know this trend in American writing mainly through the novels and stories of Mark Twain, who disingenuously fostered the belief that the distinctive English of this literature was an artful representation of actual American characters rather than what it actually was—a descendant of the literary language of fictional bumpkin gentlemen, courtly fops, and sagacious rustics of the British tradition. The forms of speech found in these American writings were, of course, connected to actual usage, but the articulation of this image was contrived from the literary past. Some features were merely fabricated from what such stereotypical characters ought to have said rather than what their prototypes did say, and this strategy, too, had a firm basis in literary tradition. Vernacular literature thus created and sustained an image of the language (as Dickens did for Cockney in the interchange of *w* and *v* in Sam Weller's speech; see Sivertsen 1960, 123; Wyld 1936, 292). Sometimes close to and sometimes remote from the facts of American language behavior, nineteenth-century "dialect literature" in the United States helped to establish the idea of a distinctively "American" English (see Burkett 1978).

In addition to Tutuola, other African writers have created a postcolonial literature with a distinctively "African" flavor, particularly in the plays, novels, and stories associated with Onitsha in eastern Nigeria. In Achebe's nostalgic recollection of the place, he calls it "the crossroads of the world."

> Onitsha was a place of schools—day schools and night schools, mission schools and private schools, grammar schools and commercial institutes, a city of one-room academies and backyard colleges. It had the best, the indifferent and the deplorable. Its major industry was retail trading and the next was education, and the two sometimes got mixed up. Onitsha was a self-confident place where a man would not be deterred even by insufficient learning from aspiring to teach and improve his fellows—and making a little profit as well. (Achebe 1975, 92)

The "pamphlet literature" of Onitsha has evoked an internationally produced interpretative criticism; the authors of Onitsha parallel earlier American efforts to use (and invent) a language of "the people" (see Asomugha 1981; Lindfors 1979; Obiechina 1972, 1973, 1990). Some of it apparently naive and some distinctly sophisticated, this writing has pioneered a genuine and successful technique to alter English for African expression, drawing (as did its American counterparts) on Biblical allusion, political rhetoric, literary quotation from English writers taught in school, and, of course, the language of real people.

Postcolonial societies can achieve linguistic independence within the anglophone world by seizing the means of expression from international norms and forcing it to serve local and national purposes. A further example of this tendency has been provided by the novel *Sozaboy*, written by the Nigerian poet, Ken Saro-Wiwa. In the preface explaining the language he has chosen for his fiction, Saro-Wiwa stated:

> Sozaboy's language is what I call "rotten English," a mixture of Nigerian pidgin English, broken English and occasional flashes of good, even idiomatic English. This language is disordered and disorderly. Born of a mediocre education and severely limited opportunities, it borrows words, patterns and images freely from the mother-tongue and finds expression in a very limited English vocabulary. To its speakers, it has the advantage of having no rules and no syntax. It thrives on lawlessness, and is part of the dislocated and discordant society in which Sozaboy must live, move and have not his being. (Saro-Wiwa 1985, iii)

Just as Stephen Daedalus declared at the end of Joyce's *Portrait of the Artist as a Young Man* that he would leave Ireland to forge a language for "the race," so Saro-Wiwa has created a distinctive literary language for Nigeria. It incorporates, rather than rejects, the mother-tongue and English, along with whatever images are available to its audience (including, of course, the echo of the King James English version of the Acts of the Apostles at the end of the declaration just quoted). Such a development follows a familiar pattern in other postcolonial anglophone societies.

Parallel development in the use of language is no more inevitable than parallel development in the economic and political spheres. The evolution of English in the United States, Canada, Australia, and other majority English-speaking nations has set an example, but not one that necessarily will be imitated (or independently invented) elsewhere. American humorists and Onitsha pamphleteers both discovered a strategy for making English the "proper" language for postcolonial societies, but they did not exhaust the possibilities of choice.

An instructive case for an alternative future for English is provided in the career of the Kenyan novelist and dramatist, Ngũgĩ wa Thiong'o. Though an undergraduate and an author of only two published short stories in 1962, James Ngugi (as he then was called) was invited to what he described as a "momentous encounter" with other "African Writers of English Expression" at Makerere University College, Kampala, Uganda (Ngũgĩ 1986, 5).

Those who attended this conference celebrated the use of English for African creative writing and projected a bright future for the language.

> *Chinua Achebe* (1964). For an African, writing in English is not without its serious set-backs. He often finds himself describing situations or modes of thought which have no direct equivalent in the English way of life. Caught in that situation he can do one of two things. He can try and contain what he wants to say within the limits of conventional English or he can try to push back those limits to accommodate his ideas. The first method can produce competent, uninspired and rather flat work. The second method can produce something new and valuable to the English language as well as to the material he is trying to put over. *But* it can also get out of hand. It can lead to *bad* English being accepted and defended as African or Nigerian. I submit that those who can do the work of extending the frontiers of English so as to accommodate African thought-patterns must do it through their mastery of English and not out of innocence. (Killam 1973, 12)
>
> *John Pepper Clark* (1966). In other words, the task for the Ijaw, and I dare say any Nigerian or African artist, writing in a European language like English, is one of finding the verbal equivalent for his characters created in their original and native context. The quest is not on the horizontal one of dialect and stress which are classifications of geography, society, and education. It is on the vertical plane of what the schoolmasters call style and register, that is, the proper manner, level, and range of dialogue and discussion. And this is a matter of rhetoric, the artistic use and conscious exploitation of language for purposes of persuasion and pleasure. (Killam 1973, 31)
>
> *Gabriel Okara* (1963). As a writer who believes in the utilization of African ideas, African philosophy and African folk-lore and imagery to the fullest extent possible, I am of the opinion the only way to use them effectively is to translate them almost literally from the African language native to the writer into whatever European language he is using as his medium of expression. (Killam 1973, 137)

In an opinion that he would soon change, Ngũgĩ celebrated the fact that the Conference "differed from the 1956 and 1959 World Congresses of Negro writers, where political discussions clouded the atmosphere" (Ngũgĩ 1962, 7).

The consensus of 1962 was challenged profoundly soon afterwards by Obiajunwa Wali.

> Perhaps the most important achievement of the last Conference of African Writers of English Expression held at Makerere College, Kampala, in June 1962, is that African literature now as defined and understood, leads nowhere. (Wali 1963,13)

Wali's arguments led to a spirited debate, not on the varieties of English but on the more fundamental question of whether to use English at all. Would African writers continue to create "a minor appendage in the main stream of European literature" (13)? Or would they accept Wali's challenge to write in African languages?

> . . . the whole uncritical acceptance of English and French as the inevitable medium for educated African writing, is misdirected, and has no chance of advancing African literature and culture. In other words, until these writers and their western midwives accept the fact that any true African literature must be written in African languages, they would be merely pursuing a dead end, which can only lead to sterility, uncreativity, and frustration. (Wali 1963, 14)

It was striking confirmation of his argument that the advertisement inserted to fill out the last column of Wali's essay in the English-language magazine in which it appeared announced publication of the translation by Julius K. Nyerere of Shakespeare's *Julius Caesar* into kiSwahili.

Unsurprisingly, spirited replies to Wali's essay appeared immediately across Africa.

> *Barry Reckord*. I believe the less languages the better, and wish to Christ everybody spoke Yoruba. I also believe theories of the peculiar potency of any black language are as unfounded as theories of the peculiar potency of blacks. Both are propagated by nationalists and racists to suit their book. (1963, 7)
>
> *Ezekiel Mphahlele*. There will thus be no reason why any language should wait for its own people to write originally in it in order to develop it as a literary medium. A writer must choose the medium that suits him best. (1963, 9)

> *Gerald Moore.* The development of the vernaculars must be left to those who
> are content with a vernacular audience. (1963, 9)
>
> *Edward C. Okwu.* . . . my contention then is that producing what may be called
> Nigerian Literature does not depend on the language a writer has used. The
> important criterion, apart from the very obvious ones about the nationality
> of the authorship and the setting of the writing, is that the Nigerian situation
> should be authentically handled. (1966, 291)

These responses did not go far to soothe the anxiety that Wali had created;
having endured many patronizing superlatives from Anglo-American critics,
the writers who met at Makerere found themselves obliged to assert their
African "authenticity" against the accusation that their very adoption of English was, as Thomas Davis had long before alleged, "the worst badge of
conquest."

For Ngũgĩ, the question turned again and again to the alternative raised
by Wali and by another East African writer, Peter Nazareth: "One way of
escaping the stranglehold of colonial English is not to write in English at all"
(Nazareth 1978, 23). Twenty years after the Makerere conference, Ngũgĩ
defined the creative writing it celebrated as "the literature of the petty-bour-
geoise born of the colonial schools and universities" (1986, 20). Beginning
in 1977, Ngũgĩ turned principles into practice by writing plays, novels, and
books for children in his mother-tongue, Gĩkũyũ. In 1986, he published a
final collection of "explanatory prose" in English; this work contains the
following declaration:

> This book, *Decolonising the Mind*, is my farewell to English as a vehicle
> for any of my writings. From now on it is Gĩkũyũ and Kiswahili all the way.
>
> However, I hope that through the age old medium of translation I shall be
> able to continue dialogue with all. (1986, xiv)

Ngũgĩ's decision is likely to become an increasingly popular answer to the
questions and contradictions raised by postcolonial English.

Postcolonial Englishes have emerged from the residue of the Anglo-
American political empires, sometimes with a local flavor to international
expression, sometimes with vividly localized characteristics. Yet the question of the continued use of English remains open to various possibilities
ranging from naturalizing the language to rejecting it. The image of English
and the ideology that attaches to it remain influential for future use of the
language. The cultural conflict swirling around the use of English is suc-

cinctly captured in this expression from the scattered island nations of the southern Pacific Ocean.

> The formal educational systems (whether British, New Zealand, Australian, American, or French) that were established by the colonisers in our islands all had one main feature in common: they were based on the arrogantly-mistaken racist assumption that the cultures of the colonisers were superior (and preferable) to ours. Education was therefore devoted to civilising us, to cutting us away from the roots of our cultures, from what the colonisers viewed as darkness, superstition, barbarism and savagery. . . . If we may not be as yet the most artistically creative region on our spaceship, we possess the potential to become the most artistically creative. There are more than 1,200 indigenous languages, plus English, French, Hindi, Spanish, and various forms of pidgin with which to catch and interpret the void, reinterpret our past, create new historical and sociological visions of Oceania, and compose songs, poems, plays and other oral and written literature. (Wendt 1982, 210, 212)

Just how this conflict of values will be resolved is by no means certain, particularly when those who reject English for some other language are so seldom heard in an anglophone community deaf to their voices.

Literary uses of English, which have been stressed in this chapter, do not entirely predict the future use or shape of the language, however much writers like to recall Shelley's dictum that "poets are the unacknowledged legislators of the world." Yet where poetry, drama, and fiction are not created, language lacks sustaining power. They are essential to its future vitality and a major factor in determining its image.

Chapter 7

English Improved

In order to enhance its image, observers of English from very early times have proposed improvements. Often such proposals are impelled by a rage for tidiness, a desire to impose consistency and order on a language that has been seen as unruly and disheveled. Sometimes Greek or Latin have been invoked as models of linguistic excellence against which to measure the state of English. Earlier stages of the language, when the wellsprings were flowing with greater purity, have also yielded ideals. The shortcomings of English in comparison to other living languages have been anatomized in the hope of importing the virtues of those languages. More modest proposers have urged mechanisms to call a halt to language change. If English cannot be improved, they believe, at least further decay and disorder can be stemmed by "fixing" the language and protecting it against future deterioration.

Improvements are often alleged to have practical consequences—making the language a more edifying vehicle for thought, a more efficient medium of expression, a more instructive object of study for the young and the foreign. Those who concoct and promulgate such ideas have seen themselves as contributing to the common welfare. Often, they begin proposals in hope only to abandon them in gloom. No better examplar of this progress from optimism to despair can be found than Samuel Johnson, who declared in the Preface to his *Dictionary* of 1755:

> Those who have been persuaded to think well of my design, require that it should fix our language, and put a stop to those alterations which time and chance have hitherto been suffered to make in it without opposition. With this consequence I will confess that I flattered myself for a while; but now begin to fear that I have indulged expectation which neither reason nor experience can justify. When we see men grow old and die at a certain time one after another,

from century to century, we laugh at the elixir that promises to prolong life to a thousand years; and with equal justice may the lexicographer be derided, who being able to produce no example of a nation that has preserved their words and phrases from mutability, shall imagine that his dictionary can embalm his language, and secure it from corruption and decay, that it is in his power to change sublunary nature, or clear the world at once from folly, vanity, and affectation. (Johnson [1755] 1974, 9)

Although Johnson abandoned his effort to put a stop to language change, many improvers have not been so daunted by the difficulties such an enterprise entails. The mere impracticality of much proposed linguistic improvement does not diminish the zeal of its advocates.

The English spelling system, above all other aspects of the language, has been the focal domain for improvement. In fact, new ideas about spelling were mooted before most people recognized spelling as a system. About 1200, the Augustinian canon, Robert Orm, invented a spelling whose most notable feature was the doubling of consonants after short vowels in closed syllables (e.g., *itt* 'it'). Orm left no surviving explanation of what motivated his system (though he wrote at length on the value of presenting Biblical stories in English rather than Latin), but it is clear from his practice that he wished to make spelling consistent and to reform it to reflect pronunciation. Orm may have wished spelling to influence the delivery of preachers and thus to foster a style for church services that would be consistent and stable across England (see Scragg 1974, 29). Though not an influential attempt at reform since there is no evidence that anyone else adopted them, Orm's proposals anticipate those of later advocates of change.

The first spelling reformer to reach a wide audience was Thomas Smith (1513–77), a diplomat, lawyer, and influential academic. First interested in the pronunciation of ancient Greek, he campaigned (with John Cheke) to persuade English scholars to adopt the pronunciation of ancient Greek devised by Erasmus. Having won against the doughty opposition of conservatives, Smith turned his attention to English spelling. Spelling practices as he found them (about 1542, though his book on the subject was not published until 1568) seemed to him "absurd, foolish, stupid, and therefore censured by the true, the good, the wise, and the learned" (Smith [1568]1968, fol. A1v). He fulminated against "silent" letters and complained that the same sounds have different spellings and different sounds are spelled with the same letters. Blame for this confusion he levelled at the French who had destroyed the rational spelling of Old English after the Norman Conquest.

Only a reformed alphabet, with additional characters, could bring the system to the ideal of a phonetic system. In Smith's view, the result would lift spelling out of chaos and allow users of the language to express themselves rationally.

The best known of Smith's immediate successors, William Bullokar (ca. 1531–1609), had more concrete and practical goals in proposing reforms. Like those who followed him, Bullokar promised great benefits from small alterations; his hopes were copiously expressed in the lengthy title of his volume.

> *Bullokars* Booke at large, for the *Amendment* of *Orthographie* for English speech: wherein, a most perfect supplie is made, for the wantes and double *sounde of letters in the olde Orthographie, with Examples for* same, with the easie conference and vse of both Orthographies, *to saue expences in Bookes for a time, vntill this amendment grow to a generall vse, for* the easie, speedie, and perfect reading and writing of English, (the speech not changed, as some vntruly and maliciously, or at the least ignorantlie blow abroade) by the which amendement the same Authour hath also framed a ruled Grammar, to be imprinted heereafter, for the same speech, to no small commoditie of the English Nation, not only to come to easie, speedie, and perfect vse of our owne language, but also to their easie, speedie and readie entrance into the secretes of other Languages, and easie and speedie pathway to all Straungers, to vse our Language, heeretofore very hard vnto them, to no small profite and credite to this our Nation, and stay therevnto in the weightiest causes. (Bullokar [1580b]1977, title page)

The basic themes for reform were here established: economy in printing English books (by eliminating "silent" letters); efficiency in learning reading and writing (since a phonetic alphabet is alleged to be easier to grasp); effortless learning of foreign languages by English speakers (since Bullokar proposed to write these other languages in his spelling system); efficacy for foreign learners (since spelling becomes the key to pronunciation).

Bullokar's claims for his reforms were ardently presented in a pamphlet published to support the longer work: youth will learn to read and write English "in a quarter of the time, that they haue learned in time past"; perfect spelling "may be learned in six weeks by a childe of fiue yeeres of age"; foreigners may "studie Inglish speech priuately in their chambers: yea at home in their owne countries, to their great delight, and credite of our language, so long time vnperfect, and therefore accounted in time past barbarous" (Bullokar [1580a]1966, 15). All of these benefits, he claimed, would yield "no small profit and credit to this our nation."

"Be-Spelling: Dis-covering and Releasing Archimagical Powers of Words" (Daly and Caputi 1987, 15). The focus of reform in efforts to improve English has been its spelling. Illustration copyright © 1987 Sudie Rakusin. Reprinted by permission of the artist. Originally published in Daly and Caputi 1987.

Bullokar's title also makes clear that he had encountered opposition even before his system appeared in print. Two years earlier, he had given a public demonstration of the spelling and circulated specimens, and the response had not been enthusiastic. The learned had resisted his modifications, and Mulcaster, for instance, declared that "the remedie it self is more dangerous then the disease" ([1582]1970, 97). Like so many of his successors in spelling reform, Bullokar hoped that the larger, disinterested public would welcome and adopt the changes. His system was phonetic, but he kept the new spelling familiar by employing diacritical marks arrayed around the usual letters of the alphabet and, thus, hoped to satisfy those who wished new spellings to be at once familiar and yet founded on speech.

During the seventeenth century, much linguistic theorizing was invested in the search for a universal philosophical language that would be freed from the imperfections of all actual human languages (see Cohen 1977). Having attempted to "ascertain" unruly English, scholars found a way out of its semantic and grammatical defects by imagining a "real character" in which words and things would stand in an orderly and "natural" relationship as they had in the prelapsarian language of Eden. These efforts had some bearing on thinking about English, but for the most part they formed a separate line of development toward the modern disciplines of psychology and logic. Imperfections, whether specific to English or general attributes of human languages, were the point of departure for speculation and systems. New schemes for spelling along the lines established by Smith and Bullokar were occasionally published, but they drew little sympathetic notice (see Zachrisson 1931–32, 12).

Typical of later reforms were those suggested by Thomas Cooke (1703–56), who was persuaded of the excellence of Latin as a model. ("We can not hope," he wrote, "ever to arrive to any Part of Speech parallel to that of the (Latin] Gerunds" [1742, 304].) Cooke found virtue in making the affixes of English consistent, and, in his *Proposals for Perfecting the English Language* (1729), he wrote approvingly of *shined* and *strived* (in place of *shone* and *strove*), of *mans* as the plural of *man*, and of *gooder* and *goodest* (instead of *better* and *best*). With these changes and a few spelling reforms, he alleged that "the Facility of learning our Language would be much greater than it is to a Foreigner" (Cooke 1742, 306). If the "Quantitys of Words in our poetical Compositions" were fixed, the result would be a "just Prosody" based on stressed syllables and long vowels. Such modifications, he believed, would have an important effect in making English endure.

> I submit not these Proposals to such Authors as have no Views beyond the
> Grave in their Productions, or who know not what constitutes a Language, but
> to those who wish no Bounds to their Fame; nay, a more generous Passion than
> the Thirst of Glory should fire them to the Endeavour of transmiting their Works
> to Posterity, the Desire and laudable Pride of contributing to the Delight and
> Profit of thousands yet unborn; which can not be without an Obedience to such
> Laws of Speech as must support the Language. If such Laws are obeyed, the
> Language will preserve the Works of Genius, and the Works preserve the
> Language. (Cooke 1742, 307)

Like other reformers, Cooke expected grand effects from small amendments;
like Bullokar, he believed that his modifications in spelling would put a halt
to language change and thus arrest deterioration in language. Perhaps lacking
confidence in his convictions, Cooke did not employ his new spelling in
either his treatise or his poems. In offering his proposals to the public, he had
fulfilled sufficiently his desire to improve the language.

In the mid-eighteenth century, Thomas Sheridan (1719–88), having
failed as an actor and theatre manager, turned his attention to education. In
lectures delivered throughout Britain, he urged that schoolchildren and adults
give greater attention to the English language and to elocution and oratory.
Awarded honorary degrees by both Oxford and Cambridge, he became an
influential figure and enjoyed the financial support of patrons and of the
government. In 1762, Sheridan appended to his *Course of Lectures on Elocution* a "Dissertation on the State of Language in other Countries, But More
Particularly in Our Own, and its Consequences." Though he did not wish to
alter the intrinsic nature of English, he provided an argument for the improvement in its use that led to actual reforms, at least in educational practices.

Like Cooke, Sheridan held up the example of antiquity. In a lengthy
series of comparisons, he noted that the Greeks "employed their chief care
and attention about their *living tongue*"; the English devote themselves primarily to their written language (Sheridan [1762]1968, 163). Such neglect
of training in spoken English leads to dire consequences:

> *We* are taught to deliver our own exercises, or the works of others, with little
> or no variation of voice, or else with some disagreeable discordant cant, applied
> to all sentences alike; without any accompaniments of looks or gesture, or else
> with such as are improper, ungraceful, or disgusting. (164)

A phonetic spelling system benefited the Greeks in learning correct pronunciation (and foreigners found it easy to learn Greek). And "the Greeks studied

no language but their own" while English pupils "employ the best part of [their] time in the study of other languages, to the utter neglect of our own" (168). For English speakers to aspire to the greatness of classical Greece (which seemed to Sheridan an indisputably excellent objective), "there can be no object of such importance to any nation as the improvement, and regulation of their language, since it is in vain without that to expect the improvement and regulation of the minds of the natives" (169). Rome, too, he wrote, achieved greatness by the assiduous and systematic cultivation of the Latin language.

Having established the necessity for reforms and the benefits to be derived from them, Sheridan made a series of practical proposals: introducing instruction in English at Oxford and Cambridge for the benefit of future school teachers; raising the practice of elocution and grammatical study of English to a position equal to that enjoyed by the classical languages; forming a committee of "a sufficient number of men of rank, fortune, and abilities" to fund teachers of English (202); awarding prizes in schools and at the universities for excellence in English oratory. All of these efforts would have three benefits for the nation: uniformity of pronunciation throughout Britain and its colonies; an improved standard of eloquence in public life and in the church; and "the refining, ascertaining, and establishing the English language on a durable basis" (206). As further consequences of his proposals, Sheridan foresaw a general improvement in civility and morality. "Odious distinctions" among social classes and regions under British sovereignty would be removed (225); foreigners would find it easier to learn English; the clarity of speech to ensue would "contribute much to the ease and pleasure of society, and improvement of politeness" (224).

Though much distressed by unphonetic English spelling, Sheridan was too practical to suggest radical reforms. Instead he set about compiling a two-volume *General Dictionary of the English Language, One Main Object of Which is to Establish a Plain and Permanent Standard of Pronunciation* (1780). Earlier lexicographers had provided occasional pronunciations, but Sheridan was the first to respell every entry to indicate both stress and sound. In general, he followed educated usage as the norm and thus entered such words as *cordial* with either *d* or *j* as the consonant of the second syllable; *literature* with *ch* as the first consonant of the last syllable; and *medicine* pronounced with two syllables (as in present-day British English). Sheridan's successor, John Walker, was more prescriptive and idealistic. In his *Critical Pronouncing Dictionary and Expositor of the English Language* (1791), Walker prescribed only the *d* in *cordial*, only the *t* in *literature*, and only the three-syllable pronunciation of *medicine* (as in present-day U.S. English; see Landau 1984, 58). The notion that dictionaries provide a "standard of pronunciation," however, begins with Sheridan, and it is owing to his influence and to methods of teaching spelling after 1800 that the "values" of individual syllables as spelled have come to be regarded by many English speakers as ultimately authoritative for spoken usage—at least most of the time.

Not satisfied to end his campaign with the *Dictionary*, Sheridan went on to publish a spelling book. His preface reiterates the goals for which he consistently worked.

> . . . wherever English is taught, all may attain a uniformity in spelling; but, with respect to pronunciation, it is left wholly to chance, depending entirely upon the common mode of utterance in the several places of their birth and education. Thus, the same individual books, when read aloud, are pronounced in a quite different manner by the natives of Scotland, Ireland, Wales, Yorkshire, and all the several counties of England; nay, in the very metropolis there are two different dialects, one current in the city, and the other at the court end of the town. In all which places English is pronounced according to the corrupt dialect of speech, established by the vulgar in their respective places of abode. (Sheridan [1786] 1968, v–vi)

His speller, he thought, would improve English by fostering a common pronunciation, at least for ceremonial occasions of speaking. With the influence of his lectures, his *Dictionary*, and his schoolbooks (all of which were widely imitated by successors), Sheridan's exhortations toward English eloquence led to consequential "improvements" in English pronunciation whereas more radical proposals for spelling reform had been without discernable influence. His notion that enunciation would eventually eliminate the distinctions of region and social class arose from a desire to foster linguistic upward mobility and egalitarianism. This impulse toward social change through linguistic reform became a dominant idea in subsequent proposals.

Nonetheless, radical solutions to the perceived problem of English orthography were not wanting as the century drew to a close. Sheridan's near contemporary, James Elphinston (1721–1809), was a projector who attracted patronage for his books but scorn from the critics and amused condescension from his friends (among them Samuel Johnson). Like many in his day, he was impressed by the success of the French in promoting their language, and he attributed the "diffusion" of the French language to spelling reforms made by the French academy. Arguing that the English should do likewise, Elphinston published volumes in his reformed spelling to illustrate the benefits that would arise from change.

> Hwen dhe essence ov a language (hwich iz its complete system ov sound) is braught by rascional nature, in dhe foolnes ov time, to' maturity; it becoms dhe duty ov man to' perform hiz part (dhe sole part, widh hwich he iz entrusted) in dhe ascertainment ov human speech; dhat ov first investigating from dhe purest livving practice, dhe hoal system ov real or audibel propriety in hiz language; and dhen ov repprezenting dhat propriety, by dhe moast expressive system ov litterary symbols; so to' picture speech, az nearly az possibel, in dhe exact state ov perfeccion she may hav attained: dhat dhus he may proppagate abraud, az wel as perpettuate at home, dhe purity, he haz been at length so happy to' compas; may secure alike dhe purified language from relapsing into' barbarism, and from degennerating into' corrupcion; may raiz her to' her just rank among pollished languages, hwile he renders her dhe wordhy vehikel ov his nacions wizdom and attainments, to' remotest ages. (Elphinston 1787, 1:ix–x)

Like Sheridan, Elphinston hoped to raise English eloquence to new heights. He elevated as models neither the folk nor the aristocracy as earlier writers had done. Instead, he looked to the middle classes to achieve ideals of purity, thwart tendencies toward degeneration and barbarism, and preserve the wisdom of his own day "to' remotest ages." For models of the "purest livving practice," he recommended (in words he translated from a French theorist in these matters) "such members ov dhe Metroppolis, az hav had dhe good– fortune, (hweddher from dellicate edducacion, or from incorruptibel taste) ov keeping equally free from grocenes, and from affectacion" (1787, 1:xiii). Only a phonetic spelling system, he believed, could diffuse the excellence of these ideal speakers as "dhe tribunal ov Use" (1:349) to the provinces and beyond Britain to the larger world.

Undaunted by criticism, Elphinston published two subsequent abridge- ments of his proposals, a translation of Latin moral maxims, and eight vol- umes of correspondence "between Geniusses ov boath Sexes and James Elphiston"—all written in his reformed spelling. Of the last of these, one reviewer, less censorious than those usually attracted to his work, declared:

> We dispute not with him the propriety of his spelling; that is, whether it may not represent the sounds that are pronounced, better than that which is actually in use, (though here we could mention many points in which we differ;) but we can assure the respectable author, that the attempt to overturn so totally the whole form of a language, is of all others the most impracticable. His knowl-

edge of the world, at the age of 72, . . . might assure him of this truth; but it is not at seventy-two that men learn to give up fancies they have long cherished. (Review of James Elphinston's *Fifty Years' Correspondence*, 1795, 18)

More typical was the view that "all will not do. So violent a change never will, or can be made, in the form of a whole language" (Review of James Elphinston's *A Minniature of Inglish Orthoggraphy*, 1796, 564). Yet the themes that Elphinston advanced in his imagery—to propagate and perpetuate English—match the contemporary ideals of many in artistic and political life: revolutionary change leading to imminent perfection; energy and fervor leading to a new age of ideal social order.

With so many improvements in English spelling connected with such practical goals as better teaching and learning, uniformity of pronunciation and spelling, and preservation and diffusion of the language, it is surprising to find reforms suggested on purely aesthetic grounds. John Pinkerton (1758–1826), however, supplied that want and urged radical reforms on his friends—among them Horace Walpole, Edward Gibbon, and Walter Scott. One of the oddest of his books was *Letters of Literature* (1785), in which he proposed drastic improvements for English. He declared that "the English tongue is sufficiently strong, rich, and universal; musicalness and softness are the only qualities it wants" (Heron 1785, 237). These defects could be remedied by making as many English words as possible end in vowels, either by selecting synonyms to replace the "unmusical" offenders (e.g., *also* for *likewise* and *felicity* for *happiness*) or by adding vowels to existing words (hence, *eggo* for *egg* and *cupo* for *cup*). He regarded *ess* as "the most horrid of all terminations" (243) and thus English plurals presented a difficult obstacle to his program. This problem he solved by proposing that *-a* be used for "all plurals," so *pens* would be replaced by *pena* and *papers* by *papera*. Even greater harmony could be achieved by making adjectives agree with their nouns in termination: *orientala manuscripta* for *oriental manuscripts* and *mya morninga devotiona* for *my morning devotions*. Such modifications, Pinkerton argued, would "give a language more perfect in melody than any yet seen"; lest anyone take him for a radical, he declared that "most of the alterations in the specimen are not *innovations*, but *restorations of our ancient language*" (266).

This proposal was subsequently dismissed by Pinkerton himself, declaring that it had been "written in early youth" and expressed "many juvenile crude ideas, long since abandoned by its author" (Pinkerton 1798, 117n). In a kindly letter, Horace Walpole praised Pinkerton's book as "full of good sense, brightly delivered," yet he dissented from the proposed language reforms not least because they would make all English poetry "defective in metre." But Walpole's main objection was to the impossibility of change in a language that had reached the elegance of a "refined age."

> To change *s* for *a* in the plural number of our substantives and adjectives would be so violent an alteration, that I believe neither the power of Power, nor the power of Genius would be able to effect it. In most cases I am convinced that very strong innovations are more likely to make impression than small and almost imperceptible differences, as in religion, medicine, politics, etc., but I do not think that language can be treated in the same manner, especially in a refined age. When a nation first emerges from barbarism, two or three masterly writers may operate wonders; and the fewer the number of writers, as the number is small at such a period, the more absolute is their authority. But when a country has been polishing itself for two or three centuries, and when consequently authors are innumerable, the most supereminent genius (or whoever is esteemed so, though without foundation) possesses very limited empire, and is far from meeting implicit obedience. (Lewis 1937–83, 16:264)

Though Pinkerton's ideas attracted little notice, Walpole's confident indifference to the likelihood of further innovation in English was not the prevailing sentiment of the century that followed.

Perhaps the most influential of the innovators of the new century was Pinkerton's contemporary, Noah Webster (1758–1843), the Massachusetts schoolteacher who set out to alter English and make it properly American. Spelling reform was only part of Webster's agenda for perfecting English, but it was to be the most effective part. In 1806, his *Compendious Dictionary* included in its subtitle various claims to superiority, including "the orthography is, in some instances, corrected." Noting that prior reforms had been too extreme for ready acceptance, Webster declared:

> The correct principle respecting changes in orthography seems to lie between these extremes of opinion. No great changes should ever be made at once, nor should any change be made which violates established principles, creates great inconvenience, or obliterates the radicals of the language. But gradual changes to accommodate the written to the spoken language, when they occasion none of these evils, and especially when they purify words from corruptions, improve the regular analogies of a language and illustrate etymology, are not only proper, but indispensable. ([1806] 1970, vii)

What is notable is that so many of the changes Webster proposed became normative in American English and that some even influenced British usage: removal of the *k* from such words as *logick* and *musick*, substitution of *k* for *que* in *cheque* and *risque*, *er* spellings in *centre* and *metre*, *s* rather than *c* in *defence* and *pretence*, removal of *u* from *favour* and *honour*. Even so, Webster did not prevail in every instance in the classes he chose for general treatment: *opaque* remains rather than his proposed *opake; theatre* continues as a high-toned variant of *theater*. His successful reforms took hold in part because they promoted spellings already current among some spellers. Where he was more inventive, he was less successful. Thus, he did not persuade others to employ *medicin* for *medicine*, *Mishigan* for *Michigan*, *pinchers* for *pincers*, *soop* for *soup*, or *vinyard* for *vineyard*. Unlike his predecessors, however, Webster was unwilling to leave his proposals in the hands of an indifferent public. By campaigning for adoption of his schoolbooks and, especially, for endorsements of his *American Dictionary* of 1828, Webster popularized these usages, but he was not satisfied to urge them at second hand, and he traveled to printers throughout New England to publicize his spellings. Because many of these spellings were adopted, they became familiar to U.S. readers. Webster was neither the first nor the last of spelling reformers; he was, however, the most influential.

Spelling was not the only aspect of English that troubled those who shaped opinion about the language in the nineteenth century. A balance between copiousness (the language enhanced through borrowing and word creation) and purity (the use of long-established English) had been struck in the seventeenth century, but the most desirable mixture of the two remained a subject for debate thereafter. With the rise of modern science in the nineteenth century, Greek and Latin provided the basis for what was to become the "international scientific vocabulary." Since they were not affected by widespread colloquial use, words from these classical sources were thought to have greater exactness and precision than traditional vernacular terms. (As with more exotic foreign borrowings, celebrators of English have left the impression that "scientific" words have come directly from Greek and Latin; in fact, a great many have been imported from other European vernaculars where they had first been put to modern use.)

Under the impact of "scientific" borrowing, long-established names for plants and animals were treated as folk terms unworthy of scientific taxonomy, however charming or familiar they might be. (The use of *folk* in patronizing or disparaging contrast to sophisticated ideas and practices is a good index to the substitution of *science* for traditional knowledge: *folk-belief*

[1892], *folk-etymology* [1883], *folk-faith* [1850], *folk-law* [1884], *folk-lore* [1846], *folk-medicine* [1898], *folk-poetry* [1892].) Since the *folk* have occupied a special place in the Romantic paradigm, reflecting an idealization of rural life and national character, vocabulary actually or apparently from "traditional" sources continues to emerge as a kind of counterscience, for instance *aftercure* 'convalescence' (1901), *maiden's wreath* '*Francoa ramosa*' (1893), *nitwittery* 'imbecility' (1936), *wicca* 'sorcery' (1970). Such terms did not, however, count as science, and consequently English has developed an array of parallel terms reflecting two differently valued domains, one official, the other informal or non-technical: *angioplasty* and *balloon procedure*, *integrated circuit* and *computer chip*, *lexical item* and *word*, *oncogenetic* and *tumor causing*, *plate tectonics* and *continental drift*.

The names of the emerging sciences were borrowed or coined in the seventeenth and eighteenth centuries, but general awareness of them and of their specialist vocabularies came only in the nineteenth century. One measure of the effect of science on the larger community of English users can be found in the derisive use of *ology* as a quasi-independent word, a rearguard action of the belle-lettred against the innovations of the scientists: "Sublime discoveries in the abstruce sciences of insect-ology, mite-ology, and nothing-ology" (1803); "the contemplation, either of physicology, or commonsensology" (1805); "this is the Ology of the day" (1823). *Ist* and *ism* in quasi-independent use reflect the same hostility to specialized doctrines and theories: "Ists and Isms are rather growing a weariness" (1841; see *OED*, s. v. "*ology*" and "*ism*").

Writing in 1851, Richard Chenevix Trench surveyed English vocabulary and wearily declaimed:

> Of the words to which each of these [philosophical, theological, and scientific] has in turn given birth, many, it is true, have never travelled beyond their own peculiar sphere, having remained purely technical, or scientific, or theological to the last; but many, too, have passed over from the laboratory and the school, from the cloister and the pulpit, into everyday use, and have, with the ideas which they incorporate, become the common heritage of all. For however hard and repulsive a front any study or science may present to the great body of those who are as laymen in regard of it, there is yet inevitably such a detrition as this continually going forward. . . . (Trench 1891, 199)

When in 1857 Trench gave a series of lectures to the Philological Society of London in support of amending the deficiencies in English dictionaries, he explicitly excluded scientific and technical language from the scope of the project.

> Nothing is easier than to turn to modern treatises on chemistry or electricity, or on some other of the sciences which hardly or not at all existed half a century ago, or which, if they existed, have yet been in later times wholly new-named— as botany, for example,—and to transplant new terms from these by the hundred and the thousand, with which to crowd and deform the pages of a Dictionary; and then to boast of the vast increase of words which it has gained over its predecessors. The labour is little more than that of transcription, but the gain is nought. It is indeed, less than nought; for it is not merely that half a dozen genuine English words recovered from our old authors would be a greater gain, a more real advance toward the completion of our vocabulary than a hundred or a thousand of these; but additions of this kind are mere disfigurements of the work which they profess to complete. (1860, 57–58)

No more telling evidence of the linguistic innovations spawned by scientists could be offered than Trench's denunciation of them. Antiquarian enthusiasm for "half a dozen genuine English words" was contrasted to the unnumbered innovations in scientific vocabulary. When science became preoccupied with the deficiencies of English and the need for terminology, the remedy was found in coining new terms from Greek and Latin sources, regardless of opposition by Trench and his ilk.

Thrusting aside existing terms and creating in their place a jargon of the initiated, available only to those who, through long apprenticeship, were admitted to the coterie of the adept, scientific English thus met a need to improve and enhance the language. In opposition to this trend, interest was revived in the "Saxon" elements of the English wordstock in the hope that "plainness" would make language available to everyone. Consequently, the nineteenth century revived the debate that had been apparently settled in the seventeenth with Sprat's recommendation of a "native easiness" for scientific discourse. Once again the language of "wits" and "scholars" challenged that of "Artizans, Countrymen, and Merchants."

An emblematic figure in this debate was William Barnes (1801–86), Dorset poet, schoolteacher, and philologist who taught himself some sixty languages (see Chedzoy 1985; Jacobs 1952). Beset nearly all his life by poverty, Barnes nonetheless triumphed over difficult circumstances, and his linguistic writings reached an international audience. Just a month after the failure of the boys' school he had founded in Dorchester, he was visited by

Prince Lucien Bonaparte (himself an accomplished philologist and eager to meet the author of accounts of the early history of English). He corresponded with influential members of the Philological Society, though he was never invited to join that learned body. His poetry was popular, especially when he read it to local audiences whose dialect he employed in stanzas modeled on Saxon, Welsh, and Persian verse forms; these efforts gained him the praise of Tennyson and, later, Thomas Hardy, who as a boy had come to admire the venerable and eccentric Barnes. His magazine articles, schoolbooks, and linguistic volumes reached a wide but usually skeptical audience. Like many improvers of English, he proposed ideals that seemed to his contemporaries worthy but unattainable.

Barnes's first public declaration of his ideas appeared in the *Gentleman's Magazine* in 1830, where he joined others in a series of miscellaneous essays headlined "Stray Thoughts on Language."

> Since the use of language is to communicate our thoughts to each other, I think that the language which is the most perspicuous (the most easily understood), and the most simple (the most easily learnt), is the best. But if we use ten thousand borrowed words, of which an Englishman has to learn the meaning and sound, instead of as many English ones, of which he knows the meaning and sound without seeking them, we make our language less perspicuous and simple, and consequently less excellent. It may be said that the borrowed words are understood by well-educated people, which I will allow to some extent; but they are critically understood by those only who know the languages from which they are borrowed; and it is no commendation to the English tongue, to say that one must learn three or four others to understand it. ("Dilettante" 1830, 501)

To the argument that borrowed words fill gaps in English, Barnes replied that compounds can be formed from native elements that will supply the necessity for innovation. Borrowing, he wrote, is a "proof of national inferiority" (as though English people found their own language inadequate to their purposes); "it renders our language less simple, less perspicuous, less pure, less regular, and fit only for learned people to converse with each other in" (502); it also wastes the time of the young who are obliged to learn words instead of facts. To amend these faults, he proposed that existing borrowed words be replaced by old words revived or by innovations from native sources. Thus *ornithology* "should be" *birdlore*, an *ornithologist* a *birdloreman*, and *ornithological* replaced by *birdlearned*. A *laboratory* would better be called a *workstead* and an *aviary* a *birdstead*. At the conclusion of his brief essay, Barnes declared:

> . . . I hope these observations will meet the eyes of some scholars who may be
> better able, and no less willing than I am, to stop the contemptible system of
> *Gallicising, Latinizing* and *Hellenizing* our language, now so extremely com-
> mon, that it is likely to make it in a few years a medly understood *critically*
> only by a few professors of the dead and living languages. (503)

These ideas continued to animate Barnes's writing for the next half century.

In a schoolbook published in 1869, Barnes carried his theorizing into
practice by using words of Germanic origin in place of conventional Latin-
Romance vocabulary (e.g., *inbringing* from *importation*, *landfolk* for *people*).

> English has become a more mongrel speech by the needless inbringing of words
> from Latin, Greek, and French, instead of words which might have been found
> in its older form, or in the speech of landfolk over all England, or might have
> been formed from its own roots and stems, as wanting words have been formed
> in German and other purer tongues.
>
> Thence English has become so much harder to learn, that, in its foreign-
> worded fulness, it is a speech only for the more learned, and foreign to un-
> schooled men, so that the sermon and book are half lost to their minds: whereas
> in Tuscany and in the west of Ireland, or in Wales, the speech of the upper ranks
> is that of the cottage, and the well-worded book of the higher mind needs no
> list of hard words to open its meaning to the lower. (Barnes 1869, 101)

In all of these writings, Barnes was a strenuous advocate of the "speech of
landfolk," and so he praised the "Saxon" terms applied by working men who
built the tramways and railways and deplored the innovations "when the
railway was taken into the hands of more learned men" and *terminus* was
employed instead of "rail-end, or way-end, or outending" (105–6). When
ordinary people attend church services—a special concern for Barnes since
he had managed, through sacrifice and struggle, to obtain a divinity degree
from Cambridge and ordination in the Church of England—"the Latin and
Greek mingled-speech of the pulpit is often one ground on which the poor
leave their church, where the preaching is, as they call it, too high for them"
(106). In later works on *speech-craft* 'grammar' and *rede-craft* 'logic,' Barnes's usage became even more painstakingly nativist; for instance, for *proper
noun* he substituted *one-head thing-name* and for *hypothetical proposition*
the term *fore-begged thought-putting*.

Like Verstegan before him, Barnes failed to win favor for his innovations, but his appeal to "purity" in English met with considerable favor.

(Thus in reviews of his *Speech–Craft*, critics approved of his attempt to "deal a blow at some of the blunders and absurdities of modern English speech" and suggested that readers "will have a kindly feeling for the chivalrous attempt which is made . . . to preserve the purity of our mother tongue" [quoted in Baron 1982a, 36].) William Morris and Gerard Manley Hopkins both experimented poetically with "Saxon" elements in English vocabulary and prosody, and the emerging practice of instructing the young in English composition established ideas about "Latinate" and "Anglo-Saxon" English that still persist. Thus Barnes proposed ideals that were founded on democratic ideas.

Less extreme improvers continued to work along the lines of Barnes's argument that the Germanic portion of the English vocabulary is meritorious and the Latin-Romance flawed. Plain, blunt, short words give everyone a doorway to English; complex, abstract, and arcane words reflect a desire to obfuscate. Reduced to this simplistic contrast, Barnes's proposals continue to be influential, even if his neologisms are mostly forgotten. The opposing position, however, was often articulated, and critics argued that hard words are necessary for hard thoughts. In 1839, Thomas De Quincey wrote in response to theories like Barnes's:

> Let us recognise with thankfulness that fortunate inheritance of collateral wealth which, by inoculating our Anglo-Saxon stem with the mixed dialect of Neustria, laid open an avenue mediately through which the whole opulence of Roman, and ultimately of Grecian, thought plays freely through the pulses of our native English. (De Quincey 1889–90, 14:151)

In a similar effort in 1874, Fitzedward Hall scorned such saxonizing as "Retrogressive English."

> Is a word derived to us from the Anglo-Saxon, or from Scandinavia, intrinsically better than a word which we owe to the Latin? Those there are who unhesitatingly deem it to be so; yet of reason in support of their preference we have never discovered so much as a shadow. The one may deserve the option, or the other may deserve it, according to circumstances, but on this ground only. Try as we might, we could not turn the Latin, Greek, and Keltic out of our speech. Our lingual hybridism is ineradicable. And what if it is! Was the Anglo-Saxon invented by autochthones who lived in a happy corner by themselves, uncontaminated by the talk of their neighbours? Latin is a composite, Greek is a composite, Sanskrit is a composite. So is English; and, solely from being the completest mongrel of all, it is the most expressive of all. (Hall 1874, 327)

This argument for the excellence of English was not an attempt to improve the language but a celebration of it as it then existed. Yet the fact that hybridism had to be defended against the proponents of native purity shows the force of Barnes's arguments and the influence of others who followed him at least part way down the path he established for improving the language.

With the mid-nineteenth-century idea that English was becoming a world language, writers began to propose reforms that would facilitate its spread. Most of the alterations were directed at the spelling system on the familiar grounds that foreign learners would acquire English quickly and that a more phonetic spelling would speed them in their learning. As efficiency became an obsession for the commercially minded, the time-consuming task of learning to read and write English once again struck proposers as a reason for reforming the language. The benefits to be achieved by language change were great indeed, and arguments on behalf of one and another still-born scheme continued well into the twentieth century.

1870.

Objekts: Too fasil·itait Lerning too Reed,
            Too maik Lerning too Spel unneces·eseri,
            Too asim·ilait Reeding and Reiting too Heerring and Speeking,
            Too maik dhi Risee·vd Proanunsiai·shen
            ov Ingglish akses·ibl too *aul* Reederz,
            Proavin·shel and Foren.

Meenz: Leev dhi Oald Speling untuch·t
            Introadeu·s along·seid ov dhi Oald Speling
            a Neu Aurthog·rafi, konsis·ting ov dhi
            Oald Leterz euzd invai·rriabli in dhair
            best noan sensez.
              Emploi· dhi Neu Speling in Skoolz too
            Teech Reeding in *boath* Aurthog·rafiz.
                      (A. J. Ellis; quoted in Zachrisson 1931–32,15–16)

1894. Let the philological associations therefore, which have hitherto made so little progress in the attempt to reform our spelling, try the experiment of some reform in pronunciation as a preliminary step, by insisting on the true names of the vowels, and by publishing a list of words in which the true and proper force of the vowels, where perverted, may be profitably restored. And without waiting for such a list, let educated men, in whom a new pronunciation will not be ascribed to illiteracy, at once begin the reform. The seeming confusion which would thus be produced would be, in reality, the first step toward a true and permanent order in our own language, and would also bring the promise of ending the confusion of Babel for the nations of the earth. (Porter 1894, 130)

1928. Key-Way was originated by the writer who now offers it to all mankind, confident its ultimate adoption will lead to world unity, international understanding and co-operation, and through these avenues aid in bringing the human race into the ways of universal peace, progress and happiness. . . .

Key-Way English is a new world-wide language and intercommunicating epoch marking service of general utility; designed to promote intellectual, social and moral intercourse and so increase the friendship and welfare of all mankind.

It is a new and distinctive system of simple marks intended to supercede all other language symbols. The code consists of only five plain marks called keys, which perfectly represent every letter and numeral used to write, type, print and figure, and to convey thoughts by means of the English language.

If true, as doubtless it is, that languages are the economic bonds which bind the people of nations together, why would not one language equally as well and economically serve to bind all nations and peoples of the world together? Misunderstandings between nations using different languages are often the cause of wars. The people of one nation and language are intolerant of the people of another, and act toward each other with suspicion, prejudice and jealousy, quite differently from what they would if all used only one language. Different languages create endless confusion, lack of confidence and even hate; these are only a few of the many objectionable things Key-Way English aims to remedy. (Irish 1928, 5, 9)

1928. While English is spreading rapidly throughout the world, it is the opinion of experts in several countries that the language, if left to itself, will degenerate into dialects in foreign countries, especially in the East. Hence,

World English, a simplified English, which will in no way affect Standard English, is essential for the protection of the purity of our language; in addition to its need as the universal auxiliary lingual medium—a secondary language for all nations. (Hamilton 1928, 3)

1929. This is only the beginning. Owning the copyrights and controlling the "Änjelika" affairs over the entire world, the accruing profits will make this movement a mighty influence and power for righteousness, purity, unity[,] peace, and harmony among men. The "Änjelika" movement will become a universal blessing, as the English speaking peoples are the most enlightened and advanced in civilization, science and culture in the world today. . . .

Adopting the regenerated English, attired in modern apparel, we have at least fifty percent or one-half of Hebrew origin, which leads us back to our original mother tongue, spoken by God to our first parents, Adam and Eve; and used by Father Abraham in prayer and conversation, by the poet David when he sang, and by our Saviour in his sermon on the mount, and by the apostle Peter in that great sermon on the day of Pentecost.

This fact should and will arouse enthusiasm among all denominations for its adoption and speedy dissemination all over the world. Just think, how easy and delightful our missionary endeavors will be and our intercourse in conferences and assemblies among the denominations and nationalities all over the whole world, when a universal language has come into general use. (Hallner 1929, 11, 30)

1946. The experiences of the last four years have sharpened the recognition by all peoples that there is a world requirement, which it would be folly in the extreme to neglect further. They must be given the power of readily learning and understanding, the wants, wishes and hopes of races with whom they must co-operate, if world peace is to be placed on a secure basis. They must be provided with a means of discussion and of personal approach, common to all. (Barr 1946, 3)

1947. The above figures [estimating savings accruing from a reformed writing system] refer to this country, excluding Eire. In the case of the United States, its population is about three times that of this country, whilst the consumption of paper per head is infinitely greater—consider the size of the newspapers, including the huge Sunday editions and the size of magazines, made bulky by the numerous and large advertisements in them. To put the saving for the United States at £360,000,000 or $1,440,000,000 per annum, being four times that for Great Britain, is reasonable. (Ridge-Beedle 1947, 37)

1955. The conventional English is the language that is used mostly throughout the world, and I believe that if we meet the rest of the peoples part-way, with a simplified form, the English language can soon become the language of the world.

Anyone who uses *Simplify-ed English* can be easily understood by those who speak only the conventional language.

Simplify-ed English is so easy that the English speaking people can learn it in one day.

When speaking, you follow eight rules; when writing, you follow twelve rules.

A simple international language can save us much time and trouble. It would facilitate world trade, increase traveling, help eradicate race hatred, and maintain peace. (Fiumedoro 1955, 1)

Such have been the various claims brought forward in support of a reformed and improved English. The imagined benefits have been enlarged, and the trouble attendant on change minimized. Though many of these efforts were little regarded, modern opinion has spasmodically favored the idea that *something* be done.

In the nineteenth century, spelling reform gained impetus from the phonetic shorthand developed by Isaac Pitman (1813–1897) and publicized through *Stenographic Shorthand* (1837) and many popular works including an edition of the New Testament. Such efforts led naturally in the direction of revised alphabets for English, which Pitman believed would facilitate "the education of the poor" (Scragg 1974, 108). In 1869, the Philological Society endorsed the principle that reform was desirable, and in 1879 the British Spelling Reform Association was founded and attracted the support of eminent literary and political figures. Prominent scholars expressed support with varying degrees of warmth—J. A. H. Murray, Walter W. Skeat, Henry Sweet, all of whom were founders of "scientific" English philology. In 1906, the Simplified Spelling Board was incorporated in the United States with a substantial endowment from Andrew Carnegie and with public endorsement from Theodore Roosevelt, Samuel Clemens, and other luminaries. Much of the activity of these organizations—Americans were served by the Simplified Spelling Society and the Spelling Reform Association in addition to the Board—consisted of public declarations of the benefits to be derived from one or another of the many systems. (Carnegie himself eventually became disillusioned with the society's expansive banquets, speeches, and disputes among the various factions of the movement; the administrators of his endowment terminated their support in 1931.) The writings of the many warring proposers illustrate the almost limitless optimism that animated discussions about reform, and new orthographic systems were presented time and again to an indifferent public under such names as Glossic, Dimidiun, Romo, Anglic, Nue Speling, Regularized Inglish, Britic, Cut Spelling, and Shavian (named for George Bernard Shaw, who left a bequest to fund the design of a new alphabet). In 1886, the American Philological Society and the Philological Society of London endorsed a list of three hundred newly spelled words, and in 1893 the Modern Language Association of America added its approval (Baron 1982b). Virtually none of these proposed words achieved any considerable currency, though the *Chicago Tribune* espoused and employed its own list of "modernized" spellings from 1935 until the 1950s (Mencken 1967, 490–91).

In Britain, the acme of the spelling reformers' efforts came in 1953, when the House of Commons voted 65 to 53 in favor of a private member's bill introduced by Mont Follick (1888–1958) in collaboration with James Pitman, designer of the Initial Teaching Alphabet and grandson of Isaac Pitman (whose proposals began the modern debate on the subject). This legislation urged that an alternative alphabet be introduced in schools to hasten the task of learning to read and write. Its sponsors eventually withdrew the bill, after extensive debate, on the assurance from the Minister of Education that she would offer "her interest, good will and good wishes" in support of research investigating the efficacy of such systems. Though little came of this effort in the financially austere years of the early 1950s, Pitman's *i.t.a.* did enjoy some popularity in schools in the 1960s, before vanishing from most primary reading programs.

Mont Follick was a representative Edwardian figure, full of imaginative schemes to add the final touches to the perfection of English established in the Victorian era. His revisions to English grammar (treated on pp. 204–5) were breath-taking in their audacity, and the flavor of his personality emerges in his description of the first blossoming of his ideas.

> We have a language here which is spread throughout the world. What is the only thing holding up the English language from becoming the universal language, the *lingua franca* of the whole world? It is the spelling.
>
> . . . I started this [campaign for reform] in 1908. I remember walking up the esplanade, at Biarritz, with Bernard Shaw and outlining my idea to him. We were almost on the verge of war even then, and I said, "If we had English as an international language, it would wipe out all this argument of war." Bernard Shaw asked me how I proposed to do it, and I replied, "By altering the spelling." Upon which his comment was, "You poor idiot!" Since then Bernard Shaw himself has become convinced of it, but he wants to go further, he wants to scrap the alphabet and introduce 42 symbols. I want to maintain the alphabet. I have told him that what he wants to do is impossible. What he is talking about may come to pass in another two centuries.
>
> Mine was a lone voice in the world in 1908, but now there are thousands of us—millions of us—all thinking along the same lines. (Follick 1946, 12, 14)

Perhaps overly optimistic about the zeal and number of his followers, Follick continued his campaigns for reform with undiminished ardor until the end of his life. Like Shaw, he left a bequest to support continued efforts in the direction of spelling reform, an obligation somewhat uneasily accepted by the University of Manchester.

Though spelling has almost always been seen as the ugliest of the blemishes that mar the image of English, other notorious aspects of the language have been considered to need remedy. Less impressed than Britons by the need to keep the language of Shakespeare and Milton alive, Americans have been more audacious in suggesting alterations. Among the most extreme proposals were those offered by Elias Molee, born in Wisconsin in

1845 where he "grew up among American, German, Irish and Scandinavian neighbors" (1888, 11). This youthful experience of multilingualism eventually convinced him of the need for a "union" language that he described in a third-person memoir.

> Wherever he found in any of the other languages some feature in which he thought it excelled the English, he longed to see it appropriated by his adopted language, the English. We are here building up an American nationality out of elements contributed by various nations. It will be a grand nation. Why cannot our language also draw to itself the best features of allied tongues and conquer the world? (1888, 12)

To effect this purpose, Molee proposed three alterations: a phonetic spelling, replacement of Latin-Romance words by revived English or newly borrowed Germanic vocabulary, and "the largest possible regularity of grammar." The resulting perfected language he called variously *Amerikan* (1888), *Germanic-English* (1888), *Pure Saxon English* (1890), *Tutonish* (1902), and *Altutonish* (1911). In addition to his energetic pamphleteering, Molee translated Ibsen's *Doll's House* into his language; the title of one of his works captures the essence of his proposals (quoted here verbatim): *"Altutonish (pangerman): ein (a) union spiek (language), makn up of deuch, english, skandinavish & hollandi, for to agenferein (reunite) al tutonish folka (people) into ein spiek mitin (within) feivte (50) jiera (years)."* Though alleging himself to be "more conservative than reformers as a class" (1888, 16), Molee offered proposals that were unusually extensive (see Baron 1982a, 39–43, and 1982b, 182–86).

Molee's motives for his new language were nationalistic (in his wish for a distinctive new language for the United States), racist (in his belief that "the pure German, Scandinavian and Irish" [27] were superior to the English), and practical (in his eagerness to save the time and money wasted in teaching and writing). Like Barnes, he was persuaded that English discriminates against those who do not know the Greek and Latin and that "present English is [the] poor child's enemy."

> It looks to me as if the English language were constructed by some eccentric, rich and learned bachelors who had nothing else to do but hunt up the meaning of words in dictionaries and to spell. It is remarkable that so busy people should have so time-wasting language. England has had too little sympathy with the middle classes. So unsympathetic a language cannot go unpunished. The result

will be comparative degradation. The United States will not always have a virgin soil, England cannot always live on the sweets of other lands. Germany, Russia and China, with their self-explaining, understanding-helping and memory-helping languages, which they are continually systematizing and enriching, will before long leave us behind with our wheat, corn, hogs, railroads, money bags and incomprehensible words and regard us as Indian princes for our wealth. The world is marching away from the English and Turkish principle of borrowing foreign and unrelated words. A race-feeling is being awakened in all great peoples, which partly manifests itself in language purification. Will it not pay for us Americans also to purify and systematize? (1888, 56)

Molee's reforms were systematic ones and covered all the domains of English he found defective: spelling, pronunciation, vocabulary, and grammar. Like others who have attempted to improve the language, he had the good of the community uppermost in mind: "I desire the American people to be more independent and to strike out for themselves in language and literature, as our forefathers did in government" (289).

A similar mania for improvement energized the efforts of W. Jones Cuthbertson, self-declared Secretary of the World Language Society, headquartered in San Francisco. Like so many others, he saw the unstable social order in Europe following the First World War as an opportunity for enduring reforms and the adoption of a common language. Like Molee, he was motivated by democratic impulses. Scientists, he noted, had established a "worldwide language" through nomenclature derived from classical sources, but the object of language improvement should affect "the great uneducated mass."

> For whom are we to make this language? For the great mass of the World's people or for a few thinkers? We say, decidedly for the great mass of the people; otherwise it cannot become a GENERAL language.
>
> For these people we want an easy, very simple, short, we might say an inartistic language: one easily understood and pickt up by the great uneducated mass, who are too ignorant to go into the intricacies of scientific grammar or into subtle shades of meanings of words and affixes. We want a Tongue that can be spoken by Chinese, Finns, Lascars, Arabs, and Negros as well as by all the Aryan peoples, and be able to be written by the Stenografers of all nationalities. (1919, 8)

The proposed language to satisfy these conditions he called GAB. In many of its features, GAB suggests that Cuthbertson had an imperfect knowledge of Pidgin (e.g., *sabe* 'understand; used on both sides of the Pacific,' *me luvd* for *I loved* and *me b luvd* for *I was loved*) and a respect for American colloquial expressions (e.g., *bust* 'explode,' *brer* 'brother,' *eets* 'meals,' *gal* 'girl,' *get me* 'comprehend my idea,' *git* 'to make oneself scarce,' and *unc* 'uncle' [all Cuthbertson's glosses]). Though somewhat apologetic about the "uncouthness and rudeness of GAB," Cuthbertson was eager to "push it along" so it could fulfill the need for a world language. What would be accomplished, he thought, was "bringing all the Peoples in touch with one another, annihilating distances and thus doing away with dislikes and prejudices due to isolation" (28).

The same impulse toward international democracy motivated the proposals of William Arthur (1860–1945), a prosperous Nebraska building contractor who had, in 1905, written a futuristic pamphlet on the shape of an "ideal city" and was thoroughly infected with utopian idealism. Like Molee and Cuthbertson, he believed that the learned had alienated ordinary people from their own language.

> The great dictionary of Oxford got as far as the letter E in thirty years. It is past sh in 1920. For 99 percent of the English-speaking people it is useless and will be so when it reaches Z. "Learning" has betrayed the millions of children who spend only a few years in school and have to waste two of them learning to spell. What to them are manuscript Bibles or Oxford dictionaries with 450,000 words? The dead learning of the universities, the meanness of their conduct, must be brushed aside and way made for the COMMON PEOPLE. We do not respect a glutton who gorges himself while hungry people surround his table; the time must come when the intellectual glutton will be even more despised. On condition that bread and butter are given to all he may eat all the pie, pastry and pate de foie gras he pleases, but not otherwise. The dangerous autocracy of Germany made great progress because, with all its faults and crimes, it stood for and used modern scientific methods and paid less attention to Virgil and Aristotle and Homer than the leaders in some other countries. But as if to show that literacy by itself without a moral curb may be used for deviltry, we saw Germany present us with 1914 to 1918, and nearly every German can read.
>
> If this world English crusade means anything at all, it stands for 99 per cent of the people and gives scorn for scorn to bigoted, selfish "learning." We need thinkers and doers instead of memories that grope among the dead. "Mummies will keep; they are well preserved men."
>
> So much the greater honor to the university forces, there and here, who stood for and worked for a modern English in the past. In doing this they were working to defeat Germany before 1914, so far as language goes—and that is further than many think. (Arthur 1920, 9–10)

Arthur's pamphlet seems not to have reached a wide audience, but the sentiments he expressed were very much representative of a generation of Americans enraged by the carnage of the Great War and the betrayal of democracy achieved through language bigotry.

In Britain, the democratic impulse was less fervid at the opening of the twentieth century, but the notion that language change might facilitate commerce was a popular one, later enlarged into a belief that an international language would prevent warfare. Mont Follick's spelling reforms were motivated by these ideas, but having tinkered he gained confidence and proposed to rebuild language from its foundation. His espousal of linguistic improvement continued as he became a prosperous proprietor of an English-language school in London. He was particularly distressed by the difficulties that foreign learners encountered in acquiring English. In a book written in 1914, though not published until 1934, he proclaimed familiar arguments that English could only be fitted for universal use with a reformed spelling and when "all superfluous grammatical modifications" are done away with and "irregularities . . . substituted by regular formations" (1934, 179). The task was, he declared, "to reduce the English language to pidgin-English, or scientifically to raise pidgin-English to the dignity of a language" (179).

Following a lengthy critique of English grammar, Follick proposed two strategies for improvement, one "radical," the other "moderate."

The radical one would be as follows:—
(1) *Articles:* Suppression of both [definite and indefinite articles].
(2) *Nouns:* Do away with plurals [e.g., *six book*] and reform feminine [by the use of *-ess, gentlemaness*]. Suppression of the Saxon genitive (possessive case) [e.g., *the books of the man*].
(3) *Pronouns:* Do away with cases [e.g., *me* for *I, me, my, myself, mine*]. Suppression of genders [e.g., *he* for *he, she, it, his, hers, him, her*]. Change *this* into *thit*. Suppress *so* and *one* as pronouns; also *some, no,* and *none*.
(4) *Adjectives:* Rectify some numbers that are different from the rest [e.g., *twoten* for *twelve, twoty* for *twenty*]. Arrange the degrees of comparison [e.g., *good, more good, most good* for *good, better, best*]. Suppress *many* and *little*.
(5) *Verbs:* Suppression of imperfect and future [e.g., *I see it yesterday* for *I saw it yesterday; I go tomorrow* for *I shall go tomorrow*]. Do away with the forms *shall* and *should*. Suppression of the subjunctive and all the persons of the imperative mood except the second [e.g., *Take it* for *Let us take it, Let him take it*]. Use gerund without preposition [e.g., *I can*

break the chalk stepping on it]. Use of the present infinitive without the preposition *to* [e.g., *See is believe* for *To see is to believe*]. Present infinitive to be used as verbal noun instead of gerund [e.g., *See is believe* for *Seeing is believing*]. Reform the verbs *to be* and *to have* [by reducing drastically their variant forms]. Complete verbs *must* and *can* [e.g., *I can do it* for *I am able to do it* and *I must do it* for *I am obliged to do it*]. Suppress the verbs *may* and *do*. Suppress *s* in present tense. Make the termination of the past participle uniform (*ed, d, t*) [e.g., *breaked* for *broken*].

(6) *Adverbs:* Do away with the use of pure adjectives as pure adverbs, and pure adverbs as pure adjectives. Do away with the use of *well* with verb *to be*. Suppression of the word *yet*. Position of adverb in sentence to be fixed.

(7) *Conjunctions:* Suppress *either, neither, whether*, and *both* (in the disjunctives *both—and*). Change *than* into *that* or *as*.

(8) *Prepositions:* Do away with the use of adverbs and prepositions in equal form. Use of prepositions with present infinitive instead of with gerund. Do away with *so as to* and *in order to* as reinforcements of the infinitive. Suppress either *by* or *for*. Preposition *of* not to govern possessive case.

But [Follick writes in a startling departure from the direction of change just proposed], before and above all, every part of speech should have its own particular distinguishing feature. It should have either a prefix or suffix to distinguish it from the other parts of speech. (1934, 237–38; examples supplied from elsewhere in his book)

The zeal for this extraordinary reform of English grammar was founded in idealism captivated by consistency. Follick hoped that this transformation in which everything would be made clear by "its own distinguishing feature" would improve the language sufficiently to eliminate difficulties for foreign learners and redound to their advantage and to that of the language. What he did not appreciate was that his consistent and unchanging structure was unlike any known human language.

England's closest approach to an institutionalized academy came in another of the Edwardian attempts to improve English. As early as 1900, Robert Bridges (1844–1930)—selected Poet Laureate in 1913—began linguistic conversations with Henry Bradley, the coeditor of the *OED*. Bridges was convinced that English was in "a condition of advancing decay" (1910, 49) and alarmed that "decay is always pushing in, because of the laziness of the speaker" (48). Like other self-appointed improvers of English, Bridges thought that something could be done to reverse the decline of the language by adopting "a good-looking phonetic alphabet" that he concocted from some characters of his own invention and from "an old Anglo-Saxon fount [sic], which was lying disused at the Clarendon Press" (52). In 1913, Bridges founded the Society for Pure English, but its flowering was delayed for the duration of the war. When publication of its "tracts" commenced in 1919, Bridges had attracted a distinguished roster of members, mainly from the British universities but including poets and politicians (among them the prime minister, A. J. Balfour). A full, distinct statement of the society's purpose was delayed until Bridges finally completed a tract on "The Society's Work" in 1925. *Pure* did not, he asserted, mean "*Teutonic*, as William Barnes would have intended it" (3), but he was oblique in defining what it did mean. Nonetheless, as the use of *tract* for its pamphlets implied, the society arose from moral earnestness and the belief that the perilous state of the language "is a substantial imperious fact that entails a vast responsibility and imposes on our humanity the duty to do what we can to make our current speech as good a means as possible for the intercommunication of ideas" (4).

Having reviewed the possible defects of the language (including "the chance that the overruling dialect was not the one that in certain particulars had attained the best solution" [4]), Bridges pointed to the peril for English posed by "other-speaking races."

> It would seem that no other language can ever have had its central force so dissipated—and even this does not exhaust the description of our special peril, because there is furthermore this most obnoxious condition, namely, that wherever our countrymen are settled abroad there are alongside of them communities of other-speaking races, who, maintaining among themselves their native speech, learn yet enough of ours to mutilate it, and establishing among themselves all kinds of blundering corruptions, through habitual intercourse infect therewith the neighbouring English. We can see this menace without any guess as to what may come of it, and in the United States, where it is most evident, it is natural that despair should encourage a blind optimism, expressed—as I redd [a spelling reform Bridges continued to employ with Bradley's approbation] it in the *New York Times*—in some such jaunty phrase as this, that *the old Lady may be trusted to take care of herself*. But, whatever sort of speech might naturally arise, it is extremely unlikely that the unknown accidental linguistic profits would outbalance the calculable loss. (5)

Despite his prescriptive views, Bridges attracted the most eminent academic philologists to his society, and their contributions dominate the tracts, even though the founder did not always agree with their penchant for uncensorious description. What he most approved were the writings of H. W. Fowler, "an instinctive grammatical moralizer" (a label applied by Otto Jespersen and happily accepted by Fowler [1927b, 193]).

While Logan Pearsall Smith generously attributed the entire management of the society to Bridges in his memorial notice (1931, 500), Bradley was clearly a moderating influence on what was published in the tracts and an anchor to Bridges's impulses for linguistic reform. Ironically, in light of Bridges's initial ideas, the society eventually published William A. Craigie's *Problems of Spelling Reform* (1944), an effective argument laying out the futility of the enterprise. Thus Bridges's anxieties were effectively dismissed, at least for academic linguists, just before the society was brought to an end.

The ideals that the society espoused were those of the previous century: foreign borrowings should be rapidly adjusted to English pronunciation if they were to be admitted at all; new terms should be formed from native elements, not from Greek or Latin; "a uniform and town-bred standard of speech" was snuffing out rural dialects whose disappearance was a matter for regret; in pronunciation, English people should "protect as far as possible the old harmonious cadences of our traditional speech" (Society for Pure English 1919, 7–10). The prospectus of 1913 elevates the folk at the expense of the learned.

> Now, believing that language is or should be democratic both in character and origin, and that its best word-makers are the uneducated, and not the educated classes, we would prefer the vivid popular terms to the artificial creations of scientists. (1919, 9)

Virtually none of the tracts dealt with these professed themes of the society, and nothing was heard from (or about) the English of the uneducated. Instead, Bridges and his collaborators expressed a political position on language issues: suspicion about Americans and "other-speaking races"; contempt for scientific vocabulary; and delight in worrying minute questions (such as sentence-ending prepositions or the "fused participle," which animated several tracts). The *New York Times* regarded the work of the society as "addressed mainly and reproachfully to the newspapers" ("To Journalists" 1923, 22). When a group of Britons and Americans sympathetic to the Society's ends proposed an international body to foster "the ideal of a single standard language for all English-speaking peoples" (Grattan 1927, 431), Bridges sabotaged the idea (Smith 1931, 497–98).

Before long, opposition to the society arose in another quarter. Writing a tract of his own, *Impenetrability, or The Proper Habit of English*, Robert Graves asserted:

> The "Society for Pure English," recently formed by the Poet Laureate, is getting a good deal of support at this moment, and is the literary equivalent of political Fascism. But at no period have the cultured classes been able to force the habit of tidiness on the nation as a whole. Ben Jonsons, John Drydens, Alexander Popes, Joseph Addisons, Samuel Johnsons, and Matthew Arnolds have only succeeded in civilising the outer crust of the national hasty-pudding. The imaginative genius of the uneducated and half-educated masses will not be denied expression. (Graves 1926, 30–31)

With Bridges's death in 1930, the society began to recede from public notice. Nonetheless, it served for a generation as a forum for serious discussion of linguistic questions. What began with Bridges's impulse toward an "aesthetic phonetic script" ended with the modern conviction—articulated religiously by most academic linguists—that what people say about language is mostly nonsense and what they do with it is beyond effective intervention or improvement. Language change, in this view, flows according to strong currents deep within the language; it is a process of impersonal "drift."

Not all linguistic improvers were impractical dreamers, though that is an impression easily gained from reading many of their proposals. In 1929, moved by a similar sense of urgency that motivated other reformers of his time, C. K. Ogden (1889–1957) completed a plan for "Basic English" to achieve two purposes.

> 1. To serve as an international auxiliary language; that is to say, a second language for use throughout the world in general communication, commerce, and science.
> 2. To provide a rational introduction to normal English; both as a first step, complete in itself, for those whose natural language is not English, and as a grammatical introduction, encouraging clarity of thought and expression, for English-speaking peoples at any state of proficiency. (1934, 4)

The expanded name for Basic reveals the scope of Ogden's plan: British American Scientific International Commercial English. Like most other proposers, Ogden stressed that his version of English was "not unduly revolutionary," and he declined to enter the debate about spelling reform while expressing sympathy for the reformers. The key to his argument was simplicity: a vocabulary of 850 ordinary English words and a grammar so simple that "the entire conjugation of verb-forms and pronouns occupies a single page" (5).

Unlike many others, Ogden was an effective promoter of his system. Operating from the Orthological Institute he founded in Cambridge, he soon issued a series of pamphlets promoting his copyrighted system, produced textbooks, compiled a dictionary (with equivalents of full-scale English in Basic), and issued "translations" of stories, periodical essays, business letters, political discussions, and *Stories from the Bible*. He even provided a patented *panopticon* or "word wheel" to allow learners to arrange simple sentences by rotating the concentric disks on which words were printed. As Noah Webster had done so effectively before him, Ogden solicited endorsements from public figures in Britain and abroad, and they expressed great enthusiasm for the system. H. G. Wells, in *The Shape of Things to Come* (1933), even projected a future in which Basic was the decisive factor in the spread of English; Wells optimistically estimated that Basic made "it possible for any person from another country who had a ready memory to get to the point of talking and writing quite good English in two or three weeks" (quoted in Ogden 1934, 299).

Ogden combined a desire for reform with considerable ability as a promoter and the drive to sustain his campaign. He found financial support from foundations and enthusiastic helpers in many countries. But more important than the talents that carried him forward in such practical matters was solid intellectual grounding arising from his long and thoughtful interest in international communication, one begun while he was still an undergraduate at Cambridge. He had visited schools in Europe, India, and the United States, and in 1923 produced a philosophical work on the relation of language to thought, *The Meaning of Meaning*. His collaborator in that volume, I. A. Richards, joined him in the preparation and publicity of Basic. In *Basic English and Its Uses* (1943), Richards expounded the ideology of simplified English for use in a postwar world. Striking a patriotic chord, Richards reminded his readers that Rudolph Hess had predicted that English would become "a minor Germanic dialect of no world importance" once the Nazis had established the thousand-year Reich (23). Richards's very different idea of a pacific world was fully articulated in a vision of future human communication in which Basic English played a crucial role without disturbing the sensibilities of "those of us who are born to the language of Shakespeare and Milton" (6). Richards was too tactful, and too sensitive to prevailing opinion, to declare in 1943 what Ogden had written a decade earlier: "What the World needs most is about 1,000 more dead languages—and one more alive" (Ogden 1934, 18).

Critics of Basic English found that some of the claims made for simplification were exaggerated. *Today* could hardly be excluded from the 850-word vocabulary on the grounds that it consisted of the Basic words *to* and *day*; nor could *well-off* be fairly claimed to combine the Basic elements *well* and *off* (examples from Aiken 1933). As a result of Ogden's attempt to reduce polysemous words, Basic is relatively impoverished in verbs (or "names of operations" as Ogden chose to call them); thus *I take an interest in fiction* is the Basic equivalent of "I am interested in fiction" (1934, 102), and *We get money for a living* of "We earn money for a living" (95). He was particularly chary of verbs with contradictory senses (like *want*), and, while the resulting paraphrases were sometimes cumbersome (for instance, "She has a desire for work"), they were usually unambiguous. Though Basic lacks the bizarre qualities of most kinds of "improved" English, the paraphrases in Basic seem occasionally forced: *milk-vessel* (= breast), *putting a body (dead person) under the earth* (= funeral), *yellow flower powder* (= pollen) (see Ogden 1932). While native speakers have trouble limiting themselves to the rigid rules of Basic, the prose written in it is not drastically different from that of "normal" English as long as routine subjects are under consideration. For scientific English, Ogden merely proposed incorporating "a large vocabulary of completely international technical words, operated stylistically by the 850 words of Basic" (Ogden 1931, 17).

With Richards's help, Ogden provided a vehicle for many people to learn English and to gain confidence in their ability to comprehend English texts. Primarily a transitional teaching language for nonanglophone learners, Basic was a successful improvement for that specific purpose. Ogden's claim that it would also encourage "clarity of thought and expression for English-speaking peoples at any state of proficiency," however, did not arouse much interest from the public, though George Orwell observed in 1944 that Basic "can act as a sort of corrective to the oratory of statesmen and publicists. High-sounding phrases," he wrote, "when translated into Basic, are often deflated in a surprising way" (Orwell and Angus 1970, 3:244).

The desire for improvement in English has not diminished since Basic English achieved popularity, though Basic is no longer fashionable and few eminent scholars or public figures espouse spelling reform, as did so many of their counterparts from 1870 to 1930. If schemes to reform and improve the language have diminished, it is partly the result of the belief that English is already the universal language and that no special provisions need be made for children (who still find learning to read difficult) or for the foreign (whose languages tend more and more to be regarded with indifference or irritation). Even so, new proposals occasionally emerge. In 1981, Randolph Quirk mooted the idea of "Nuclear English" as yet another means of encouraging nonnative speakers to learn the language (Quirk 1982, 37–53). Its principal feature involves the avoidance of "the most frequent items . . . since they are the most polysemous" (45). Quirk's simplifications concentrate on the grammatical system, particularly on relative clauses and the mood system of the verb phrase, but nothing is allowed that would have to be unlearned as students move from Nuclear to full-scale English. Like Ogden and Richards, Quirk does not wish to distress the sensibilities of native speakers with his innovations. What is most striking, however, is his departure from the usual idea that English needs to be altered as a means of bringing foreigners into the English-language community.

> The emblematic consumers of Nuclear English should not be seen as Indonesian children in a village school room, but as Italian and Japanese company directors engaged in negotiating an agreement. (44)

What is different in this "emblematic" situation is that the participants in the discourse where Nuclear English is used are not anglophones. Virtually all earlier proposals were designed to bring foreigners into communication with English-speaking peoples—in Bullokar's words, to provide an "easie and speedie pathway to all Straungers to vse our Language." Quirk celebrates the idea that these "Straungers" employ "our language" for their own purposes, and it is evidently a source of pride that foreigners use English. (Quirk's idea is not entirely new; in 1940, J. Hubert Jagger wrote with evident satisfaction that "when the foreign ministers of Germany and Italy [von Ribbentrop and Ciano] meet, they find it most convenient to speak to one another in English" [Jagger 1940,127].)

With the idea that English is the undisputed world language, the desire to improve its spelling, vocabulary, or grammar in wholesale ways has consequently diminished. Most of those whose ideas so far have occupied attention in this chapter seem almost comic in their fervor or pitiful in their failure to influence English. Modern conventional wisdom declares that, in a language community as large as English has become, it is impossible for individuals to deflect the direction or impede the pace of linguistic change. In its summary of the efforts of purists, one of the principal histories of the language was at pains "to point out the danger and the futility of trying to prevent the natural developments of language" (Baugh and Cable 1978, 330). Yet quite recent trends in English vocabulary show that sustained and widespread campaigns may not be quite so futile as the conventional academic wisdom maintains.

One such development contrary to the principle of inevitable "natural development" is found in the success of African-Americans in persuading other Americans to shift the vocabulary used to describe them. This trend began with the substitution of formerly derisive *Black* for the long-traditional *Negro*, a change encouraged by the names of such organizations as the *Black Muslims* (first attested in print in 1960) and *Black Panthers* (1965) and the evolution of *Black Nationalism* (1964), *Black Power* (1966), and *Black Studies* (1969). Further attention to the problem of naming resulted in the revival and widespread use of *Afro-American*, (1853), *Aframerican* (1910), and the currently prevalent *African-American*. This example demonstrated to others in pursuit of social change that English (or at least its respectable public use) was not immune to explicit influence. Thus in 1965, the term *sexist* was formed on the model of *racist* (1932), and critics of social discrimination brought forth, in 1968, the term *sexism* on the model of *racism* (1936). (*Racialist* and *racialism* are the prior terms, both coined in this century.)

As the analysis of sexism evolved, language reform became a focal part of the feminist social agenda. The result has been efforts to purge English of male bias and to achieve language that is *inclusive* or *gender-free* in representing male and female. In parallel to African-Americans renaming themselves, feminist language reformers have urged *woman* in place of *girl* (except for female children) and denigrated *lady*, which has been "banned from the approved lexicon" (Maggio 1989, 76). Using *man* and *mankind* to refer to human beings both male and female has been strenuously criticized, and in 1975 job titles were revised in U. S. government statistical documents: *firefighter* for *fireman*, *mailcarrier* for *mailman*, *police officer* for *policeman*, and *supervisor* for *foreman*. Most of these alterations involved popularizing terms already in use, but creativity in reform was not thereby satisfied. Established techniques of English word formation were brought to bear in improving the language: compounding (in such examples as *anchorperson* [1977], *birthname* 'maiden name' [1983], *chairperson* [1971], *craftsperson* [1976], and *humanslaughter* [1983]) and creation (in *herstory* 'history' [1973], *misterectomy* [1987], *Miz* [1972], and *waitron* [1980]). *Wimmin*, though occasionally employed earlier by nonfeminist writers, was reinvented as a spelling to remove *-man* from *women*. Inventions to supply a third-person singular generic pronoun for English—a perennial concern of language improvers since the eighteenth century—added to the eighty already devised: *e, hes, himorher, on, (s)he, s/he, shem, thon,* and many more (see Baron 1986, 190–216). The quest for the singular pronoun, however, continues, for none of the creations has been employed extensively outside the writings of its inventor. Even so, feminist linguistic "improvers" have shaped style guides for many publishers and broadcasters, a development reminiscent of Noah Webster's influence on the nineteenth-century United States.

The ideologies of those who have attempted to improve English have profoundly shaped the climate of opinion about the language and provided a basis for present-day observers to comment on its features. Individually they often offer impracticable solutions to the problems they perceive. But what motivates radical reform has parallels in mainstream thought: anxiety about linguistic change, concern for inefficient spelling conventions, distress about regional and social distinctions expressed through language, hope for making English easier for children and foreign learners, optimism that respect for others can be achieved through vocabulary change.

Looking at these proposals to improve English, one is struck by their frequent absurdities and nearly universal ineffectuality. Only when the ideas for improvement were followed by a concerted campaign to change usage have they had any influence on the image of English. Noteworthy among the sucessful campaigns are those of Noah Webster (with a handful of spelling changes), African-Americans (with a relatively limited linguistic agenda), and contemporary feminists (with a program in support of thought reform through language). Among many revealing calls to action is the following from an American activist, Bobbye D. Sorrels.

> Everyone can bring her or his advocacy of nonsexism to bear on the academic community. Some of us will be asked to write articles for publications affecting the academic community, others will be asked to speak to classes, still others will enroll in classes, and all can write to authors of books, guidelines, manuals, and articles. Through all these avenues we can promote nonsexism. And, though we may sometimes feel lonely as we do so, the results reward our perseverance. A few comments to lecturers and speakers, some articles and speeches, and a few letters to authors will start ripples that will join others' ripples and eventualy swell into the waves that can wash away communication sexism. With its eradication will come the tide of a self-fulfilling prophecy of a nonsexist culture. (Sorrels 1983, 7)

Improving English, in short, need not necessarily be a futile enterprise.

Chapter 8

Imaginary English

The wish to improve English has often been expressed in programmatic statements designed to alter the language. Some writers accept uncritically the view that English is in an advanced state of decline and decay, and they expect that it will become still worse. Others are attracted to schemes for halting change, and they hope to stabilize the language and preserve it in "perfectness" forever (as Bullokar hoped his reformed spelling would). Optimism for English is a negligible theme in projections of its future.

Utopian and fantasy literature occasionally offers an idealized view of language, though, of the many social institutions such literature explores, language is seldom so central as social reform or exotic weapons systems. Nonetheless, language sometimes figures in imaginings about possible human futures. In Plato's *Republic*, for instance, poets and poetic expression were banished from the ideal state (along with certain musical forms) on the grounds that human beings need to be restrained if they are to be rational. But for exemplars of pure rationality such as the Houyhnhnms in *Gulliver's Travels* and Mr. Spock in the television series "Star Trek," ideal expression comes at the cost of affection, humor, playfulness, artistic fiction making, and impulsive expression.

Futuristic story telling sometimes speculates about language in ideal worlds. An early American novel, Mary Griffith's *Three Hundred Years Hence* (1836), anticipated a time enlightened by such developments as the emancipation of women, improved sanitation and manners, elocution schools for public speakers, and English-medium schools in China (1950, 77). But she foresaw no important change in the English of its setting, the eastern seaboard of the United States. Theodor Hertzka's *Freeland* (1890), though written in German and primarily concerned with a new economic order, described a utopian community in central Africa in which English is chosen as "the language of command, as well as that of our general intercourse" (1972, 15). Hertzka's near contemporary, William Alexander Taylor, in *Intermere* (1901–2), imagined a protagonist whose guide speaks to him "in a tongue at once familiar but wholly unknown, as paradoxical as that may sound" (1972, 16). The visitor's English is peculiarly suited to utopian society, says the guide.

> You speak English, but are not an Englishman except by partial descent. You are an American. Not a native of the eastern portion of the continent, but from west of the range of mountains which separate the Atlantic seaboard from the great central valley of the continent. You are from the tributary Ohio valley, and are, therefore, better fitted to comprehend what you will be permitted to see and hear, than the average habitant of the eastern seashore, especially of its great cities. (Taylor 1971, 17)

Since the citizens of Intermere communicate with each other through "mental conversation," language hardly arises once Taylor has alleged that British usage will be useless in the future, claimed a special virtue for Ohio valley English, and declared that the citizens of Intermere have reached perfection by solving the communication problems that create uncertainty or confusion.

Fiction of this sort projects the future as the writer's present improved. Ideals of an "evolved" English are inevitably derived from the authors' preferences and prejudices (and those of their readers). Thus, in Edward Bulwer-Lytton's utopia, *The Coming Race* (1871), the narrator discovers a "strange world, amidst the bowels of the earth" (1896, 2:273) peopled by advanced beings, the Vril-ya, who employ machinery "to an inconceivable extent in all the operations of labor within and without doors" (2:308–9). Their language, the narrator notes after discoursing on its properties, "is akin to the Aryan or Indo-Germanic" (2:326) but is able to express far more "complex ideas" than English. To explain this evolution, Bulwer-Lytton has his narrator quote the latest philological ideas on language change articulated by Max Müller (*On the Stratification of Language* [1868]) in which inflected languages are seen as the result of evolution that begins with isolating and continues with agglutinative stages. Consequently, as a language ahead of English on Müller's "evolutionary" scale, Vril-ya has more inflections.

> Should life be spared to me, I may collect into systematic form such knowledge as I acquired of this language during my sojourn amongst the Vril-ya. But what I have already said will perhaps suffice to show to genuine philological students

that a language which, preserving so many of the roots in the aboriginal form, and clearing from the immediate, but transitory, polysynthetical stage so many rude encumbrances, has attained to such a union of simplicity and compass in its final inflectional forms, must have been the gradual work of countless ages and many varieties of mind; that it contains the evidence of fusion between congenial races, and necessitated, in arriving at the shape of which I have given examples, the continuous culture of a highly thoughtful people. (2:327)

Vril-ya, in short, is a vision of English purified along the lines commended by the language improvers of the mid-nineteenth century: "aboriginal" roots retain their ancient etymons (an ideal that led Emerson to declare words to be "fossil poetry"); expression is condensed but "pregnant with meaning" (a usage of *pregnant* old in English but especially favored by Victorians reflecting on good language). By some process undescribed, Vril-ya words "beyond three syllables became proscribed as barbarous; and in proportion as the language grew thus simplified, it increased in strength, in dignity, and in sweetness" (2:321). Even so, dialect diversity caused anxiety for learned speakers of Vril-ya since among various "tribes of the same race, the original signification and beauty of sounds may become confused and deformed" (2:326). For Bulwer-Lytton and his readers, then, the fictional future language reflected commonly held notions of linguistic excellence—significant monosyllables close to supposedly universal "roots," for instance, and freedom from long or borrowed words (see Dowling 1986).

In *A Modern Utopia* (1905), H. G. Wells questioned the idea that, in future worlds, "we need suppose no linguistic impediments to intercourse" (Wells 1967, 17). Wells was sceptical of wholly rational systems (and hence of imaginary rational languages) on the grounds that the essential nature of human intellection is dynamic, evolutionary, and individual. Thus, the sort of ideal language that animated the minds of linguistic improvers of his day seemed to him quite uninteresting: a language with a perfected spelling system, wholly consistent grammatical processes, and "without ambiguity, as precise as mathematical formulae" (19). His imagined future language was based on radically different principles.

The language of Utopia will no doubt be one and indivisible; all mankind will, in the measure of their individual differences in quality, be brought into the same phase, into a common resonance of thought, but the language they will speak will still be a living tongue, an animated system of imperfections, which every individual man will infinitesimally modify. Through the universal freedom of exchange and movement, the developing change in its general spirit will be a world-wide change; that is the quality of its universality. I fancy it will be a coalesced language, a synthesis of many. Such a language as English is a coalesced language; it is a coalescence of Anglo-Saxon and Norman French and Scholar's Latin, welded into one speech more ample and more powerful and beautiful than either. The Utopian tongue might well present a more spacious coalescence, and hold in the frame of such an uninflected or slightly inflected idiom as English already presents, a profuse vocabulary into which have been cast a dozen once separate tongues, superposed and then welded together through bilingual and trilingual compromises. In the past ingenious men have speculated on the inquiry, "Which language will survive?" The question was badly put. I think now that this wedding and survival of several in a common offspring is a far more probable thing. (Wells 1967, 21–22)

The idea that the best language is "an animated system of imperfections" was a novel and insightful one; Wells allowed individual differences to persist even in an imagined state of "universal freedom of exchange and movement."

Wells's fiction in *A Modern Utopia* reflects many of the predictions laid out in his earlier work, *Anticipations* (1902), "a picture of a human community somewhere towards the year 2000" (Wells 1924, 186). In that book, he heaped scorn on the idea that the various branches of "the English-speaking people" would eventually evolve mutually unintelligible languages separating "the Australian, the Canadian of English blood, the Virginian, and the English Africander" (194). To make that assumption, he thought, was to disregard the unifying force of worldwide communications. Dialect differences within England, he observed, were fast disappearing as a result of increased literacy and population mobility; the same trends would keep English unified on a global scale. Even so, the spread of English to speakers of other languages was retarded by prejudice.

The Hindoo who is at pains to learn and use English encounters something uncommonly like hatred disguised in facetious form. He will certainly read little about himself in English that is not grossly contemptuous, to reward him for his labour. The possibilities that have existed, and that do still in a dwindling degree exist, for resolute statesmen to make English the common language of communication for all Asia south and east of the Himalayas, will have to develop of their own force or dwindle and pass away. They may quite probably pass away. There is no sign that either the English or the Americans have a sufficient sense of the importance of linguistic predominance in the future of their race to interfere with natural processes in this matter for many years to come. (1924, 200–201)

In Wells's view, prejudice might or might not "pass away," but the crucial predictor of excellence was the intellectual quality of literature. French and German, he thought, were superior to English; "the philosophical or scientific writer" in English experiences "poverty and popular neglect" (203). (This sentiment reflects Wells's own early struggles to support himself through authorship.) Even so, he foresaw that English could extend its hegemony over other languages only if those in power provided the encouragement for it to do so—to his mind, an unlikely course. For Wells, the geopolitical struggle among distinct languages described in *Anticipations*—and the question "Which language will survive?"—shortly gave way to his conception, in *A Modern Utopia*, of the "wedding and survival of several [languages] in a common offspring."

Early twentieth-century authors who imagined a future society were usually less shrewd about language than Wells had been or were simply less concerned with it. In a "clairvoyant investigation," the Theosophists Annie Besant and C. W. Leadbeater projected a future in which:

> the language which they are speaking is naturally English, since the community has arisen in an English-speaking country, but it has been modified considerably. Many participial forms have disappeared, and some of the words are different. (1913, 406)

Such vague speculations about the shape of English were, however, set in the context of a much more definite idea of its social status and international role.

> This curious altered form of English, written in a kind of short-hand with many grammalogues [i.e., words represented by a single sign], has been adopted as a universal commercial and literary language. Ordinarily educated people in every country know it in addition to their own, and indeed it is obvious that among the upper and commercial classes it is rapidly superseding the tongues of the different countries. Naturally the common people in every country still speak their old tongue, but even they recognise that the first step towards getting on in the world is to learn the universal language. The great majority of books, for example, are printed only in that, unless they are intended especially to appeal to the uneducated. In this way it is now possible for a book to have a much wider circulation than it could ever have had before. There are still university professors and learned men who know all the old languages, but they are a small minority, and all the specially good books of all languages have long ago been translated into this universal tongue.

In every country there is a large body of middle and upper class people who know no other language, or know only the few words of the language of the country which are necessary in order to communicate with servants and labourers. One thing which has greatly contributed to this change is the new and improved method of writing and printing, which was first introduced in connection with the English language and is therefore more adapted to it than others. In our community all books are printed on pale sea-green paper in dark blue ink, the theory being apparently that this is less trying to the eyes than the old scheme of black on white. The same plan is being widely adopted in the rest of the world. Civilised rule or colonisation has spread over many parts of the world which formerly were savage and chaotic; indeed almost no real savages are now to be seen. (457–58)

A universal desire to "get on" in the world through English was thus made a principle of future civilization. The imaginary future merely perpetuated the social distance between multilinguals of "the upper and commercial classes" and their monolingual "servants and labourers." Besant and Leadbeater only spiritualized the British Empire as it existed in their day. In what they imagined, they were moved by the familiar imperial expectation that English would "supersede" the languages of other nations.

Apart from H. G. Wells, speculators of the early twentieth century gave little attention to English, though an image of "futuristic" vocabulary began to emerge. Aldous Huxley's *Brave New World* (1932), for instance, provided a few technical terms to suggest the flavor of the future language— *soma* 'hallucinogenic drug,' *alpha plus intellectual*, and *epsilon minus moron*—but these examples only patched the current English wordstock onto the twenty-sixth century. Otherwise Huxley's characters, despite quite radical changes in society, communicate in an unremarkable twentieth-century English.

However tangentially, Huxley and other utopian writers created new words for new worlds, and some of these innovations have come into general use. The most dramatic was English *robot* (< Czech *robota* 'work') which first appeared early in 1923 in the translation of Karel Čapek's play, *R. U. R.*, 'Rossum's Universal Robots.' Almost immediately, *robot* took fire as an English word. By June 1923, George Bernard Shaw extended the meaning from Čapek's 'mechanical replica of a human being' to people whose work is repetitive and standardized, and in 1924 a journalist coined *robotry* to describe thoroughly predictable and routinized human behavior. *Robotize*, to designate the process by which human beings were enslaved, evolved in

1927 in the writings of Hugh MacDiarmid, Scotland's most highly regarded twentieth-century poet. By 1931, *robot* was employed as the term for a mechanized traffic signal. In 1941, Isaac Asimov had coined the term *robotics* for the technology that produces such mechanical devices and *roboticist* for the experts who design them. The development of an array of senses for *robot* and the elaboration of its derivatives took place with remarkable speed, even though *automaton* had been available for the same idea since the eighteenth century and *golom* since the end of the nineteenth century. *Robot*, then, emerged from futuristic fiction to symbolize what was troubling about life in the machine age.

Futuristic fictions have provided many similar terms that have been given subsequent real-world application: *astronaut* (1880); *spacefaring* (1959); *space flight* (1931); *spaceman* (1942); *spaceship* (1894); *space shuttle* (1960); *space sick* (1949); *spacer* 'spacevoyager' (1955), 'spacecraft' (1962); *spatial station* (1929) > *space station* (1936); *space suit* (1929); *space warp* (1936); *spaceways* (1947); and *spacewoman* (1962). The usual linguistic techniques employed to form neologisms in (and about) such fiction reveal the means of creativity that writers and readers regard as "futuristic": analogy (e.g., *planetfall* [1954] 'a landing on a planet,' cf. *landfall*; *Terran* [1953] 'inhabitant of the planet Earth,' cf. *Martian* [1883]; *timescape* [1980] 'vista or prospect over time,' cf. *landscape*), blends (e.g., *sci-fi* [1955]; *cyborg* (1962) [< cybernetic + organism]), compounding (e.g., *rocket ship* [1928], *star ship* [1934], *time travelling* [1895]), eponymy (e.g., *waldo* [1942] 'a mechanism for handling objects by remote control,' < Waldo F. Jones, a fictional inventor in a story by Robert Heinlein), and combinations created from roots and affixes used in international scientific vocabulary (e.g., *android* [1951], a word in rare earlier use apparently reinvented; *cryonics* [1967] 'preservation of human life by freezing the body' [<cry- + -onic]; *psionics* [1952] '[the study of] the paranormal' [< psi + -onic]).

Abbreviations and acronyms in fiction have paralleled those of nonfictional science and technology. *Ess Eff*, *sci-fi*, *s-f*, and *SF* for 'science fiction' is one metafictional instance of that tendency. Another is *HAL 9000*, the computer in Arthur C. Clarke's *2001: A Space Odyssey* (1968), a shortened form of "*H*euristically programmed *AL*gorithmic computer." (Clarke has vigorously denied that HAL was named by taking letters immediately prior in the alphabet to *IBM* [Clarke 1972, 78].) In this acronym, Clarke echoed the names of several early computers, the best known of which is *ENIAC* (1946) '*E*lectronic *N*umerical *I*ntegrator *A*nd *C*alculator'. Such alphabetizings have evoked a future world with troubling or sinister qualities.

So too the use of numbers for names had come to symbolize the loss of individuality (despite their uniqueness). The love story of I-330 and D-503 in Yevgeny Zamiatin's *We* (1924) was a harbinger of such futuristic naming practices in subsequent works, and combinations of abbreviations and numbers now often signal an ominous future world.

Fiction writers were not the only ones to have considered imaginary forms of English, however. In early 1938, engineers at the Westinghouse Electric & Manufacturing Company determined to create a "time capsule" as part of their exhibition for the 1939–40 New York World's Fair. The idea of encasing "historic" documents and small objects in the cornerstone of a building was a familiar one, but the Time Capsule Committee at Westinghouse created a more ambitious plan to bequeath insight into their own day to the people of the future. Determining that the capsule should remain sealed for 5,000 years, these engineers devoted most of their imagination to the physical preservation of the contents and ensured that Westinghouse products would be well represented in the trove stored for the illumination of future archaeologists.

Recently developed microfilm technology allowed the inclusion of a library of texts and pictures along with brief films and voice recordings. As an aid to interpreting them, copies of a *Book of Record of the Time Capsule* were "distributed to libraries, museums, monasteries, convents, lamaseries, temples, and other safe repositories throughout the world" (Pendray 1940, 536). This volume contained directions for finding the capsule, messages from Albert Einstein, Robert Millikan, and Thomas Mann, and a "Key to the English Language" to help the *futurians* (i.e., those living in the year 6939) decipher the stored texts. This "key" was a naive linguistic description accompanied by a list of frequent English words intended to allow the futurians to make sense of the dictionaries and extracts from encyclopedias found on the microfilm.

> After five thousand years all the spoken languages of the present time will have become extinct or so altered as to require a key for their understanding. The English language spoken in the United States today, if not replaced by some other natural or invented tongue, will have suffered complete reforming many times over through the laws of linguistic evolving—laws which though proceeding in regular paths will, because of their complexity, work the apparent result of radical havoc. (Harrington 1938, 19)

With the Rosetta stone in mind as the exemplar of an aid to linguistic decoding, a brief fable was provided with parallel translations in twenty-five lan-

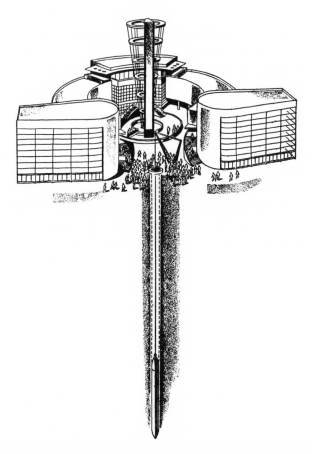

Protecting English against the erosion of time has been a recurring theme in attempts to save the language from decay. The time capsule entombed by Westinghouse at the 1939–40 New York World's Fair was an attempt to preserve Anglo-American civilization for a time when the language would be as dead as Sumerian. Illustration from Westinghouse Electric and Manufacturing Company, 1938, frontispiece.

guages and the Lord's Prayer in three hundred languages. What was remarkable about this elaborate effort, however, was the presumption that "1938 English" would have become unintelligible to the futurians through a process of "reforming," much as the languages of the "early Egyptians, Sumerians, and Babylonians" were opaque to the Time Capsule Committee (Pendray 1940, 533).

The projectors who prepared the Time Capsule were afflicted by a sense of approaching cataclysm in which written records and perhaps even inscriptions would be destroyed. (Not accidentally, the microfilm contained a photograph of Picasso's *Guernica* and newsreel pictures of the bombardment of Canton by the Japanese in June, 1938.) By their selection of material for preservation, they presumed that almost all events of 1939 would be forgotten in 5,000 years (if not sooner), that new languages would have "appeared," and that the futurians would know nothing of English (since it would have "suffered" change). Civilization might "perish," thought the science director of the fair, but "whatever creatures may be living here in the year 6939" could "rebuild" using the information found in the capsule (see Kihlstedt 1986, 112). The imagined future world must have seemed dismal indeed if the remedy to its problems lay in restoring the world of 1939. Of all the many despairing predictions about the future of the English language, theirs was perhaps the most bleak. English, in their view, might well vanish, leaving no trace behind.

The gloom of the 1930s also influenced literary futuring, and the earlier utopias in which technology and reason had solved social problems were replaced by visions of despair. In a short story published in 1933, Evelyn Waugh created a young American socialite suddenly transported, at the end of an evening of gaiety, five hundred years into the future. He finds himself on the spot from which he departed in London's West End, but every familiar landmark has become a stark ruin. (London unpopulated has been a recurrent nightmare to the British literary imagination; St. Paul's in ruins was evoked with a shudder by Thomas Gray in 1768 [Brady and Price 1961, 238], Horace Walpole in 1774 [Lewis 1937–1983, 24:62], and T. B. Macaulay [1840, 228].) In Waugh's story, Londoners are living in primitive huts raised on poles for defense from enemies and to escape the high tide that washes the mud flats of the decaying city. Some unexplained inversion of power has reduced Londoners to a subject people who extract ancient fragments from the mud and attempt to barter them for trinkets offered by black colonizers whose ships pass by on the Thames. English has changed beyond the ability of the protagonist to recognize it.

> They spoke slowly in the sing-song tones of an unlettered race who depend on oral tradition for the preservation of their lore.
>
> Their words seemed familiar yet unintelligible . . . . Occasional phrases came to him, "white," "black boss," "trade," but for the most part the jargon was without meaning. (Waugh 1936, 131,133)

Waugh's purpose in describing a future English transmuted to the language of an "unlettered race" is to put it in contrast to the liturgy that has endured without change; in his story, the celebration of the Latin Mass continues to mitigate the sorrows of English people. Later in the story, the time traveler discerns that a "black anthropologist" is painstakingly reading "familiar words with an extraordinary accent" (135–36). The words he hears are those of Shakespeare, and the death of English (as Waugh presents it) stands in contrast to the endurance of church Latin. English has not merely evolved; it has declined into a primitive jargon.

Like other utopian and dystopian writers, George Orwell did not so much predict as speculate about the future in *Nineteen Eighty-Four* (1948). As he wrote after the publication of his novel, "I do not believe that the kind of society I describe necessarily *will* arrive, but I believe (allowing of course for the fact that the book is a satire) that something resembling it *could* arrive" (Howe 1982, 287). An important element of his fiction is a provocative invention of an evolving totalitarian society and the roles of English in it. The lines of social schism between "party members" and "proles" have rigidified; the former prefer "rapid polysyllabic speech" (Howe 1982, 10), the latter a "debased" Cockney (63). The stylistic preferences of the two groups are not markedly different from the dialect differences that Orwell observed in his own day. "Party members," however, are shown as linguistic engineers, obliterating traditional usages, *Oldspeak*, and inventing new English forms, *Newspeak*.

Orwell's *Newspeak* is the best known of the various imagined forms of English, and the combining form *-speak* he invented continues a lively existence, often to indicate a scorned form of English (e.g., *creep-speak* [1960], *doublespeak* [1952]). For Orwell, *Newspeak* was an efficient and "rational" variety of English akin to the "cultivated voices" he satirized in his novel and despised in real life. Its purpose, not yet achieved at the time in which the novel is set, "was not only to provide a medium of expression for the world-view and mental habits proper to the devotees of Ingsoc, but to make all other modes of thought impossible" (Howe 1982, 198). Consistent with his broader political satire, Orwell created a kind of English that constrained imagination and enforced conformity. *Newspeak*, at least as outlined in the appendix Orwell attached to his novel, had a variety of traits designed "not so much to express meanings as to destroy them" (201). These include features that Orwell found irritating in the English of his own time: affixing in unconventional ways (of which *doubleplusungood* 'very bad' and *unperson* 'a human being declared officially nonexistent' are Orwellian examples); compounding (*crimethink*, *Newspeak* itself); creating portmanteau words, or "telescoped" words in Orwell's terminology (*artsem* 'artificial insemination,' *Minitrue* 'Ministry of Truth'). In addition, Orwell savaged the English telegraphic newspaper style found in headlines or employed in bureaucratic communications.

> times 3.12.83 reporting bb dayorder doubleplusungood refs unpersons
>   rewrite fullwise upsub antefiling.
> In Oldspeak (or standard English) this might be rendered:
>   The reporting of Big Brother's Order for the Day in the *Times* of December 3rd 1983 is extremely unsatisfactory and makes references to nonexistent persons. Rewrite it in full and submit your draft to higher authority before filing. (Howe 1982, 31)

As part of his linguistic fiction, Orwell emphasized the banal (but frightening) work of rewriting history in both "factual" and linguistic aspects to conform to evolving orthodoxy. In support of this revisionism, lexicographers were discouraged from recording new words and urged to destroy old ones, stripping them of historic associations and ideas. The result of all this work would be baseless "truth" expressed in English that had been itself debased.

Orwell's novel put into fictional practice many ideas he developed in a 1946 essay, "Politics and the English Language," which began with an arresting opening sentence that captured long-held English wisdom.

> Most people who bother with the matter at all would admit that the English language is in a bad way, but it is generally assumed that we cannot by conscious action do anything about it. (Howe 1982, 248)

As the next chapter will illustrate, the idea that "the English language is in a bad way" has been a recurring lament. Orwell's expression of this traditional complaint, however, has been unusually influential, particularly in the United States, where "Politics and the English Language" has become staple reading in universities. Recapitulating the eighteenth-century equation of a good language with a good society, Orwell connected bad English with "political and economic causes" that distressed him and many other Britons in the postwar years. Bad language and bad politics reinforced each other, Orwell opined, but he declared that it was possible to expose political dishonesty by replacing windy and unreliable abstractions with vivid and indisputable concrete ideas.

> Millions of peasants are robbed of their farms and sent trudging along the roads with no more than they can carry: this is called *transfer of population* or *rectification of frontiers*. People are imprisoned for years without trial, or shot in the back of the neck or sent to die of scurvy in Arctic lumber camps: this is called *elimination of undesirable elements*. (Howe 1982, 256)

Orwell alleged that his essay was an attack on duplicity in the uses of language, but the solutions he proposed emerged from complaints with a long history. The remedies for diseased English, however, were mainly aesthetic: be fresh, be brief, be honest. The linguistic correlates of these ideas, in his view, recommended the use of short words rather than long ones, concrete words rather than abstractions, and native terms rather than foreign borrowings. Orwell's popularity as a linguistic authority rests largely on this articulation of conventional wisdom about what constitutes the best English. In his preference for "native" words, however, Orwell went beyond the usual means for achieving an appropriately "English" style, and in an unpublished notebook he had listed "foreign words & phrases unnecessarily used in English" and (like the lexicographers in *Nineteen Eighty-Four*) assigned most of them to the "dust bin" (see Bailey 1984, 35).

Given Orwellian anxieties about the future of English, it is surprising that fantasy literature has not more frequently given this topic a prominent place. The most comprehensive survey of the linguistic aspects of such fiction reached the following conclusion.

> In general the treatment of linguistic change in science fiction is like the sky on a hazy night: a few bright spots seen through an obfuscating fog. When we look more specifically at the treatment of the future development of English, the fog does not lift. (Meyers 1980, 18)

Authors in this genre, however, face the same difficulty that "dialect" writers must cope with: the problem of intelligibility. However clearly the future of

English may be imagined, a contemporary audience must still find it readable, and short patches of the invented new English usually suffice to give its flavor.

A 1958 story, "Time Bum" by C. M. Kornbluth, reached such a solution to the intelligibility problem; a confidence-game trickster from the year 2403 has projected himself into the reader's present, and he employs an odd combination of archaism (*feoff*, glossed as 'rent') and innovation (*cimango*, alleged to be Esperanto for 'universal food'). The key to his mysterious use of English is discovered in a page from a newspaper whose dateline is July 18th, 2403.

TAIM KOP NABD:

PROSKYOOTR ASKS DETH

Patrolm'n Oskr Garth 'v thi Taim Polis w'z arest'd toodei at hiz hom, 4365 9863th Strit, and bookd at 9768th Prisint on tchardg'z 'v Polis-Ekspozh'r. Thi aledjd Ekspozh'r okur'd hwaile Garth w'z on dooti in thi Twenti-Furst Sentch'ri. It konsist'd 'v hiz admish'n too a sit'zen 'v thi Twenti-Furst Sentch'ri that thi Taim Polis ekzisted and woz op'rated fr'm thi Twenti-Fifth Sentch'ri. Thi Proskyoot'rz Ofis sed thi deth pen'lti wil be askt in vyoo 'v thi heinus neitch'r 'v thi ofens, hwitch thret'nz thi hwol fabrik 'v Twenti-Fifth-Sentch'ri eksiztens. (Kornbluth 1958, 77)

Careful reading of this passage suggests that the spellers of the twenty-fifth century have neither invented an adequate phonetic alphabet for English nor solved the inconsistency of its spelling. Even so, the fictional passage serves its purpose of suggesting a strangely "evolved" form of the language without demanding too much of the audience.

Fantasy literature almost always cloaks the familiar in the garment of universality. In his 1961 short story "Prometheus," for instance, Philip José Farmer presented a scientist, John Carmody, teaching English to a race of prelingual creatures on a distant planet. In a conversation with Dr. Holmyard, his supervisor, Carmody is compelled to justify the kind of English he has chosen.

"John, why this pidgin English?" said Holmyard. "Why the avoidance of *is* and the substitution of the nominative case for the objective with the personal pronouns?"

"Because *is* isn't necessary," replied Carmody. "Many languages get along without it, as you well know. Moreover, there's a recent tendency in English to drop it in conversational speech, and I'm just anticipating what may become a general development.

"As for teaching them lower-class English, I'm doing that because I think that the language of the illiterates will triumph. You know how hard the teachers in our schools have to struggle to overcome the tendency of their highclass students to use button-pusher's jargon." (Farmer 1971, 146)

The notion that "the language of the illiterates" is the source of unwanted innovation in English was entirely familiar to the audience for which Farmer wrote, as was the image of teachers "struggling" with recalcitrant students to enforce linguistic propriety. Nothing could have been easier than to imagine that the linguistic turmoil of the 1970s would continue into the age of space travel and that education would still be on the verge of failure. Fortunately for his fiction, however, Farmer's sense of "illiterate" usage was better than his recollection of grammatical terminology; Carmody's English plausibly "pidginizes" pronouns rather than substituting the "nominative" for the "objective" (e.g., "Me man" [154]).

The idea that "illiterates" would shape the future of English recurred in the imagined English of Anthony Burgess's *A Clockwork Orange* (1962). Nearly all prior fictional Englishes had suggested an evolution of English along lines internal to the present-day language. Burgess, however, provided his first-person *nadsat* ('teenage') narrator, Alex, with a rich array of Russian-influenced colloquialisms, and the appendix to the American edition of the novel dissected some two hundred of them: *droog* (<*drug* 'friend'), *gulliver* (<*golová* 'head'), *horrorshow* (<*khoroshó* 'good'), *smeck* (<*smekh* 'laugh'). Only teenagers in the novel employ this "nadsat talk," however; adults speak ordinary mid-twentieth-century English. Both linguistically and otherwise, adults seek quiet and stability; teenagers amuse themselves by doing "the ultraviolent."

In the course of the narrative, two doctors treating Alex through *behavior therapy* (a term first attested in English in 1959) discuss his language.

"Quaint," said Dr Brodsky, like smiling, "the dialect of the tribe. Do you know anything of its provenance, Branom?"

"Odd bits of old rhyming slang," said Dr Branom, who did not look quite so much like a friend any more. "A bit of gipsy talk, too. But most of the roots are Slav. Propaganda. Subliminal penetration."

"All right, all right, all right," said Dr Brodsky, like impatient and not interested any more. (Burgess 1972, 115)

What is striking about this conversation is the implication that violent teen-agers like Alex have been transformed from afar by superior Soviet behavior therapy into socially destructive hooligans. "Subliminal penetration" has infected Britain and unleashed the violent impulses of the young. The most sophisticated linguistic aspect of *A Clockwork Orange*, however, is the stylistic range of Alex's English. When he is treated through aversion therapy by the two doctors, his English comes to resemble that of the adults in his world; when he is restored to command of a full range of ethical choice (through "deep hypnopaedia" [Burgess 1972, 172]), Alex reverts to "nadsat talk." (*Hypnopaedia* 'sleep-teaching' was coined by Huxley in *Brave New World* and revived as a term of actual science in 1959.) Burgess's imaginary English was both rich in the sources upon which it drew and remarkable in the stylistic varieties it illustrated. In its world of rapid change and growing indifference to book learning, Alex's English shows that linguistic creativity endures.

In 1974, the English translation of Stanisław Lem's *The Futurological Congress* appeared. Like Čapek's play, the translation stimulated ideas about futuristic English. In 2039, Lem's narrator has suffered an overdose of *hallucinogens* (yet another Huxley coinage adopted in scientific English) and undergoes *vitrification* by being stored in a glass flask until a cure for his affliction has been found. In the world to which the narrator awakes, the new technologies are mainly sidelights: spray-on clothing, books that are not read but eaten, and robots. "But the language has changed the most" (Lem 1974, 73). Some phonetic evolutions are alluded to (e.g., *mychine* 'machine'), but what most interests the narrator are innovations in vocabulary.

> Some other unfamiliar expressions I've come across: threever, pingle, he-male, to widge off, palacize, cobnoddling, synthy. The newspapers advertise such products as tishets, vanilliums, nurches, autofrotts (manual). The title of a column in the city edition of the *Herald*: "I Was a Demimother." Something about an eggman who was yoked on the way to the eggplant. The big Webster isn't too helpful: "*Demimother*—like demigran, demijohn. One of two women jointly bringing a child into the world. See Polyanna, Polyandrew." "*Eggman*— from mailman (*Archaic*). A euplanner who delivers licensed human gametes (fe-male) to the home." I don't pretend to understand that. This crazy dictionary also gives synonyms that are equally incomprehensible. "*Threever*—trimorph." "*Palacize, bepalacize, empalacize*—to castellate, as on a quiz show." "*Pala-dyne*—a chivalric assuagement." "*Vanillium*—extract emphorium, portable." The worst are words which look the same but have acquired entirely different meanings. "*Expectorant*—a conception aid." "*Pederast*—artificial foot fad-

dist." *"Compensation*—mind fusion." *"Simulant*—something that doesn't exist but pretends to." Not to be confused with *"simulator*, a robot simulacrum." *"Revivalist*—a corpse, such as a murder victim, brought back to life. See also *exhumant, disintermagent, jack-in-the-grave.*" (Lem 1974, 71–72)

These imaginative coinages follow familiar English patterns: prefixing (e.g., *demimother*; suffixing (*-ant* in *exhumant, -ize* in *empalacize*); compounding (*mindjacking* 'mental abduction,' *soothseer*), neologisms akin to those of international scientific vocabulary (*ectogenesis, obliterine, torturometry, vanillium*); and portmanteau words ("A probot is a robot on probation, while a servo is one still serving time" [85]).

All these techniques for inventing a future English were pioneered in Orwell's *Nineteen Eighty-Four*, but Lem made them both more benign and funnier. What the two authors share is the conviction that language shapes perception. Orwell's totalitarians reduced freedom by limiting the ways in which ideas could be expressed; Lem's "futurologians" explore intellectual innovation through linguistic inventiveness, an approach to imaginary English anticipated by John Wilkins in *Essay towards a Real Character and a Philosophical Language* (1668). Lem's description of linguistic creativity, though satirical in intent, merits full quotation.

"Linguistic futurology investigates the future through the transformational possibilities of language," Trottelreiner explained.

"I don't understand."

"A man can control only what he comprehends, and comprehend only what he is able to put into words. The inexpressible therefore is unknowable. By examining future stages in the evolution of language we can come to learn what discoveries, changes and social revolutions the language will be capable, some day, of reflecting."

"Amazing. How exactly is this done?"

"Our research is conducted with the aid of the very largest computers, for man by himself could never keep track of all the variations. By variations of course I mean the syntagmatic-paradigmatic permutations of the language, but quantized . . ."

"Professor, please!"

"Forgive me. The Chablis is excellent, by the way. A few examples ought to make the matter clear. Give me a word, any word."

"Myself."

"Myself? H'm. Myself. All right. I'm not a computer, you understand, so this will have to be simple. Very well then—myself. My, self, mine, mind.

Mynd. Thy mind—thynd. Like ego, theego. And we makes wego. Do you see?"

"I don't see a thing."

"But its perfectly obvious! We're speaking, first, of the possibility of the merging of the mynd with the thynd, in other words the fusion of two psychic entities. Secondly, the wego. Most interesting. A collective consciousness. Produced perhaps by the multiple dissociation of the personality, a mygraine. Another word, please."

"Foot."

"Good. Onefoot, two foot. Threefooter, fourfooted. Footing, footingly, footling. Footage, befootery. Footment. And footlose gets you footless, un-footed, defeeted. Ah, defeetism. Feetish, feetus . . . feetback? Infoot and out-foot! I think we're getting somewhere. Feetality, twofootalitarianism."

"But these words have no meaning!"

"At the moment, no, but they will. Or rather, they *may* eventually acquire meaning, provided footeries and defeetism catch on. The word 'robot' meant nothing in the fifteenth century, and yet if they had had futurolinguistics then, they could have easily envisioned automata." (Lem 1974, 108–10)

Unlike most other varieties of imagined English, Lem's future language opens new lines of thought rather than closing them. His work was a satire recalling, in addition to Orwell's *Newspeakers*, Swift's mocking treatment of the imaginary scholars in *Gulliver's Travels* who devised a machine to produce random combinations of symbols from which they expect to extract meaning. What made Lem's fiction persuasive was the idea that the future can be brought into being through linguistic inventiveness. In this notion, he expressed one aspect of megalomania in ideas about English—the notion that the language is not only adequate for what now needs expression but also can free its speakers to shape their future.

Lem's apparent optimism about the future of language is unusual in fantasy literature. Despair about the future and gloom about its English, the usual theme for speculation, reappeared in Russell Hoban's novel, *Riddley Walker* (1980). In the year 4344, Riddley, the protagonist and narrator, gropes through the darkness of *Inland* 'England' after the nuclear holocaust of 1997 has destroyed civilization; he is in quest of the secrets of those who lived before the "Bad Time."

Counting counting they wer all the time. They had iron then and big fire they had towns of parpety. They had machines et numbers up. They fed them numbers and they fractiont out the Power of things. They had the Nos. of the rain bow and the Power of the air all workit out with counting which is how they got boats in the air and picters on the wind. Counting clevverness is what it wer. (Hoban 1982, 19)

Hoban has solved the problem of intelligibility for his readers by relying mainly on word forms not typical of edited English (*1st* 'first,' *clevver* 'clever,' *wd* 'would'), quasi-phonetic spelling (*barming* 'bombing,' and *parpety* 'property' from dialects lacking consonantal *r* after vowels;), and unconventional word division (*farring seakert tryer* 'foreign secretary,' *party cools* 'particles'). Yet his future English was not merely derived from literary trompe l'oeil; Hoban drew upon a range of present-day British colloquial usage: deletion of unstressed syllables (*Cambry* 'Canterbury,' *cernly* 'certainly,' *dinnit* 'didn't it?,' *lerting* 'alerting,' *terpit* 'interpret,' *wunnering* 'wondering'); simplification of final consonant clusters (*jus* 'just,' *hans* 'hands,' *musve* 'must have,' *nex* 'next'); attraction of *n* from *an* to the following word (*a nindicator* 'an indicator,' *your nemminy* 'your enemy'), various southern British sound shifts (*breeve* 'breathe,' *norf* 'north,' *teef* 'teeth'); and "linking *r*" before vowels ("the woal idear of this writing"). Hoban's English has evolved in the generations after the time when people traveled "beyont the sarvering gallack seas" ('beyond the sovereign galaxies'). Though little direct comment about Riddley's language appears in the novel, it is apparent that his evolved English mirrors the wreckage of civilization that surrounds him.

In a more positive vein, language change becomes a liberating force for human aspirations in Láadan, a language constructed by Suzette Hayden Elgin and employed in two science fiction novels, *Native Tongue* (1984) and *Native Tongue II: The Judas Rose* (1987). Known for her studies of linguistic theory and of Amerindian languages, Elgin began in 1981 to reflect on needed improvements in English.

> There occurred to me an interesting possibility within the framework of the Sapir-Whorf Hypothesis (briefly, that language structures perceptions): if women had a language adequate to express their perceptions, it might reflect a quite different reality than that perceived by men. (Elgin 1988, 3)

Her first impulse was to coin words using methods conventional in English. In thinking along these lines, she produced a few neologisms, of which the following are specimens.

acanthophile A woman who repeatedly chooses to form relationships with persons who abuse or neglect her, despite apparent unhappiness each time. (From Gr. "acanthos," "thorn.")

bordweal An artificial barrier raised to keep women out of things such as an irrelevant height requirement. (From O. E. "bord-weal," "a wall of shields.")

to granny To apply the wisdom and the experience of the elderly woman to any situation.

L-harmonics The theory whose basic hypothesis is that the purposeful language of women has, as organizing principle, a set of strategies for reducing communicative dissonance (failure of communication) to its minimum level.

scratstrak A night spent tending children, the sick, the helpless, while male members of the household sleep peacefully through it all; an ugly word coined to be ugly. You'll have no trouble pronouncing it. (Elgin 1981)

Amending the deficiencies of English to adapt usages to women's perspectives is, as the following chapter will illustrate, not an uncommon modern activity. What Elgin did next—inventing a language—was distinctly unusual.

In *Native Tongue*, Elgin created a twenty-third century society in which men have constrained social opportunities for women as a result of the "superb research" of two scientists in 1987 who provided "scientific *proof* of the inherent mental inferiority of women" (Elgin 1985, 73). Children in this community are raised as multilinguals with a "Household" language (English, French, or Swahili), other Earth languages, and an "Alien language" that they acquire in order to act as translators in the cosmopolitan society of space travel. Language learning occupies a central role, and linguistics is the science fictionalized in the novel. Unobserved until they have achieved their purpose, Linguist women seek privacy and acquire freedom through the "Encoding Project" within which they invent their own language. Because men are vigilant for signs of restiveness among them, the women's "Encoding Project" produces a grotesquely elaborate language called Langish; hidden within the linguistic deformity of Langish is Láadan. That language allows the idea of liberation, and through it the women escape male tyrrany. By means of Láadan, they change their "reality." Having no corresponding idea in their language of women's freedom or equality, men stumble unknowingly through a linguistic world in which women live freely in the reality they have invented through language.

Láadan is not English, but its features repair what Elgin sees as defective in present-day English. Some highlights suggest the new "reality" that Elgin has used her new language to invent. Láadan makes more mandatory distinctions than English (compared to the three degrees of comparison in English, Láadan has six) and more temporal ones (including both "past" and "distant past," "future" and "distant future"). Sentences contain markers that show the source of the speaker's authority (e.g., "known to X because perceived by X," "perceived by X in a dream"), the intentions of an utterance (e.g., "said neutrally," "said in fear," "said in jest"), and its emotional quality (e.g., "ecstasy," "linked empathetically with others," "in meditation"). Further emotive flavoring arises from the fact that words may contain a "borrowing" from present-day Navajo, the consonant *lh*, to designate "something unpleasant" (e.g., *dórado* 'dominate' > *dólhórado* 'dominate with evil intent'; *zho* 'sound' > *zholh* 'noise'). Pronoun forms include four degrees of relation to the speaker (neutral, beloved, honored, or despised).

These and other features are conceived to make a language superior to English in expressiveness, discrimination of relationships, and explicitness in revealing the speaker's mood and purpose. Commands in Láadan are "very rare, except to small children" (another "influence" from Navajo); "request" is the commonly used speech act for the English imperative. In short, Láadan emphasizes internal states and feelings; in interaction with others, its speakers are, perforce, attentive and polite. What Elgin has done with her invented language is to create a means of communication that is melodic (Láadan is a tone language and no consonant clusters are permitted), revelatory of its speakers' motives, and, compared to English, aimed at group cohesiveness rather than competition. The worldview projected through Láadan was thus a remedy for the linguistic brutality that Elgin attributed to conventional English usage.

All these efforts to imagine a future language have arisen within a distinctively English context, and they vividly reflect the cultural preoccupations of their times. Growing confidence in the worldwide spread of English in the nineteenth century produced fictions in which future English had become universal, though perhaps "coalesced" (in Wells's term) through contact with other languages. Twentieth-century enthusiasm for technology produced ideas about English with yet more "futuristic" and scientific vocabulary. Bitter experience of totalitarianism and urban violence brought forth visions of a debased English spoken among the ruins of civilization. An anticipated collapse of schooling and rampant illiteracy gave rise to even more apocalyptic images of the language. Only Lem and Elgin treat language change as an opportunity for improved perception and better human expression. Such optimism is rare indeed among ideas of imaginary, or actual, English.

Chapter 9

English Imperiled

Evaluations of English swing wildly between extremes of celebration and deprecation. Those who celebrate its perfection usually find some aspect in need of improvement; those who deride its imperfections often conclude that it is not much worse than other human languages or, with modest amendments, the best language ever spoken. Still others, gloomier than the rest, despair that English can achieve (or return to) perfection. All these appraisals are usually vehicles for extralinguistic speculation. Culture, whether one's own or another, is expressed through language, and commentators turn language back on itself to clinch their arguments.

From quite early times, English has been regarded as imperiled by sinister forces, sometimes nonanglophone "barbarians," but most often by members of the English-speaking community itself. The bad practices of a few are presumed to threaten the well-being of the many, and English has been seen, over and over, as on a slippery slope of decline. Those whose innovations lubricate the wheels of the careening vehicle of expression are saboteurs of values: learning, morality, civility, and reverence for the past. Community members who perpetrate unwanted innovations are treated as ignorant, immoral, rude, and indifferent to the grandeur of tradition. The use of the label *illiterate* in these fulminations and alarms is of special interest, since those whose usage is thought to put the language in peril are seldom unable to read and write; on the contrary, they are usually innovators whose literacy gives them access to and influence in the larger community. Thus freighted with polar opposites, neatly subsumed in the opposition between *literate* and *illiterate*, the preconditions of argument make discussion difficult or even impossible for those who wish to defend innovation. English speakers often find themselves cowed or silenced by arbiters of etiquette. To argue against a self-proclaimed cultural aristocracy is both to criticize the culture that is one's own and to cede, even if tacitly, the idea that these aristocrats of taste are worthy of notice.

The conditions of argument are not new ones. Where disputes arise, warring factions compete in vituperation and in assertion of superior taste and learning. A specimen typical of American debate in the mid-twentieth century pits two university professors against each other (the first paragraph is an extract from an unpublished letter of Jacques Barzun's, the second is Donald J. Lloyd's evaluation of it).

> A living culture in one nation (not to speak of one world) must insist on a standard of usage. And usage, as I need not tell you, has important social implications apart from elegance and expressiveness in literature. The work of communication in law, politics and diplomacy, in medicine, technology, and moral speculation depends on the maintenance of a medium of exchange whose values must be kept fixed, as far as possible, like those of any other reliable currency. To prevent debasement and fraud requires vigilance, and it implies the right to blame. It is not snobbery that is involved but literacy on its highest plane, and that literacy has to be protected from ignorance and sloth.
>
> It is a pity that these sentiments, so deserving of approval, should receive it from almost all educated people except those who really know something about how language works. One feels like an uncultivated slob when he dissents—one of the low, inelegant, illiterate, unthinking mob. Yet as a statement about the English language, or about standard English, it is not merely partly true and partly false, but by the consensus of most professional students of language, totally false. It is one of those monstrous errors which gain their original currency by being especially plausible at a suitable time, and maintain themselves long after the circumstances which give rise to them have vanished. Mr. Barzun's remarks are an echo from the eighteenth century; they reek with an odor mustier than the lavender of Grandmother's sachet. They have little relevance to the use of the English language in America in our day. (Lloyd 1951, 282)

Arguments conducted through such images (for instance, "*living* culture," "*reliable currency*," "*monstrous* errors," and the *musty odor* of long-cherished ideas) hardly increase understanding or lay bare fundamental principles. A dispassionate observer of such spats as these finds few arguments about language itself; rather, they are disputes about the worthiness of those who claim authority in the language community.

The kind of discourse exemplified by Barzun and Lloyd has its own long tradition. In *The Standard of Usage in English* (1908), Thomas R. Lounsbury evaluated the situation.

> There seems to have been in every period of the past, as there is now, a distinct apprehension in the minds of very many worthy persons that the English tongue is always in the condition approaching collapse, and that arduous efforts must be put forth, and put forth persistently, in order to save it from destruction. . . . These foretellers of calamity we have always had with us; it is in every way probable that we shall always have them. A certain uniformity is to be found in the attitude they exhibit towards the speech, no matter what period it is to which they belong. (2–3)

Given the stale familiarity of the claims made, and even the examples adduced, it is illuminating that anglophone culture continues to provide a ready market for books and articles rehashing the dispute. (Recent U.S. disquisitions warning that English is "in the condition approaching collapse" include Edwin Newman's *A Civil Tongue* [1976] and *Strictly Speaking* [1974], John Simon's *Paradigms Lost* (1980), Arn Tibbets and Charlene Tibbets's *What's Happening to American English?* [1978], and David Lehman's "Hastening the Decline of Grammar" [1984]. Among works that reiterate the arguments to dispute them are Harvey A. Daniels's *Famous Last Words* [1983], Jim Quinn's *American Tongue and Cheek* [1980], and Geoffrey Nunberg's "The Decline of Grammar" [1983].)

What is remarkable about the alarmists is their tendency to single out particular groups and social practices to blame for the allegedly unhealthy state of the language. The culprits vary with the times and the political viewpoint of the observer. The perpetrators of unwanted linguistic innovation include nearly everyone who does not occupy the position that observers have selected for themselves—learned, conservative, reflective, and genteel.

> *1665.* I conceive the reason both of additions to, and the corruption of the English language, as of most other tongues, has proceeded from the same causes; namely, from victories, plantations, frontieres, staples of com'erce, pedantry of schooles, affectation of travellers, translations, fancy and style of Court, vernility [= 'servility'] & mincing of citizens, pulpits, political remonstrances, theatres, shopps, &c. (Evelyn 1906, 3:309)
>
> *1712.* So that if the Choice [of linguistic arbiters] had been left to me, I would rather have trusted the Refinement of our Language, as far as it relates to Sound, to the Judgment of the Women, than of illiterate Court-Fops, half-witted-Poets, and University-Boys. For, it is plain that Women in their man-

ner of corrupting Words, do naturally discard the Consonants, as we do the Vowels. . . . Now, though I would by no means give Ladies the Trouble of advising us in the Reformation of our Language; yet I cannot help thinking, that since they have been left out of all Meetings, except Parties at Play, or where worse Designs are carried on, our Conversation hath very much degenerated. (Swift 1966, 115–16)

1731. And if these Circumstances tend to raise in our Minds a great Opinion of these *Tongues* [Greek and Latin], the contrary Circumstances contribute not a little to debase our own. We learn it from our Nurses, which are ignorant and unpolish'd Creatures; we daily speak it with all sorts of People, Tradesmen, and Peasants, and almost always about common, sometimes very mean and contemptible Matters, (tho' at present it is a little more employ'd in the Commerce of *Sciences*) and if so how can it well be, that a *Tongue* which is employ'd in common by Men of the lowest Parts, and on the meanest Subjects, should have that Place in our Esteem, with those that are dignify'd and distinguish'd by such exalted Usage? (Stackhouse [1731] 1968, 150–51)

1755. The great pest of speech is frequency of translation. No book was ever turned from one language into another, without imparting something of its native idiom; this is the most mischievous and comprehensive innovation. (Johnson [1755] 1974, C-5)

1782. At a coffee-house, near St. Paul's, where I frequently spend my evening in reading the news-papers, I am, at the beginning of a month, alarmed, disturbed, and distracted with the city-beaux calling, waiter, bring me the Euro-PEan Magazine. . . . Sometimes I hear a sprig of divinity, just slivered from college, (agreeable to the fashionable mode of throwing the emphasis as far back as the poor word will bear, that the sound may "go tripping on the tongue," without being liable to any jolts in its way, regardless of the injury done to the signification) begging Mr. Waiter to let him see the Eurōpĕăn Magazine. (A. B. 1782, 263. The writer argues on the grounds of analogy with *Asian*, *American*, and *African* that the word should be pronounced as if spelled *Europan* with second-syllable stress.)

1804. Another circumstance, just hinted at, which is peculiarly humiliating, and which, I should hope, a little recollection of the manly spirit of our ancestors would yet cause us to resent, is, that all these endeavours to expel the natives [i.e., "native" English words], and to place foreigners in their room, is not the work of scholars and critics, but of persons who have never, in any nation, been ranked among the ablest linguists. We are not beat out of our language by Royal Academies and Royal Societies, by armies of Lexicographers, and hords of Philologists, but by a combination of Milliners and of Mantua-makers, of Perfumers and of Hair-dressers, of Cabinet-makers and Upholsterers, of Taylors, and of Cooks, the fabricators of pantaloons, and the architects of pastry, by the Authors of stews, and Compilers of soups. It is from them we are humbly to receive the language in which we must dress our wives and our daughters, and furnish our houses and our wardrobes, our dinners and our desserts. It is they who are rendering Dr. Johnson's Dictionary obsolete, that they may supply its place by a Polyglott of pies and puddings, of pickles and flummeries. ("The Projector" 1804, 818)

1824. On the return of Charles from the Continent, some of his followers may really have lost their native idiom, or at least may have forgotten the graver and solider parts of it; for many were taken over in their childhood. On their return to England, nothing gave such an air of fashion as imperfection in English: it proved high breeding, it displayed the court and loyalty. Home-bred English ladies soon acquired it from their noble and brave gallants; and it became the language of the Parliament, of the Church, and of the Stage. (Landor 1891, 3:350–51)

1864. Some optimists may be disposed to ask, what is the good of this hair-splitting, and to say that English may safely be left to itself. But, if we examine the history of the language, we perceive, that, since the date of the authorized translation of the Bible,—the finest example of English,—the alterations that have taken place have been, generally, for the worse. The double negative has been abandoned, to the great injury of strength of expression. The inflexion of the preterite has been abandoned, with the use of the second person, that most forcible of all kinds of address. The affected Italianisms of the sixteenth century happily did not commend themselves to the translators of the Bible. They were succeeded by the more offensive Gallicisms of the modish eighteenth century, which, happily, could not maintain their hold. The nineteenth century has witnessed the introduction of abundant Gallicisms, Germanisms, Americanisms, colonialisms, and provincialisms; nearly all needless, or easily to be supplied by more correct words or phrases. (Quoted in Hall 1873, 279)

1867. Among writers, those who do the most mischief are the original fabricators of error, to wit: the men generally who write for the newspapers. Next to them, in order, are the authors of the vapid trashy "sensation novels" of the day. (Gould 1880, 7)

1873. Something of the like kind may be remarked in 1873, as to the men who keep the English printing press at work. Some of these are scholars, or men of strong mother wit, who in prose and poetry employ a sound Teutonic style. Others are men representing the middle class, writers who, for want of education, often use in a wrong sense the long Latinized words wherein the true penny-a-liner revels. The first class are day by day straining the foul matter from our language, and are leading us back to old springs too long unsought; perhaps they may yet keep alive our perishing Subjunctive mood. The other class are day by day pouring more sewage into the well of what can no longer be called "English undefiled." From the one quarter comes all that is lofty and noble in the literature of the day; from the other all that is mean and taudry. (Kington Oliphant 1873, 322–23)

1883. But language always deteriorates when the morals of a people become depraved, when the growth of political corruption hardens the heart and dulls the conscience of a nation; when men, and worse still when women, lose the feeling and the habit of reverence, and when the cynical sneer or the senseless ridicule of the high and low vulgar are fashionable. (Errington 1883, 593–94)

1889. Many causes exist which tend to corrupt the "well of English undefiled." The immense area over which the language now extends, in America, Asia, and Africa, removes it further from the center in Europe, and whilst English tends to become the language most widely used and spoken in all parts of the globe, it is used and spoken by men less familiar than ourselves with the literary authority which determines its accuracy and fitness. It is probable that the vernacular tongue of the colonies and dependencies of England will gradually become more remote from the original. Another cause is the immense extension and influence of the newpaper press, supplying to countless millions the only form of literature with which they are acquainted; and the newspaper press of the United States and the British colonies, as well as the inferior class of newspapers in this country, is to a large extent in the hands of writers who have no respect for propriety or reticence of language. (Reeve 1889, 349)

1894. The characters which had always substantially been called *ah*, *ay*, and *ee*, and which had represented these sounds in all languages since the invention of the alphabet, came to be sounded *ay*, *ee*, and *eye*, but a dull-eared and thick-mouthed peasantry, so persistently in familiar, daily, conversational usage and in oft-recurring words in their limited peasant vocabulary, that learning and literature, after long resisting the tendencies of illiterate speech, at length gave way, and consented to a change in the names of the characters themselves. I know not who is responsible for this ignominious surrender of the interests of the language, and of all languages, to the demands of illiterate ignorance. Doubtless, however, the schoolmaster of the period, who may be regarded as the connecting link between education and ignorance, must come in for a large share of the responsibility. But, with the change of the names of the characters representing the three leading vowel-sounds of the language, the *coup de grâce* was given to anything like phonetic system, or, indeed, to any system as regards vowel-sounds in English orthography. (Porter 1894, 120)

1906. Where shall we find the teachers, who "may do much" to restore to our children their lost inheritance? Not in Chicago's schools. Here, I can assure him, he will find dozens of schools in which not one teacher is capable of setting an example of pure and beautiful speech. Let him visit, also, our great high schools, with their marble wainscoting, tiled floors, improved fire-escapes, generously equipped gymnasium and laboratories worthy of the best colleges; he will find in each perhaps one or two noble women, bred back in old New England, who are really fit to carry the torch of enlightenment to—fifteen hundred students! A scant half-dozen more, men and women, use the best quality of Western speech; we are thankful for them. But the count has not reached ten righteous ones.

I appeal to the *Nation*: How is the case in New England itself? Some of us are sending our sons and daughters East to college, hoping thus to repair in some measure the damage done by sheer force of numbers in this huge, prosperous Philistia. Is our confidence well-placed? Shall we receive them back cleansed, purified? (Hiestand 1906, 73)

1927. The present century threatens us with a torrent of fancy words, which are forced at all hours on the consciousness of the average citizen. From the bastard French of the drapers and the crazily spelled abortions of the cosmetic-mongers, the flood is fast spreading to every trade. The senseless but snappy, catchy, and fool-snaring creations of "the great American advertising man" are no longer alien to these islands, and the lure of polysyllabic monstrosities may soon be felt here also. (Grattan 1927, 435–36)

1930. If, at the very beginning of that wave of animated photography which has swept over Europe from the West as Attila and his Huns swept over it from the East, the whole problem of the cinema industry had been treated differently . . . every boy and girl of fourteen or fifteen in this country [Britain] . . . might have proceeded thence, through the pictures, to some appreciation of drama and literature. Of that I cannot judge. But they would not have become innocent accomplices in the matricide of their mother tongue. The restraint which art imposes on itself, and which commerce does not impose upon itself, would have prevented the onset of cinemese. It is a *lingua franca*, or a *lingua calefornica*. It has devastated Europe. The subtitlers have created a wilderness and called it prose. (Knox 1930, 187–88)

1931. Mispronunciation abroad [i.e., outside the United States] is due largely to the influence exerted by the people of Oxford, who have steadily debased the coinage of English speech with emasculated voices and exaggerated idiosyncracies. . . . Nowadays in England members of audiences and critics complain that actors and actresses—especially since the war—have become so infected with what the English themselves term "the abhominable Oxford voice" that they are no longer audible on the stage. (Vizetelly 1931,149; for responses, see Chapman 1931 and 1932; Wyld 1934)

1964. Propaganda always lies, because it over-states a case, and the lies tend more and more to reside in the words used, not in the total propositions made out of those words. A "colossal" film can only be bettered by a "super-colossal" one; soon the hyperbolic forces ruin all meaning. If moderately tuneful pop-songs are described as "fabulous," what terms can be used to evaluate Beethoven's Ninth Symphony? The impressionable young—on both sides of the Atlantic—are being corrupted by the salesmen; they are being equipped with a battery of inflated words, being forced to evaluate alley-cat copulation in terms appropriate to the raptures of *Tristan and Isolde*. For the real defilers of language—the cynical inflators—a deep and dark hell is reserved. (Burgess 1964, 180)

1975. . . . . there is no doubt that real Cockney, despite all its delicious associations of pluck and humour and broadmindedness, is a very ugly wrenching of distinguishable sounds into indistinguishable. All city dialects tend to suffer from the effects of catarrh (the Cardiff snarl is sometimes called *catarrhdiff*), haste, smoking, fumes, shouting (especially against the telly), gang-speech, and protest; and some are indefensible, especially Brum [= the urban dialect of Birmingham] and (with its *fur wur and tur*) Liverpuddlian. Southern Accepted is certainly preferable to these, but why has the English of England so utterly effaced the final *r* and even the medial one? (Cottle 1975, 65–66)

1985. It must suffice to say that Black English is a separable, differentiated, fully structured spoken variety of English, not tied down to particular regions in the US, potently political in its animosity towards the structured patterns of Received American, colourful, animated, fancy, and subversive. If it is possible to see a variety of English as a threat to the acceptability of the language handed down to white Americans from the seventeenth century onward, this is it. Its dislocation of normal syntax, its patterned formulas showing disregard for the traditional shape of sentences make it at once deeply impressive and overtly threatening to currently agreed standards. (Burchfield 1985, 164)

1986. Two of the causes of decline in *all* modern European languages have been: the doctrines of linguistic "science" and the example of "experimental" art. They come together on the principle of Anything Goes—not in so many words, usually, but in unmistakable effect. (Barzun 1986, 4)

1986. Commentators fret that standards are being abandoned, that words are losing their meaning, that other languages are threatening the primacy of English, that ugly bureaucratic and scientific jargon is polluting our speech. Among the culprits linked to the demise of language are television, underfunded schools, advertising, bilingual education, and computers. (Finneran 1986, 9)

These authors allege that the excellencies of the language have been corrupted and diminished by the named enemies of good English: youth, technocrats, city dwellers, advertisers, filmmakers, teachers, journalists, translators, corrupt politicians, tailors, people who promote fashionable trends, and foreign travelers.

Coupled with these accusations is often an assertion that English achieved its fullest excellence at some earlier time. This idea has its influential beginning in Edmund Spenser, who, in 1589, declared Chaucer to be the "well of English vndefyled" (*Faerie Queene*, bk. 5, canto 2, line 32). Samuel Johnson echoed these words in determining to ornament his *Dictionary* of 1755 with "examples and authorities from the writers before the restoration [including, of course, Spenser], whose works I regard as *the wells of English undefiled*, as the pure sources of genuine diction" (Johnson [1755] 1974, C-1). Noah Webster asserted that

> it would have been fortunate for the language, had the stile of writing and the pronunciation of words been fixed, as they stood in the reign of Queen Anne and her successor. Few improvements have been made since that time; but innumerable corruptions in pronunciation have been introduced by Garrick, and in stile by Johnson, Gibbon and their imitators. (Webster [1789] 1951, 50)

A generation later, Macaulay declared that Bunyan's *Pilgrim's Progress* (1678) was the exemplar of "the fame of the old unpolluted English language" (Macaulay 1903, 1:286). Not long after Macaulay wrote, another (much less famous author) brought the ideal closer to his own time.

> . . . it is evident that the language is in a rapid course of decay; threatening utter and speedy destruction. In the advantages, supposed to have been conferred by the prevailing spirit of reform, it is plain, that our language has no participation. For the simplicity and purity of *Hooker* and *Addison*, the splendour of *Gibbon's* History, the easy elegance of his correspondence, the vigour and grandeur of *Johnson*, and the perspicuity of all, we have now substituted weak sophistry, covered by a redundancy of words, selected less for their import and application than their unusual and extraneous character; the excessive use of hyperbole; always misrepresenting, by exceeding the truth; a general affectation of foreign terms; obsolete and vulgar phrases; unnatural metaphor, forced with perpetual effort, wearing, without rewarding, the attention; and a license universally assumed of creating new words, not to be found in any dictionary, or with the sanction of any authority, by arbitrary inventions; changing substantives to verbs and verbs to substantives; or by mutilation, retaining part of a word with some alteration or addition; that must at no distant period produce a much greater change in the language than has occurred in the lapse of time since the reigns of *Elizabeth* and *James I*. (Vesey 1841, 2–3)

This combination of nostalgia and despair localizes the golden age of the language in the past. In an extreme example of antiquarian enthusiasm, Meric

Casaubon declared in 1650 that "the Saxon language is the true and genuine English language. So just as much as present-day English has receded from the old Saxon, so much has it degenerated from its native purity" (1650, 131–32). That same yearning for the Saxon also animated Gerard Manley Hopkins in 1882.

> It makes one weep to think what English might have been; for in spite of all that Shakspere and Milton have done with the compound I cannot doubt that no beauty in a language can make up for want of purity. In fact I am learning Anglosaxon and it is a vastly superior thing to what we have now. (Hopkins 1955, 162–63)

But sometimes the ideal is not so distant. Writing in 1975, Douglas Watt asserted: "The English language began to curl up and die, instead of being regenerated, sometime after the Second World War, until now it has become like, wow!, you know" (Morris 1975, xix). Kingsley Amis declared in 1980 that "till quite recently, perhaps about 1960, it was comparatively rare to find a misuse of words in the writings of the supposedly educated, among whom I include journalists and those who get their letters printed in the newspapers. But now, five minutes' reading almost anywhere will turn one up" (Amis 1980, 25).

As these comments show, evaluations of language usually reflect cultural anxieties on a larger scale, and perpetrators of "bad English" have often been blamed for other forms of alleged social misconduct. Sometimes criticism arises from purely linguistic issues; more often, language is a skirmish in a larger battle. In many assessments of English, the linguistic norm is presumed to be that of fiercely heterosexual men, and any departure by men from masculine stereotypes is treated severely. This line of attack is very old in Western societies. In Roman times, Juvenal satirized gay men and wrote scathingly of the "piping falsetto" of their language (*Second Satire*, l. 107). Adopting the linguistic styles and preferences of the gender opposite to one's own has been regularly deplored in anglophone communities as well. The following examples illustrate the flavor of this criticism.

> *1709.* They adopt all the small vanities natural to the feminine sex to such an extent that they try to speak, walk, chatter, shriek and scold as women do, aping them as well in other respects. In a certain tavern in the City, the name of which I will not mention, not wishing to bring the house into disrepute, they hold parties and regular gatherings. As soon as they arrive they begin

to behave exactly as women do, carrying on light gossip as is the custom of a merry company of real women. (Quoted in Hyde 1970, 63)

1741. . . . they had no sooner entered but the Marshall was complemented by the company with the titles of Madame and Ladyship. The man asking the occasion of these uncommon devoirs, the Marshall said it was a familiar language peculiar to the house. The man was not long there before he was more surprised than the first. The men calling one another "my dear" and hugging, kissing, and tickling each other as if they were a mixture of wanton males and females, assuming effeminate voices and airs; some telling others that they ought to be whipped for not coming to school more frequently. (*Select Trials* 1742, 2:257–58)

1742. I found between 40 and 50 men making love to one another, as they called it. Sometimes they would sit in one another's laps, kissing in a lewd manner and using their hands indecently. Then they would get up, dance, make curtsies, and mimic the voices of women, indulging in such vernacular expressions as "O, fie, Sir," "Pray, Sir," "Lord, how can you serve me so?," "I swear I'll cry out," "You're a wicked devil," "You've a bold face," and "Eh! ye little dear toad!" (*Select Trials* 1742, 3:37)

1900. The female with masculine manners is always amusing and often pitiable; but the attenuated weak-voiced neuter, the effeminate male: pity him, but blame his mother for the false training, and give scorn to the father for his indifference. . . .

The female possessed of masculine ideas of independence; the viragint who would sit in the public highways and lift up her pseudo-virile voice, proclaiming her sole right to decide questions of war or religion or the value of celibacy and the curse of women's impurity, and that disgusting antisocial being—the female sexual pervert, are simply different degrees of the same class—degenerates. (Howard 1900, 686–87)

1911. It appears that in this community there is a large number of men . . . who mostly affect the carriage, mannerisms, and speech of women; who are fond of many articles ordinarily dear to the feminine heart; who are often people of a good deal of talent; who lean to the fantastic in dress and other modes of expression, and who have a definite cult with regard to sexual life. They preach the value of non-association with women from various standpoints and yet with one another have practices which are nauseous and repulsive. Many of them speak of themselves or each other with the adoption of feminine terms, and go by girls' names or fantastic application of women's titles. They have a vocabulary and signs of recognition of their own, which serve as an introduction into their own society. The cult has produced some literature, much of which is uncomprehensible to one who cannot read between the lines, and there is considerable distribution among them of pernicious photographs. (Vice Commission of Chicago 1911, 296)

> *1926.* The other extreme—the man of broad hips and mincing gait, who vocalizes like a lady and articulates like a chatterbox, who likes to sew and knit, to ornament his clothing and decorate his face, and the woman who makes her garb approximate man's, who swaggers and swears, uses a cane and often a monocle, who goes in for horses and hunting, business and sports—everyone knows. (Review of Joseph Collins' *The Doctor Looks at Love* 1926, 74)
>
> *1965.* This is Broadway, the Great White Way, the fabled street of dreams. Barrett calls it the sewer. Down it flows the worst America has to offer in the way of degenerates, perverts and lawbreakers—to Barrett, "germs." . . . Around the corner in the alley-like darkness of 43rd Street, homosexual exhibitionists skip between Broadway and Eighth Avenue, shouting affectionate female curses at each other. (Mills 1965, 90)

For all these writers, men's use of the "mannerisms and speech of women" arouses extremely emotional evaluations. Lesbian adoption of a "pseudo-virile voice," on the other hand, does not usually excite such rage, since the "virile voice" is taken to be a norm.

Only very recently have celebratory images of Gay and Lesbian English begun to appear in print. These embrace ideals of creativity, antiquity, and "tribal tradition" so often claimed for English generally.

> *1972.* Gay slang, like black slang, enriches our language immeasurably. "Camp," "straight," and "vibrations" were once solely gay inventions that are today part of every hip vocabulary. Gay slang was invented, coined, dished and shrieked by the gay stereotypes: The flaming faggots, men who look like women, flagrant wrist-benders, the women who don't shave their legs, all those who find it difficult to be accepted for what they feel they are even within the pariah gay subculture. And they stereotype others because they themselves have been labeled offensively: They see all Italian straights as members of the Mafia, and they speak of Yiddishe Mamas with a knowing smirk. They over-dramatize words to make up for the plainness they find in their own lives; to them life is a stage with all the lights going and the audience constantly clapping for more. It's Vegas every minute! They jeer because they have been mocked; they retaliate with a barrage of their own words which ridicule women, male virility, the sanctity of marriage, everything in life from which they are divorced. (Rodgers 1972, 11–12)
>
> *1978.* Without exception, the attempts of outsiders to describe language use among various gay subgroups fail to account for the diversity and fluidity of contexts, codes, methods of acquisition, sexual and political implications, and gender-linked associations. There is some question about how to define the possible communities whose language habits can be studied. Yet the

nonverbal communication of mutual recognition among gays, the various aspects of *passing* as a straight person, and the interest in searching for a nonderogatory, nonlimiting vocabulary suggest certain areas of common interest. (Hayes 1978–79, 203)

1984. In the heart group of traditionalists lie the clues to the ancient Gay traditions, which are contained in the names, words, puns, and special phrases; in the gestures, intonations, lisping, swaggering body language; in the feathery costumes, rings, tatoos, leather jackets of Gay transvestism; in the derogatory names *faggot, queen, dyke, queer, fairy, bulldagger.* In these fragments rest the remnants of ancient Gay tribal traditions: the social functions, offices and domains, the stories of origin and magical powers, of rebellions and sorcery, of witches, wizards, gods, spirits and shamanism, warriors and wars. (Grahn 1984, 86)

Enforcing "correct" behavior through language is, of course, a primary means of social control within the English-language community. Homophobia (and homophilia) thus have linguistic correlates that mesh with broader social patterns of conduct and mirror ideas about "proper" English (see Hayes 1978–79).

While linguistic defects (e.g., an unphonetic spelling) have been alleged to put English in peril, the battleground of warring ideologies lies mainly in social class and in gender stereotypes. Social-class differences have given rise to a library of usage manuals and scholarly studies to interpret them. Until very recently, however, gender differences have been neglected, though they provide deep insights into preferences and anxieties about English.

In the so-called Proverbs of Alfred (1150), the writer declared that women are *word-wod* 'word-mad' and unable to control their tongues (Arngart 1955, 102). Demureness, taciturnity, and silence are the expected womanly virtues; loquacity, candor, and reiteration are their corresponding vices. (These latter speech habits were often viewed as admired traits of men's speech.) Proper forms of female behavior have been explicitly taught in courtesy books and child-rearing manuals from very early times (Bornstein 1978), and women who have departed from such social ideals have been regarded as somehow remarkable and held up for occasional praise (if they women were powerful) and frequent blame (if they were not). In general, the nature and quality of instruction for young women in the use of their language has not much changed from that prescribed by Robert Codrington (1601–65) in his treatise, *Youths Behavior, or Decency in Conversation Amongst Women* (1665).

Though earlier writers had commented on the status of individual usages, Robert Baker was the first to gather "errors" and to suggest their systematic emendation in *Reflections on the English Language* (1770). With the nineteenth century, such compilations appeared in increasing numbers. Illustration from James Dabney McCabe, *National Encyclopedia of Business and Social Forms* (Chicago: G. W. Borland, 1879), 38.

> The true Vertue of Silence cannot be too much commended. It is such a quality that I want words to express its worth: I cannot well tell which I should most commend to Gentlewomen, either Speech or Silence, since the one of them doth too much, and the other too little; Speech enricheth, and corrupteth, but Silence is poor, but honest. I am not so much against Discourse, as vain pratling, which consumes time, and profiteth no body. Speech indeed is one of the blessings of Nature, but to ride still on the top of it is too vehement. They that use it are at great pains in feeding hungry ears, and to speak properly are the very Bellows to kindle laughter; and they are not only guilty of this fault, but they are unsafe and dangerous, their words discovering their mind, and negligently betraying to every eye the sight of their heart. (Codrington 1664, 140)

In these words and those that follow, Codrington never explains what misfortunes might follow from a woman's silence; instead he concentrates on the perils that flow from her decision to speak at all.

Codrington exemplifies the virulent antifeminism of his day, and he and his contemporaries were quick to find Biblical warrants to silence women. If that were not enough, proverb lore abounded to show that women's speech violated the natural order. Joseph Swetnam, for example, elaborated an abundance of such folk wisdom in 1615.

There is no woman but either she hath a long tongue, or a longing tooth, and they are two ill neighbours, if they dwell together: for the one will lighten thy purse, if it be still pleased, and the other will waken thee from thy sleepe, if it be not charmed. Is it not strange of what kinde of metall a womans tongue is made of? that neither correction can chastise nor faire meanes quiet: for there is a kinde of venome in it, that neither by faire meanes nor foule they are to be ruled. All beasts by man are made tame; it is but a small thing, and seldome seene, but it is often heard, to the terror and vtter confusion of many a man. (Swetnam 1615, 40)

Similarly, in 1650, Moses à Vauts carried misogyny even further in a tract titled *The Husband's Authority Unvail'd*.

If the Tongue of a *Clamorous Woman* be allowed to walke at large, a Man may be brought to such an Exigent; that he shall not have a quiet Corner in his own house or Heart to retire himself unto, for Prayer or any Exercise of Piety; but be forced out into the Fields, Woods, or Caves . . . least his humiliation (as *Davids*) be both interrupted and reproached. (64)

Vauts's title was amplified by his promise to explain "Whether it be fit or lawfull for a *good Man* to beat his *bad Wife*" (to which question he provided an affirmative answer), but such accusations were not restricted to works designed to endorse the brutal behavior of men toward women. Thus, Hanna Wolley, in *The Gentlewoman's Companion* (1675), advised:

It is true (Ladies) your tongues are held your defensive armour, but you never detract more from your honour than when you give too much liberty to that slippery glib member. That Ivory guard or garrison, which impales your tongue, doth caution and instruct you, to put a restraint on your Speech. In much talk you must of necessity commit much error, as it leaves some tincture of vain-glory, which proclaims the proud heart from whence it proceeded, or some taste of scurrility, which displays the wanton heart from whence it streamed. (42)

That silence is an especially womanly virtue remains an important part of language culture even today.

Conflicts between the ideal and the real in the language of women are, of course, a frequent theme for the literary imagination. Portia, in *The Merchant of Venice*, disguises herself as a man in order to exercise the functions of a judge, and the male disguise gives her linguistic as well as juridical authority. When Becky Sharp leaves school at the beginning of Thackeray's *Vanity Fair*, she hurls her copy of Johnson's *Dictionary* from the coach window, thus illustrating her liberation from the ruled language of school and from the other social constraints that institution had imposed upon her. The degree of personal freedom permitted for women has a linguistic component that is an index of other opportunities that men provide or deny.

Until very recently, discussions of women's English presumed that male usage is the norm and female English a deviation from it. These observations fall into four principal groups: women speak a flawed variety of the language; women use a more refined (or otherwise superior) form of English; women are victims of linguistic oppression; women are prisoners of patriarchal English. As with other types of perceived social diversity, each of these characterizations is founded on the idea that difference leads to disharmony and to linguistic discord. In the first view, women's defective English harms the community. In the second, their superior English civilizes naturally brutish men, but it also limits women's scope for linguistic creativity and innovation. In the third, their segregation from many linguistic domains through enforced propriety unfairly restricts their contribution to the common language, and their "delicacy" creates euphemism and evasion in the use of English. In the fourth, women are unable to express themselves fully, since patriarchal English is not a suitable vehicle of expression for them. All four have distinctive histories.

An early articulation of the view that women speak a flawed variety of English was expressed by Thomas Elyot in 1531; governesses should be chosen to ensure "that they speke none englisshe but that / whiche is cleane / polite / perfectly / and articulately pronounced / omittinge no lettre or sillable as folisshe women often times do of a wantonness / wherby diuerse noble men / and gentilmennes chyldren (as I do at this daye knowe) haue attained corrupte and foule pronuntiation" (see p. 35). The kind of guidance Elyot expected writing to provide for the improvement of speech was simply unavailable to women, for in his day, British women were seldom educated in basic literacy. When Henry VIII came to the throne in 1509, only 1 percent of adult women were literate; no more than 10 percent of adult women were literate before 1600, and it was well into the nineteenth century before women's literacy increased to 50 percent. Progress toward universal literacy was not steady, and the same economic recession that spurred emigration to the Americas at the end of the sixteenth century was accompanied by a reduction in schooling that influenced both men and women but particularly women, since they were viewed as less economically important and thus less in need of education. The gap between literacy rates for men and women reached a difference of 30 percent in the mid-eighteenth century, and that gap began to close in Britain only after universal primary education was provided in 1870. Because most women were illiterate, they did not participate significantly in the rise of the newly borrowed learned vocabulary introduced into English in Tudor and Stuart times, but there is evidence that women wished to be part of that linguistic development. Thus, Robert Cawdrey, the compiler of the first general monolingual English dictionary (1604), was a shrewd judge of the market when he declared that the hard words he defined "were gathered for the benefit & helpe of Ladies, Gentlewomen, or any other vnskillful persons."

Since education was driven by economic motives, women were not generally offered the full range of English eloquence. There were few opportunities for them in the church, in politics, or in positions newly opening as the commercial world began to take on a recognizably modern form. In *The Arte of English Poesie* (1589), George Puttenham declared that "our chiefe purpose herein is for the learning of Ladies and young Gentlewomen, or idle Courtiers, desirous to become skilful in their owne mother tongue" (1936, 158), but the lessons he taught were directed to economically frivolous uses of language—anagrams and verses—"commendable inough and a meete study for Ladies, neither bringing them any great gayne nor any great losse vnlesse it be of idle time" (108). Women, he alleged, were intellectually unsuited to "tedious doctrines and schollarly methodes of discipline" (159) since they had no access to the foundations of useful eloquence found in Latin oratory and poetry. Thus, the ideal of women's English was highly constrained and practically useless, parallel to the skills of needlework that occupied the talents of generations of gentlewomen.

The paradox that women's limited linguistic competence allowed them greater (and more dangerous) linguistic creativity was an idea asserted by male writers typified by Chesterfield who in 1754 used an abusive metaphor in his dissection of "the incontinency of female eloquence." His feigned praise conceals a typically antifeminist notion of women and their language.

> Language is indisputably the more immediate province of the fair sex: there they shine, there they excel. The torrents of their eloquence, especially in the vituperative way, stun all opposition, and bear away, in one promiscuous heap, nouns, verbs, moods, and tenses. If words are wanting, which indeed happens but seldom, indignation instantly makes new ones; and I have often known four or five syllables that never met one another before, hastily and fortuitously jumbled into some word of mighty import. (Stanhope 1777, 2:170–71)

His ironic stance—calling women "the enrichers, the patronesses, and the harmonizers of our language" (174)—is to be understood in the context of his linguistic conservatism and his denunciation of most linguistic innovation (see Neumann 1946). For Chesterfield, women's English was a threat to the purity and stability of the language—defined from a male perspective.

A second idea—that women use a more refined variety of English—emerged from the quite different educational practices thought fit for boys and for girls. Beginning in the seventeenth century, women writers alleged that a classical education diverted boys from excellence in English while girls, not burdened with the study of Greek and Latin, were much more likely to achieve it. An essay attributed to Judith Drake and published in 1697 was an early exponent of this idea.

> I have often thought that the not teaching Women Latin and Greek, was an advantage to them, if it were rightly consider'd, and might be improv'd to a great heigth. For Girles after they can Read and Write (if they be of any Fashion) are taught such things as take not up their whole time, and not being suffer'd to run about at liberty as Boys, are furnish'd among other toys with Books, such as *Romances, Novels, Plays* and *Poems*; which though they read carelessly only for Diversion, yet unawares to them, give 'em very early a considerable Command both of Words and Sense; which are further improv'd by their making and receiving Visits with their Mothers, which gives them betimes the opportunity of imitating, conversing with, and knowing the manner and address of elder Persons. These I take to be the true Reasons why a Girl of Fifteen is reckon'd as Ripe as a Boy of One and Twenty, and not any natural forwardness of Maturity, as some People would have it. These advantages the Education of Boys deprives them of, who drudge away the Vigour of their Memories at Words, useless ever after to most of them, and at Seventeen or Eighteen are to begin their Alphabet of Sense, and are but where the Girles were at Nine or Ten. Yet because they have learnt Latin and Greek, reject with scorn all *English* Books their best helps, and lay aside their Latin ones, as if they were already Masters of all that Learning, and so hoist sail for the wide World without a Compass to Steer by. (Drake 1697, 57–58)

Within this analysis are two presumptions: that women are more skillful at English because of their early exposure to contemporary good usage as practiced by the "fashionable" and that even exposure to carelessly read English works of fiction is more linguistically profitable than extended study of Greek and Latin classics.

Writing in 1753, Lady Mary Wortley Montagu, in a letter to her daughter on the education of Lady Mary's granddaughter, reflected on her own neglect of the daughter's education. Since the granddaughter was physically deformed and not thought a likely marriage prospect, Lady Mary believed no harm would come from her being given a classical education. Even so, the girl should do all in her power to conceal whatever mastery of the learned languages she had acquired.

> The second caution to be given her (and which is most absolutely necessary) is to conceal whatever Learning she attains, with as much solicitude as she would hide crookedness or lameness. The parade of it can only serve to draw on her the envy, and consequently the most inveterate Hatred, of all he and she Fools, which will certainly be at least three parts in four of all her Acquaintance. The use of knowledge in our Sex (beside the amusement of Solitude) is to moderate the passions and learn to be contented with a small expence, which are the certain effects of a studious Life and, it may be, preferable even to that Fame which Men have engross'd to themselves and will not suffer us to share. (Halsband 1967, 3:22–23)

Concealing one's learning meant constraining one's language, and men embraced the idea that women's English was impoverished. "Flawed" English (evaluated from a masculine perspective) came to be an expected part of feminine conduct as well as a self-confirming principle of linguistic difference. When she published the first English thesaurus in 1794, Hester Lynch Piozzi felt obliged to acknowledge this prejudice and to apologize that a woman had approached the sacred precincts of philological study.

> If then to the selection of words in conversation and elegant colloquial language a book may give assistance, the Author, with that deference she so justly owes a generous public, modestly offers her's; persuaded that, while men teach to write with propriety, a woman may at worst be qualified—through long practice—to direct the choice of phrases in familiar talk. (Piozzi [1794] 1968, 1:ii)

In short, if women have any claim to knowledge of English, it arises only from the most trivial uses of it.

The view that women use a more refined form of English emerges in a fully developed form in the eighteenth century. Though Chesterfield's allegation persisted that "incontinent" women were grammatical chuckleheads, women came to be praised for refinement and taste in linguistic matters (though most often for their social grace rather than for discernment and intelligence).

Writing a dialogue on poetry in 1718, Charles Gildon presented an array of characters including one "Manilia" who "has an Inclination to the Muses, so she has, in her Performances, no small Force of unassisted Nature." But since "she is thoroughly acquainted with no Language but her own" (i.e., she lacks a classical education), she cannot put her own compositions or those of others in the larger context of the literature of antiquity (ix). Her interlocutor is "Laudon," a man of taste and erudition who leads her toward a fuller understanding of poetry. Manilia alleges that the beauty of dramatic art lies in "the Colouring, and Shades, and Lights, properly dispos'd"; to this argument Laudon disdainfully replies:

> I confess . . . I am not surpriz'd to hear this from a fair Lady, since that Sex has a mighty *Tendre* for *fine Things* and *fine Language*, as they call it; but it is because they see few Tragedies on our Stage, which are eminent for the greater and more solid Beauties; yet it must be own'd they have declar'd for Things of another Nature in some; I'll only instance their general and still continued Approbation of the *Orphan*. (Gildon 1718, 1:224)

Having disposed of women's unworthy interest in soppy melodrama, Laudon discloses the true source of poetic beauty, the plot. Yet what is striking is that he allows that women have a special *tendre* 'fondness' for fine language even though it is a minor attribute of dramatic excellence; from such concessions to women's taste emerged the notion that judgment about language was, at least in its superficial aspects, a special quality of women's perception.

This idea that women employ a superior form of English became a staple of late eighteenth-century observations. Robert Baker, for instance, declared in 1770:

> Women of polite Education, who are used to good Company, though they have studied Grammar no more than this Servant-maid, talk, if not quite correctly, yet more correctly than such Men in ordinary Life as have passed some Years at a Latin-school. (Baker [1770] 1968, xv)

Even so, praise was often grudging, presented not so much to celebrate the "natural" correctness of uneducated women as to point out the futility of a "classical" education for men. In the nineteenth century, however, the cult of pure womanhood appeared, and with it a special emphasis on language. Writing in 1836, Roland G. Hazard elevated the praise of women's English to an unparalleled level of celebration.

... in the sex of finer mould, who are elevated above these degrading influences, whose feelings are more pure, whose sentiments are more refined, and whose spirits are more ethereal, it [the faculty of language] manifests itself with a softened splendor, to which that of angels may well be supposed only another step in the scale of a magnificent progression.

It is to the superiority which woman has in this expressive language,—and to her command of this direct avenue to the finer feelings,—that we must attribute her influence in refining and softening the asperities of our nature. And it is owing to the possession of this element of moral elevation that, while the finest and strongest reasoning of philosophy has, in this respect, accomplished so little, woman has accomplished so much. (Hazard 1857, 36–37)

With this extravagant praise, the idea of women's perfection made their alleged solecisms even more blameworthy than in the prior century, when men observing women's English were convinced of their linguistic incapacity.

If women "naturally" spoke better than men, any lapse from idealized usage was so much the more objectionable. Describing the consequences of linguistic upward mobility (for which he coins the derisive term *get-on-itiveness*), an anonymous writer in 1842 ironically declared:

The tongue is proverbially an ungovernable member, and in no instance is it more so than in its relation to conventional politeness. Not that to pass muster in the highest society, it is absolutely necessary to be always quite accurate in grammar; nor in every instance to avoid those forms of speech which are esteemed among the educated as vulgarities. The early intercourse between ladies and their waiting-maids opens a wide door to the adoption of solecisms by the highest ranks of females, which, on that account, do not derogate. Indeed, when women of undoubted rank and distinction are permitted to think with their abigails, there is nothing so extraordinary in their taking the privilege of using their phraseology. "Oh, mys," and "did you evers," with many other nursery slipslops, are so far from objectionable, that we should advise the better educated candidates for distinction, to practise attentively the peculiar intonation and accent with which these elegant expletives should be introduced. ("Contributions" 1842, 216)

Just as Elyot had been concerned to protect young gentlemen from the linguistic contagion of nursemaids, so this author scolds the solecisms "women of undoubted rank and distinction" have caught from their *abigails* 'lady's maids.' The norm against which this childish nursery English is to be measured is that of the "educated," even though "better educated" women are inclined to employ fashionable "vulgarieties."

Other observers reluctantly proclaimed women's English superior to men's. James Fenimore Cooper celebrated women for mitigating the natural harshness of the English language, but ten years afterwards declared that American women, "contrary to the general law in such matters, . . . have a less agreeable utterance than the men, a defect that great care should be taken to remedy, as the nursery is the birth-place of so many of our habits" (Cooper 1931, 110–11; see Baron 1986, 74). The traits that Cooper finds to praise in men's English—deliberate and clear speech, matching words to the subject— should be characteristic of women since they "are the natural agents in maintaining the refinement of a people" (116). Such idealizations, of course, expose women to social condemnation, since those who fail to exercise the admired traits of English are subject to even more severe criticism than men. This fact of social life was explained by an anonymous author of a usage volume published in London in 1826.

> Young ladies require not to be informed how indispensible correct speaking is to them; for unless they possess this accomplishment, music, dancing, a fine carriage, or an elegant taste for dressing, will be thrown into the shade. A vulgar expression will at once give evidence of a glaring deficiency, and fix a blot on their taste and their accomplishments, which will not be easily effaced from the memory of an observer. A few hours careful study, with an attentive practice of our rules and examples, would not only prevent this, but would unfailingly produce ever after, a favourable impression of character and accomplishment. (*Vulgarities* 1826, 6)

Error-free English, therefore, was an accomplishment far more necessary than music, dancing, or the other social graces, since a false note or a missed step would not have the same likelihood of fixing "a blot on their taste" or calling a woman's character into question.

Writing in 1840, Thomas De Quincey also praised "the purity of female English," but his celebration carried an important reservation.

> Would you desire at this day to read our noble language in its native beauty, picturesque from idiomatic propriety, racy in its phraseology, delicate yet sinewy in its composition, steal the mail-bags, and break open all the letters in female handwriting. Three out of four will have been written by that class of women who have the most leisure and the most interest in a correspondence by the post: that class who combine more of intelligence, cultivation, and of

thoughtfulness, than any other in Europe—the class of unmarried women above twenty-five—an increasing class; women who, from mere dignity of character, have renounced all prospects of conjugal and parental life, rather than descent into habits unsuitable to their birth. Women capable of such sacrifices, and marked by such strength of mind, may be expected to think with deep feeling, and to express themselves (unless where they have been too much biased by bookish connexions) with natural grace. Not impossibly these same women, if required to come forward in some public character, might write ill and affectedly. They would then have their free natural movement of thought distorted into some accommodation to artificial standards, amongst which they might happen to select a bad one for imitation. But in their letters they write under the benefit of their natural advantages; not warped, on the one hand, into that constraint or awkwardness which is the inevitable effect of conscious exposure to public gaze; yet, on the other, not left to vacancy or the chills of apathy, but sustained by some deep sympathy between themselves and their correspondents. (De Quincey 1889–90, 10:145–46)

This small cadre of unmarried women of gentle "birth" was allowed to be especially "pure" in their use of English, but only in the domain of personal correspondence and not in language that would be subject to "public gaze." Women, in De Quincey's view as in Gildon's, are "naturals" who owe their skill to their being sheltered from distorting influences of the world. Like other citizens regarded as speaking especially "pure English," usually people in isolated and impoverished communities, such leisured women have little beyond the quality of their English to recommend them.

As this doctrine of the purity of women's speech became fully articulated, commentators stressed the vulnerability of women caught in linguistic informality.

Never speak of "lots" of things. Some young men allow themselves a diffusive license of speech, and of quotation, which has introduced many words into colloquial style that do not at all tend to improve or dignify the language, and which, when heard from *ladies'* lips, become absolute vulgarisms. A young man may talk recklessly of "lots of bargains," "lots of money," "lots of fellows," "lots of fun," &c., but a lady may *not*. Men may indulge in any latitude of expression within the bounds of sense and decorum, but woman has a narrower range—even her mirth must be subjected to the rules of good taste. It may be naive, but must never be grotesque. It is not that we would have *primness* in the sex, but we would have refinement. Women are the purer and the more ornamental part of life, and when *they* degenerate, the Poetry of Life is gone. (Gwynne 1856, 103)

A SOUND LIKE "THE GABBLE OF A GOOSE"

The great American language may "listen good" to us, but nevertheless, a Spanish critic assures us, it grates on more delicate ears—and it is fearfully illogical besides.

During the nineteenth century, women's English was subject to more and more censure. American writers who had spent time in Europe returned home to abuse the English of American women. European men joined the chorus. This cartoon was drawn to illustrate the reaction of a Madrid-born Spanish-American who first encountered American English as a youth (Blanco 1924b, 46): "The sound of her speech gave me a cold shock, a painful sensation of disillusion; it sounded so much like the cackle of a goose" (1924a, 342). More recently Burchfield has pilloried an American woman visiting Oxford for having said, "Is this the main drag, Edwin?" (Burchfield and Aarsleff 1988, 27).

A usage manual published in Philadelphia in 1868 made this point even more painfully clear.

> Slang is especially offensive in woman, to whom we are pleased to ascribe delicacy of taste. Yet how often do we not hear her introduce it into conversation! "He has the stamps," said, lately, in a public place, a young woman who would have been mortified to think that she had produced a bad impression even in a bystander. (Bache 1868, 19–20)

(The slang thus overheard by this "bystander" was the use of *stamps* to refer to paper money, an ephemeral term just then becoming current.)

The notion that *American* women were particularly likely to disappoint in matters of linguistic purity and were prone to various shameful forms of expression became, at the end of the nineteenth century, a subject upon which American men found themselves compelled to expatiate.

> What is it that has so vitiated the voices of most "American" men, and still more of most "American" women? For there is no doubt that the fairer sex are in this respect the least to be admired. Among fifty men you will find perhaps ten or a dozen who will open their mouths and speak clearly and freely; but among fifty women not more than two or three.
>
> This it is chiefly which here so diminishes the charms of that sex which in England delights the ear even more than it does the eye. Among the general public here, the public of the railway car and the hotel, the woman who has not this vice is a rare exception. You shall see a lovely, bright creature, with all the external evidences of culture about her, a woman who will carry you captive so long as she is silent; but let her open her pretty lips, and she shall pierce your ear with a mean, thin, nasal, rasping tone, by which at once you are disenchanted. An Englishwoman, even of the lower classes, will delight you with the rich, sweet, smooth, and yet firm and crisp tones in which she utters what may perhaps be very bad "grammar." (White 1880, 93–94)

Similarly, William Dean Howells alarmed magazine readers in 1906 with the idea that flaws in just one woman's English could lead a foreign visitor to wholesale condemnation of American English.

> Yet, what is it gives the cultivated sojourner, or the transitory stranger among us the impression that our women are of slovenly and uncouth utterance, and that the exceptions are so few as not to affect the general impression? . . . A young lady twanging or whiffling in an open trolley-car, or snuffling or whining

on a hotel veranda, will lodge in the ear of the listener a discomfort, which all
her companions, when they trill sweetly as hermit-thrushes, or murmur softly
as doves in immemorial elms, cannot remove. (Howells 1906, 930)

Because of the expectation that women's usage would manifest particular
"delicacy of taste" and lyricism, the stereotype of women as speakers of
"pure English" put them in even greater danger of censure than the earlier
theory that vilified their defective English.

At the same time Howells was fulminating against the "slovenly and
uncouth utterance" of American women, Henry James added his "European"
affirmation.

> For even more striking to me, at this recent hour and under the impression of a
> wider view and more evidence, than the fact itself of the crudity of tone of my
> countrywomen in general, was the immunity from comment, from any shadow
> of criticism, that it serenely enjoys. This sinister circumstance of the social
> silence surrounding them was really what had constituted my key, as I had
> called it, to the license of the poor children—poor children of the rich—who,
> under expensive tuition, tuition of a cost often so startling to "European" ears,
> were vociferating over the Boston gutters. The supremely interesting thing was
> that, even at the fountain-head of our native culture, nobody, and least of all
> their remunerated instructors, seemed to doubt for a moment that these were
> good formative conditions. The imagination attuned to the "European" view of
> what is good and what is bad for growing creatures of the more sensitive sex,
> recoils in dismay before the conception thus involved in the duties and the
> standards, the general authority and quality, of such strange presiding pre-
> ceptresses. (James 1906–7, 18)

For James, the "sinister circumstance of the social silence" about women's
usage thrust them from their "proper" place as social arbiters of proper
English. "Ladies' culture-clubs," as James disparagingly called them, had
arisen throughout the United States, and in them women endeavored to
educate themselves in subjects to which male-dominated institutions of learning had denied them access. All such attempts to join men's conversation
about history, beauty, and culture were doomed, opined James, since women
had not first perfected their language.

> The ladies' culture-club is the most publicly taken engagement, surely, that
> ever was. It engages for those things which in the ancient world, as it survives
> around us, are held to come *after* the habit of harmonious speech, and assumed,

by the same stroke, to be discussable only in its terms and with its aid; an air
of grotesqueness attaching inevitably to their preceding it or dispensing with it.
(James 1906–7, 1105)

The doctrine of the special "purity" of women's English was turned back to
thwart women's aspirations. Failing to speak correctly became, in James's
argument, a justification for denying women access to the knowledge.

Even if delicacy of taste had become generally admired in men and
women alike by the early twentieth century, the obligation to sustain delicacy
increasingly was regarded as a particularly female duty. In his much vilified
essay on "The Woman" (1921), Otto Jespersen stated this expectation in a
way that made it appear to be a general law of human society.

> There can be no doubt that women exercise a great and universal influence
> on linguistic development through their instinctive shrinking from coarse and
> gross expressions and their preference for refined and (in certain spheres) veiled
> and indirect expressions. (Jespersen 1964a, 246)

Such "praise" for refinement makes women responsible for euphemism, indi-
rection, evasion, and vagueness when occasions call for blunt, frank, bald,
and even unpleasant assertions. By celebrating the purity of women's English, such observers placed them and their language on the fringe of conversation about the most important social issues and the most valued social
occasions for speaking. Putting women on a pedestal of linguistic idealism
was a deliberate and consequential way of limiting their mobility.

A third notion of women's English suggests that women are simultaneously inferior users of the language *and* superior through greater refinement and sensitivity. This view asserts that women are *different* because their
opportunities for hearty vulgarity or effectual eloquence are constrained in
male-dominated culture. In a patriarchal society, that difference is presumed
to be part of the natural order of things, and so women rightly experience
linguistic restraints that are not compelling for men. In his influential *Arte
of Rhetorique* (1560), Thomas Wilson incidentally displays this principle in
an illustration of the faults of orators who arrange their ideas in the "wrong"
order.

> Some will set the Cart before the horse, as thus. My mother and my father are
> both at home, as though the good man of the house did weare no breches, or
> that the graie Mare were the better Horse. And what though it often so hap-

peneth (God wot the more pitty) yet in speaking at the least, let vs keepe a
naturall order, and set the man before the woman for maners sake. ([1560]
1909,167)

In other words, though women may sometimes "rule" at home, decency and
tact require that this circumstance be glossed over and hence it is proper to
write "My father and my mother are both at home."

Anglo-American attacks on patriarchy and its linguistic offspring developed fully with the rise of modern feminist advocacy around the issue of
the right of women to vote. In her chapter on "Sex Dialects" in *The Old-
Fashioned Woman* (1913), Elsie Clews Parsons noted that women were socially segregated and thus linguistically deprived.

> Excluded from statecraft as well as from theology, women have naturally been
> ignorant of the dialect of politics . . . . Women are also unlearned in the dialects
> of business and trade, of war and its machines, and of sport. Few women
> understand the slang of Wall Street or are able to read stock quotations. How
> many women remain sufficiently unbewildered by new terms to go on listening
> when men begin to discuss the balance of trade or the theory of a central bank?
> Military expressions are rarely used by a woman and she is as uncertain in her
> reference to the parts of pistol or rifle as in her handling of them. Football,
> baseball, boats, horses, cards, drink, all have their technical vocabularies, and
> bits of them often come to be understood and adapted to other exegencies of
> description by the layman, seldom by the laywoman. In critical circles, in fact,
> her use of race track, gambling, or tippling slang would be deplored, since it
> suggests a knowledge of "sport" "distinctly unbecoming." (Parsons 1913, 153–
> 54)

Parsons found this deliberate deprivation of women a matter for righteous
anger. "Of such sacrosanct lingo we may be sure the women are kept in
ignorance, shut out as they are from the pursuit or calling itself" (150).

A leap forward from the idea that women are denied access to the entire
range of English emerges in a fourth perspective, the notion that English
itself is not well suited to women's favored modes of expression since they
have not participated fully in its development. Once women are fluent in the
"sacrosanct lingo" of men, they find themselves uncomfortably constrained
by the very nature of English.

> *Gertrude Stein* (1927). Patriarchal poetry needs rectification and there about it.
> Come to a distance and it still bears their name. (Stein 1953, 264)

Virginia Woolf (1929). But it is still true that before a woman can write exactly as she wishes to write, she has many difficulties to face. To begin with, there is the technical difficulty—so simple, apparently; in reality, so baffling—that the very form of the sentence does not fit her. It is a sentence made by men; it is too loose, too heavy, too pompous for a woman's use. Yet in a novel, which covers so wide a stretch of ground, an ordinary and usual type of sentence has to be found to carry the reader on easily and naturally from one end of the book to the other. And this a woman must make for herself, altering and adapting the current sentence until she writes one that takes the natural shape of her thought without crushing or distorting it. (Woolf 1980, 48)

Adrienne Rich (1971). Both the victimization and the anger experienced by women are real, and have real sources, everywhere in the environment, built into society, language, the structures of thought. They will go on being tapped and explored by poets, among others. (Rich 1979, 49)

For a woman to express herself fully, she needs to change the language to suit her distinct sensibility and purposes.

The image of English as a male-dominated and consequently a flawed mode of expression has come to be regarded as nearly axiomatic among the adherents of late twentieth-century feminism.

What all this comes down to is that the male bias of English did not have to be fostered by a conspiracy. It came about through the working of a familiar principle: power tends to corrupt. English is male-oriented because it evolved through centuries of patriarchy to meet the needs of partriarchy. Those in power tend to try to stay there, and those out of power, to make the best of what they are allotted. But because women's image of themselves is changing, language is changing in response. (Miller and Swift 1977, 87)

Such a notion compels those who state it to face the paradox that the vehicle by which they express these ideas is the very same patriarchal English that constrains them. As a consequence of the English language, women's "elemental powers of communication" are short-circuited.

The sadosocietal system fixes and freezes women's Elemental Powers of Communication, confining their expression to "appropriate" stereotypic activities, such as those assigned to wives and mothers, nurses, schoolmarms, hostesses, and efficient do-gooders. Thus enslaved by the snoolish rules and rulers, women become complicit in the stunting and fragmentation of our Selves. A phallically fixed wife and mother keeps pop on his pedestal and nurtures future faithful followers of fatherland's rules/roles. A nurse whose loyalty is to physicians and patriarchal medicine is a servant of disease-causing agents. A female teacher, whether she works in a nursery school or in a Ph.D. program, who uncritically transmits the dogmas of doublethink is an agent of maledom's mindbinding. (Daly and Caputi 1987, 8–9)

English, in this view, is reformed and restored by being changed through the introduction of *new words*, defined in Mary Daly and Jane Caputi's *Wickedary* as: "words of Gynocentric communication—many of which are not 'new' in the old sense (materially) but New in a New sense, having different meanings because they are Heard and Spoken in New ways" (Daly and Caputi 1987, 84, 86).

Attacks by feminists on the bias of English quickly go beyond an inventory of linguistic faults to identify the malefactors who have caused them. Thus recent psychological studies trace the most damaging forms of social conduct to male speech and assign positive values to women's English. Women are alleged to display cooperation, engagement, and "person-orienta-tion" while men manifest individualism, aloofness, and "object-orientation." In friendly conversation women are claimed to use the pronouns *you* and *we* far more than men (who are more likely to employ *I* and *me*); women give signs of interest and attention (while men tend to challenge others for domi-nance); women begin to speak by acknowledging others and linking their contributions to what others have said (while men change the subject). This analysis supports the image that women's English is typified by socially valued motives: consideration for others, cooperation in the elaboration of ideas, and concern for orderly social relations (see Lakoff 1975; Maltz and Borker 1982). It suggests that Virginia Woolf was right in asserting "that both in life and in art the values of a woman are not the values of a man" (1980, 49); patriarchal language distorts the best of human nature. English, imperiled by sexism, can be redeemed only through reforming conduct and linguistic manners. That these claims seem so plausible to so many may well be a result of their connection to currently "correct" ideas about gender equality. Their resemblance to a long history of language manipulation might well invite further reflection.

Chapter 10

Proper English

The survey so far provided demonstrates over and over the ways in which cultural anxieties and aspirations are reflected in statements about English. In the early sixteenth century, when Britain was isolated, impoverished, and incidental to European intellectual and economic life, English speakers despaired that their language could ever be stabilized, ascertained, or exported. Rising democratic impulses late in the eighteenth century produced another set of ideologies: English might be spread abroad, especially to North America, and provide a new voice for political freedom and for exuberance freed from the restraints of dying institutions. Imperial dreams of the nineteenth century made it possible to imagine that English speakers could travel around the world, assisted everywhere by people like themselves "in taste, in opinions, in morals, and in intellect" (see p. 138). Political emergence of former dependencies did not quell that impulse, and anglophones at the end of the twentieth century are still persuaded that their language is the inevitable vehicle worldwide for development, innovation, and hope. In modern times, nearly every invention has been construed as a means to spread English; "electric communication, steamships" (1894, see p. 117); "aviation, motion pictures, and the wireless telephone" (1929, see p. 119); "mass communication and the spread of computer technology" (Finneran 1986, 13); "the communications satellite" (1990, see p. 121). Poets were viewed as the leaders in perfecting and diffusing the language during the Renaissance; today, the leadership has fallen to technicians.

Optimism about the language has never quite overcome doubts and uncertainties. For some, the language itself contains the infection of debilitating disease: an imperfect spelling system obscuring its use; unpredictable grammatical processes warping the ideal of predictable regularity; a vocabulary deteriorating through unrestrained borrowing and neologism. For others, its expressions mirror a disgraceful and unredeemed history of racism, gender bias, and political oppression; these "entrenched attitudes" cry out for change (see Bailey 1990, 87). Still others fear that imprecise usage by successive generations of innovators leads inexorably to chaos when "the language of the illiterates will triumph" (see p. 229). Regretful memories of a golden past when English poured forth from a clear spring of pure expression mingle with doubts that the language will ever recover from the assaults of its enemies—enemies as various as the ignorant (who foist yet new errors on the unsuspecting genteel) and the young (who perpetually wrest usage to their own terrible purposes).

Writing in 1926, Robert Graves saw the need for "a review of those classroom commonplaces on the peculiar nature of English which . . . have for years been copied from one blackboard to another without due inquiry into their truth" (6–7). Academic blackboards and the media dependent upon them continue to repeat those commonplaces, not because they are true but because they are usually familiar and occasionally comforting. Currently received wisdom about English is perhaps nowhere better expressed than in the opening chapter of Robert Claiborne's popular book, *Our Marvelous Native Tongue* (1983), "The Importance of Speaking English: A Most Extraordinary Language." Claiborne's candor in celebrating the virtues of English is matched by his willingness to present familiar ideas in a lively style. As he writes in his preface: "where (as occasionally happened) I have had to choose between academic precision and readability, I have unhesitatingly picked the latter" (viii). He does not, of course, intend to promulgate error, only to unleash his enthusiasm from the bondage of "academic" qualification. By being "readable," he expresses contemporary images in a particularly bald form.

Antiquity is a source of pride for Claiborne: "The story of the life and times of English, from perhaps eight thousand years ago to the present, is both a long and a fascinating one" (7). In this estimate of eight thousand years, Claiborne draws his readers into the reaches of linguistic reconstruction, deep into the heart of Proto-Indo-European, and finds there "English." English is thus among the oldest languages, a tongue earlier than the most ancient written records far in the distant past. In elaborating this idea, Claiborne adds: "English borrowings from other Indo-European tongues come from the modern or relatively modern members of the family" (29). In this "family," English is construed to be the senior language, only borrowing from "modern members" once it had consolidated and identified itself. Such a view is far from the conventional academic idea that English coalesced recently among a tiny tribe living in a geographical bywater. *Old* languages, of course, are like *old* families; one is of the same antiquity as another. To be an *old* family, or an *old* language, is in some indistinct way to be better.

The *OED* declares the use of *old* to refer to "things which have always existed" as *poetic*, and this poetic usage invokes the romanticized history of everyday life that is so essential a part of anglophone culture. Idries Shah, a shrewd observer of present-day Britain, sees the incongruity in a title—for a book describing the supposed early hominid Piltdown skull—*The Earliest Englishman* (Shah 1987, 15). But the English are not likely to recognize the eccentricity of identifying prehistoric Homo sapiens with present-day Britons. Antiquity is a badge of honor worn, in the case of Claibourne's *marvelous* language, upon the tongue.

The idea that English is remarkable for its antiquity was elaborated early in the seventeenth century. When Verstegan, Carew, and Sprat used the word *natural* to describe a "natural way of speaking" or *naturally* to express the connection between words and ideas or emotions, they did not have in mind the arbitrary convention that modern linguists claim is the link between sign and referent; instead, they meant that the link between sound and sense in English had been given by *Nature*. If others express themselves differently, it is their misfortune to be wrong. Hence, Renaissance historians were at pains to explain the antiquity of English in Biblical terms, and if not all were willing to embrace Becanus's view that "Teutonic" was the language of Eden, they were not reluctant to locate its roots in Biblical history. Certainly the idea that Danes and Normans had deflected English people from their divinely ordained destiny was not unpopular, and the twentieth-century notion of Aryan superiority was founded in these seventeenth-century opinions.

Writing in 1642, John Hare declared England to be a "primitive nation," by which he meant that it was *original*, a human community established from the beginning.

> [S]he is a primitive nation, and vaunts her descent to be from no other place, than from the top of Nimrod's tower, where was made the first division of mankind into nations; she derives not herself, (like those of her neighbours that boast so much of their great birth) from the conquered relicks of ruined Troy, whence also Virgil took so much pains to deduce his Romans, or from any other nation; but, as most conceive, the first transmigration, that the Teutones made, was, as is aforesaid, from the building of Babel. . . . (Hare 1810, 93)

Hare bitterly regretted that English had been "un-teutonised" as a consequence of "one unfortunate battle," the one at Hastings in 1066 (99). He
proposed the eradication of "Normanising" from the political and cultural
scene of his day, including reform of the language. It appeared at the end of
his bill of particulars:

> 5. That our language be cleared of the Norman and French invasion upon it,
> and depravation of it, by purging it of all words and terms of that descent,
> supplying it from the old Saxon and the learned tongues, and otherwise correct-
> ing it, whereby it may be advanced to the quality of an honourable and sufficient
> language, than which there is scarce a greater point in a nation's honour and
> happiness. (103)

These notions are too pernicious to dismiss with the relatively neutral term
ethnocentrism. "Restoring" a racially pure language to suit a racially "primitive" nation is an idea that reached its most extreme and dreadful consequence in Hitler's Reich, and its appearance in images of English has not
been sufficiently acknowledged.

Claiborne's "perhaps eight thousand years ago" is the modern equivalent of the descent from Babel so comforting to seventeenth-century thinkers.
By giving English the cachet of antiquity, he invests its speakers with a sense
of their own superiority. In so doing, he invokes disinterested rationality:

> some readers will suspect me of exaggeration if not outright cultural chauvin-
> ism. Can I really be claiming that English is not merely a great language but the
> greatest? Yes, that is exactly what I'm saying—and I don't consider myself any
> sort of chauvinist. (Claiborne 1983, 6)

Adducing cultural evidences for the superiority of anglophone nations,
Claiborne cites literary excellence and political institutions. These claims,
too, have a long history: Carew celebrating English authors as equal to
those of ancient Greece and Rome (see p. 43); American patriots on the
eve of revolution anticipating for their country an English achieving "its
highest perfection, with every other branch of human knowledge" (see p.
103); zealous imperialists of the mid-nineteenth century celebrating British
superiority and connecting English to evidences of "the God of providence"
(see p. 107), "the vigor of the race that uses it" (see p. 109), and "the
revolutions of science, the progress of free institutions, and the developments of civilization generally" (see p. 108). Claiborne's assertions of supe-

riority are merely old notions in a new guise; accepting them uncritically invites speakers of English to bask in their present-day glory without considering how in their older forms these notions justified slavery, exploitation, and conquest.

A characteristic of late twentieth-century popular culture is a fascination with fictionalized history through "theme parks," "historical" villages, and "documentary" films and television programs. Such reconstructions are cleansed of inconvenient realism in order to match modern ideas of "long ago"; thus, sewage, sickness, slavery, and squalor are all rigorously excluded. Such presentations invite viewers to invent a past from which problems of the present are erased while problems of the past are silently corrected. That past becomes *our* past, a collective memory that defines what is *ours*. So too, the *our* in Claiborne's title—*Our Marvelous Native Tongue*—invokes what Patrick Wright calls "a transhistorical national identity going by the name of 'we'" (1985, 163). English is not a language that people happen to speak; it is *our* language, *marvelous* for its lengthy history and varied excellencies. It is "the treasure of our tongue" of which Samuel Daniel wrote in 1599.

This love affair with the past expresses itself in images, and the idea of "traditional" usage exercises an overpowering attraction, especially for those discontented with the present. The late nineteenth-century travel writer C. M. Doughty conceived such an intense dislike of the "Victorian English" of his own day that he attempted to compose in a style that would "continue the older tradition of Chaucer and Spenser, resisting to my power the decadence of the English language" (Hogarth 1928, 114; Hopkins 1955, 283–84; Taylor 1939). In flying from present "decadence" to past glory, writers of Doughty's taste find the sources of true English to lie in its Old English vocabulary even though thousands of words derived from Latin and French have a claim to antiquity. Since there has been a continuous flow of borrowings and adaptations from Latin and French, anglophones have not acquired the "depth perception" to distinguish ancient loans from recent imports (so, for instance, without special study speakers do not recognize that *schism* became English in the fourteenth century, *synchronism* in the sixteenth, *synergism* in the eighteenth, and *syndicalism* in the twentieth). Given this uncertainty about the actual age of English words, then, *archaism* has the special sense, not of being, but of *seeming* old.

Nativism in linguistic preference began among the sixteenth-century rhetoricians who drew their ideas from Cicero's theories of oratory. One of the first principles of diction in the Ciceronian tradition was thus articulated in 1560 by Thomas Wilson: "that such words as we vse, should be proper vnto the tongue wherein wee speake" ([1560]1909, 165). Though he had distinct notions of what was *proper* to English, Wilson himself was no saxonizing purist. However, the seed of his idea grew into doctrine. John Cheke, Wilson's contemporary, declared: "I am of this opinion, that our own tongue should be written clean and pure, unmix'd and unmangeled with borrowing of other tongues . . . " (1954, 538). When he turned his hand to translating a portion of the New Testament, Cheke's preference for "our own tongue" affected his choice of vocabulary: *crossed* for *crucified, freschman* for *proselyte, hundreder* for *centurion, wizards* for *magi* (Gray 1988, 116). Verstegan's urging that *scypman* replace *mariner* followed the same tradition (see p. 41), and a share of Puritan "plainness" expressed itself in vocabulary actually or apparently from Old English sources. William Barnes was even more ambitious in his plan to saxonize the vocabulary through such substitutions as *inbringing* for *importation* (see p. 194), and that impulse toward "pure, unmix'd and unmangeled" English still persists.

Inventing "old" terms rather than reviving them became a hallmark of English vocabulary among writers who have favored "antique" or "rustic" diction. The impulse toward a native vocabulary resulted in such pseudo-archaic innovations as: *derring-do* 'manhood and chivalry' (1579), *dispart* 'part with' (1828), *malgrace* 'something unbecoming' (1882), *passen* 'pass' (1748), *raptril* 'rascal' (1843), *swan's bath* 'the sea' (1865), and *war-fain* 'eager to fight' (1876). Some old prefixes have been mimicked in such inventions: *a-* in *aplenty* (1830; on the pattern of the genuinely old *afresh* and *anew*); *be-* in *behear* (1600; resembling *beseech* and *beset*); and *y-* (< Old English *ge-*) in *ybord* (1768), *yclinge* (1620), *yminted* (1835), and *ysprinkled* (1867). As a literary device, archaism, whether fabricated or genuine, has been particularly attractive to authors invoking a purer past language—Spenser, Chatterton, Scott, Coleridge, Morris, Hopkins, and Tolkien (among many others). In its most extreme form, it attracts the attention of the learned; thus C. T. Onions offered this opinion of the use of *Ye* 'the' in modern contexts.

> It is still often used pseudo-archaically, jocularly, or vulgarly (pronounced as *ye*), e.g., in Lewis Carroll's "Ye Carpette Knyghte," and in shop-signs like Ye Olde Booke Shoppe. (*OED*, s. v. "Y")

R. W. Burchfield, Onion's student and successor as editor of the *Oxford English Dictionary*, was similarly scornful of this long-standing, though inauthentic, expression of archaism.

olde, *a*. An affected form of OLD *a*., supposed to be archaic and usu. employed to suggest (spurious) antiquity, *esp*. in collocations often also archaistically spelt, as *olde Englisch(e), Englysche, worlde, worldy*. (*OED*)

The late nineteenth century even acquired a term for this stylistic tendency, *Wardour Street English*: "a perfectly modern article with a sham appearance of the real antique about it" (quoted in *OED*, s. v. "*Wardour Street*"). (Wardour Street, formerly a district of antique dealers, gave its name to a variety of English, a coinage formed on the model of *billingsgate* 'coarsely abusive language' [< Billingsgate fish market, 1652] and *Grub Street* 'literary hack-work' [1630].)

If Wardour Street English was too much of a good thing, it was at least allowed to be an error on the side of virtue. In what was to become a modern stylistic maxim, the Fowler brothers declared in 1906: "**Prefer the Saxon word** to the Romance" (7). In *A Dictionary of Modern English Usage* (1926–) —"an epoch-making book in the strict sense of that overworked phrase" (Gowers 1965, iii)—this sentiment was elaborated in extended essays on *Anti-Saxonism* and *Saxonism*, but with a caveat.

> The wisdom of this nationalism in language—at least in so thoroughly composite a language as English—is very questionable; we may well doubt whether it benefits the language, & that it does not benefit the style of the individual, who may or may not be prepared to sacrifice himself for the public good, is pretty clear. (Fowler 1927, 514)

Such skepticism about "the follies of Saxonism" (Fowler 1927, 26) has not often afflicted successors who have regarded the original formulation as a first principle. Orwell, for instance, worried that Latin and Romance borrowings seemed to "gain ground from their Anglo-Saxon opposite numbers" (Howe 1982, 252); Peter Farb wrote of the difference "between the Latinate upper-class speech and the Anglo-Saxon of the common people" (1975, 28); Strunk and White asserted: "Anglo-Saxon is a livelier tongue than Latin, so use Anglo-Saxon words" (1979, 76–77). Like Wardour Street English, "Anglo-Saxon" qualities are not necessarily founded in historical fact. So too *Old English* has long been employed "in popular use . . . vaguely to all obsolete [or old-seeming] forms of the language" (*OED*). Thus *copy* (< French, pre-1338) counts as "Anglo-Saxon" while *replica* (< Italian, 1834) does not; *quart* (< French, pre-1325) not *liter* (< French, 1797); *ridiculous* (< Latin, 1550) not *risible* (< Latin, 1557), *stay* (< French, 1440) not *remain* (<

French, pre-1425). *Anglo-Saxon* or *Saxon* have thus come to describe words from any source that are 'plain, unvarnished, forthright' (*OED*) or 'language that is blunt, monosyllabic, and often rude or vulgar' (Flexner 1987, 81). For many stylists and reformers, whatever can be accomplished to uproot words derived from Latin and French is to be welcomed. Thus, Samuel Johnson described a word employed by his "undefiled" Spenser as "a French word which with many more is now happily disused" (1755, s. v. "*souvenance*"), perpetuating the old idea that "as much as present-day English has receded from the old Saxon, so much has it degenerated from its native purity."

"Antiquity" as a virtue of the English language thus emerges as a significant part of the image of the language. But the fact of antiquity is one thing; its uses are another, and "educated" people have been expected to employ antiquity to their own advantage in presenting themselves as "discriminating" users of English. Highly refined national and class distinctions have been built around etymological nuance, and hence it is that one of the most forceful arguments against spelling reform has been "the obvious Inconvenience of utterly destroying our Etymology" (Swift 1966, 114). Repelled by linguistic snobbery founded on "exact" usage, Elias Molee opined in 1888: "It looks to me as if the English language were constructed by some eccentric, rich and learned bachelors who had nothing else to do but hunt up the meaning of words in dictionaries and to spell" (see p. 201; this description applied aptly to Molee's successors at reform, the Fowler brothers).

Not surprisingly, social radicals have recognized a "refined" sense of linguistic antiquity as a device that masks opposition to political change, and they suggest innovations to liberate expression from the prejudices of the *pointy-headed* (1968) and the *phallocentric* (1927): "The dead learning of the universities, the meanness of their conduct must be brushed aside and way made for the COMMON PEOPLE" (see p. 203); "Under phallocracy, grammar is an instrument of social control" (Daly and Caputi 1987, 24). Linguistic history and the "antiquity" of English, they correctly discern, have justified politically reactionary ideologies.

Yet the same linguistic material may be used to justify incompatible social values. In considering the gradual loss of the suffix *-ess*, for instance, Richard Chenevix Trench presented in 1857 the following revealing analysis.

> The designation of a female person by changing "er" into "ess," as "flatterer," "flatteress," or by the addition of "ess," as "captain," "captainess," was once much more common than it is now. The language is rapidly abdicating its

Whether women are best served by a distinctive vocabulary for their pursuits remains a matter for debate. Illustration from a Peggy Mills comic strip, ca. 1930. See Hofstadter 1985.

rights in this matter. But these forms, though now many of them obsolete, are very indicative of the former wealth of the language, and have good claim to be registered [in a dictionary]. (Trench 1860, 24)

By describing English as a monarch (*abdicating* rights) and by implying present poverty descended from *former wealth*, Trench demonstrated how history could be used to justify the social construction of a particular ideal. Modern readers are likely to view his analysis as constraining the social aspirations of others—in this case women who see nothing to be gained in irrelevant gender distinctions or who find the use of *-ess* demeaning in, for example, *sleeress* (< *slayer*) or *soveraintess* (< *sovereign*)—Trench's examples. To Trench's contemporaries, however, another interpretation was possible. Writing in *Godey's Lady's Book* in 1865, an anonymous author responded to Trench by welcoming the "revival" or creation of titles formed with -*ess* that would make women separately equal. *Americaness*, *paintress*, *professoress*, and *presidentess* were examples independently coined to illustrate the idea (quoted in Mencken 1960c, 590–91). Such titles were construed to give special dignity to women's roles by "following the analogies of *our* language" (italics added). Both sides of the argument drew upon the "analogies" of English and found confirmation for their views in "antiquity."

A second recurring argument in favor of English extends from the praise of antiquity to celebration of copiousness. Through its long history, the argument runs, English has accumulated an enormous wordstock, and that fact is construed as evidence of its general excellence and even its unqualified superiority to other languages. Claiborne, once again, expresses the received wisdom.

> The total number of English words lies somewhere between 400,000—the number of current entries in the largest English dictionaries—and 600,000—the largest figure that any expert is willing to be quoted on. By comparison, the biggest French dictionaries have only about 150,000 entries, the biggest Russian ones a mere 130,000. (1983, 5)

Though the arithmetic varies from generation to generation, the number of words attributed to English has always been substantial and always larger than the vocabulary size of other, less fortunate nations. Puncturing the swollen pride of anglophone superiority, Idries Shah points out the absurdity of "the English statement, seen so often in print, that English has one of the largest vocabularies of all (nearly half a million words) 'though the average educated person uses only one per cent of these'" (1987, 52). "Words" in such computations are mere tokens rather than expressions for use, and thus their number is meaningless as an index of culture. An unreflecting sense of superiority is all that allows one to claim special virtue for an abstraction named English. Yet Claiborne presses unequivocally forward in asserting that an enormous vocabulary is a signal merit.

> Words . . . are a kind of natural resource; it is impossible to have too many of them. Not, indeed, that any one of us will ever get around to using more than a fraction of our enormous thesaurus ("treasury"—from Greek) of words, not least because tens of thousands of them are intelligible only to specialists. But even the fraction in general use endows us with a uniquely rich assortment of synonyms on almost any subject under the sun: words that mean more or less

THE "UNDESIRABLES."

SHADE OF ABRAHAM LINCOLN.—I stand among you, good people. *My* father could never have passed!

Demands for literacy in English have increased over the last century as Anglo-American culture has come to regard reading, writing, and computation as essential skills for more and more citizens. Unsatisfied with the rate of assimilation to English of immigrants, U.S. nativists have succeeded in declaring English "the official language" of various states. In 1986, Californians passed such a measure in a state-wide referendum supported by nearly three out of four voters. At the same time, the California legislature discussed regulations to "make standard English instruction part of the school level planning, implementation, and program review processes" (Assembly Bill no. 2655 [January 13, 1986], Senate Bill no. 2372 [February 21, 1986]). See Fishman 1986, Baron 1990. Illustration from *Puck* 75 (March 21, 1914): 2.

the same thing, yet each of which possesses its own special qualities of sound and rhythm and shade of meaning. (1983, 5)

There is nothing intrinsic in English to justify Claiborne's comparison of the wordstock to such "natural resources" as petroleum reserves or mineral deposits. All languages are open to borrowing, and all provide a mechanism for creating and expressing new meanings. English is distinctive only in having devoted so much investment in archiving the words that have been used in the past. Big dictionaries are nothing but storerooms with infrequently visited and dusty corners. Celebrating the size of the English vocabulary is a tribute to the lexical accumulation that has been gathered in the last two centuries. Yet an unreflecting triumphalism founded on dictionaries is regularly offered as evidence for the "uniquely rich" perfection of English and expressed in such bald assertions as: "We have by far the largest vocabulary of any language" (Cottle 1975,15).

Just as the idea of antiquity has spawned a series of doctrines about the virtues of English and nuances of its use, so the idea of copiousness has resulted in conclusions affecting those thought to have relatively small vocabularies: foreigners generally, primitive peoples in particular, and English speakers remote from sources of power and authority. The decade of the 1860s was an especially fertile one for the development of these ideas, but they remain influential even today.

> *1851.* Fearful indeed is the impress of degradation which is stamped on the language of the savage, more fearful perhaps even than that which is stamped upon his form. When wholly letting go the truth, when long and greatly sinning against light and conscience, a people has thus gone the downward way, has been scattered off by some violent catastrophe from those regions of the world which are the seats of advance and progress, and driven to its remote isles and further corners, then as one nobler thought, one spiritual idea after another has perished from it, the words also that expressed these have perished too. As one habit of civilization has been let go after another, the words which those habits demanded have dropped as well, first out of use, and then out of memory, and thus after a while have been wholly lost. (Trench 1891, 17–18)
>
> *1860.* It must be obvious even from this extremely cursory glance that our English, enriched with French, Latin, Greek, and other words, and formed into complicated sentences by rules of grammatical construction, is an unknown tongue to the masses, especially in some districts. . . . It is not merely the peasantry of rural districts that are thus ignorant. The lower middle

classes of our large towns are deplorably so, and many of higher position too; but because they can express themselves tolerably in speaking or writing on the business of their every-day life, which requires no extensive vocabulary or complicated paragraphs, it is taken for granted that they understand all that can possibly be said to them in the language which we call English. (Foster 1860,19)

1861. A country Clergyman informed me, that he believed the labourers in his parish had not 300 words in their vocabulary, and a recent article in the *Quarterly* extends the statements to the great mass of our rural population. It is well known that forty-nine per cent of our people never enter any place of worship; and though other causes may and do contribute to this neglect of religious observances, the almost total ignorance of literary English is not the least. I know I shall be referred to the crowds that run after popular preachers, to the well-filled lecture-rooms of Mechanics' Institutes, to the success which has crowned "public readings," to the habits of study amongst the working-classes, as proved by the large sales of the Book-hawking Society, and to the very great intelligence of our operatives, as shown in their conversation, speeches and publications. I grant all this, and yet I do not retract a word, as unconsidered or exaggerated. The skilled artisan and the rough ploughman cannot be classed together; it is of the latter that I speak: and I appeal to the Clergy, to Schoolmasters, Inspectors of Schools, District Visitors, Chaplains of prisons, to all who are brought into contact with the lower orders of this country, whether it is possible to exaggerate the amount of darkness which prevails. (D'Orsey 1861,15)

1863. Language is a thrifty housewife. If we consider the variety of ideas that were expressed by the one root *spas* [in, e.g., *auspicious, respectable, respite*, etc.], it is easy to see that with 500 such roots a dictionary might have been formed sufficient to satisfy the wants, however extravagant, of her husband—the human mind. If each root yielded fifty derivatives, we should have 25,000 words. Now, we are told by a country clergyman, that some of the labourers in his parish did not use more than 300 words in their daily conversation. . . . A well-educated person in England, who has been at a public school and at the university, who reads his Bible, his Shakespeare, the *Times*, and all the books of Mudie's Library, seldom uses more than about 3,000 or 4,000 words in actual conversation. Accurate thinkers and close reasoners, who avoid vague and general expressions, and wait till they find the word that exactly fits their meaning, employ a larger stock; and eloquent speakers may rise to a command of 10,000. (Müller 1899, 377–79)

1865. But *why* should it be held impossible that man once existed with nothing but the merest rudiments of speech? There are whole nations *even now* which, if the testimony of travellers is to be accepted, possess very little more. Nor, indeed, is it necessary to look to the remotest parts of the earth to find how very few are the words which are *necessary* to express the wants of men. Mr. D'Orsey mentions that some of his parishioners had not a vocabulary of more than 300 words; and although the assertion has been widely disputed, I should certainly be inclined to confirm it out of my own experience. I once listened for a long time together to the conversation of three peasants who were gathering apples among the boughs of an orchard, and as far as I could conjecture, the whole number of words they used did not exceed a hundred; the same word was made to serve a multitude of purposes, and the same coarse expletives recurred with a horrible frequency in the place of every single part of speech, and with every variety of meaning which the meagre context was capable of supplying. Repeated observation has since then confirmed the impression. If this be so in Christian and highly-civilised England in the nineteenth century, what may not have been perhaps ten thousand years before the Savior was born into the world? (Farrar 1865, 58–59)

1897. For when we consider that the average man uses about five hundred words, it is appalling to think how pitiably we have degenerated from the copiousness of our ancestors. (Wood 1897, 295)

1918. One of the things which has helped to make America a great nation is the English language. In a part of South America there are to-day people whose language has only several hundred words, and no word for any numeral above two. There are other people, living in North America, who have no written language except that of pictures. The first people are the Brazilian Indians, the second are our Alaska Eskimos. But even if you did not know who these people were, you would feel sure that you would not care to live among them. Only a backward race could get along with languages like these. (Turkington 1918, 43–44)

1926. The average person in America to-day uses about 2,500 words in ordinary speech. The well-educated person uses between 10,000 and 13,000 words. Shakespeare, whose vocabulary is regarded as the largest ever used by any one individual, used about 15,000 words. But to yield once more to temptation to contrast, there are savage people still existing who find a few dozen words wholly adequate for all their needs. (Eichler 1926, 25)

1940. In vocabulary and in grammar the mark of the language of the uneducated is its poverty. The user of Vulgar English seems less sensitive in his impressions, less keen in his realizations, and more incomplete in his representations. (Fries 1940, 288)

1968. Also, language in the lower class is not as flexible a means of communication as in the middle class. It is not as readily adapted to the subtleties of the particular situations, but consists more of a relatively small repertoire of stereotyped phrases and expressions which are used rather loosely without much effort to achieve a subtle correspondence between perception and verbal expression. Much of lower-class language consists of a kind of incidental "emotional" accompaniment to action here and now. In contrast, middle-class language, rather than being a mere accompaniment to ongoing activity, serves more to represent things and events not immediately present. Thus middle-class language is more abstract and necessarily somewhat more flexible, detailed, and subtle in its descriptive aspects. (Jensen 1968, 118–19)

While it is no longer fashionable to speak of "savage people" or the "lower orders," the cultural presuppositions remain influential. So-called standardized testing is founded on the idea that vocabulary size is an accurate measure of intelligence and promise. The ideas flowing from Trench and D'Orsey have been refuted regularly by empirical study, declared "obviously wrong" (Jespersen n.d., 225), characterized as "the peasant-vocabulary-myth" (Nice 1926, 1), and dismissed as "nonsense" (Mencken 1960c, 348). Even so, they persist as cultural myths about the perfections of English—and the imperfections of some of its speakers.

One consequence of grandiose claims for English has been to stigmatize the inarticulate. Word coiners have created a rich array of distinctions for the purpose: *balubutient* 'stammering, stuttering' (1642), *barbarism* 'the use of words or expressions not in accordance with the classical standard of a language' (1579), *cacology* 'bad speaking, bad choice of words; vicious pronunciation' (1775); *cacophony* 'ill, harsh, or unpleasing sound, (in words) a vitious utterance or pronunciation' (1656), *solecism* 'an impropriety or irregularity in speech' (1577), *tardiloquent* 'slow speech' (1623), *titubate* 'stammer' (1623), *traulism* 'stuttering' (1589), *ungrammatical* 'not in accord with the rules of grammar' (1654), *vulgarism* 'a colloquialism of a low or unrefined character' (1746). In addition, *broken* (1599), *inarticulate* (1603), *mispronunciation* (1530), and *vicious* (1589) were applied to varieties of English at the same time. These terms have been used since to criticize usages that differ from the "refined" norm.

Another conclusion drawn from the "huge" English lexicon resulted in an emphasis on the social distance between country and city dwellers. This notion has been illustrated often in previous chapters (in, for instance, Puttenham's scorn of the speech of "any vplandish village or corner of a Realme"). Until the late eighteenth century, rural dialects in Britain were widely held to be impoverished, and Thomas Gray's imagined "mute inglorious Milton" in the country churchyard had not only been silenced by death but also by the supposed linguistic penury of country life. In the English-speaking world of the nineteenth century, under the influence of Rousseau, a new myth of "peasant eloquence" emerged. From this perspective, rural dialects expressed ideas beyond the reach of the effete English of urban and educated people.

> *1800*. Humble and rustic life was generally chosen [as the subject for poetry], because, in that condition, the central passions of the heart find a better soil in which they can attain their maturity, and are less under restraint, and speak a plainer and more emphatic language; because in that condition of life our elementary feelings co-exist in a state of greater simplicity, and, consequently, may be more accurately contemplated, and more forcefully communicated; because the manners or rural life germinate from those elementary feelings, and, from the necessary character of rural occupations, are more easily comprehended, and are more durable; and, lastly, because in that condition the passions of men are incorporated with the beautiful and permanent forms of nature. The language, too, of these men has been adopted (purified indeed from what appear to be its real defects, from all lasting and rational causes of dislike or disgust) because such men hourly communicate with the best objects from which the best part of language is originally derived; and because, from their rank in society and the sameness and narrow circle of their intercourse, being less under the influence of social vanity, they convey their feelings and notions in simple and unelaborated expressions. (Wordsworth [1800] 1952, 336)
>
> *1865*. Our peasants still speak good Old-English words pregnant with meaning. Living out of doors, their words breathe an out-of-door air. Their images are picturesque and full of life. . . . Our peasantry still remain in many respects in an early stage of society. Hence they retain so many of those primitive words, language-marks, by which we may measure the flow and ebb of our language. On the other hand, our artificial life in large towns is emasculating our speech. The strong metaphor has become faded. The color is washed out with rose-water. ("Poetry of Provincialisms" 1865, 434)
>
> *1885*. Language, be it remembered, is not an abstract construction of the learned, or of dictionary-makers, but is something arising out of the work, needs, ties, joys, affections, tastes, of long generations of humanity, and has its bases broad and low, close to the ground. Its final decisions are made by the masses, people nearest the concrete, having most to do with actual land and sea. (Whitman [1885] 1969, 55)

Though distinctively nineteenth century in character, these notions of the eloquent peasant and the "arid society" of the educated still find occasional expression.

> *1984*. The responsibility of "the white man's burden" began to corrupt the very resources of European energy, so that English and European culture generally

became a *veneer* culture rather than the living culture of the people. It became the cultural expression of the elite. The organisations that were established in those arid societies—the *Oxford Dictionary*, *The Times* newspaper, the B.B.C.—all of these monoliths were set up in order to protect the empire and create a model for what was correct or not.

The submerged people, on the other hand, had all this volcanic energy, this energy of the hurricane with them and an oral tradition and a tradition of communal participation. They had to express themselves completely, not *just* through the written word or established institutions and computers. They had to express themselves in a way which would communicate with other *people*, not communicate through artifice. (Brathwaite 1984)

While expressed nowadays in more subtle forms, this romanticizing of folk speech remains a force, even among commentators who, at the same time, hold that the English of "ordinary" people is limited. In this view, though the "folk" are far less verbose than the sophisticated and urbane, they may be nonetheless *emphatic*, *forceful*, *pregnant*, or even *volcanic*. Patronizing as these comments often are, they suggest that there are virtues in "few words," as long as they are the right ones.

Not satisfied with celebrating the antiquity and copiousness of English, observers have also located in the language a distinctive character. Thus Claiborne, in a typically modern vein, acknowledges a fashionable cultural relativism in his celebration of the perfections of English.

Whether any culture can be shown to be "better" overall than any other is doubtful. But it is a matter of historical record that certain cultures have been better *at certain things* than others. (1983, 6)

From the Renaissance forward, observers have characterized English according to the special virtues that they found distinctive in their own times and anatomized the habits of mind for which English was especially suited.

1711. I have only considered our Language as it shows the Genius and natural Temper of the *English*, which is modest, thoughtful and sincere. . . . (Addison 1966,105)

1731. The Strength, the Life, the Vigour of our Tongue, the Softness of its Cadence in some Words, and the rapid Concurrence of its harsher Consonants in others, give Grief and Rage their different Turns, and are mightily assistant to the Poet's Passion. (Stackhouse [1731] 1968, 178)

1854. Well may we be allowed to indulge in a noble admiration of it; for, no language has such a history, no language has such a basis and superstructure as the English; and we may say also, no language has such a people to speak it. What a majestic literature, in prose and poetry, has been built upon it. What royal gems it holds, displaying them with princely mien, right worthily. The annals of the world may safely be challenged to furnish a superior literature, if an equal. (Review of Peter Mark Roget's *Thesaurus of English Words* 1854, 537)

1856. The English language is by far the noblest now spoken—probably ever spoken—upon this earth. It is the speech for orators and poets, the speech of the household, for business, for liberty, and for common sense. It is a language for great individuals as well as great nations. (Whitman 1856, 1)

1862. We believe it is Grimm who gives the preference to the English among modern languages, because, like the Duke of Wellington's army in Spain, it can go anywhere and do anything. There is no purpose to which it cannot turn its hand. Like the German, it is good for poetry; like the French, it is good for prose; if the words are well picked and chosen, as by Burns and Moore, it is even good for song. Of all modern languages, it is probably the most hardy, because it clips its words close to the root, and can live and thrive in all climates. When mixed with other tongues—as French in Canada, and French and German in the United States—it has a knack of superseding them. And yet it is a language in which the original structural beauty has been sacrificed more than perhaps any other. It is a thoroughly unprincipled language; not in the sense that the French say "perfide Albion," but in having no fixed principles of grammar. It is not a dainty feeder, but derives its words and phrases from all sources, and digests them into its own body, only requiring that they should be available for expressing its meanings. Those who look at it all round may find fault, but they cannot deny that it works well and wears well. It is like the English Constitution in this respect, and perhaps also the English Church, full of inconsistencies and anomalies, yet flourishing in defiance of theory. It is like the English nation, the most oddly governed in the world, but withal the most loyal, orderly, and free. (Swayne 1862, 368)

1867. The English language is endowed with a higher vitality than any other now spoken upon the globe, and begs, borrows, steals, and assimilates words wherever it can find them, without any other rule of accretion than that the new word shall either express a new idea or render an old one more tersely and completely than before. ("Inroads" 1867, 399)

1879. We started this investigation with intent to show the inferiority of the English language as compared with Greek, Latin, French, and German; but, finding that it contains the cream and essence of its predecessors and cotemporaries, that its grammar is simpler than any we have studied, and that its records and literature are more successive and complete than those of any other tongue—we must acknowledge the fact, in order to be true to our convictions. (Weisse 1879, 6)

1888. The crowning recommendation of the English language for universality is the simplicity of its grammar. In this respect English is immeasurably superior not only to other national tongues, but also to every form of artificial language that has been devised. The various moods and tenses, declensions and conjugations, which burden other grammars have practically no existence for us. . . . English is happily almost free from these, but it presents a solitary example of such freedom, as if the language had been predestined to universality, and by this means made ready for its great function. An English word expresses a thought definitely, absolutely, fixedly; the words of an inflected language are unsteady in the mind, and they veer to point after point of the logical compass, under the influence of the little rudders of grammatical inflection. (Bell 1888, 292)

1905. Nevertheless, there is one expression that continually comes to my mind whenever I think of the English language and compare it with others: it seems to me positively and expressly *masculine*, it is the language of a grown-up man and has very little childish or feminine about it. (Jespersen n.d., 2)

1919. For the rest, the English language reflects many of the special characteristics of the English people. We are a very reserved race, very conservative, and we dislike any ostentation either in manner, dress or speech. Our language is not rich in expressions of cordial welcome; a "glad to see you" is as much as we can place against the Frenchman's "enchanted" or "charmed." (Classen 1919, 263)

1922. Schoolmasters do what they can, but their methods are often unpopular; those who speak our language are for the most part freedom-loving, careless, illogical, and easily captivated by novelty. They think very little about their speech-inheritance, and when they do think they are apt to conclude that it can look after itself as it did in the time of their fathers. (Newbolt 1923, 13)

1929. If English be not to-day a world language, it might not be erratic to deduce from what is, what will be, in the course of time, given the same law of accomplishment and progress. Moreover, if we look directly at the nature of English, as a tongue among other tongues, it can be asserted with little fear of contradiction that it is a language of masculine powers, a Germanic speech in derivation having the vigor the word implies, capable of producing effects wherein strength blends with music, and the rugged Anglo-Saxon backbone of its framework is clothed with a sonorous beauty largely borrowed from the Greek, Latin and other foreign sources. Nobody who knows whereof he speaks would ever dream of calling English a weak, undistinguishable tongue, or one in the slightest degree imitative or closely paralleled; an echo rather than a voice. Its resonant resources are too well known to need defense. (Burton 1929, 261–62)

1934. Whether we like it or not, we have a middle-aged, perhaps an old, language upon our tongues—and the only ways to be rid of it are to kill it in a social cataclysm, or to hasten its normal tendency toward dissolution by artificial measures. In these uneasy middle reaches, all of us dream of the fountain of youth; but we may as well stoically face the fact that a young language is never to be the portion of any man who now speaks English. (Laing 1934, 64)

1940. The speech of the English people is inextricably bound up with our public and private character. We made and are making it, and it has maintained and is maintaining us. It is us. It would not have been what it is if we had not been a practical race, a race that placed substance before form, a race that had obtained and loved freedom, that believed in the dignity of the common man and the inalienable right of each person to happiness and the means of livelihood: a race that believed in the political and legal equality of all men, and in the sovereignty of the law. It enshrines our ideals of character and conduct, our humanity, our hopes of immortality, our rationality—and irrationality—and all our aspirations—and prejudices—as surely as our literature does. Those who in the future will speak it, whether they are our descendants or from whatever race they come and whatever tongue their ancestors have spoken, will come under its influence, and will acquire the type of mind of which it is, in its spoken and written forms, the outward expression and audible and visible shape. (Jagger 1940, 189)

1982. I am talking about majority problems of language in a democratic state, problems of a currency that someone has stolen and hidden away and then homogenized into an official "English" language that can only express nonevents involving nobody responsible, or lies. If we lived in a democratic state our language would have to hurtle, fly, curse, and sing, in all the common American names, all the undeniable and representative and participating voices of everybody here. We would not tolerate the language of the powerful and, thereby, lose all respect for words, *per se.* We would make our language conform to the truth of our many selves and we would make our language lead us into the equality of power that a democratic state must represent. (Jordan 1985, 30)

1984. For English is a killer. . . . It is English that has killed off Cumbric, Cornish, Norn, and Manx. It is English that has now totally replaced Irish as a first language in Northern Ireland. And it is English that constitutes such a major threat to Welsh and to Scottish Gaelic, and to French in the Channel Islands, that their long-term future must be considered to be very greatly at risk. (Price 1984, 170)

1986. For on our former, flexible and clear Anglo-Latin-French, which we call American English, the überwältigend academic fog has descended and we grope about, our minds damp and moving in circles. Similar forms of the blight have struck the other languages of Western civilization, with the inevitable result of a growing inability to think sharp and straight about anything—whence half our "prahblems." (Barzun 1986, 130)

Linguistic change over the three centuries encompassed by these evaluations cannot explain so many different ideas about the special perfections of English. A dispassionate observer could hardly imagine that the same language were being described: *modest* and *practical* yet *passionate* and *princely*; *grown-up* and *vital* yet *weak* and *old*; a force for *liberty* and *equality* yet a *killer*; *vigorous* and admirable for *common sense* and *logic* yet *blighted* in ways obscuring thought.

Observations about English are a mirror that commentators hold up to themselves; they reflect prejudice and hope, bigotry and pride, scorn and celebration. They offer insights into the social conditions that produced them. Many of them pretend to offer evidence for anglophone superiority in all fields of human endeavor. Many have justified the most pernicious forms of injustice. Few withstand rigorous and dispassionate scrutiny. English is, after all, a language much like all the others.

References

A. B. 1782. "To the Editors." *European Magazine* 2 (October): 263–64.

Aberigh-Mackay, George. 1881. *Twenty-One Days in India, or the Tour of Sir Ali Baba, K. C. B.*. 1829. 3d ed. London: W. H. Allen.

A. C. C. 1829. "Corruptions of the English Language." *Gentleman's Magazine* 99 (February): 121–23.

Achebe, Chinua. 1975. *Morning Yet on Creation Day*. London: Heinemann.

Adams, John. 1852. "Letter to the President of Congress" (Amsterdam, September 5, 1780). In *The Works of John Adams*, ed. Charles Francis Adams, 7:249–51. Boston: Little, Brown.

Addison, Joseph. 1966. "Spectator 135." [1711]. In *The English Language: Essays by English & American Men Of Letters, 1490–1839*, ed. W. F. Bolton, 102–6. Cambridge: Cambridge University Press.

Agnew, John A. 1981. "Linguistic Shift and the Politics of Language: The Case of the Celtic Languages of the British Isles." *Language Problems and Language Planning* 5: 1–10.

Aiken, Janet Rankin. 1933. "'Basic' and World English." *American Speech* 8 (4): 17–21.

Aitken, A. J. 1985. "A History of Scots." Prefatory essay in *The Concise Scots Dictionary*, ed. Mairi Robinson, ix–xvi. Aberdeen: Aberdeen University Press.

Alderson, Albert William. 1908. *The Extinction in Perpetuity of Armaments and War*. London: P. S. King and Son.

———. 1955. *The Only Way to Everlasting Peace*. London: Alderson.

Algeo, John T. 1960. "Korean Bamboo English." *American Speech* 35:117–23.

Allen, David O. 1853–54. "The State and Prospects of the English Language in India." *Journal of the American Oriental Society* 4:265–75.

Allen, Harold B. 1985. "Attitudes of the National Council of Teachers of English." In *The English Language Today*, ed. Sidney Greenbaum, 139–46. Oxford: Pergamon Press, 1985.

An American. 1774. "To the Literati of America." *Royal American Magazine* 1:6–7.

Amis, Kingsley. 1980. "Getting It Wrong." In *The State of the Language*, ed. Leonard Michaels and Christopher Ricks, 24–33. Berkeley: University of California Press.

Armah, Ayi Kwei. 1985. "Our Language Problem." *West Africa* (April 29): 831–32.

Arngart, Olof Sigfrid, ed. 1955. *The Proverbs of Alfred*. Lund: C. W. K. Gleerup.

Arthur, William. 1905. *A Well-Ordered Household; or, The Ideal City*. Omaha: William Arthur.

———. 1920. *World English: A Maker of Peace, An Enemy of War*. Omaha: William Arthur.

Asomugha, C. N. C. 1981. *Nigerian Slangs: A Dictionary of Slangs and Unconventional English Used in Nigeria*. Onitsha, Nigeria: ABIC Publishers.

Aston, Margaret. 1963. "A Kent Approver of 1440." *Bulletin of the Institute of Historical Research* 36:86–90.

Atkinson, George Francklin. 1860. *"Curry & Rice," on Forty Plates; or, The Ingredients of Social Life at "Our Station" in India*. 3d ed. London: Day and Son.

Avis, Walter S., ed. 1967. *A Dictionary of Canadianisms on Historical Principles*. Toronto: W. J. Gage.

Axon, William E. A. 1888. "English the Dominant Language of the Future." In *Stray Chapters in Literature, Folk-lore, and Archaeology* 199–210. London: John Heywood.

Babbitt, E. H. 1907–8. "The Geography of the Great Languages: The Steady Advance of English as a Universal Written Language, and Its Relation to Literacy." *The World's Work* 15:9903–7.

Bache, R. M. 1868. *Vulgarisms and other Errors of Speech*. Philadelphia: Claxton, Remsen and Haffelfinger.

Bailey, Richard W. 1984. "George Orwell and the English Language." In *The Future of Nineteen Eighty-Four*, ed. Ejner J. Jensen, 24–46. Ann Arbor: University of Michigan Press.

———. 1985. "The Conquests of English." In *The English Language Today*, ed. Sidney Greenbaum, 9–19. Oxford: Pergamon.

———. 1990. "English at Its Twilight." In *The State of the Language*, ed. Christopher Ricks and Leonard Michaels, 83–94. Berkeley: University of California Press.

———, and Manfred Görlach, eds. 1982. *English as a World Language*. Ann Arbor: University of Michigan Press.

Bailyn, Bernard. 1986a. *The Peopling of British North America: An Introduction*. New York: Knopf.

———. 1986b. *Voyagers to the West: A Passage in the Peopling of America on the Eve of the Revolution*. New York: Knopf.

Baker, Robert. [1770] 1968. *Reflections on the English Language*. Facsimile ed. English Linguistics,1500–1800, no. 87. Menston: Scholar Press.

Baldensperger, Fernand. 1917. "Une prédiction inédite sur l'avenir de la langue des Etats-Unis (Roland de la Platiére, 1789)." *Modern Philology* 15:475–76.

Barnard, John, and Paul Hammond. 1984. "Dryden and a Poem for Lewis Maidwell." *Times Literary Supplement*, May 25, 586.

Barnes, William. 1869. *Early England and the Saxon-English*. London: John Russell Smith.

Barnes, William. *See* "Dilettante."

Barnhart, Robert K., ed. 1988. *The Barnhart Dictionary of Etymology*. Bronx, N.Y.: H. W. Wilson.

————, Sol Steinmetz, and Clarence L. Barnhart. 1990. *The Barnhart Dictionary of New English*. Bronx, N.Y.: H. W. Wilson.

Baron, Dennis E. 1982a. *Going Native: The Regeneration of Saxon English*. Publication of the American Dialect Society, no. 69. University, Ala.: University of Alabama Press.

————. 1982b. *Grammar and Good Taste: Reforming the American Language*. New Haven: Yale University Press.

————. 1986. *Grammar and Gender*. New Haven: Yale University Press.

————. 1990. *The English-Only Question: An Official Language for Americans?* New Haven: Yale University Press.

Barr, Robert. 1946. *Spoken English as an Auxiliary World Language*. Melbourne: Fitzroy City Press.

Barry, Jerome B. 1927. "A Little Brown Language." *American Speech* 3:14–20.

Barzun, Jacques. 1986. *A Word or Two Before You Go. . . .* Middletown, Conn.: Wesleyan University Press.

Batsleer, Janet, Tony Davies, Rebecca O'Rourke, and Chris Weedon. 1985. *Rewriting English: Cultural Politics of Gender and Class*. London and New York: Methuen.

Baugh, Albert C., and Thomas Cable. 1978. *A History of the English Language*. 3d. ed. Englewood Cliffs, N.J.: Prentice-Hall.

Bede. 1958. *Bede's Ecclesiastical History of the English Nation*. London: J. M. Dent and Sons.

Bell, Alan. 1977. "The Language of Radio News in Auckland: A Sociolinguistic Study of Style, Audience, and Subediting Variation." Ph.D. diss., University of Auckland.

————, and Janet Holmes, eds. 1990. *New Zealand Ways of Speaking English*. Philadelphia: Multilingual Matters.

Bell, A. Melville. 1888. "The Claims of the English Language to Universality." *Science* 12:291–93.

Bell, Ralcy Husted. 1909. *The Changing Values of English Speech*. New York: Hinds, Noble and Eldredge.

Berndt, Rolf. 1965. "The Linguistic Situation in England from the Norman Conquest to the Loss of Normandy (1066–1204)." *Philologica Pragensa* 8:145–63.

Besant, Annie, and C. W. Leadbeater. 1913. *Man: Whence, How and Whither (A Record of Clairvoyant Investigation)*. London: Theosophical Publishing Society.

Bhatt, B. D., and J. C. Aggarwal, eds. 1977. *Educational Documents in India (1813–1977)*. New Delhi: Arya Book Depot.

Blair, Walter, and Raven I. McDavid, Jr., eds. 1983. *The Mirth of a Nation: America's Great Dialect Humor*. Minneapolis: University of Minnesota Press.

Blanco, Enrique. 1924a. "American as a World-Language." *Literary Digest International Book Review* 2:341–43.

————. 1924b. "American versus Spanish as a World Language." *Literary Digest* 81:46–48.

Bligh, William. 1976. *The Log of H. M. S. Providence, 1791–93*. Facsimile ed. Guildford, Surrey: Genesis Publications.

Bliss, Alan J. 1977. "The Emergence of Modern English Dialects in Ireland." In *The English Language in Ireland*, ed. Diarmaid Ó Muirithe, 7–19. Dublin: Mercier Press.

————. 1979. *Spoken English in Ireland, 1600–1740*. Dublin: Dolmen Press.

Bloomfield, Leonard. 1933. *Language*. New York: Holt, Rinehart and Winston.

————. 1944. "Secondary and Tertiary Responses to Language." *Language* 20:45–55.

Blunt, John Henry, ed. 1873. *The Myroure of oure Ladye* [ca. 1450]. Early English Text Society, extra series, vol. 19. London: N. Trübner.

Blyden, Edward W. 1967. *Christianity, Islam, and the Negro Race*. Edinburgh: Edinburgh University Press.

Bobbins, G. N. D. [ca.1951]. *The Twilight of English*. Cape Town: Maskew Miller, Ltd.

Boorde, Andrew. [1542] 1870. *The Fyrst Boke of the Introduction of Knowledge*. Ed. F. J. Furnivall. Early English Text Society, extra series, vol. 10. London: N. Trübner.

"Borealis" [pseudonym]. 1836. "English Language in America." *Southern Literary Messenger* 2:110–11.

Bornstein, Diane. 1978. "As Meek as a Maid: A Historical Perspective on Language for Women in Courtesy Books from the Middle Ages to *Seventeen Magazine*." In *Women's Language and Style*, ed. Douglas Butturff and Edmund L. Epstein, 132–38. Akron, Ohio: L & S Books.

Bown, Lalage, ed. 1973. *Two Centuries of African English: A Survey and Anthology of Non-Fictional English Prose by African Writers since 1769*. London: Heinemann.

Brackebusch, W. 1868. *Is English Destined to Become the Universal Language of the World?: An Inaugural Dissertation for Obtaining the Degree of Doctor of Philosophy in the University of Göttingen*. Göttingen: W. F. Kaestner.

Bradford, William. 1952. *Of Plymouth Plantation* [1620–47]. Ed. Samuel Eliot Morison. New York: Knopf.

Bradshaw, James. 1847. *A Scheme for Making the English Language the International Language of the World*. London: Brain.

Brady, Frank, and Martin Price. 1961. *English Prose and Poetry 1660–1800: A Selection*. New York: Holt, Rinehart and Winston.

Branford, Jean. 1987. *A Dictionary of South African English*. 3d. ed. Cape Town: Oxford University Press.

Brathwaite, Edward Kamau. 1984. "Interview." In Chris Searle, *Words Unchained: Language and Revolution in Grenada*, 232–39. London: Zed Books.

Bridges, Robert. 1910. "On the Present State of English Pronunciation." *Essays and Studies* 1:42–69.

————. 1925. *The Society's Work*. Society for Pure English, tract no. 21. Oxford: Clarendon Press.

Brink, André. 1983. "English and the Afrikaans Writer" [1976]. In *Writing in a State of Siege: Essays on Politics and Literature*, 96–115. New York: Summit Books.

Briton, M. 1740. "An Apology for the English Language." *London Magazine* 9: 598–601.

Bullokar, William. [1580a] 1966. *A Short Introduction or Guiding to Print, Write, and Reade Inglish Speech.* Facsimile. Ed. Bror Danielsson and Robin C. Alston. Leeds: University of Leeds, School of English.

———. 1977. *Booke at Large* [1580b] and *Bref Grammar for English* [1586]. Delmar, N.Y.: Scholars' Facsimiles and Reprints.

Bulwer-Lytton, Edward. 1896. *Kenelm Chillingly: His Adventures and Opinions; to which is added, The Coming Race.* 2 vols. Boston: Little, Brown.

Burchfield, Robert. 1985. *The English Language.* Oxford: Oxford University Press.

———, ed. 1986. *The New Zealand Pocket Oxford Dictionary.* Auckland: Oxford University Press.

———, and Hans Aarleff. 1988. *The Oxford English Dictionary and the State of the Language.* Washington, D.C.: Library of Congress.

Burgess, Anthony. 1964. *Language Made Plain.* New York: Thomas Y. Crowell.

———. 1972. *A Clockwork Orange* [1962]. New York: Ballantine Books.

Burkett, Eva M. 1978. *American English Dialects in Literature.* Metuchen, N.J.: Scarecrow Press.

Burnley, J. D. 1989. "Sources of Standardisation in Later Middle English." In *Standardizing English: Essays in the History of Language Change in Honor of John Hurt Fisher*, ed. Joseph B. Trahern, Jr., 23–41. Knoxville: University of Tennessee Press.

Burton, Richard. 1929. *Why Do You Talk Like That?* Indianapolis: Bobbs-Merrill.

Burton, Richard F. 1875. *Ultima Thule; or, A Summer in Iceland.* 2 vols. London: William P. Nimmo.

Butler, Guy. 1975. "The Language of the Conqueror on the Lips of the Conquered is the Language of Slaves." *Theoria* (Pietermaritzburg) 45:1–11.

Cable, Thomas. 1984. "The Rise of Written Standard English." In *The Emergence of National Languages*, ed. Aldo Scaglione, 77–94. Ravenna: Longo Editore.

Cameron, Angus. 1985. "The Boundaries of Old English Literature." In *The Anglo-Saxons: Synthesis and Achievement*, ed. J. Douglas Woods and David A. E. Pelteret, 27–36. Waterloo, Ontario: Wilfrid Laurier University Press.

Camden, William. 1984. *Remains Concerning Britain.* Ed. R. D. Dunn. Toronto: University of Toronto Press.

Campbell, N. A. 1889. "Protection for Our Language." *North American Review* 149:127–28.

Candolle, Alphonse de. 1875. "On a Dominant Language for Science." In *Annual Report of the Board of Regents of the Smithsonian Institution for 1874*, 239–48. Washington, D.C.: Government Printing Office. Translation of chap. 5 of his *Histoire des science et des savants depuis dieux siècles* (Geneva, 1873).

"Canton-English." 1857. *Household Words* 15:450–52.

Carver, Craig. 1987. *American Regional Dialects: A Word Geography.* Ann Arbor: University of Michigan Press.

Casaubon, Meric. 1650. *De Quatuor Linguis.* London: J. Flesher.

Cawdrey, Robert. [1604] 1966. *A Table Alphabeticall.* Facsimile. Ed. Robert A. Peters. Gainesville, Fla.: Scholars' Facsimiles and Reprints.

Caxton, William. 1966. Prologue to his translation of *Eneydos* [1490]. In *The English*

Language: Essays by English and American Men of Letters, 1490–1839, ed. W. F. Bolton, 1–4. Cambridge: Cambridge University Press.

Chapman, R. W. 1931. "English Pronunciation." *Saturday Review of Literature* 7:841–42.

———. 1932. *"Oxford" English*. Society for Pure English, tract 37. Oxford: Clarendon Press.

Chaterjee, Bankin Chandra. 1986. In *Sociological Essays: Utilitarianism and Positivism in Bengal*, ed. and trans. S. N. Mukherjee and Marian Maddern. Calcutta: Rddhi India.

Chedzoy, Alan. 1985. *William Barnes: A Life of the Dorset Poet*. Stanbridge, Dorset: Dovecote Press.

Cheke, John. 1954. "A Letter of Sir J[ohn] Cheke's to his Loving Friend Maister Thomas Hoby" [1557]. In *The Renaissance in England*, ed. Hyder E. Rollins and Herschel Baker, 538–39. Boston: D. C. Heath.

Chinweizu, Onwuchekwa Jemie, and Ihechukwu Madubuike. 1980. *Toward the Decolonization of African Literature: African Fiction and Poetry and Their Critics*. Enugu, Nigeria: Fourth Dimension Publishing Co..

Claiborne, Robert. 1983. *Our Marvelous Native Tongue: The Life and Times of the English Language*. New York: Times Books. Republished in an anglicized edition as *The History of Our Marvellous Native Tongue*. London: Bloomsbury, 1990.

Clark, Cecily. 1981. "Another Late Fourteenth-Century Case of Dialect Awareness." *English Studies* 62:504–5.

Clark, Gregory R. 1990. *Words of the Vietnam War: The Slang, Jargon, Abbreviations, Acronyms, Nomenclature, Nicknames, Pseudonyms, Slogans, Specs, Euphemisms, Double-Talk, Chants, and Names and Places of the Era of the United States Involvement in Vietnam*. Jefferson, N.C.: McFarland.

Clarke, Arthur C. 1972. *The Lost Worlds of 2001*. London: Sidgwick and Jackson.

Classen, Ernest. 1919. *Outlines of the History of the English Language*. London: Macmillan.

Clinch, Bryan J. 1902. "The New Language Despotism in the Philippines." *American Catholic Quarterly Review* 27:369–88.

Coates, Jennifer. 1986. *Women, Men and Language*. London and New York: Longman.

[Codrington, Robert.] 1664. *The Second Part of Youths Behaviour, or Decency in Conversation Amongst Women*. London: W. Lee.

Cody, Sherwin. 1918. *The Sherwin Cody 100% Self-Correcting Course in English Language*. Port Washington, N.Y.: Morrill Cody.

Cohen, Murray. 1977. *Sensible Words: Linguistic Practice in England, 1640–1785*. Baltimore: Johns Hopkins University Press.

Coles, E[lisha]. [1676] 1971. *An English Dictionary*. Facsimile. English Linguistics, 1500–1800, no. 268. Menston: Scholar Press.

Collins, Harold Reeves. 1968. *The New English of the Onitsha Chapbooks*. Athens: Ohio University, Papers in International Studies, Africa Series, no. 1.

"Contributions to a Fashionable Vocabulary." 1842. *New Monthly Magazine* 66:213–21.

Cook, James. 1784. *A Voyage to the Pacific Ocean*. London: G. Nicol and T. Cadell.

————. 1971. *The Explorations of Captain James Cook in the Pacific as Told by Selections of His Own Journals, 1768–1779*. Ed. A. Grenfell Price. New York: Dover.

Cooke, Thomas. 1742. *Original Poems . . . to which are added: Proposals for Perfecting the English Language*. 2d ed. London: T. Jackson.

Cooper, James Fenimore. 1931. *The American Democrat* [1838]. New York: Knopf.

Coote, Edmund. [1596] 1968. *The English Schoole-Maister*. Facsimile. English Linguistics, 1500–1800, no 98. Menston: Scholar Press.

Corcoran, T. 1923. "How English May Be Taught Without Anglicising." *Irish Monthly* 51:269–73.

Cottle, Basil. 1975. *The Plight of English: Ambiguities, Cacophonies and Other Violations of Our Language*. New Rochelle, N.Y.: Arlington House.

Craigie, William A. 1944. *Problems of Spelling Reform*. Society for Pure English, tract 63. Oxford: Clarendon Press.

Cressy, David. 1980. *Literacy and the Social Order: Reading and Writing in Tudor and Stuart England*. Cambridge: Cambridge University Press.

Croft, Herbert. [1797] 1968. *A Letter from Germany to the Princess Royal of England; on the English and German Languages*. Facsimile. English Linguistics, 1500–1800, no. 101. Menston: Scholar Press.

Crowley, Tony. 1989. *The Politics of Discourse: The Standard Language Question in British Cultural Debates*. London: Macmillan.

Crummell, Alexander. 1862. "The English Language in Liberia." In *The Future of Africa*, 9–54. New York: Charles Scribner.

Cunningham, Peter Miller. 1827. *Two Years in New South Wales*. 2 vols. London: Henry Colburn.

Curtis, Edmund, and R. B. McDowell, eds. 1943. *Irish Historical Documents, 1172–1922*. London: Methuen.

Cuthbertson, W. Jones. 1919. *Standard World Language for International Use*. San Francisco: W. Jones Cuthbertson.

Dallas, Robert C. 1968. *The History of the Maroons* [1803]. 2 vols. London: Frank Cass and Company.

Daly, Mary, and Jane Caputi. 1987. *Webster's First New Intergalactic Wickedary of the English Language*. Boston: Beacon Press.

Daniel, Samuel. 1950. *Poems and A Defence of Ryme*. Ed. Arthur Colby Sprague. London: Routledge and Kegan Paul.

Daniels, Harvey A. 1983. *Famous Last Words: The American Language Crisis Reconsidered*. Carbondale: Southern Illinois University Press.

Danielsson, Bror. 1955. *John Hart's Works on English Orthography and Pronunciation*. Pt. 1. Stockholm: Almqvist and Wiksell.

Dante. 1973. *Literary Criticism of Dante Alighieri*. Trans. and ed. Robert S. Haller. Lincoln: University of Nebraska Press.

Darrach, Marie L. 1930. "Manila and English." *Commonweal*, August 20, 401–3.

Davis, Thomas. [1914] 1982. *Thomas Davis: Selections from His Prose and Poetry*. Repr. ed. London: Gresham Publishing Co.

De Quincey, Thomas. 1889–90. *The Collected Writings of Thomas De Quincey*. Ed. David Masson. 14 vols. Edinburgh: Adam and Charles Black.

Derricke, John. [1581] 1883. *The Image of Irelande*. Facsimile ed. Edinburgh: A. and C. Black.

Devitt, Amy J. 1990. *Standardizing Written English: Diffusion in the Case of Scotland, 1520–1659*. Cambridge: Cambridge University Press.

De Witt, Marguerite E. [1924]. *EuphonEnglish in America*. New York: E. P. Dutton.

"Dilettante" [William Barnes]. 1830. "Corruptions of the English Language." *Gentleman's Magazine* 100 (June): 501–3.

Dillard, Joey L. 1985. *Toward a Social History of American English*. Contributions to the Sociology of Language, no. 39. Berlin: Mouton.

Dixon, James. [1822] 1984. *Narrative of a Voyage to New South Wales and Van Dieman's Land in the Ship Skelton During the Year 1820*. Facsimile ed. Hobart: Melanie Publications.

Dobson, E. J. [1955] 1969. "Early Modern Standard English." In *Approaches to English Historical Linguistics*, ed. Roger Lass, 419–39. New York: Holt, Rinehart and Winston.

Domínguez, C. Villalobos. 1929. "The Language of the Future." *Living Age* 337 (September 15): 105–10.

D'Orsey, Alexander J. D. 1861. *The Study of the English Language an Essential Part of a University Course*. Cambridge: Deighton, Bell, and Company.

Dowling, Linda. 1986. *Language and Decadence in the Victorian Fin de Siècle*. Princeton: Princeton University Press.

Eclectikwn, Eis [pseudonym]. 1846. *Language in Relation to Commerce, Missions, and Government; England's Ascendancy and the World's Destiny*. Manchester: A. Burgess.

[Drake, Judith?]. 1697. *An Essay in the Defence of the Female Sex*. London: A. Roper and E. Wilkinson.

Edwards, Bryan. 1819. *The History, Civil and Commercial, of the British West Indies*. 5th ed. 5 vols. London: T. Miller.

Egan, Pierce. 1821. *Life in London: The True History of Tom and Jerry*. London: Sherwood, Neely, and Jones.

Eichler, Lillian. 1926. *Well-Bred English*. Garden City, N.Y.: Doubleday, Page and Company.

Elgin, Suzette Haden. 1981. "Some Proposed Additions to the Glossary of Needed Lexical Items for the Expression of Women's Perceptions." *Lonesome Node* 1, no.1 (September/October).

———. 1985. *Native Tongue*. London: Women's Press.

———. 1987. *Native Tongue II: The Judas Rose*. New York: DAW Books.

———. 1988. *A First Dictionary and Grammar of Láadan*. Ed. Diane Martin. 2d ed. Madison, Wisc.: Society for the Furtherance and Study of Fantasy and Science Fiction.

Ellis, P. Berresford. 1974. *The Cornish Language and Its Literature*. London: Routledge and Kegan Paul.

Elphinston, James. 1787. *Propriety Ascertained in Her Picture; or, Inglish Speech and Spelling Rendered Mutual Guides*. 2 vols. London: Jon Walter.

Elyot, Thomas. [1531] 1970. *The Boke Named the Gouernour*. Facsimile. English Linguistics, 1500–1800, no. 246. Menston: Scholar Press.

"English Dialects." 1836. *Quarterly Review* 55 (February): 354–87.

"The English Language." 1867. *London Quarterly Review* 28:269–92.

"The English Language in America." 1860. *North American Magazine* 91:507–28.

Errington, Dudley. 1883. "Fashionable English." *Gentleman's Magazine* 254:576–94.

Evelyn, John. 1906. *Diary of John Evelyn*. Ed. William Bray and Henry B. Wheatley. 5 vols. London: Bickers and Son.

Farb, Peter. 1975. *Word Play: What Happens When People Talk*. New York: Bantam Books.

Farmer, Philip José. 1971. *Down in the Black Gang, and Others*. Garden City, N.Y.: Nelson Doubleday.

Farrar, Frederic William. 1865. *Chapters on Language*. London: Longmans, Green and Company.

Feister, Lois M. 1973. "Linguistic Communication between the Dutch and Indians in New Netherland, 1609–1664." *Ethnohistory* 20:25–38.

"Filipinos Learn Readily." 1901. *New York Times*, December 26, p. 6, col. 7.

Finkenstaedt, Thomas, and Dieter Wolff. 1973. *Ordered Profusion: Studies in Dictionaries and the English Lexicon*. Heidelberg: Carl Winter.

Finneran, Kevin. 1986. "The Future of the English Language." *Futurist* 20 (July–August): 9–13.

Fishman, Joshua A., ed. 1986. *The Question of an Official Language: Language Rights and the English Language Amendment*. Berlin, New York, Amsterdam: Mouton De Gruyter.

Fiumedoro, Ali. 1955. *Simplify-ed English: A Language for World Use*. Boston: Ali's World.

F[lecknoe], R[ichard]. 1665. *A True and Faithful Account of What Was Observed in Ten Years Travells into the Principal Places of Europe, Asia, Africa, and America*. London: William Crook.

Flexner, Stuart Berg. 1987. *The Random House Dictionary of the English Language*. 2d ed. New York: Random House.

Follick, Mont. 1934. *The Influence of English*. London: Williams and Norgate.

———. 1946. *Can English Become a Truly International Language?* World Unity Pamphlets, no. 1. London: Jason Press.

Fonblanque, Albany de. 1881. "The English of America." *Tinsley's Magazine* 29:330–34.

Fonlon, Bernard. 1969. "The Language Problem in Cameroon (A Historical Perspective)." *Abbia* 22 (May–August): 5–40.

[Foster, Margaret]. 1860. "English, Literary and Vernacular." *London Review* 15 (October): 1–30.

Fowler, H. W. 1926–. *A Dictionary of Modern English Usage*. Oxford: Clarendon Press.

———. 1927. "On -*ing*: Professor Jespersen and 'The Instinctive Grammatical Moralizer.'" Society for Pure English, tract 26, 192–96. Oxford: Clarendon Press.

———, and F. G. Fowler. 1906. *The King's English*. Oxford: Clarendon Press.

Franklin, Margaret Ann. 1976. *Black and White Australians*. South Yarra, Victoria: Heinemann Educational Australia.

Fréine, Seán de. 1977. "The Dominance of the English Language in the Nineteenth Century." In *The English Language in Ireland*, ed. Diarmaid Ó Muirithe, 71–87. Dublin and Cork: Mercier Press.

Freitag, Robert E. 1990. "An English Speaking World?" *Michigan Alumnus* 97 (2): 7.

Friel, Brian. 1981. *Translations*. Boston: Faber and Faber.

Fries, Charles C. 1927. *The Study of the English Language*. New York: Thomas Nelson and Sons.

———. 1940. *American English Grammar*. New York: Appleton-Century-Crofts.

"The Future of the English Language." 1894. *Chambers's Journal* 71:294–96.

Gandhi, Mohandas K. 1958. *Evil Wrought by the English Medium*. Ed. R. K. Prabhu. Ahmedabad: Navajivan.

Gaster, Theodor H. 1969. *Myth, Legend, and Custom in the Old Testament*. New York: Harper and Row.

Gerald of Wales. 1984. *The Journey through Wales and the Description of Wales*. Trans. Lewis Thorpe. Harmondsworth: Penguin Books.

Gildon, Charles. 1718. *The Complete Art of Poetry*. 2 vols. London: Charles Rivington.

Gill, Alexander. [1621] 1903. *Logonomia Anglica*. Ed. Otto L. Jiriczek. Strassburg: Karl J. Trübner.

Gladstone, W. E. 1885. "Mr. Gladstone on George Washington and the Future of English-speaking Peoples." *Times* (London), February 18, p. 7, col. 4.

Gneuss, Helmut. 1972. "The Origin of Standard Old English and Æthelwold's School at Winchester." *Anglo-Saxon England* 1:63–83.

Goddard, Ives. 1977. "Some Early Examples of American Indian Pidgin English from New England." *International Journal of American Linguistics* 43:37–41.

———. 1978. "A Further Note on Pidgin English." *International Journal of American Linguistics* 44:73.

Gookin, Daniel. 1792. *Historical Collections of the Indians in New England*. Boston: Belknap and Hall.

Gordon, Elizabeth. 1983. "New Zealand English Pronunciation: An Investigation into some Early Written Records." *Te Reo* 26:29–42.

———, and Tony Deverson. 1985. *New Zealand English: An Introduction to New Zealand Speech and Usage*. Auckland: Heinemann.

Gould, Edward S. 1880. *Good English; or, Popular Errors in Language* [1867]. Rev. ed. New York: A. C. Armstrong and Son.

Gowers, Ernest, rev. and ed. 1965. *A Dictionary of Modern English Usage by H. W. Fowler*. Oxford: Oxford University Press.

Grahn, Judy. 1984. *Another Mother Tongue: Gay Words, Gay Worlds*. Boston: Beacon Press.

Grattan, J. H. G. 1927. "On Anglo-American Cultivation of Standard English." *Review of English Studies* 3:430–41.

Graves, Robert. 1926. *Impenetrability, or The Proper Habit of English*. London: Hogarth Press.

Gray, Douglas. 1983. "Captain Cook and the English Vocabulary." In *Five-Hundred Years of Words and Sounds: A Festschrift for Eric Dobson,* ed. E. G. Stanley and Douglas Gray, 49–62. Cambridge: Brewer.

———. 1988. "A Note on Sixteenth-Century Purism." In *Words for Robert Burchfield's Sixty-Fifth Birthday,* ed. E. G. Stanley and T. F. Hoad, 103–19. Cambridge: Brewer.

[Green, John]. [1615] 1941. *A Refvtation of the Apology for Actors.* Facsimile. Ed. Richard H. Perkinson. New York: Scholars' Facsimiles and Reprints.

Griffith, Mary. 1950. *Three Hundred Years Hence* [1836]. Philadelphia: Prime Press.

Grimm, Jakob. [1851] 1965. "Über den Ursprung der Sprache." Repr. in *Kleineren Shrifte,* 1:255–98. Hildesheim: Georg Olms Verlag.

Grose, Francis. 1963. *A Classical Dictionary of the Vulgar Tongue* [1796]. Ed. Eric Partridge. New York: Barnes and Noble.

Gwynne, Parry. 1856. *A Word to the Wise; or, Hints on the Current Improprieties of Expression in Writing and Speaking* [1852]. In *Conversation: Its Faults and Its Graces,* ed. Andrew P. Peabody, 61–108. Boston: James Munroe and Company.

Haines, C. R. 1935. "Will English Be the Universal Language?" *Quarterly Review* 264:47–64.

Hakluyt, Richard. 1985. *Voyages and Discoveries.* Ed. Jack Beeching. Harmondsworth: Penguin.

Hall, Fitzedward. 1873. *Modern English.* New York: Scribner, Armstrong, and Company.

———. 1874. Review of *The Sources of Standard English* by T. L. Kington Oliphant. *North American Magazine* 119:308–31.

Hall, Ivan Parker. 1973. *Mori Arinori.* Cambridge, Mass.: Harvard University Press.

Halliday, M. A. K. 1978. "Antilanguages." [1976]. In *Language as Social Semiotic: The Social Interpretation of Language and Meaning,* 164–82. Baltimore: University Park Press.

Hallner, Andrew. 1929. *Änjelika: The English Language Transformed into Phonetic Orthography Becoming the World Language.* Turlock, Calif.: California Publishing House.

Halsband, Robert, ed. 1967. *The Complete Letters of Lady Mary Wortley Montagu.* 3 vols. Oxford: Clarendon Press.

Hamilton, J[ames] W. 1928. *World or Cosmo English.* 2d ed. St. Paul: J. W. Hamilton.

Hancock, Ian. 1984. "Romani and Angloromani." In *Language in the British Isles,* ed. Peter Trudgill, 367–83. Cambridge: Cambridge University Press.

Hansard. 1979–80. "The English Language: Deterioration in Usage." *The Parliamentary Debates: House of Lords,* 5th ser., 403 (4th vol. of Session 1979–80): 131–95.

Hare, John. 1810. *St. Edward's Ghost, or Anti-Normanism* [1642]. Repr. in *The Harleian Miscellany,* 6:90–106. London: Robert Dutton.

[Hare, Julius Charles.] 1832. "On English Orthography." *Philological Museum* 1:640–78.

Harrington, John P. 1938. "A Key to the English Language." In *The Book of the*

Record of the Time Capsule, 19–28. New York: Westinghouse Electric and Manufacturing Company.

Harris, Martyn. 1987. "Developing One's Haspirations." *Daily Telegraph* (London), December 23, 14.

Harrison, H. W. 1943. *Exit Babel*. London: W. H. Allen.

Hatcher, John. 1977. *Plague, Population and the English Economy, 1348–1530*. London: Macmillan.

Hayes, Alfred E. 1920. "The English Language and International Trade." *Journal of the Royal Society of Arts* 63:198–209.

Hayes, Joseph J. 1978–79. "Language and Language Behavior of Lesbian Women and Gay Men: A Selected Bibliography." *Journal of Homosexuality* 4:201–12, 299–309.

Hazard, Rowland G. 1857. *Essay on Language, and Other Papers*. Boston: Phillips, Sampson and Company.

Heath, Shirley Brice. 1980. "Standard English: Biography of a Symbol." In *Standards and Dialects in English*, ed. Timothy Shopen and Joseph M. Williams, 3–32. Cambridge, Mass.: Winthrop Publishers.

Heron, Robert [John Pinkerton]. 1785. *Letters of Literature*. London: G. G. J. and J. Robinson.

Hertzka, Theodor. 1972. *Freeland: A Social Anticipation* [1890]. Trans. Arthur Ransom. New York: Gordon Press.

Hewes, John. [1624] 1972. *A Perfect Survey of the English Tongue*. Facsimile. English Linguistics, 1500–1800, no. 336. Menston: Scholar Press.

Heywood, Thomas. [1612] 1941. *An Apology for Actors*. Facsimile. Ed. Richard H. Perkinson. New York: Scholars' Facsimiles and Reprints.

Hiestand, Sarah Willard. 1906. "Slovenly Speaking of English." *Nation* 82 (January 25): 72–73.

Hoban, Russell. 1982. *Riddley Walker*. New York: Washington Square Press.

Hofstadter, Douglas R. 1985. "A Person Paper on Purity in Language." In his *Metamagical Themas: Questing for the Essence of Mind and Pattern*, 159–67. Toronto: Bantam Books.

Hogarth, D. G. 1928. *The Life of Charles M. Doughty*. London: Oxford University Press.

Hoggart, Richard. 1990. *A Sort of Clowning: Life and Times, 1940–1959*. London: Chatto and Windus.

Honey, John. 1989. *Does Accent Matter? The Pygmalion Factor*. Boston: Faber and Faber.

Hopkins, Gerard Manley. 1955. *The Letters of Gerard Manley Hopkins to Robert Bridges*. Ed. Claude Colleer Abbott. 2d rev. imp. London: Oxford University Press.

Hornadge, Bill. 1980. *The Australian Slanguage: A Look at What We Say and How We Say It*. North Ryde: Methuen Australia.

Horrocks, Roger. 1985. "Creating a Feature-Film Industry." *Journal of Popular Culture* 18:149–58.

[Hotten, John Camden]. 1874. *The Slang Dictionary: Etymological, Historical and Anecdotal*. London: Chatto and Windus.

Howard, Philip. 1985. *The State of the Language: English Observed*. New York: Oxford University Press.

Howard, William Lee. 1900. "Effeminate Men and Masculine Women." *New York Medical Journal* 77:686–87.

Howe, Irving, ed. 1982. *Orwell's* "Nineteen Eighty-Four": *Text, Sources, Criticism*. 2d ed. New York: Harcourt Brace Jovanovich.

Howells, William Dean. 1906. "Our Daily Speech." *Harper's Bazaar* 40:930–34.

Hughes, Arthur, and Peter Trudgill. 1979. *English Accents and Dialects: An Introduction to Social and Regional Varieties of British English*. Baltimore: University Park Press.

Hume, David. 1932. Letter to Edward Gibbon, 24 October 1767. In *The Letters of David Hume*, ed. J. Y. T. Greig, 2:170–71. Oxford: Clarendon Press.

Huxley, Aldous. 1932. *Brave New World*. London: Chatto and Windus.

Hyde, Douglas. [1894] 1973. "The Necessity for De-Anglicizing Ireland." In *The Revival of Irish Literature*, by Charles Gaven Duffy, George Sigerson, and Douglas Hyde, 115–61. New York: Lemmas.

Hyde, H. Montgomery. 1970. *The Love That Dared Not Speak Its Name*. Boston: Little, Brown.

"Inroads upon English." 1867. *Blackwood's Magazine* 102:399–417.

Irish, W. E. 1928. *Key-Way English as a World Language*. Cleveland: W. E. Irish.

Islam, Sirajul, ed. 1978. *Bangladesh District Records: Chittagong, 1760–1787*. Dhaka: University of Dhaka.

Jacobs, Willis D. 1952. *William Barnes, Linguist*. University of New Mexico Publications in Language and Literature, no. 9. Albuquerque: University of New Mexico Press.

Jagger, J. Hubert. 1940. *English in the Future*. London: Thomas Nelson and Sons.

James, Henry. 1906–7. "The Speech of American Women." *Harper's Bazaar* 40:979–82, 1103–6; 41:17–21, 113–17.

Jászi, Oscar. 1929. *The Dissolution of the Habsburg Monarchy*. Chicago: University of Chicago Press.

Jensen, Arthur R. "Social Class and Verbal Learning." In *Social Class, Race, and Psychological Development*, ed. Martin Deutsch, Irwin Katz, and Arthur R. Jensen, 115–74. New York: Holt, Rinehart and Winston.

Jespersen, Otto. N.d. *Growth and Structure of the English Language* [1905]. 9th ed. Garden City, N.Y.: Doubleday Anchor Books.

———. 1964a. *Language: Its Nature, Development, and Origin* [1922]. New York: W. W. Norton.

———. 1964b. *Mankind, Nation and Individual from a Linguistic Point of View* [1925]. Bloomington: Indiana University Press.

Jeyifo, Biodun. 1984. "Soyinka at 50." *West Africa* (August 27): 1729–31.

Johnson, Samuel. [1755] 1974. *A Dictionary of the English Language*. 2 vols. Facsimile. London: Times Books.

Jones, Daniel. 1946. *An English Pronouncing Dictionary*. 7th ed. New York: E. P. Dutton.

Jones, Richard Foster. 1953. *The Triumph of the English Language*. Stanford: Stanford University Press.

Jones-Quartey, K. A. B. 1949. "Our Language and Literature Problem." *Africana* 1 (3): 23–24.

Jonson, Ben. [1640] 1972. *The English Grammar*. Facsimile. English Linguistics, 1500–1800, no. 349. Menston: Scholar Press.

———. 1981. *The Complete Plays of Ben Jonson*. Ed. G. A. Wilkes. Oxford: Clarendon Press.

Jordan, June. 1985. *On Call: Political Essays*. Boston: South End Press.

"To Journalists." 1923. Society for Pure English, tract 14, 21–22. Oxford: Clarendon Press.

Juvenal. 1958. *The Satires*. Trans. Rolfe Humphries. Bloomington: Indiana University Press.

Kachru, Braj B. 1986. *The Alchemy of English: The Spread, Functions and Models of Non-Native Englishes*. Oxford: Pergamon Institute of English.

Kashoki, Mubanga E. 1970. "Writer, Forget Your Tribal Language." *Jewel of Africa* 3:28–36.

Kelly, Thomas. 1981. *For Advancement of Learning: The University of Liverpool, 1881–1981*. Liverpool: Liverpool University Press.

Kihlstedt, Folke T. 1986. "Utopia Realized: The World's Fairs of the 1930s." In *Imagining Tomorrow: History, Technology, and the American Future*, ed. Joseph J. Corn, 97–118. Cambridge, Mass.: MIT Press.

Killam, G. D., ed. 1973. *African Writers on African Writing*. Evanston: Northwestern University Press.

Kington Oliphant, T. L. 1873. *The Sources of Standard English*. London: Macmillan.

Kinney, Coates. 1873. "Japanning the English Language." *Galaxy*, August: 188–95.

Kirch, Max S. 1959. "Scandinavian Influence on English Syntax." *PMLA* 74:503–10.

Knoflech, Augustin. 1890. *Sound English: A Language for the World*. New York: G. E. Stechert.

Knox, E. V. 1930. "Cinema English." *Living Age* 338 (April 1):187–89.

Kornbluth, C. M. 1958. *A Mile Beyond the Moon*. Garden City, N.Y.: Doubleday and Company.

Kramarae, Cheris, and Paula A. Treichler. 1985. *A Feminist Dictionary*. Boston: Pandora Press.

Labov, William. 1966. *The Social Stratification of English in New York City*. Washington, D. C.: Center for Applied Linguistics.

———. 1982. "Building on Empirical Foundations." In *Perspectives on Historical Linguistics*, ed. Winifred P. Lehmann and Yakov Malkiel, 17–92. Amsterdam: John Benjamins.

———, Malcah Yaeger, and Richard Steiner. 1972. *A Quantitative Study of Sound Change in Progress*. 2 vols. Philadelphia: U. S. Regional Survey.

Laing, Alexander Kinnan. 1934. *Wine and Physic: A Poem and Six Essays on the Fate of Our Language*. New York: Farrar and Rinehart.

Lakoff, Robin. 1975. *Language and Woman's Place*. New York: Harper and Row.

Lal, P., ed. 1969. *Modern Indian Poetry in English*. Calcutta: Writers Workshop.

Landau, Sidney I. 1984. *Dictionaries: The Art and Craft of Lexicography*. New York: Charles Scribner's Sons.

Landor, Walter Savage. 1891. *Imaginary Conversations*. Ed. Charles G. Crump. 6 vols. London: J. M. Dent.

Larik, K. M. 1981–82. "English as an International Language." *Ariel* (Jamshoro) 7:75–80.

Lee, Joseph. 1973. *The Modernisation of Irish Society, 1848–1918*. Dublin: Gill and Macmillan.

Leechman, Douglas, and Robert A. Hall, Jr. 1955. "American Indian Pidgin English: Attestations and Grammatical Peculiarities." *American Speech* 30:163–71.

Lehman, David. 1984. "Hastening the Decline of Grammar." *New Criterion* 3 (May): 82–86.

Leitner, Gerhard. 1982. "The Consolidation of 'Educated Southern English' as a Model in the Early 20th Century." *IRAL* 20:91–107.

Leland, Charles G. 1892. *Pidgin-English Sing-Song, or Songs and Stories in the China-English Dialect*. 3d ed. London: Kegan Paul, Trench, Trübner and Company. [This small work was continually reprinted in both London and Philadelphia (by J. P. Lippincott), reaching a 10th edition in 1924.]

Lem, Stanisław. 1974. *The Futurological Congress (from the Memoirs of Ijon Tichy)*. Trans. Michael Kandel. New York: Seabury Press.

[Leslie, Charles.] 1740. *A New History of Jamaica*. 2d ed. London: T. Hodges.

The Letters of T on the Employment of the English Language as a Medium for Native Education. 1834. Calcutta: n. p.

Lewis, W. S., et al., eds. 1937–83. *The Yale Edition of Horace Walpole's Correspondence*. 43 vols. New Haven: Yale University Press.

Li, Dun J., ed. 1969. *China in Transition: 1517–1911*. New York: Van Nostrand Reinhold.

Lifton, Robert Jay. 1974. *Home from the War*. New York: Simon and Schuster.

Lindfors, Bernth, comp. 1979. *Black African Literature in English: A Guide to Information Sources*. Detroit: Gale Research Company.

Llamazon, Teodoro A. 1969. *Standard Filipino English*. Manila: Ateneo University Press.

L'Isle, William. 1638. *Divers Ancient Monvments in the Saxon Tongue*. London: Francis Eglesfield.

Lloyd, Donald J. 1951. "Snobs, Slobs and the English Language." *American Scholar* 21:279–88.

Lloyd, R[ichard] J. 1895. "Standard English." *Die Neueren Sprachen* 2:52–53.

———. 1897. "Can the English Tongue Be Preserved?" *Westminster Review* 147:286–92.

Lounsbury, Thomas R. 1904. *The Standard of Pronunciation in English*. New York: Harper and Brothers.

———. 1908. *The Standard of Usage in English*. New York: Harper and Brothers.

Lyons, John. 1968. *Introduction to Theoretical Linguistics*. Cambridge: Cambridge University Press.

Lyons, Martyn. 1981. "Politics and Patois: The Linguistic Policy of the French Revolution." *Australian Journal of French Studies* 18:264–81.

Macaulay, Thomas Babington. 1840. Review of Leopold Ranke's *Ecclesiastical and Political History of the Popes of Rome*. *Edinburgh Review* 72:227–58.

———. 1903. *Critical and Historical Essays Contributed to the* Edinburgh Review *by*

Lord Macaulay. Ed. F. C. Montague. 3 vols. London: Methuen and Company.

———. 1952. *Macaulay: Prose and Poetry*. Ed. G. M. Young. Cambridge, Mass.: Harvard University Press.

McClure, J. Derrick. 1981. "Scottis, Inglis, Suddroun: Language Labels and Language Attitudes." In *Proceedings of the Third International Conference on Scottish Language and Literature (Medieval and Renaissance)*, ed. Roderick J. Lyall and Felicity Riddy, 52–69. Stirling and Glasgow: Department of Scottish Literature, University of Glasgow.

McCormick, E. H. 1977. *Omai: Pacific Envoy*. Auckland: Auckland University Press.

McGeorge, Colin. 1984. "Hear Our Voices We Entreat: Schools and the 'Colonial Twang,' 1880–1930." *New Zealand Journal of History* 18:3–18.

McGhee, George C. 1974. "English—Best Hope for a World Language." *Saturday Review World* 2 (November 30): 6, 57.

McMullan, John L. 1984. *The Canting Crew: London's Criminal Underworld, 1550–1700*. New Brunswick, N.J.: Rutgers University Press.

Maggio, Rosalie. 1989. *The Nonsexist Word Finder: A Dictionary of Gender-Free Usage*. Boston: Beacon Press.

Mahaffy, J. P. 1893. "The Modern Babel." *Nineteenth Century* 40:782–96.

Malkiel, Yakov. 1976. "Changes in the European Languages under a New Set of Sociolinguistic Circumstances." In *First Images of America: The Impact of the New World on the Old*, ed. Fredi Chiappelli, 2:581–93. Berkeley: University of California Press.

Malone, Kemp. 1928. "The International Council for English." *American Speech* 3:261–75.

———. 1942. "Observations on the Word 'Standard.'" *American Speech* 17:235–38.

Maltz, Daniel N., and Ruth A. Borker. 1982. "A Cultural Approach to Male-Female Miscommunication." In *Language and Social Identity*, ed. John J. Gumperz, 196–216. Cambridge: Cambridge University Press.

Marckwardt, Albert H. 1935. "The High-School Teacher and a Standard of Usage." *English Journal* 24:283–91.

———. 1971. "The Concept of Standard English." In *The Discovery of English: NCTE Distinguished Lectures*, 15–36. Urbana, Ill.: National Council of Teachers of English.

March, Francis Andrew. 1861. *The English Language: A New Speech*. New York: W. H. Bidwell.

———. 1888. "A Universal Language." *Forum* 5:445–53.

Marriott, John A. R. 1932. *The English in India: A Problem of Politics*. Oxford: Clarendon Press.

Marsh, Ngaio. 1978. "It's Not What We Say . . . ." *New Zealand Listener* 90 (October 14):23.

Mashabela, Harry. 1983. "Isintu is a Self-Denial." *Frontline* 3 (8): 17.

Massie, James William. 1840. *Continental India*. 2 vols. London: Thomas Ward.

Mathews, Mitford M., ed. 1931. *The Beginnings of American English: Essays and Comments*. Chicago: University of Chicago Press.

————. 1951. *A Dictionary of Americanisms on Historical Principles*. Chicago: University of Chicago Press.

Matthews, Brander. 1898–99. "The Future of the English Language." *Munsey's Magazine* 20:100–105.

————. 1900. "The Future Literary Centre of the English Language." *Bookman* 12:238–42.

————. 1908. "English as a World-Language." *Century Magazine* 76:430–35.

Maurault, Joseph Pierre Anselme. 1866. *Histoire des Abenakis*. [Sorel, Québec]: Gazette de Sorel.

Mazrui, Ali A. 1973. "The English Language and the Origins of African Nationalism." In *Varieties of Present-day English*, ed. Richard W. Bailey and Jay L. Robinson, 57–70. New York: Macmillan.

Mencken, H. L. 1960a. *The American Language* (1936). 4th ed. New York: Alfred A. Knopf.

————. 1960b. *The American Language: Supplement I* (1945). New York: Alfred A. Knopf.

————. 1960c. *The American Language: Supplement II* (1948). New York: Alfred A. Knopf.

————. 1967. *The American Language*. Rev. Raven I. McDavid, Jr. New York: Knopf.

Meyers, Walter E. 1980. *Aliens and Linguists: Language Study and Science Fiction*. Athens: University of Georgia Press.

Miège, Guy. [1688] 1969. *The English Grammar; or, The Grounds and Genius of the English Tongue*. Facsimile. English Linguistics, 1500–1800, no. 152. Menston: Scholar Press.

Miller, Casey, and Kate Swift. 1977. *Words and Women*. Garden City, N.Y.: Anchor Books.

Mills, James. 1965. "The Detective." *Life* 59 (December 3): 90–122.

Moberly, George H., ed. 1881. *Venerabilis Baedae, Historia Ecclesiastica Gentis Anglorum*. Oxford: Clarendon Press.

"A Modest Proposal." 1873. *New York Times*, January 16, p. 4, col. 5.

Molee, Elias. 1888. *Plea for an American Language, or Germanic-English*. Chicago: John Anderson and Company.

Moore, Francis. 1840. *A Voyage to Georgia, Begun in the Year 1735*. Repr. *Collections of the Georgia Historical Society* 1:79–152.

Moore, Gerald. 1963. "The Dead End of African Literature." *Transition* 11:9.

Morris, Richard, ed. 1875. *Cursor Mundi*. Early English Text Society, o.s. 59. London: Trübner.

Morris, William, and Mary Morris. 1975. *Harper Dictionary of Contemporary Usage*. New York: Harper and Row.

Moynihan, Maurice, ed. 1980. *Speeches and Statements by Eamon De Valera, 1917–73*. Dublin: Gill and Macmillan.

Mphahlele, Ezekiel. 1963. "The Dead End of African Literature." *Transition* 11:7–11.

Mühlhäusler, Peter. 1982. "Tok Pisin in Papua New Guinea." In *English as a World Language*, ed. Richard W. Bailey and Manfred Görlach, 439–66. Ann Arbor: University of Michigan Press.

Mulcaster, Richard. [1582] 1970. *The First Part of the Elementarie VVhich Entreateth Chefelie of the Right Writing of Our English Tung*. Facsimile. English Linguistics, 1500–1800, no 219. Menston: Scholar Press.

Müller, F. Max. 1868. *On the Stratification of Language*. London: Longmans, Green, Reader, and Dyer.

———. [1861–62] 1899. *The Science of Language*. 2 vols. London: Longmans, Green, and Company.

Murison, David. 1979. "The Historical Background." In *Languages of Scotland*, ed. A. J. Aitken and Tom McArthur, 2–13. Edinburgh: Chambers.

Murray, Lindley. 1816. *English Grammar, Adapted to the Different Classes of Learners*. Cooperstown, N.Y.: H. and E. Phinney.

Nashe, Thomas. 1966. *The Works of Thomas Nashe*. Ed. Ronald B. McKerrow and rev. F. P. Wilson. Oxford: Basil Blackwell.

Nazareth, Peter. 1978. "The Social Responsibility of the East African Writer." In *The Third World Writer: His Social Responsibility*, 1–31. Nairobi: Kenya Literature Bureau.

Ndebele, Njabulo S. 1986. "The English Language and Social Change." Paper presented at the jubilee conference of the English Academy of Southern Africa, Johannesburg.

Neumann, J. H. 1946. "Chesterfield and the Standard of Usage in English." *Modern Language Quarterly* 7:463–75.

"The New English Empire." 1986. *Economist* 301 (December 20): 127–31.

Newbolt, Henry. 1923. "The Future of the English Language." *Transactions of the Royal Society of Literature of the United Kingdom*, n.s., 3:1–16.

Newman, Edwin. 1974. *Strictly Speaking: Will America Be the Death of English?* Indianapolis: Bobbs-Merrill.

———. 1976. *A Civil Tongue*. Indianapolis: Bobbs-Merrill.

Ngugi, J. T. [Ngũgĩ wa Thiong'o]. 1962. "A Kenyan at the Conference." *Transition* 5:7.

Ngũgĩ wa Thiong'o. 1986. *Decolonising the Mind: The Politics of Language in African Literature*. London: James Currey.

Nice, Margaret Morse. 1926. "On the Size of Vocabularies." *American Speech* 2:1–7.

Nicklin, T[homas]. 1925. *Standard English Pronunciation with Some Notes on Accidence and Syntax*. Oxford: Clarendon Press. [This is the title shown on the title-page; embossed on the cover is an alternative title by which the book is sometimes catalogued, *The Sounds of Standard English*.]

Nihalani, Paroo, R. K. Tongue, and Priya Hosali. 1979. [*Indian and British English*]. Delhi: Oxford University Press.

Norman, Arthur M. Z. 1954. "Linguistic Aspects of the Mores of U. S. Occupation and Security Forces in Japan." *American Speech* 29:301–2.

———. 1955. "Bamboo English: The Japanese Influence upon American Speech in Japan." *American Speech* 30:44–48.

Nugent, Maria Skinner. 1907. *Lady Nugent's Journal: Jamaica One Hundred Years Ago*. Ed. Frank Cundall. London: Adam and Charles Black.

Nunberg, Geoffrey. 1983. "The Decline of Grammar: An Argument for a Middle Way between Permissiveness and Traditionalism." *Atlantic* 252 (December): 31–46.

Obiechina, Emmanuel N. 1972. *Onitsha Market Literature*. London: Heinemann.

————. 1973. *An African Popular Literature: A Study of Onitsha Market Pamphlets.* Cambridge: Cambridge University Press.

————. 1990. *Language and Theme: Essays on African Literature.* Washington, D.C.: Howard University Press.

O'Brien, Conor Cruise. 1982. "Revolution and the Shaping of Modern Ireland." In *The Celtic Consciousness*, ed. Robert O'Driscoll, 427–35. New York: George Braziller.

Ogden, C. K. 1931. *Basic English Applied (Science).* London: Kegan Paul, Trench, Trubner and Company.

————. 1932. *The Basic Dictionary.* London: Kegan Paul, Trench, Trubner and Company.

————. 1934. *The System of Basic English.* New York: Harcourt, Brace.

Okeke-Ezigbo, Emeka. 1982. "The Role of the Nigerian Writer in a Carthaginian Society." *Okike* 21:28–37.

Okwu, Edward C. 1966. "A Language of Expression for Nigerian Literature." *Nigeria Magazine* 91:289–92, 313–15.

Ó Murchù, Máirtin. 1985. *The Irish Language.* Dublin: Department of Foreign Affairs and Bord na Gaeilge.

Orwell, Sonia, and Ian Angus, eds. 1970. *The Collected Essays, Journalism and Letters of George Orwell.* 4 vols. Harmondsworth: Penguin Books.

Osselton, N. E. 1958. *Branded Words in English Dictionaries before Johnson.* Groningen Studies in English, no. 7. Groningen: J. B. Wolters.

"Our Language Destined to be Universal." 1855. *Democratic Review* 35:306–13.

Palmer, Harold E. 1969. *A Grammar of Spoken English.* 3d ed. Cambridge: W. Heffer and Sons.

Palsgrave, John, trans. 1540. *The Comedye of Acolastus.* London: Berthelet.

Pankhurst, Estelle Sylvia. 1927. *Delphos, or the Future of International Language.* London: Kegan Paul, Trench, Trubner, and Company.

Parry, Albert. 1946. "The English Language, Oriental Style." *American Mercury* 62:286–91.

Parsons, Elsie Clews. 1913. *The Old-Fashioned Woman: Primitive Fancies about the Sex.* New York: G. P. Putnam's Sons.

Pedantius. 1631. London: Robert Nylbourn.

Pei, Mario. 1958. *One Language for the World.* New York: Devin-Adair.

Pendray, G. Edward. 1940. "The Story of the Time Capsule." *Annual Report of the Smithsonian Institution for 1939*, 533–53. Washington, D.C.: Smithsonian Institution.

Perren, G. E., and Michael F. Holloway. 1965. *Language and Communication in the Commonwealth.* Commonwealth Education Liaison Committee. London: H. M. Stationery Office.

Pinkerton, John. "Walpoliana" [selection 100]. *Monthly Magazine* 6:117–18.

Pinkerton, John. *See* Heron, Robert.

Piozzi, Hester Lynch. [1794] 1968. *British Synonymy; or, An Attempt at Regulating the Choice of Words in Familiar Conversation.* 2 vols. Facsimile. *English Linguistics, 1500–1800*, no. 113. Menston: Scholar Press.

Pitman, James. 1969. "The Late Dr. Mont Follick—An Appraisal." In *Alphabets for English*, ed. W. Haas, 14–49. Manchester: Manchester University Press.

Platt, John, and Heidi Weber. 1980. *English in Singapore and Malaysia: Status, Features, Functions.* Kuala Lumpur: Oxford University Press.

"The Poetry of Provincialisms." 1865. *Eclectic Magazine,* n.s. 2:433–42.

Porter, D. G. 1894. "English as a Universal Tongue." *Journal of Social Science* 32:117–30.

Pottle, Frederick A., and Charles H. Bennett, eds. 1936. *Boswell's Journal of a Tour to the Hebrides.* New York: Viking Press.

Price, Glanville. 1984. *The Languages of Britain.* London: Edward Arnold.

Proctor, Richard A. 1881. "English and American English." *Gentleman's Magazine,* n.s. 27:156–76.

"The Projector." 1804. "Essay on the English Language." *Gentleman's Magazine* 72:816–19.

Puttenham, George. 1936. *The Arte of English Poesie.* Ed. Gladys Doidge Willcock and Alice Walker. Cambridge: At the University Press.

Quinn, David Beers. 1955. *The Roanoke Voyages, 1584–1590.* 2 vols. London: Hakluyt Society.

———. 1985. *Set Fair for Roanoke: Voyages and Colonies, 1584–1606.* Chapel Hill: University of North Carolina Press.

Quinn, Jim. 1980. *American Tongue and Cheek: A Populist Guide to Our Language.* New York: Pantheon Books.

Quirk, Randolph. 1982. *Style and Communication in the English Language.* London: Edward Arnold.

———. 1985. "The English Language in a Global Context." In *English in the World: Teaching and Learning the Language and Literatures,* ed. Randolph Quirk and H. G. Widdowson, 1–6. Cambridge: Cambridge University Press.

Ramson, W. S., ed. 1988. *The Australian National Dictionary.* Melbourne: Oxford University Press.

Read, Allen Walker. 1934. "The Philological Society of New York." *American Speech* 9:131–36.

———. 1935. "Amphi-Atlantic English." *English Studies* 17:161–78.

———. 1947. "The Identification of the Speech of Americans in England." Paper presented at the meeting of the Linguistic Society of America, Ann Arbor.

———. 1979. "Milestones in the Branching of British and American English." Lecture presented at Vanderbilt University, Nashville.

Read, Hollis. 1849. *The Hand of God in History; or, Divine Providence Historically Illustrated in the Extension and Establishment of Christianity.* Hartford: H. Huntington.

Reckord, Barry. 1965. "The Dead End of African Literature." *Transition* 11:7.

[Reeve, Henry]. 1889. "The Literature and the Language of the Age." *Edinburgh Review* 169:328–50.

Reinberg, Linda. 1991. *In the Field: The Language of the Vietnam War.* New York: Facts on File.

Remy, Charles F. 1900. "Where the Best English is Spoken." *School Review* 8:414–21.

"Résolution de linguistique." 1959. *Présence Africaine* 24–25:397–98.

Review of Bradshaw's *Scheme* (q.v.). 1848. *The Athenaeum,* no. 1056 (January 22): 82.

Review of Joseph Collins' *The Doctor Looks at Love*. 1926. *New York Times Book Review*, October 24, 74.

Review of James Elphinston's *Fifty Year's Correspondence*. 1795. *British Critic* 5:18–20.

Review of James Elphinston's *A Minniature of Inglish Orthoggraphy*. 1796. *British Critic* 8:564.

Review of George P. Marsh's *Lectures on the English Language*. 1860. *North American Review* 91:507–28.

Review of Peter Mark Roget's *Thesaurus of English Words*. 1854. *Christian Review* 19:529–43.

Rich, Adrienne. 1979. *On Lies, Secrets, and Silence: Selected Prose, 1966–1976*. New York: Norton.

Richards, I. A. 1943. *Basic English and Its Uses*. New York: Norton.

Ridge-Beedle, Peter D. 1947. *Why Not English?: A New Alphabet for the English Language*. Glasgow: Stratford Press.

Rivarol, Antoine de. 1929. *Discours sur l'universalité de la langue française* [1784]. Ed. Marcel Hervier. Paris: Librairie Delagrave.

Rodgers, Bruce. 1972. *The Queens' Vernacular: A Gay Lexicon*. San Francisco: Straight Arrow Books.

Rollins, Hyder E., and Herschel Baker, eds. 1954. *The Renaissance in England*. Boston: D. C. Heath.

Rolph, Thomas. 1836. *Observations Made during a Visit in the West Indies and a Tour through the United States of America, in Parts of the Years 1832–33; together with a Statistical Account of Upper Canada*. Dundas, Upper Canada: G. Heyworth Hackstaff.

Rose, Cowper. 1829. *Four Years in Southern Africa*. London: Henry Colburn and Richard Bentley.

Russel, W[illiam] P. 1801. *Multum in Parvo; or A Brief Display of More than a Thousand Errors in Each of the Undermentiond Writers; Johnson, Sheridan, Walker, Nares, Perry, Entick (and in the Works of Other Philologists)*. London: Barrett.

S. H. 1853. "Jacob Grimm on the Genius and Vocation of the English Language." *Notes and Queries* 7:125–26.

Salgado, Gamini. 1972. *Cony-Catchers and Bawdy Baskets: An Anthology of Elizabethan Low Life*. Harmondsworth: Penguin.

———. 1977. *The Elizabethan Underworld*. London: J. M. Dent and Sons.

Salisbury, Neal. 1974. "Red Puritans: The 'Praying Indians' of Massachusetts Bay and John Eliot." *William and Mary Quarterly* 31:27–54.

Sampson, Geoffrey. 1980. *Schools of Linguistics*. Stanford: Stanford University Press.

Sanoff, Alvin P., and Lucia Solorzano. 1985. "English: Out to Conquer the World." *U.S. News and World Report*, February 18, 49–57.

Sapir, Edward. [1921] 1949. *Language: An Introduction to the Study of Speech*. New York: Harvest Books.

Saro-Wiwa, Ken. 1985. *Sozaboy*. Port Harcourt, Nigeria: Saros International Publishers.

Savage, W. H. 1833. *The Vulgarisms and Improprieties of the English Language*. London: T. S. Porter.

Scott, Fred Newton. 1926. *The Standard of American Speech and Other Papers*. Boston: Allyn and Bacon.

Scragg, D. G. 1974. *A History of English Spelling*. Mont Follick Series, no. 3. Manchester: Manchester University Press.

Select Trials for Murders, Roberies, Rape, Sodomy, Coining, and Other Offenses at the Sessions-House in the Old Bailey, 1740–1742. 1742. 3 vols. London: L. Gilliver et al.

Senghor, Léopold S. 1975. "The Essence of Language: English and French." *Culture* 2 (2): 75–98.

Sewall, Samuel. 1886. *Letter-Book*. 2 vols. Collections of the Massachusetts Historical Society, 6th ser., vols. 1–2. Boston: Published by the Society.

Sey, Kofi Abokah. 1973. *Ghanaian English: An Exploratory Survey*. London: Macmillan.

Shah, Idries. 1987. *Adventures, Facts and Fantasy in Darkest England*. London: Octagon Press.

"Shall English Become a Dead Language?" 1897. *Spectator* 78 (May 1): 620–21.

Sharp, Andrew. 1963. *The Discovery of Australia*. Oxford: Clarendon Press.

Sheridan, Thomas. [1762] 1968. *A Course of Lectures on Elocution*. Facsimile. New York: Benjamin Blom.

———. 1780. *A General Dictionary of the English Language*. 2 vols. London: J. Dodsley.

———. [1786] 1968. *Elements of English*. Facsimile. English Linguistics, 1600–1800, no. 120. Menston: Scholar Press.

Shuffelton, Frank. 1976. "Indian Devils and Pilgrim Fathers: Squanto, Hobomok, and the English Conception of Indian Religion." *New England Quarterly* 49 (1): 108–16.

Silliman, Benjamin. 1812. *A Journal of Travels in England, Holland, and Scotland, and of Two Passages over the Atlantic, in the years 1805 and 1806*. 2 vols. Boston: T. B. Wait and Company.

Simon, John. 1980. *Paradigms Lost: Reflections on Literacy and Its Decline*. New York: C. N. Potter.

Simpson, W. 1873. "China's Future Place in Philology." *Macmillan's Magazine* 29 (November):45–48.

Sivertsen, Eva. 1960. *Cockney Phonology*. Oslo Studies in English, no. 8. Oslo: Oslo University Press.

Smith, John. 1624. *The Generall Historie of Virginia, New-England, and the Summer Isles*. London: Michael Sparkes.

———. 1986. *The Complete Works of Captain John Smith (1580–1631)*. 3 vols. Ed. Philip L. Barbour. Chapel Hill: University of North Carolina Press.

Smith, Logan Pearsall. 1931. "Robert Bridges: Recollections." Society for Pure English, tract 35. Oxford: Clarendon Press.

Smith, Thomas. [1568] 1968. *De Recta et Emendata Linguae Anglicae Scriptione, Dialogus*. Facsimile. English Linguistics, 1500–1800, no. 109. Menston: Scholar Press.

Society for Pure English. 1919. *Preliminary Announcement & List of Members*. Tract no. 1. Oxford: Clarendon Press.

"Some Thoughts on the English Language." 1766. *Annual Register*, 194–97.

Sorrels, Bobbye D. 1983. *The Nonsexist Communicator: Solving the Problems of Gender and Awkwardness in Modern English*. Englewood Cliffs, N.J.: Prentice-Hall.

Soyinka, Wole. 1971. "The Choice and Use of Language." *Cultural Events in Africa* 75:3–6.

———. 1979. "We Africans Must Speak in One Tongue." *Afrika* (Munich) 20 (9): 22–23.

Spencer, John. 1971. "Colonial Language Policies and Their Legacies." In *Current Trends in Linguistics: Linguistics in Sub-Saharan Africa*, ed. Thomas A. Sebeok, 537–47. The Hague: Mouton.

Spenser, Edmund. 1932–49. *The Works of Edmund Spenser: A Variorum Edition*. 9 vols. Ed. Edwin Greenlaw et al. Baltimore: Johns Hopkins University Press.

Sprat, Thomas. [1667] 1958. *History of the Royal Society*. Ed. Jackson I. Cope and Harold Whitmore Jones. St. Louis: Washington University Studies.

Stackhouse, Thomas. [1731] 1968. *Reflections on the Nature and Property of Languages*. Facsimile. English Linguistics, 1500–1800, no. 111. Menston: Scholar Press.

Stanhope, Philip Dormer, Fourth Earl of Chesterfield. 1777. *Miscellaneous Works*. 3 vols. Dublin: W. Watson.

[Stead, W. H.] 1897. "The Topic of the Month: A Plea for the Queen's English." *Review of Reviews* 15:338–39.

Stein, Gertrude. 1953. *Bee Time Vine, and Other Pieces [1913–27]*. New Haven: Yale University Press.

Struble, George G. 1929. "Bamboo English." *American Speech* 4:276–85.

Strunk, William, Jr., and E. B. White. 1979. *The Elements of Style*. 3d ed. New York: Macmillan.

[Swayne, G. C.] 1862. "Characteristics of Language." *Blackwood's Edinburgh Magazine* 91:360–75.

Sweet, Henry. 1877. *A Handbook of Phonetics*. Oxford: Clarendon Press.

[Swetnam, Joseph.] 1615. *The Araignment of Lewd, Idle, Froward, and Vnconstant Women*. London: Thomas Archer.

Swift, Jonathan. 1966. "A Proposal for Correcting, Improving and Ascertaining the English Tongue" [1712]. In *The English Language: Essays by English and American Men of Letters, 1490–1839*, ed. W. F. Bolton, 107–23. Cambridge: Cambridge University Press.

Taylor, Walt. 1939. *Doughty's English*. Society for Pure English, tract 51. Oxford: Clarendon Press.

Taylor, William Alexander. 1971. *Intermere [1901–02]*. Facsimile. New York: Arno Press.

Thomas, Aaron. 1968. *The Newfoundland Journal of Aaron Thomas*. Ed. Jean M. Murray. London: Longmans.

Thomason, Sarah Grey. 1979. "On Interpreting 'The Indian Interpreter.'" *Language and Society* 9:167–93.

Thomson, R. L. 1984. "The History of the Celtic Languages in the British Isles." In

Language in the British Isles, ed. Peter Trudgill, 241–58. Cambridge: Cambridge University Press.

Tibbets, Arn, and Charlene Tibbets. 1978. *What's Happening to American English?* New York: Charles Scribner's Sons.

Toon, Thomas. 1983. *The Politics of Early Old English Sound Change.* New York: Academic Press.

Trench, Richard Chenevix. 1860. *On Some Deficiencies in Our English Dictionaries.* London: John W. Parker and Son.

———. 1891. *On the Study of Words* [1851]. New York: Macmillan.

Trevisa, John. 1869. *Polychronicon Ranulphi Higden, Monachi Cestrensis; together with the English Translations of John Trevisa and of an Unknown Writer of the Fifteenth Century.* 9 vols. Ed. Churchill Babington. London: Longmans, Green, and Company.

Turkington, Grace A. 1918. *My Country: A Textbook in Civics and Patriotism for Young Americans.* Boston: Ginn and Company.

Upton, M. G. 1873. "The English as a Universal Language." *Overland Monthly* 11 (October): 324–29.

Vauts, Moses à. 1650. *The Husband's Authority Unveil'd.* London: Robert Bostock.

Verstegan, Richard. [1605] 1976. *A Restitution of Decayed Intelligence.* Facsimile. English Recusant Literature, 1558–1640, no 323. Ilkley, Yorkshire: Scholar Press.

Vesey, Francis. 1841. *Decline of the English Language.* London: Saunders and Benning.

Vice Commission of Chicago. 1911. *The Social Evil in Chicago: A Study of Existing Conditions.* Chicago: Gunthrop-Warren.

Vindex Anglicus: or, The Perfections of the English Language Defended and Asserted. 1644. Wing STC, no. V461. Oxford: H. Hall. [Repr. in *The Harleian Miscellany* 5 (1810): 428–34.]

Vizetelly, Frank H. 1931. "A Matter of Pronunciation" *Atlantic Monthly* 147 (February): 148–51.

The Vulgarities of Speech Corrected; with Elegant Expressions for Provincial and Vulgar English, Scots, and Irish; for the Use of Those Who are Unacquainted with Grammar. 1826. London: James Bulcock.

Waddell, Hope Masterton. 1970. *Twenty-Nine Years in the West Indies and Central Africa* [1863]. London: Frank Cass.

Wali, Obiajunwa. 1963. "The Dead End of African Literature?" *Transition* 10:13–15.

Walker, John. 1791. *A Critical Pronouncing Dictionary and Expositor of the English Language.* London: Robinson and Cadell.

Waller, Edmund. 1904. "Of English Verse." In *The Poems of Edmund Waller,* ed. G. Thorn Drury, 2:69–70. London: George Routledge and Sons.

Watts, T[homas]. 1850. "On the Probable Future Position of the English Language." *Proceedings of the Philological Society* 4:207–14.

Waugh, Evelyn. 1936. *Mr. Loveday's Little Outing and Other Sad Stories.* London: Chapman and Hall.

Webster, Grant. 1960. "Korean Bamboo English Once More." *American Speech* 35:261–65.

Webster, Noah. 1843. *A Collection of Papers on Political, Literary, and Moral Subjects by Noah Webster, LL. D.* New York: Webster and Clark.

———. [1789] 1951. *Dissertations on the English Language.* Facsimile. Gainesville, Fla.: Scholars' Facsimiles and Reprints.

———. [1806] 1970. *A Compendious Dictionary of the English Language.* Facsimile. New York: Bounty Books.

Weisse, John A. 1879. *Origin, Progress and Destiny of the English Language and Literature.* New York: J. W. Bouton.

Wells, H. G. 1924. *Anticipations and Other Papers.* London: T. Fisher Unwin.

———. 1967. *A Modern Utopia* [1905]. Lincoln: University of Nebraska Press.

Wendt, Albert. 1982. "Towards a New Oceania." In *Writers in East-West Encounter: New Cultural Bearings,* ed. Guy Amirthanayagam, 202–15. London: Macmillan.

Westinghouse Electric and Manufacturing Company. 1938. *The Book of Record of the Time Capsule of Cupaloy.* New York: Westinghouse.

White, Richard Grant. 1880. *Every-Day English.* Boston and New York: Houghton Mifflin Company.

Whiteley, W. H. 1971. "Language Policies of Independent African States." In *Current Trends in Linguistics: Linguistics in Sub-Saharan Africa,* ed. Thomas A. Sebeok, 548–58. The Hague: Mouton.

Whitman, Walt. 1856. "America's Mightiest Inheritance." *Life Illustrated,* no. 76 (April 12): 185–86.

———. [1885] 1969. "Slang in America." In *The English Language: Essays by Linguists and Men of Letters, 1858–1964,* ed. W. F. Bolton and David Crystal, 54–58. Cambridge: At the University Press.

"Why English is So Easy to Mangle." 1985. *U. S. News & World Report* 98 (February 18): 53.

Wilkie, Franc B. 1880. *Sketches beyond the Sea.* 2d ed. Chicago: Belford, Clarke and Company.

Williams, Raymond. 1961. "The Growth of 'Standard English.'" In *The Long Revolution,* 214–29. New York: Columbia University Press.

———. 1983. *Keywords: A Vocabulary of Culture and Society.* Rev. ed. New York: Oxford University Press.

Williams, Roger. 1863. "Letter to John Winthrop." *Collections of the Massachusetts Historical Society,* ser. 4, 6:214–17.

Wilson, Thomas. [1560] 1909. *Arte of Rhetorique.* Ed. G. H. Mair. Oxford: Clarendon Press.

Wolley, Hannah. 1675. *The Gentlewoman's Companion.* London: A. Maxwell.

Wood, D. N. C. 1977. "Elizabethan English and Richard Carew." *Neophilolgus* 61:304–15.

Wood, Francis A. 1897. "Indo-European Root-Formation." *Journal of Germanic Philology* 1:280–309.

Woolf, Virginia. 1980. *Women and Writing.* Ed. Michèle Barrett. New York: Harcourt Brace Jovanovich.

Wordsworth, William. [1800] 1952. *Preface to* "Lyrical Ballads." In *Criticism: The Major Texts,* ed. Walter Jackson Bate, 335–46. New York: Harcourt, Brace and Company.

Wright, Arnold. 1891. *Baboo English as 'tis Writ, Being Curiosities of Indian Journalism*. London: T. Fisher Unwin.

Wright, Patrick. 1985. *On Living in an Old Country: The National Past in Contemporary Britain*. London: Verso.

Wrigley, Edward A., and Roger S. Schofield. 1981. *The Population History of England, 1541–1871*. London: Edward Arnold.

Wurm, Stephen A. 1984. "Pidgin English in the Pacific Area." *Diogenes* 127:101–12.

Wyld, Henry Cecil. 1914. "Class Dialect and Standard English." In *A Miscellany Presented to John Macdonald Mackay, LL.D.*, ed. Oliver Elton, 283–91. Liverpool: At the University Press.

———. 1934. *The Best English: A Claim for the Superiority of Received Standard English*. Society for Pure English, tract 39. Oxford: Clarendon Press.

———. 1936. *A History of Modern Colloquial English*. 3d ed. Oxford: Basil Blackwell.

Yule, Emma Sarepta. 1925. "The English Language in the Philippines." *American Speech* 1:111–20.

Yule, Henry, and A. C. Burnell, eds. [1903] 1968. *Hobson-Jobson: A Glossary of Colloquial Anglo-Indian Words and Phrases* [1886]. New ed. by William Crooke. Facsimile. New York: Humanities Press.

Zachrisson, R. E. 1931–32. "Four Hundred Years of English Spelling Reform." *Studia Neophilologica* 4:1–69.

Zincke, Foster Barham. 1883. *The Plough and the Dollar, or The Englishry of a Century Hence*. London: Kegan Paul, Trench and Company.

Name Index

Subject Index

DATE DUE

07/13/98			
1/18/01			
DEC 0 3 2003			
GAYLORD			PRINTED IN U.S.A.